TIME® LIFE BOOKS Complete *Book of* Redecorating & Remodeling

Other Publications

DO IT YOURSELF
The Time-Life Complete Gardener
Home Repair and Improvement
The Art of Woodworking
Fix It Yourself

COOKING
Weight Watchers® Smart Choice Recipe Collection
Great Taste~Low Fat
Williams-Sonoma Kitchen Library

HISTORY
What Life Was Like
The American Story
Voices of the Civil War
The American Indians
Lost Civilizations
Mysteries of the Unknown
Time Frame
The Civil War
Cultural Atlas

SCIENCE/NATURE
Voyage Through the Universe

TIME-LIFE KIDS
Library of First Questions and Answers
A Child's First Library of Learning
I Love Math
Nature Company Discoveries
Understanding Science & Nature

Printed in Canada

*For information on and a full description of any
of the Time-Life Books series listed above, please
call 1-800-621-7026 or write:*

Reader Information
Time-Life Customer Service
P.O. Box C-32068
Richmond, Virginia 23261-2068

The Consultants

Jeff Palumbo is a registered journeyman
carpenter who has a home-building and
remodeling business in northern Virginia.
His interest in carpentry was sparked by
his grandfather, a master carpenter with
more than 50 years' experience. Palumbo
teaches in the Fairfax County Adult Education Program.

Mark M. Steele is a professional home in-
spector in the Washington, D.C., area. He
has developed and conducted training pro-
grams in home-ownership skills for first-time
homeowners. He appears frequently on tele-
vision and radio as an expert in home repair
and consumer topics.

William Covey has been active in the floorcovering industry for more than 30 years. He
founded the Northern Virginia Floorcovering
Association in 1984 and is an active execu-
tive board member of the Virginia Floorcovering Association. He owns Covey's Carpet
and Drapes, Inc., and is part owner of Tech-
nical Flooring Services, both located in
Springfield, Virginia.

Joe Teets is a master electrician/contractor.
Currently in the Office of Adult and Com-
munity Education for the Fairfax County
Public Schools, he has been involved in
apprenticeship training as an instructor
and coordinator since 1985.

TIME® LIFE BOOKS Complete *Book of* Redecorating & Remodeling

BY THE EDITORS OF TIME-LIFE BOOKS, ALEXANDRIA, VIRGINIA

CONTENTS

PAINTING

1

Painting is not only one of the easiest and most cost-effective ways to breathe new life into a room, it is also a powerful tool for creating visual effects and emotional ambiance. Color can trick the eye, with light colors opening up a room and dark colors making large rooms cozier. Whether you combine paint with wallpaper, paneling, and other finishes, or just use it alone for its simple beauty, paint is the basis for a successful decorating project.

To help you get started, you'll find a primer on painting tools, sandpaper, and protective gear. This chapter also discusses stripping off old paint and repairing defects in existing paint jobs, as well as preparing wood knots, wallboard, and old plaster walls for a fresh coat of paint. We'll teach you how to prep a room for painting, including masking windows, covering light fixtures, and removing hardware. Step-by-step instructions guide you through proper painting techniques, and a list of precautions and safety tips provides necessary information to ensure a safe, successful paint job. Potential problem areas like doors, windows, cabinets, and louvers are no problem at all once you learn a few tricks of the trade. On pages 10-11 you'll find a special color and paint guide to help you with your redecorating needs.

Once you've finished painting, we'll show you the proper ways to clean your equipment, remove dried paint from glass, and store paints and solvents for touchups and future paint jobs.

A red wall perfectly accents the classic, formal style of this dining room. Rich and warm, red reacts well with different lighting—cheerful when caught in the sunlight, dramatic in low or accent lighting.

Yellow paint works perfectly in this room, adding warmth while accenting the unique architecture and height of the ceiling. With the bright colors repeated in the fabrics, the room radiates sunshine.

You need not limit your walls to one color. Here, the unique combination of cool blues and pale greens creates a calm atmosphere. The color changes highlight the wall's unusual angles and accent the central fireplace.

The simple use of pink paint on the lower third of this wall adds warmth to the cool plaster and softness to the rough textures of this rustic room.

Understanding Color

A favorite project for do-it-yourselfers, painting is one of the most creative ways to set a certain mood, disguise or enhance particular architectural elements, or carry a motif throughout the house. A basic understanding of color concepts combined with mindful use of interior paint opens up a fascinating array of decorating possibilities.

Visually, color is experienced in hue, value, and intensity. Hue is simply another name for color itself and refers to the basic color families that blend into one another to form an interrelated circle or color wheel. Value refers to a color's relative lightness or darkness. Colors lightened with white are known as tints, and those blended with black are called shades. Adding gray to a color makes it a tone. Intensity, also known as saturation, describes a color's richness or purity. Painting a room with a color high in value—such as pale blue—makes it seem larger. Conversely, using a highly saturated or low in value color—like royal blue—makes a room seem smaller and cozier. A low ceiling seems higher if it's painted with a color slightly paler than the surrounding walls.

A color's "temperature" can also help alter a room's perceived size as well as set a certain mood. Warm colors like red, orange, and yellow seem to advance, which increases the apparent size and vibrancy of the colored surface and makes a room look smaller. Warm colors are particularly good choices to "warm up" north-facing rooms that

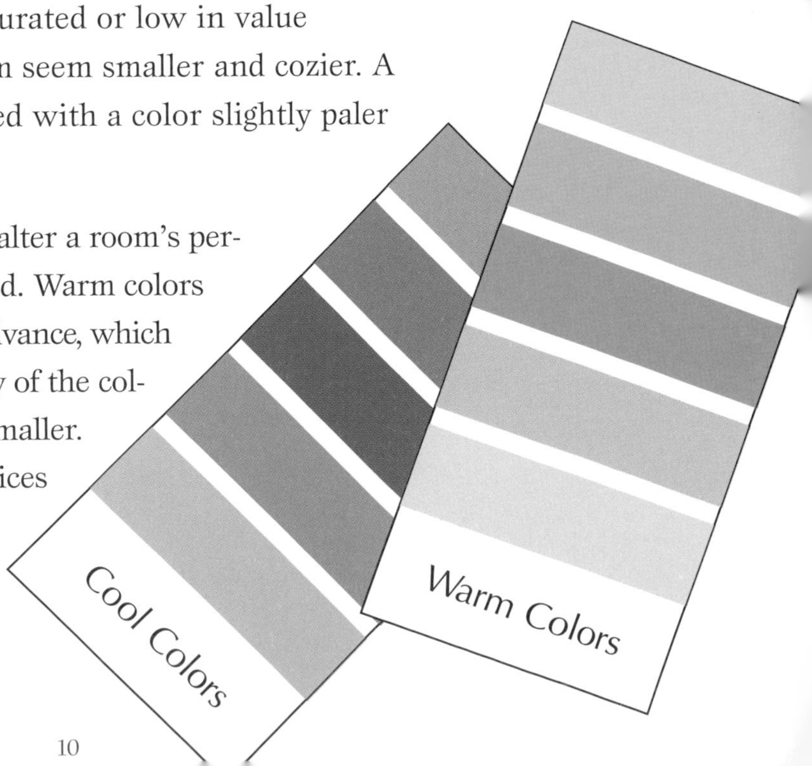

Cool Colors

Warm Colors

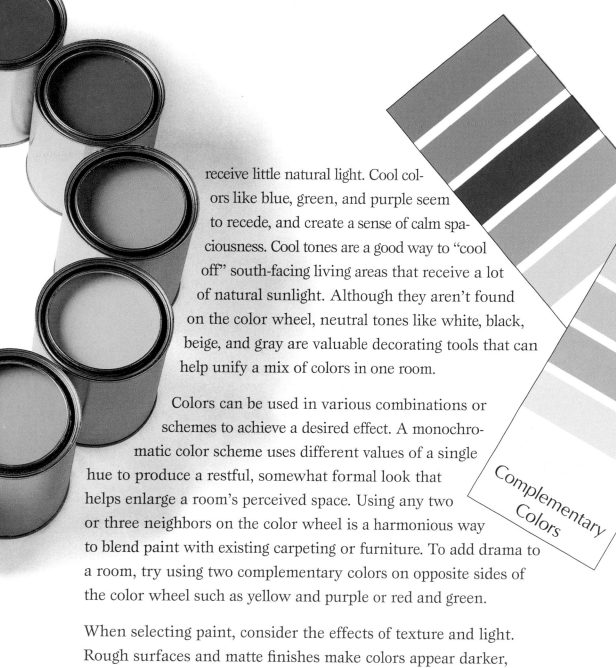

receive little natural light. Cool colors like blue, green, and purple seem to recede, and create a sense of calm spaciousness. Cool tones are a good way to "cool off" south-facing living areas that receive a lot of natural sunlight. Although they aren't found on the color wheel, neutral tones like white, black, beige, and gray are valuable decorating tools that can help unify a mix of colors in one room.

Colors can be used in various combinations or schemes to achieve a desired effect. A monochromatic color scheme uses different values of a single hue to produce a restful, somewhat formal look that helps enlarge a room's perceived space. Using any two or three neighbors on the color wheel is a harmonious way to blend paint with existing carpeting or furniture. To add drama to a room, try using two complementary colors on opposite sides of the color wheel such as yellow and purple or red and green.

When selecting paint, consider the effects of texture and light. Rough surfaces and matte finishes make colors appear darker, because irregular texture produces shadow and absorbs light. The same color can look very different in the daylight and in the evening. If you use paint chips to choose colors, bear in mind that the color will appear stronger on the wall than on the sample. Flat paint finishes absorb light, while semi-gloss and high-gloss finishes reflect light and can make a room seem brighter. To add interest to any painted surface, see page 43 for tips on sponging, ragging, and other creative applications of paint.

A Tool Kit for Painting

Like most jobs, painting requires a variety of tools and materials. General-purpose items—such as a hammer, a screwdriver, a sturdy knife, a can opener, and masking tape—you probably already have on hand. For cleaning up, you'll need rags and metal containers such as coffee cans or loaf pans.

You may, however, need to purchase many of the tools that are shown here, as well as other items. Buy drop cloths to protect both furniture and floors from paint drips and spatters. You'll also need a sanding block and several grades of sandpaper to smooth repairs to walls and woodwork, and a sponge to clean up dust and dirt and to wash down previously painted walls. As an auxiliary container for paint, a medium-size rustproof pail is ideal.

Appropriate protective gear includes rubber gloves, goggles, and a dust mask. A respirator may be necessary with a few toxic paint removers.

CAULKING GUN

Tools for repairing surfaces.
For patching wallboard, plaster, and trim before painting, you will need both stiff- and flexible-blade putty knives, and a wide-blade putty knife for taping wallboard. Extensive filling of joints around trim and baseboards requires a caulking gun.

6" PUTTY KNIFE

3" PUTTY KNIFE

$1\frac{1}{4}$" PUTTY KNIFE

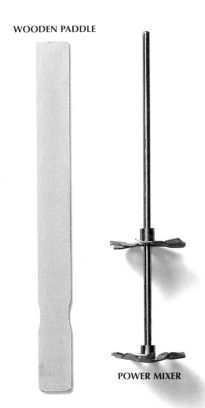

WOODEN PADDLE

POWER MIXER

Mixing tools.
Paint must be stirred thoroughly to cover surfaces evenly. For small quantities, wooden paddles are satisfactory, but a power mixer driven by an electric drill works faster, especially when blending large quantities.

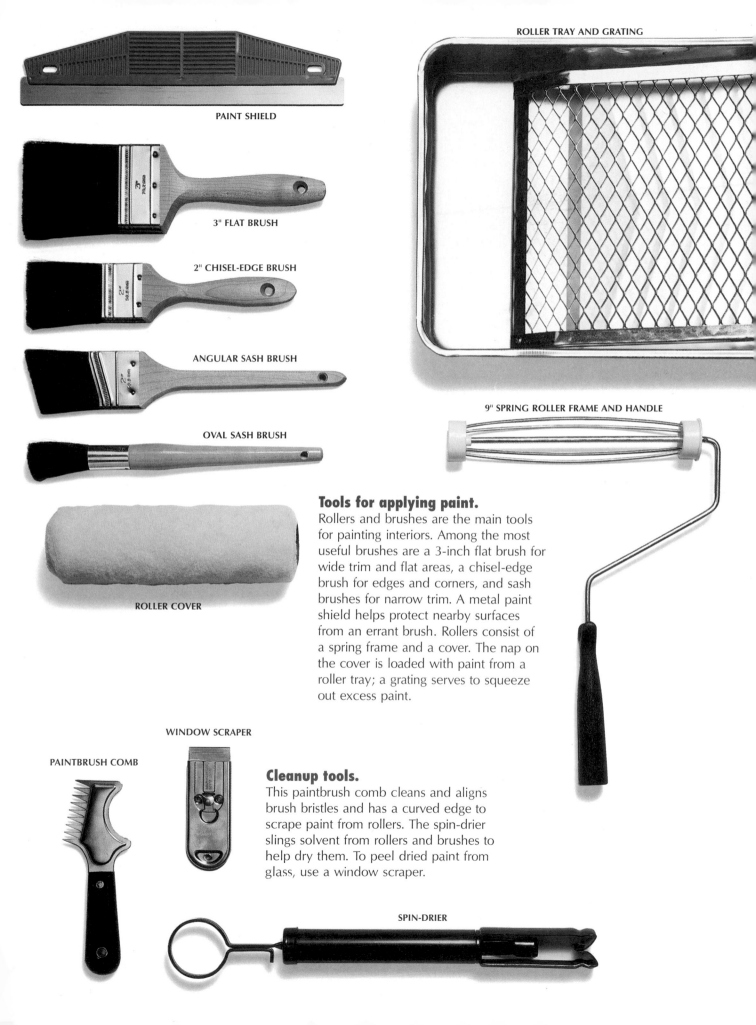

PAINT SHIELD

ROLLER TRAY AND GRATING

3" FLAT BRUSH

2" CHISEL-EDGE BRUSH

ANGULAR SASH BRUSH

OVAL SASH BRUSH

9" SPRING ROLLER FRAME AND HANDLE

ROLLER COVER

Tools for applying paint.

Rollers and brushes are the main tools for painting interiors. Among the most useful brushes are a 3-inch flat brush for wide trim and flat areas, a chisel-edge brush for edges and corners, and sash brushes for narrow trim. A metal paint shield helps protect nearby surfaces from an errant brush. Rollers consist of a spring frame and a cover. The nap on the cover is loaded with paint from a roller tray; a grating serves to squeeze out excess paint.

WINDOW SCRAPER

PAINTBRUSH COMB

Cleanup tools.

This paintbrush comb cleans and aligns brush bristles and has a curved edge to scrape paint from rollers. The spin-drier slings solvent from rollers and brushes to help dry them. To peel dried paint from glass, use a window scraper.

SPIN-DRIER

Surface Preparation

The durability of any paint job depends largely on the care with which you have prepared the surfaces before you apply the paint.

For virgin wallboard, plaster, or wood, first dust the surface thoroughly, then brush a coat of primer on surfaces that you plan to paint *(pages 322-325)*.

If you are working with finished surfaces, try to ascertain whether the material beneath the finish is wallboard or plaster, and the type of surface covering that was used *(pages 320-325)*. Such information will determine how you proceed with preparation treatments and will help you to select the proper undercoatings, primers, and paints. Next, inspect the room thoroughly for damage that may call for repairs.

Dealing with Old Paint: Check for blistering, cracking, or peeling paint and scrape it off *(pages 16-17)* or remove it with a nylon paint stripper that is fitted to an electric drill. If it is necessary for you to remove many layers of paint, consider using a heat gun. When the damaged paint is near window glass, strip it with a chemical paint remover rather than risk breaking the glass with a power tool *(page 17)*.

Concealing Flaws: Repair damaged wallboard or plaster *(pages 20-33)*, and fill in gouges, holes, and cracks in walls and trim. When choosing a filler, read the label to be sure the product is compatible with the finish you plan to use.

Build up depressions and conceal nails with spackling compound. Use the same material to repair short open joints; longer gaps—along a baseboard, for example—are better caulked than patched with spackling compound.

On surfaces that are bare and those that have been painted, follow repair work with a thorough sanding. Electric sanders speed the work, but for small areas, a sanding block works well *(opposite)*.

Special Surfaces: New paint will not adhere properly to glossy surfaces; dull such finishes by raising a nap with sandpaper or a liquid deglosser. Strip off wallpaper *(pages 58-61)* or prepare it for painting *(page 19)*. If floor wax has adhered to baseboards, take it off with wax remover. Brush rust from radiators, pipes, and heat ducts, and clean mildew from damp places . Interior brick and garage and basement surfaces require special preparations.

Cleaning: Dirt, grease, and even fingerprints can prevent new paint from adhering firmly. A good washing down with a heavy-duty household detergent just before painting will usually suffice for finished walls and woodwork. Finally, be sure that surfaces are completely dry before painting.

 *Paint strippers, solvents, and cleaning agents can* CAUTION *give off harmful fumes. Follow the advice on page 35.*

 TOOLS

Putty knives (flexible- and stiff-blade)
Inexpensive paint-brush
Sharp knife
Long-nose pliers
Nail set
Hammer

 **MATERIALS**

Sandpaper (fine- and medium-grit)
Spackling compound
Wood putty
Wood filler
Primer
Paint remover

Paint solvent
Shellac
Caulk
Wallpaper primer-sealer

🪖 **SAFETY TIPS**

Protect your hands from cleaning agents and paint solvents. Wear rubber gloves and goggles to apply paint remover, and add a respirator if the product contains methylene chloride. When sanding, wear a dust mask.

Safety Measures for Lead and Asbestos

Lead and asbestos, known health hazards, pervade houses constructed, remodeled, or redecorated before 1978. Test all painted surfaces for lead with a kit available at hardware stores, or call your local health department or environmental protection agency (EPA) for other options. Asbestos was once a component of insulation, wallboard, joint compound, acoustic or decorative ceiling and wall materials, heat-proofing materials, and resilient flooring installed before 1986. Mist such materials with a solution of 1 teaspoon low-sudsing detergent per quart of water, then remove small samples for testing at a certified lab.

When the job is large and indoors or you suffer from cardiac or respiratory problems or don't tolerate heat well, hire a licensed professional. If you choose to do the job yourself, follow these guidelines:

! Keep children, pregnant women, and pets out of the work area.

! Indoors, seal off the area from the rest of the house with 6-mil polyethylene sheeting and duct tape. Turn off forced-air systems, and cover rugs and furniture that can't be removed with more sheeting and tape.

! Wear protective clothing (available at safety-equipment or paint stores) and a dual-cartridge respirator with high efficiency particulate air (HFPA) filters.

! Never sand asbestos-laden materials or use a power tool to cut them; instead, mist them with the detergent solution and cut them with a hand tool. If you must use a sander on lead-painted surfaces, use one equipped with a HEPA-filter vacuum.

! Avoid tracking dust from the work area into other parts of the house, and take off protective clothing and shoes before leaving the area. Shower and wash your hair immediately; wash clothing separately.

! When you finish indoors, mist the plastic and roll it up; dispose of materials as directed by your local health department or EPA office.

SANDING TECHNIQUES

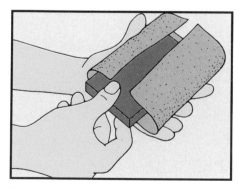

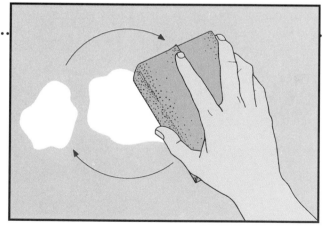

1. Making a sanding block.
You can buy a ready-made sanding block, but a homemade one works just as well.
◆ From a scrap of 1-by-3 or 1-by-4 board, cut a block 4 or 5 inches long.
◆ Cut a rectangle of sandpaper large enough to encircle the block. For previously painted surfaces, start with medium-grit sandpaper then proceed to fine-grit paper; for virgin wood, use only fine-grit paper.
◆ Wrap the paper around the block with the grit side out.

2. Sanding flat areas.
◆ Make sure that all loose paint is removed from the area to be sanded (pages 16-17) and that any patching compounds are completely dry.
◆ Grasp the block firmly, holding the sandpaper snugly around it.
◆ On a painted surface, sand with a gentle, circular motion, and feather the edges of the area by blending the old paint or patching materials into the surrounding surface; on bare wood, work in straight strokes along the grain.
◆ Tap the sandpaper frequently on a hard surface to remove accumulated residue, and replace the paper when it becomes clogged or worn out.

A sanding edge for intricate jobs.
◆ Fold a 6-inch square of sandpaper into quarters to make a sharp sanding edge *(above, left)*.
◆ Place the edge against the surface to be sanded *(above, right)*, and gently rub the paper over the surface to blend the edges of patching material or old paint with the surrounding surface.
◆ Refold the paper as necessary to make fresh edges.

REPAIRING FLAWS IN PAINT

Scraping paint.
Insert the edge of a $1\frac{1}{4}$-inch-wide putty knife under the loose paint *(left)*, and being careful not to gouge the surface, scrape with a pushing motion. For large areas, use the scraper that is shown on page 56.

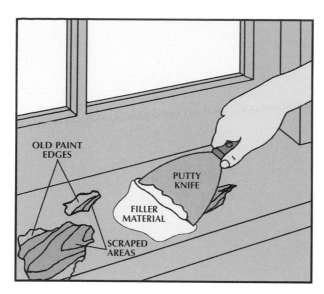

Filling in depressions.
◆ Apply spackling compound to a small depression with a flexible-blade putty knife; use a wide-blade putty knife for extensive filling.
◆ When the filler has dried, sand it flush with the surface.
◆ Spot-prime all scraped or filled areas before repainting *(pages 322-325).*

STRIPPING OLD PAINT

1. Applying paint remover.
On most surfaces, a paste-type, water-base remover is safest. However, water in the paint remover may lift or buckle a wood veneer; use a solvent-base remover instead.
◆ Protect the surrounding area with a thick layer of newspaper.
◆ With a clean, inexpensive paintbrush, spread a generous amount of remover on the area to be stripped. Work with short strokes, brushing in one direction, and do not cover an area more than 2 feet square at one time.

2. Scraping off the paint.
◆ When the paint begins to blister and wrinkle, peel it off with a putty knife.
◆ As you remove the paint, clean the knife frequently with newspaper.
◆ When all paint is off, clean the bare surface using a wash of water or solvent as the label directs.
◆ Wait for the surface to dry, then smooth it lightly with fine-grit sandpaper.

TENDING TO WOOD KNOTS

Preparing the surface.
◆ Scrape off any hardened resin with a sharp paring knife or similar utensil and clean the area with turpentine.
◆ If the knot is loose, remove it with long-nose pliers and fill the hole with wood putty or wood filler.

To conceal a protruding knot that you cannot remove, build up the surrounding area with putty or filler and sand to an unobtrusive slope.

Sealing a knot.
◆ Sand the surface lightly, then paint it with thinned shellac.
◆ When the shellac is dry, sand the surface lightly once more.

TRIM AND MOLDING

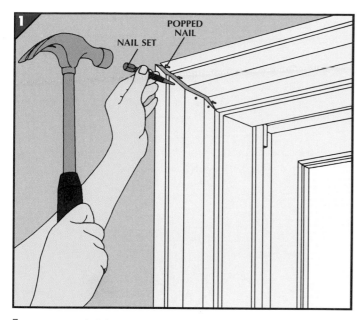

1. Countersinking a nail.
◆ Place a nail set on the popped nailhead, with the shaft perpendicular to the surface *(above)*.
◆ Strike the set with a hammer to embed the head about $\frac{1}{8}$ inch below the surface.

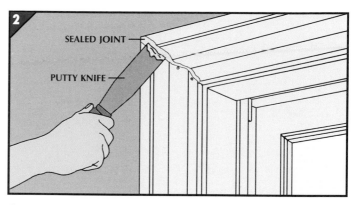

2. Filling a hole or joint.
With a flexible-blade putty knife, fill the nail holes with spackling compound or wood putty, depending on the surface you are preparing *(page 14)*.

◆ For slightly opened joints around window frames and doorframes *(above)*, apply spackling compound or wood putty, roughly shaping it to match the molding contours if the gap is wide. Caulk longer joints *(page 14)*.
◆ After the filler dries, check it for shrinkage and add more if needed.
◆ Sand the dried patches with fine-grit sandpaper.

PAINTING OVER WALLPAPER

There are a number of sound reasons for stripping off wallpaper before painting *(pages 58-61)*. Painstaking preparation counters most of them, but not all. For example, the design of a textured paper may show through the paint. And if you paint over several layers of paper, the combined weight of the layers and the paint may cause the paper to fall off the wall.

If you decide to paint a wallpapered surface, observe these principles: the paper must adhere firmly to the wall, it must be clean and grease free *(page 99)*, any imperfections in the paper must be repaired *(pages 96-99)*, and the surface must be treated with a wallpaper primer-sealer.

To patch an area of torn or missing wallpaper, first glue down any loose edges. Then cover the area with two thin layers of spackling compound, letting it dry between layers.

Apply the material with a wide-blade putty knife, extending the compound slightly beyond the edge of the damaged area. When the second layer is dry, sand the patch so that it is flush with the surrounding wallpaper.

If you wish to disguise a wallpapered surface, sand down the seams, then use the technique above to conceal them with spackling compound. Next, gently sand the entire surface of the wallpaper. Doing so raises a slight nap on the surface, so it will look less like painted-over wallpaper when the work is finished.

Vinyl- or plastic-coated paper will not hold paint, and wallpaper dyes may bleed through. Paint also can soften the adhesive holding the paper to the wall. To overcome these obstacles, coat all types of wallpaper with a wallpaper primer-sealer before painting.

Before painting a room, correct all defects in walls and ceilings. Wallboard can be repaired using the techniques on the following pages; plaster repairs are covered on pages 28 to 33.

Hiding Nails and Seams: Wallboard fastened with nails sometimes pulls away from the studs, causing the nails to protrude or pop. A popped nail can be reseated and covered *(opposite)*. If a seam between wallboard panels has opened, the gap can be bridged with conventional paper tape or fiberglass-mesh tape *(pages 22-23)*.

Patching Holes: You can fill dents in wallboard with vinyl spackling compound and a putty knife that is wider than the depression. The same remedy applies to small nail holes and others up to $\frac{1}{4}$-inch in diameter. For holes up to an inch across, stuff in a wad of newspaper to give the compound something to adhere to. Larger holes—up to 6 inches across—require a more substantial backing of wire screening fastened to the inside of the wallboard *(pages 23-24)*. Sections of damaged wallboard wider than 6 inches can be cut out and replaced with a patch *(pages 25-27)*.

 TOOLS

Hammer
Putty knives
Sanding block
Metal file
Finishing knife
  (10")

Scissors
Wallboard saw
Utility knife
Carpenter's square
Electric drill

 **MATERIALS**

Nails
Joint compound
Sandpaper (fine-grit)
Scrap wood
Wallboard joint tape
  (paper or fiber-
  glass)

Wire screening
String
Patching plaster
Dowel
1 x 3s
Dry-wall screws
  ($1\frac{1}{4}$", $1\frac{5}{8}$")
Wallboard
Wood screws (3")

 SAFETY TIPS

Protect your eyes with goggles when hammering, drilling, or sawing, and wear a respirator while sanding.

RESEATING POPPED NAILS

1. Securing and dimpling the nail.
Hammer the nail flush with the wallboard. Then carefully drive the nail a fraction of an inch below the surface, so the hammer's face creates a small depression, or dimple, in the surrounding wallboard without breaking the surface. (A driven and dimpled nail is shown to the right of the joint here.)

If the nail refuses to stay put, insert a new nail 2 inches directly above or below it. Dimple the new nail, then reseat the original one.

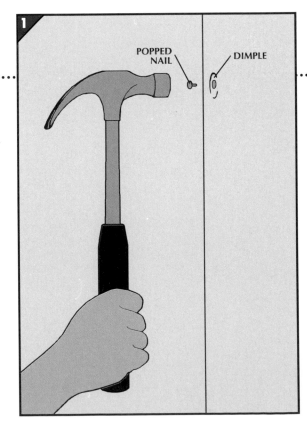

POPPED NAIL

DIMPLE

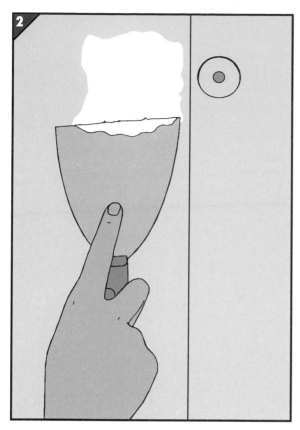

2. Patching the dimples.

◆ Apply a thin, smooth layer of joint compound over each dimple with a putty knife *(above)*. Let the compound dry; as it does, its color will change from dark to light beige.

◆ Apply a second layer of joint compound over a slightly larger area than the first layer.

◆ Smooth out any rough spots, especially at the edges, and let the patch dry.

3. Leveling the surface.

◆ Gently sand the patches with fine-grit sandpaper wrapped around a sanding block. For smoothest results, rub the block across the patch in a circular motion.

◆ Feather the edges of the patches *(page 15)*, and clear away the dust before repainting.

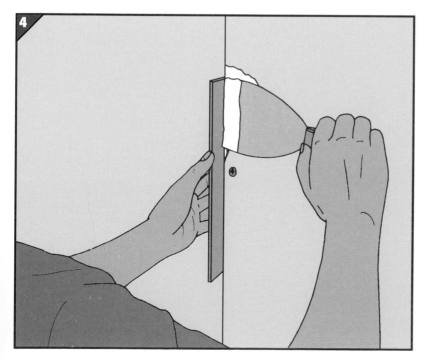

4. Rebuilding a corner.

◆ If the corner bead has been damaged, reseat it with $1\frac{5}{8}$-inch dry-wall screws and flatten any protruding bends with a metal file.

◆ Roughen the damaged surface on each side of the corner with coarse sandpaper, then brush clean and dampen.

◆ Holding a flat piece of wood against one side of the corner, apply joint compound to the other *(left)*. Reverse sides and repeat, taking care not to dent the fresh joint compound.

◆ Scrape off excess compound and let the area dry for 24 hours.

◆ Repeat this step as required, using fine-grit sandpaper on a sanding block to smooth the patch after each coat.

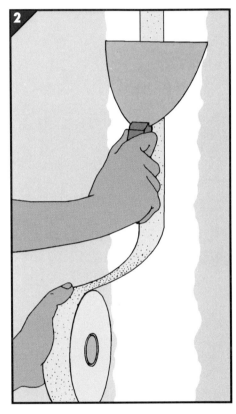

1. Filling the joints.

◆ Remove any loose or damaged tape and crumbled joint compound from between the sections of wallboard.

◆ Spread a $\frac{1}{8}$-inch-thick layer of joint compound directly over the joint with a 6-inch-wide putty knife, pressing the knife firmly against the wallboard to force the compound into the joint.

A QUICKER JOINT WITH FIBERGLASS TAPE

Although perforated paper tape is the traditional material for covering wallboard joints, you can save some time by using fiberglass-mesh tape instead. Because this product is sticky on one side, you do not have to first apply joint compound to the seam for attachment. Simply stretch the mesh tape along the joint, pressing it down so that it adheres, then follow Steps 3 and 4 to finish the seam.

FIBERGLASS-MESH TAPE

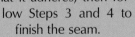

2. Applying the tape.

Before the joint compound dries, cover the filled seam with a single, unbroken piece of joint tape as follows:

◆ Roll out a 2-foot section of perforated paper joint tape.

◆ Center the end of the tape over the top of the joint, and press it into the joint compound.

◆ With the tape in one hand and the knife in the other, draw the knife over the tape at a 45-degree angle to embed it in the joint compound (above). Unroll more tape in 2-foot sections as needed. If the tape wrinkles or veers away from the joint, lift it up carefully and recenter it.

◆ At the end of the seam, cut the tape from the roll.

When repairing only a short section of a joint, slightly overlap the ends of the old tape with the new tape.

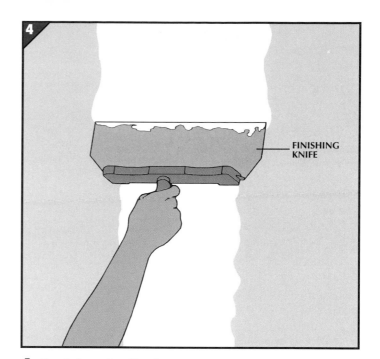

FINISHING KNIFE

3. Covering the tape.
◆ Apply a thin, smooth layer of joint compound over the tape *(above)*. Use enough compound to extend this second layer about an inch beyond the edges of the layer applied in Step 1.
◆ Let the patch dry completely. Unless the weather is humid, this should take about 24 hours.

4. Applying the final coat.
This completion of the repair goes fastest if you use a 10-inch finishing knife instead of the 6-inch putty knife.
◆ Smooth on a very thin finish coat of joint compound in a layer about 10 to 12 inches wide.
◆ Let the patch dry.
◆ Sand the area with fine-grit sandpaper wrapped around a sanding block, feathering the edges *(page 15)*.

FILLING HOLES IN WALLBOARD

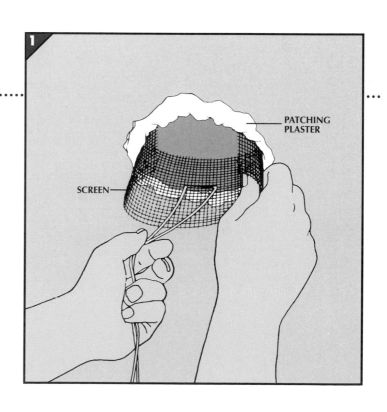

PATCHING PLASTER

SCREEN

1. Patching large holes.
◆ Remove the loose or torn wallboard around the opening.
◆ Cut a piece of wire screening that is slightly larger than the hole. Thread a length of string through the middle of the screen.
◆ Wet the inside edges of the hole with water and apply patching plaster to them. Then spread plaster on the inside of the wallboard, around the hole edge.
◆ Insert the screen through the hole *(right)*. Pulling the ends of the string gently, draw the screening flat against the inside of the hole and embed it in the fresh plaster.

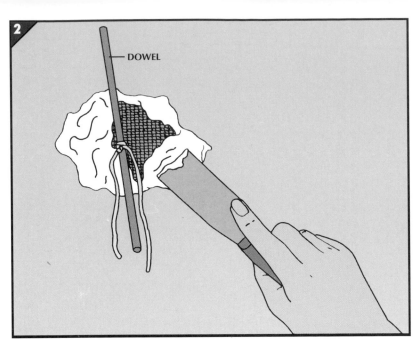

2. Initial filling.
◆ Secure the screen by placing a dowel across the opening and tying the ends of the string firmly around it.
◆ Fill the hole with plaster to a level almost—but not quite—flush with the wallboard surface *(left)*. Leave only a small gap around the string.
◆ Turn the dowel slightly to increase tension on the string and screen.
◆ Let the plaster set for 30 minutes.

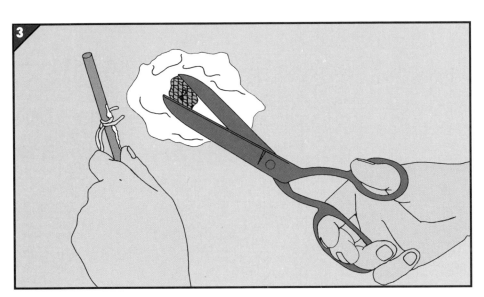

3. Removing the dowel.
◆ Cut the string as close to the screen as possible and then remove the dowel *(left)*.
◆ Wet the edges of the remaining gap and fill the gap with fresh plaster.
◆ Plaster over the entire patch to bring it flush with the wallboard surface.
◆ Allow the patch to set.

4. Final sealing.
◆ With a wide-blade putty knife, spread joint or spackling compound over the patch. Extend this final layer beyond the edges of the previous layer with long, smooth sweeps of the knife.
◆ Let the patch dry for about 24 hours.
◆ Finally, sand the patch with fine-grit sandpaper wrapped around a sanding block. Feather the edges of the patch *(page 15)*.

REPAIRING EXTENSIVE DAMAGE

1. Cutting out the damage.
◆ With a carpenter's square, pencil a rectangle around the damaged area.
◆ Cut along the edges of the rectangle using a wallboard saw or a keyhole saw. With a wallboard saw *(right)*, start the cut by forcing the pointed tip of the saw blade through the wallboard. Drill holes at the corners for a keyhole saw. As you saw around the damage, do not let the cutout drop behind the wall.
◆ Use the cutout as a pattern for a patch that is made from wallboard of the same thickness.
◆ From a 1-by-3, make two braces for the patch, each about 5 inches longer than the height of the opening in the wall.

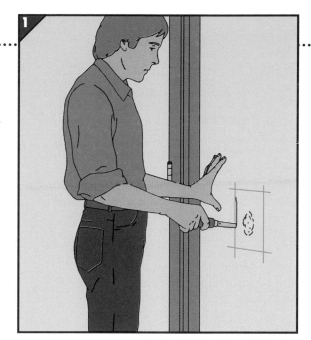

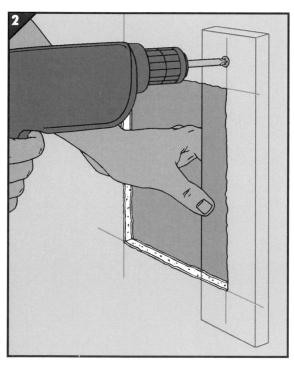

2. Installing the braces.
◆ Hold a 1-by-3 brace behind the wall so that it extends equally above and below the opening and is half hidden by the side of the opening.
◆ Drive a 1¼-inch dry-wall screw through the wall and into the brace, positioning the screw in line with the side of the hole and about 1 inch above it *(above)*. Drive a second screw below the opening.
◆ For holes taller than 8 inches, drive an additional screw along the side.
◆ Install the second brace on the opposite side of the opening the same way.
◆ Slip the wallboard patch into the opening, and screw it to the braces in the four corners and opposite any screws along the sides.

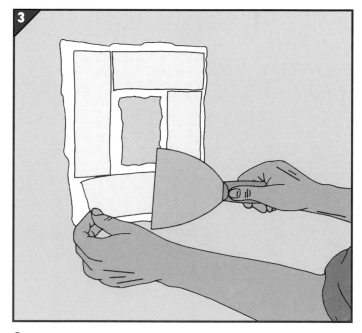

3. Taping the edges of the hole.
◆ Cover the screws and edges of the patch with joint compound, then embed strips of paper tape around the edges of the hole *(above)*.
◆ Using an 8-inch dry-wall knife, stroke the surface of the joint compound from the center of the patch outward, tapering the edges of the patch to the level of the surrounding wall.
◆ Allow the patch to dry for 24 hours, then apply a second coat, feathering the edges.
◆ Once the patch has dried, smooth it with fine-grit sandpaper on a sanding block, feathering the edges *(page 15)*.

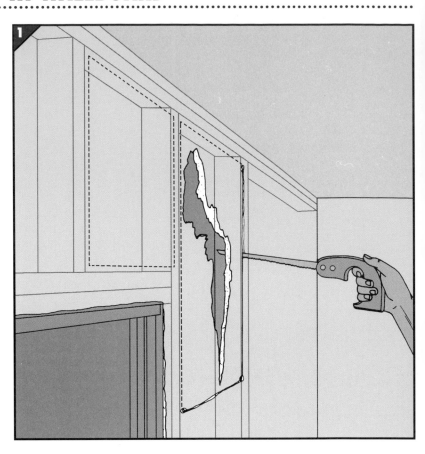

1. Cutting between studs and joists.

◆ Locate the position of the nearest stud or joist on each side of the hole *(page 326).*

◆ Using a carpenter's square, mark an opening with 90-degree corners to be cut around the hole. Draw along the inside edges of the two studs or joists that flank the hole, and along any framing members between them. If a stud frames a window or door as shown here, continue the marks to the next stud: Doing so avoids a joint in line with the opening, which would otherwise be subject to cracking from repeated opening and closing. Where a hole lies within 16 inches of an inside corner, draw to the end of the panel to avoid forming a new joint too close to the corner.

◆ Remove any wood trim within the marked-off area. If there are electrical fixtures or outlets, turn off power and unscrew cover plates.

◆ Cut out sections of wallboard between framing members with a wallboard saw or a keyhole saw *(right).*

2. Removing attached or blocked pieces.

Switch to a utility knife to remove wallboard attached to studs or joists or if you encounter obstructions in the wall (such as insulation or firestops).

◆ Cut through the sections, using a straightedge as a guide *(left).*

◆ Take out any screws or nails and chip off any wallboard mounted with adhesive.

◆ Cut away joint tape and torn surface paper with the utility knife.

◆ At an inside corner, pull out pieces of wallboard wedged in the butted joint.

◆ Sand uneven edges around the opening with coarse sandpaper on a sanding block and brush debris from the exposed framing, cleaning it for the patch.

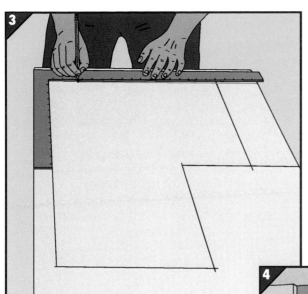

3. Making the patch.

◆ Measure each side of the opening as well as the sizes and positions of any electrical boxes, or door-frames or window frames, within it *(page 134)*.

◆ Transfer the measurements to a panel of the same type and thickness as the damaged wallboard, using a carpenter's square to ensure 90-degree corners *(left)*. Exclude the panel's tapered edges from the patch unless an edge of the opening falls at an inside corner.

◆ Cut out the patch, positioning the saw blade on the outline's inner edge; for an opening within the patch, cut just outside the line.

4. Adding cleats.

◆ For fastening the patch, cut 2-by-4 cleats to fit alongside the joists or studs at the edges of the opening. Where possible, cut the cleats 2 to 3 inches longer than the opening.

◆ Secure the cleats flush with the studs or joists using 3-inch wood screws driven every 4 to 6 inches along the cleat *(right)*.

5. Installing the patch.

◆ Before positioning the patch, mark the location of any exposed stud or joist on the wall or ceiling near the opening.

◆ Fit the patch in the opening and drive $1\frac{5}{8}$-inch dry-wall screws through the patch about every 6 inches into each cleat, stud, or joist, starting at the middle and working to the edges *(left)*. Do not screw the patch to a top plate or a soleplate.

◆ Finish the repair as described in Step 3 on page 25.

A wall or ceiling finished in plaster requires different repair techniques than one covered in wallboard, though some of the same materials are used for both. For example, small defects in either surface are filled with vinyl spackling compound or joint compound, and large areas are patched with wallboard.

To repair cracks and holes, clear away damaged material to expose the wood or metal lath behind the plaster, fill the opening with joint compound, and sand the area flush with the wall *(pages 30-31)*. Undercutting the edge of a hole will help hold the compound in place *(page 31)*. When patching large holes with wallboard, take particular care not to damage surrounding plaster *(pages 32-33)*.

 TOOLS

Can opener
Dry-wall knives
Putty knives
Chalk line
Hammer
Cold chisel
Keyhole saw
Electric drill

 **MATERIALS**

Joint compound
Joint tape (paper and
  fiberglass)
Patching plaster
Sandpaper
Plaster washers

Plywood ($\frac{1}{4}$")
Shims
Dry-wall screws
  (1", $1\frac{5}{8}$")
Wallboard
Construction
  adhesive

 SAFETY TIPS

Protect your eyes with goggles when hammering, drilling, sawing, or chipping plaster, and add a hard hat for overhead work. Wear a respirator while sanding.

REPAIRING A HAIRLINE CRACK IN PLASTER

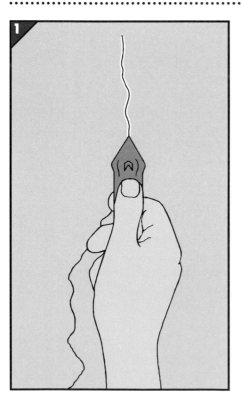

1. Cleaning.
◆ With the tip of a can opener, clear away loose plaster along the edges of the crack *(left)* so that the patching material will have a sound surface to grip.
◆ Remove a bit of the firm plaster at each end of the crack. This will keep the crack from extending farther in the future.
◆ Clear all dust out of the crack.

2. Sealing.
◆ Wet the crack and the surrounding area.
◆ Spread joint or spackling compound along the entire length of the crack. Make sure the patching material fills the crack completely and overlaps the solid edges.
◆ Let the patch dry for a day or so. If it shrinks, add another layer and allow it to dry.
◆ Sand the patch smooth.

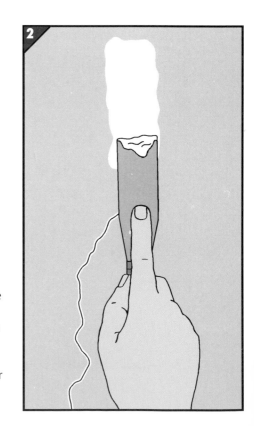

FILLING CRACKS

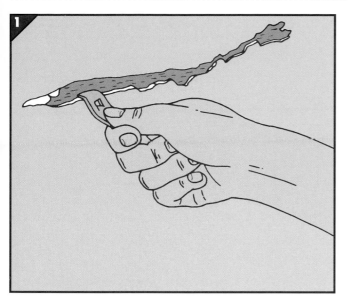

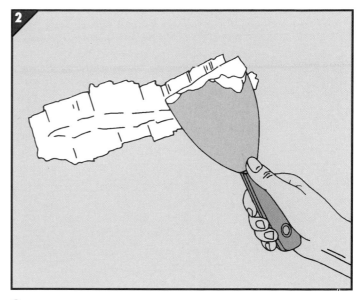

1. Preparing the crack.

This procedure applies to cracks comparable to the one shown here. Narrower cracks in sound walls do not require taping *(Step 3)*.

◆ To help lock the patching material in place, scrape some of the plaster from behind the edges; a can opener works well *(above)*. Doing so makes the crack wider at the base than at the surface.

◆ Brush out dust and loose plaster, then dampen the interior surfaces of the crack.

2. Filling the crack.

◆ Using a 5-inch dry-wall knife, pack joint compound into the crack, working it behind the undercut edges.

◆ Stroke the knife back and forth across the crack *(above)* until it is completely filled, then draw the knife along the crack to bring the patch surface flush with the wall.

◆ Allow the patch to dry for 24 hours.

3. Reinforcing the patch with tape.

◆ Cut a piece of fiberglass tape 2 inches longer than the crack.

◆ Spread a wide layer of joint compound over the crack.

◆ Press the tape into the compound, then run the knife blade along the tape to set it in place *(left)*.

◆ Allow the area to dry, then apply a second coat, feathering the edges.

◆ After the patch dries, sand it smooth.

PATCHING A SMALL HOLE

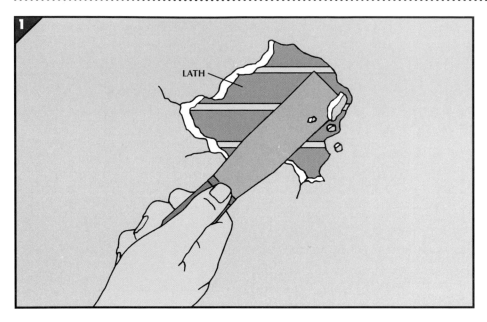

LATH

1. Preparation.
With a putty knife, clear away any loose or crumbling plaster from the edges of the hole, leaving sound plaster all around. If this enlarges the hole to more than 6 inches across, or if you find damaged lath underneath the plaster, call in a professional to complete the repair.

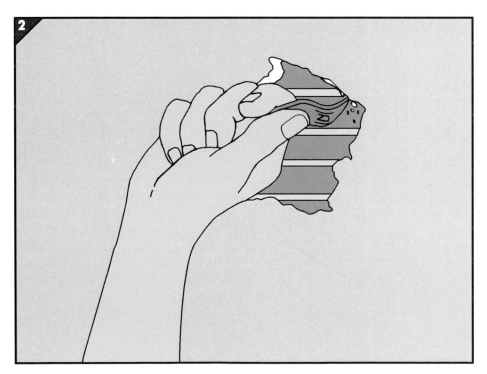

2. Undercutting.
◆ Using a can opener, undercut the edges to make the hole wider at the lath than it is at the surface *(left)*.
◆ Clear the plaster dust from the hole.

3. Applying the first layer.

◆ Moisten the edges of the hole and, if it is made of wood, the lath.

◆ Apply patching plaster to the edges, then fill the rest of the hole with plaster to about $\frac{1}{4}$ inch below the surface.

◆ While the plaster is still wet, score its surface *(right)*. The scoring will provide a better gripping surface for the next layer of plaster.

◆ Let the plaster set for 30 minutes.

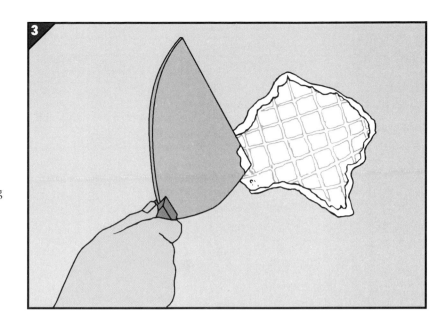

4. Applying the second layer.

◆ Dampen the scored layer and 2 or 3 inches of undamaged surface around the hole.

◆ Fill the hole to the surface with plaster, spreading it an inch or so beyond the hole's edges.

◆ Draw the knife blade evenly over the patched area to smooth it.

◆ Let the plaster set.

5. Completing the patch.

◆ Cover the filled hole with a smooth layer of joint or spackling compound *(above)*. Spread the material an inch or so beyond the edges of the patching plaster.

◆ Let the patch dry for several days.

◆ Sand the area smooth and feather the edges of the patch into the surrounding surface *(page 15)*.

WALLBOARD FOR LARGER FLAWS

1. Removing the plaster.

◆ Snap a chalk line to form a rectangle that encompasses the damage.

◆ To protect sound plaster from damage while clearing deteriorated plaster from the rectangle, screw plaster washers just outside the chalked lines.

◆ Score the plaster along the chalked lines with a utility knife; then, with a hammer and cold chisel, remove the damaged plaster within the rectangle *(above)*.

> ⚠ **CAUTION** *When chiseling plaster, work in small sections and tap the chisel gently. Excessive force can loosen plaster beyond the plaster washers.*

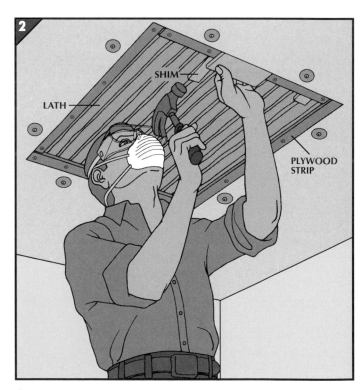

2. Attaching plywood strips.

◆ Cut strips of $\frac{1}{4}$-inch plywood, 1 inch wide.

◆ Edge each opening with the strips, loosely fastened with $1\frac{5}{8}$-inch dry-wall screws driven partway into the lath.

◆ Shim the strips to position a scrap of wallboard flush with the plaster *(above)*. Tighten the screws.

◆ Trim the protruding shims with a keyhole saw.

3. Installing the patch.

◆ Cut a piece of wallboard to fit the rectangle.

◆ Apply a bead of construction adhesive to each plywood strip, then press the wallboard against the adhesive.

◆ Fasten the wallboard to the plywood strips with 1-inch dry-wall screws 6 inches apart, starting at the corners *(left)*.

4. Taping the joints.

◆ With a 6-inch-wide dry-wall knife, spread a $\frac{1}{8}$-inch-thick layer of joint compound over all the joints *(right)*.

◆ Embed perforated-paper joint tape in the wet compound and run the knife over it, squeezing out excess material. Let the compound dry for 24 hours.

◆ Scrape off any ridges with the knife and apply a second layer of joint compound, called a block coat, with a 12-inch dry-wall knife centered on the joint. Allow the joint compound 24 hours to dry.

◆ Apply a final skim coat of compound with the 12-inch knife, feathering the material to a distance of 12 inches on both sides of the joint.

◆ When the compound is dry, smooth all the joints with fine-grit sandpaper.

Protecting Against Paint Splatters

Thoroughly preparing a room before you paint is well worth the time and effort. Doing so not only shields room contents from the inevitable splattering of paint, but saves time when cleaning up and results in a neater job. The only tool you'll need is a screwdriver.

Begin by shifting furniture into the middle of the room and covering it with drop cloths. Cover the floor as well, taping newspaper along the baseboards. Newspaper also makes an excellent shield for radiators and other objects that can't be removed.

Electrical: Turn off the circuit breakers or unscrew the fuses for the room. Unscrew switch plates and receptacle covers *(page 92)*, tape the screws to the plates, and set them near their original positions. If you wish, you can write the new paint brand, color, and type on a piece of masking tape and stick it to the back of one of the plates for future reference.

Loosen screws that secure light fixtures so that they stand away from the surface, allowing you to paint behind them later with a brush *(pages 40-41)*. Tape plastic around the fixtures, and make sure not to turn them on while the plastic is in place.

Smooth away ridges of old paint around the openings with sandpaper, taking care to observe the precautions for dealing with lead and asbestos that are outlined on page 15. Turn the electricity back on for illumination if it is necessary, but exercise caution when painting around the openings.

Hardware: Uninterrupted surfaces are easier to paint than those with obstructions, so remove as much hardware as possible—unless, of course, the objects themselves are to be painted. You may wish to take off items such as window-sash locks, strike plates, and cabinet handles. Masking tape will protect parts that are not easily removed, such as hinges, locks, and thermostats. Doorknobs can be removed or masked.

Window Glass: Many painters use the technique called beading, which is shown on page 41, for window sashes and dividers, but you might wish to protect the glass instead. Run masking tape around the edges of the panes, leaving a $\frac{1}{16}$-inch gap between the edge of the tape and the wood or metal so that paint can form a seal on the glass. This will prevent condensation from damaging the frame. When you are finished painting, peel the tape away.

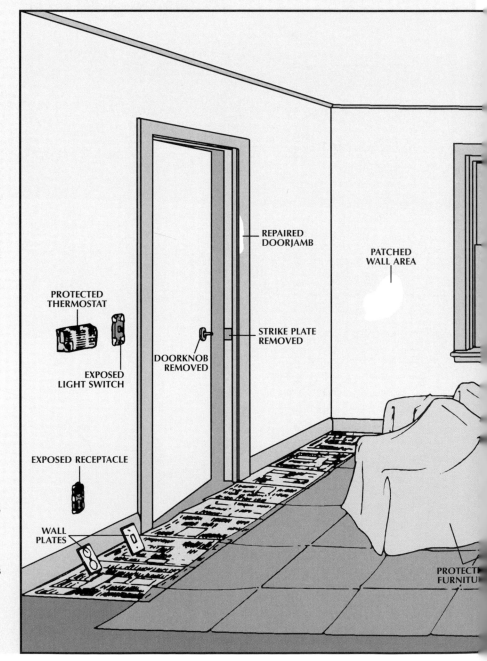

PROTECTED THERMOSTAT

EXPOSED LIGHT SWITCH

EXPOSED RECEPTACLE

WALL PLATES

DOORKNOB REMOVED

REPAIRED DOORJAMB

STRIKE PLATE REMOVED

PATCHED WALL AREA

PROTECT FURNITU

Drop cloths   Sandpaper
Newspaper   Rags
Masking tape
Plastic sheets

Preparing a room for painting.

The illustration below indicates the wide range of repairs and preparation that may be required before painting begins. Most repairs, such as patching cracks and holes or sealing wood joints *(pages 14-33),* will be necessary only from time to time.

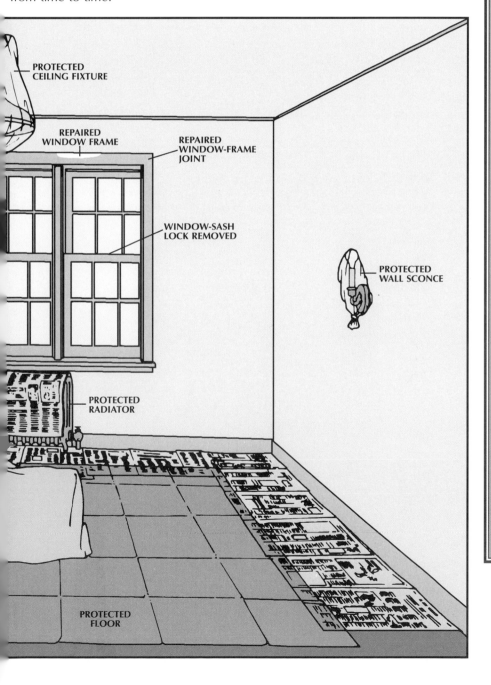

PROTECTED
CEILING FIXTURE

REPAIRED
WINDOW FRAME

REPAIRED
WINDOW-FRAME
JOINT

WINDOW-SASH
LOCK REMOVED

PROTECTED
WALL SCONCE

PROTECTED
RADIATOR

PROTECTED
FLOOR

Painting the Safe Way

Many products used in painting are toxic. Water-base products, such as latex paint, are the safest, but like most chemicals they contain poisonous ingredients. Use special care in handling solvent-base coatings such as alkyd paints, as well as related products like thinners, varnishes, and strippers. The fumes of some are so toxic that you may need a respirator approved by the National Institute of Occupational Safety and Health. Many of these products are highly flammable—some even require that you extinguish gas range or water-heater pilot lights before beginning work. In addition, follow these precautions:

✔ Keep children and pets out of the work area.

✔ Read labels of products for special requirements, and keep the labels on hand should you need to call a doctor.

✔ Work only in a ventilated room. Open doors and windows, and use fans to dispel fumes.

✔ When painting a ceiling, work in a position that prevents paint from falling in your eyes.

✔ Wash any coating off your skin as soon as you can, and scrub up carefully after each session.

✔ Immediately clean paint off an animal's skin or fur—it can do serious harm, especially if the animal tries to lick it off. Wash away latex paint with plain water. Remove alkyd paint with a cloth soaked in mineral oil or cooking oil. Never use turpentine or any other powerful paint solvent: it will burn the animal's skin and will be doubly dangerous if the animal licks it off.

✔ Dispose of all paint, solvents, and other toxic chemicals in an approved manner. Call your local sanitation department or environmental protection office for advice.

The two major tools for any painting job are the roller and the brush. Rollers are by far the easier to use. They require none of the special handling necessary with brushes and can paint a wall or ceiling twice as fast as a brush can. On the other hand, brushes are more versatile, and most jobs need at least some brushwork to paint areas unreachable with a roller.

Choosing a Brush or Roller:
While a single roller may suffice for an entire job *(page 37)*, you will need more than one brush. Consult the guide on page 13 to see the different kinds of brushes.

You must also match the applicator to the paint. Natural bristles and fibers lose resiliency as they absorb water from latex paint, so use synthetics with latex-base coverings. For alkyd-base paints, either a natural or a synthetic material is fine.

Preparing the Paint: Pigments sink rapidly to the bottom of a can of paint, the solvent rising to the top. So unless the paint has just been machine-agitated at the dealer's, mix it thoroughly before using *(page 38)*. Before doing so, however, check the paint to see if a skin has formed across the top. If so, use the procedure on page 38 to remove it. Never attempt to stir a skin back into the rest of the paint; the skin is insoluble, and stirring will only break it into tiny bits that show up on a newly painted surface.

Do not paint out of the original container. Instead, pour the paint into a pail, and keep the original can closed, so that the paint is less likely to dry out, get dirty, or spill. The tips on page 39 show how to keep paint clean and minimize drips and spills when pouring paint and moving it around as you work.

Using a Brush: For the neatest results and to stave off fatigue, hold the brush correctly. The long, thin handle of a sash brush, for example, is most effectively grasped with the fingers, much as you would hold a pencil. The thick "beaver-tail" handles of wider brushes, however, are best held with the whole hand, as you would hold a tennis racket. Whatever the handle style, periodically switch hands or grips to keep your hands from getting tired.

In addition to the basic up-and-down brush stroke *(page 40)*, there are two important techniques. The first is "cutting in," or painting a strip in corners between two surfaces of matching colors *(page 41)*. At wall and ceiling edges where two colors meet, or on the narrow dividers between windowpanes, a technique called beading allows you to paint a sharp edge *(page 41)*.

 TOOLS

Paintbrushes
Roller cover
Roller frame
Extension handle
Roller with drop shield
Pail
Paint stirrer
Electric drill with mixer blade
Hammer
Paint shield
Corner roller
Paint pad
Roller pan with grating

 **MATERIALS**

Paint
Cheesecloth
Wire screening
Paper plate
Finishing nail
Aluminum foil

 SAFETY TIPS

To minimize inhalation of paint fumes, always work in a well-ventilated area. When using alkyd-base paints and solvents, protect your hands with latex gloves.

BRUSHES AND ROLLERS

A design for efficient painting.
Whether natural or synthetic, the bristles of a typical paintbrush are frayed at the working end to hold as much paint as possible *(inset)*. At the other end, they are embedded in hard plastic, which is anchored to the brush handle by a metal band called a ferrule. Inside the ferrule, a spacer spreads the bristles at the base to create a thick, springy brush edge.

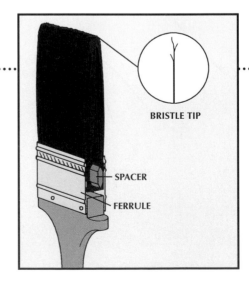

BRISTLE TIP

SPACER

FERRULE

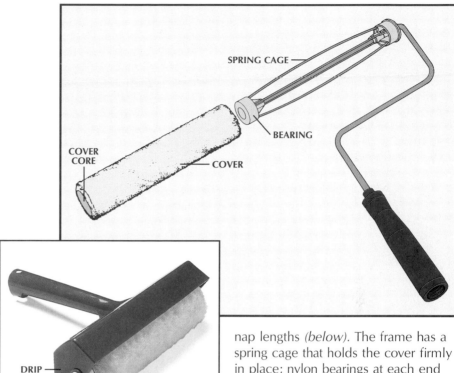

Anatomy of a roller.

Rollers consist of a cover and a frame, usually sold separately. Made of lamb's wool or synthetic fibers, the cover winds around a central core of plastic or cardboard and comes in a variety of nap lengths *(below)*. The frame has a spring cage that holds the cover firmly in place; nylon bearings at each end of the frame allow the cover to roll smoothly. To reach ceilings and high walls without standing on a ladder, screw an extension pole into the handle's threaded end.

For jobs where dripping paint may be a problem—such as when painting ceilings—purchase a roller frame with a built-in drip shield *(inset)*.

Choosing a nap.

Roller covers are available in three kinds of nap: short, medium, and long. Short nap, about $\frac{1}{4}$ inch deep, holds less paint than the others but leaves a thin, smooth coating that is ideal for glossy paint. All-purpose medium nap, between $\frac{1}{2}$ and $\frac{3}{4}$ inches deep, holds any type of paint well and produces a softly stippled effect. Long nap, from 1 to $1\frac{1}{4}$ inches deep, is good for working a thick coat of paint into textured or porous surfaces and leaves behind deep stipples in the paint.

Roller covers need no special preparation unless you are using glossy paint and a new, short-nap roller. In that case, prime the roller by sloshing it in soapy water to remove loose strands of material. Rinse the cover thoroughly and dry it completely before you begin.

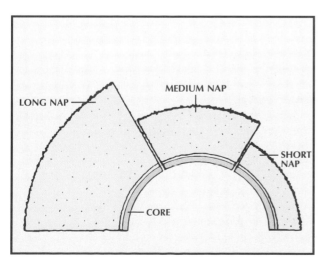

PREPARING THE PAINT

Manual mixing.
◆ Pour the top third of the paint—the thinnest portion—into a pail.
◆ Stir the remaining paint to a uniform consistency with a wooden or plastic paddle.
◆ Gradually return the thinner paint to the can, stirring continuously until the paint is thoroughly mixed *(left)*.
◆ Pour the mixed paint from can to pail and back several times for a final, thorough blending.

TRICKS OF THE TRADE

A Better Stirring Stick

To make a wooden or plastic paint stirrer more effective, drill a few $\frac{1}{4}$- or $\frac{3}{8}$-inch holes along its length. As you stir the paint, the holes generate extra turbulence—resulting in quicker mixing.

Power mixing.
While faster than manual mixing, this technique requires more care, since you must keep the mixer's spinning metal blades from damaging the can's rustproof coating.
◆ Secure a two-bladed mixer to the chuck of a variable-speed drill and adjust the drill's trigger stop for a low speed.
◆ With the drill off, lower the mixer into the can until it touches bottom. Then raise it a few inches, keeping both blades submerged.
◆ Turn on the drill, and move the mixer around the can for a minute or two *(right)*. To avoid splatters, turn off the drill before withdrawing the mixer.

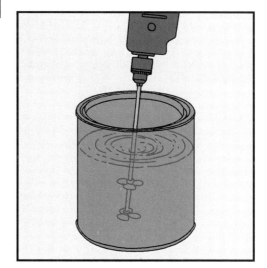

PAINT FILTERS AND DRIP CONTROL

Removing paint skin.
◆ Drape cheesecloth over a bucket, and secure the cloth to the rim with string or a rubber band.
◆ Gently separate the skin from the side of the paint can with a paddle.
◆ Pour the paint through the filter *(right)*, then discard the cloth and paint debris.
◆ Mix the remaining paint as described above; it is not affected by the loss of the material in the skin.

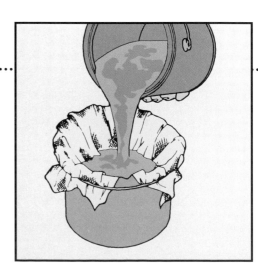

Keeping the paint clean.
This method is simpler than trying to fish out a brush bristle or other contaminant that falls into the paint.
◆ Cut a piece of window screening to the size of the paint-pail opening.
◆ Drop the screen onto the surface. The screen will sink, taking any debris to the bottom and trapping it there.

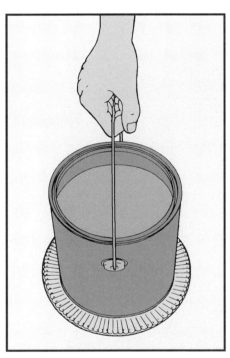

Drip-proofing the can.
A plastic-coated paper plate makes a simple drip guard. To ensure that the guard is always in place, secure the plate to the bottom of the can with loops of masking tape.

Preventing an overflow.
To keep the U-shaped rim of a paint can from filling with paint and overflowing, punch several nail holes around its circumference. Paint caught in the rim will then drain into the can, which can still be sealed for storage because the lid covers the holes. Keep the nail handy to reopen any holes that clog up with paint. Do not use this trick with cans smaller than a gallon; it may deform the rim, preventing the lid from making a tight seal.

BRUSHWORK BASICS

Loading the brush.
This technique helps prevent overloading and reduces the likelihood that paint will run under the ferrule, where dried paint can ruin the brush.
◆ Dip the bristles into the paint no more than halfway.
◆ Tap the ferrule gently against the rim of the pail to remove excess paint. Do not wipe the brush across the pail rim; doing so removes too much paint.

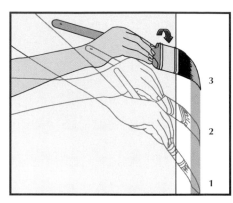

A feathered brush stroke.
Make the length of each stroke about double the length of the bristles. Wherever possible, end the stroke in the wet paint of a previously painted section.
◆ Start the brush stroke with the flat side of the brush angled low to the surface (1).
◆ As you move the brush, increase the angle gradually (2).
◆ End the stroke by drawing the brush up and off the surface with a slight twist (3); the brush should leave a thin, feathered edge of paint.
◆ If one stroke covers the surface satisfactorily, move on to an adjacent area. Otherwise, repaint the area with a second stroke.

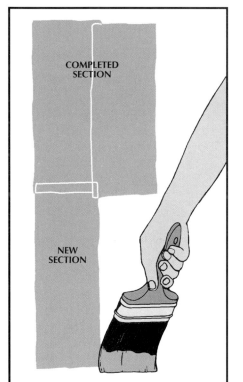

Painting in sections.
Cover a large surface in sections, each about two brush widths across and two bristle lengths long. With slow-drying paints, you can experiment with painting larger sections.
◆ Paint the first section, using up-and-down strokes combined with the feathering technique shown above.
◆ Then move to an adjacent section, working toward and into the completed area of wet paint (left).

Guarding as you go.
A metal or plastic paint shield, available where paint is sold, protects surfaces you do not want painted.
◆ Hold the edge of the shield against the surface you want to protect. If there is a gap at the boundary, such as often occurs between walls and baseboards or walls and carpets, gently push the shield into it.
◆ While holding the paint shield in place with one hand, paint along the length of the shield with the other hand (left).
◆ Remove the shield and wipe it clean. Then reposition the shield and paint the next section.

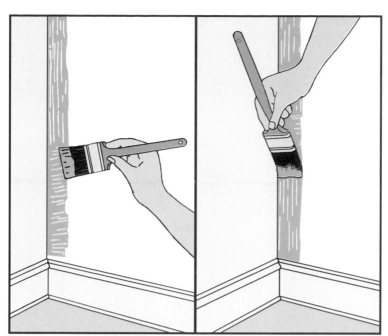

Cutting in.
◆ Make four or five 2-inch-long overlapping brush strokes perpendicular to the edge of the wall or ceiling *(far left)*. (At the bottom of the wall, make the last stroke about $\frac{1}{2}$ inch above the baseboard.)
◆ Smooth over the brush strokes with one long stroke. Wherever possible, end the stroke in an area of wet paint *(near left)* and use it to cover the small gap above a baseboard.
◆ Repeat this procedure along the edge of the adjacent wall or ceiling.

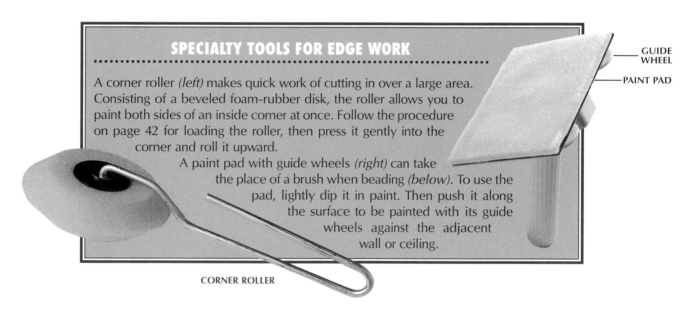

SPECIALTY TOOLS FOR EDGE WORK
• •

A corner roller *(left)* makes quick work of cutting in over a large area. Consisting of a beveled foam-rubber disk, the roller allows you to paint both sides of an inside corner at once. Follow the procedure on page 42 for loading the roller, then press it gently into the corner and roll it upward.

A paint pad with guide wheels *(right)* can take the place of a brush when beading *(below)*. To use the pad, lightly dip it in paint. Then push it along the surface to be painted with its guide wheels against the adjacent wall or ceiling.

GUIDE WHEEL

PAINT PAD

CORNER ROLLER

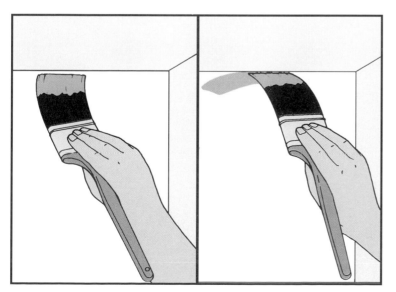

Beading.
This procedure works best with a stiff-bristled trim brush.
◆ Grasp the brush as shown here.
◆ Press the bristle tips against the surface near the edge, forcing a thin line of paint, called a bead, to emerge at the bristle tips *(far left)*.
◆ Then, in one smooth, steady motion, draw the bristle tips along a line about $\frac{1}{16}$ inch from the edge of the surface you are painting *(near left)*. Doing so forces the paint bead just to the edge of the surface.

LOADING A ROLLER

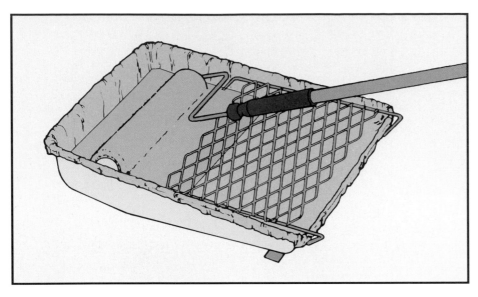

Distributing the paint evenly.
◆ Line a roller pan with aluminum foil to facilitate cleanup, then fill the well halfway with paint.
◆ Dip the roller in the paint, then roll it down the sloped grating, stopping short of the well. Repeat this two or three times.
◆ Dip the roller into the paint once more and roll it on the grating until the nap has been evenly saturated.

AN INITIAL ZIGZAG

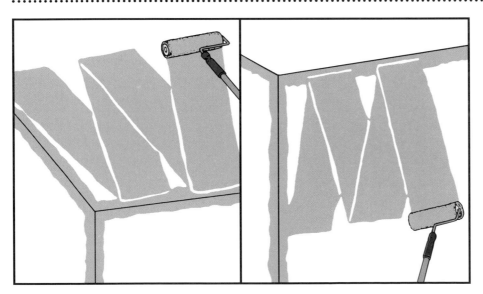

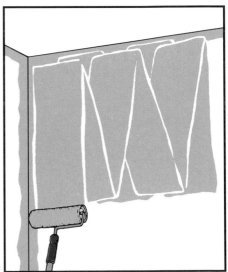

1. Starting a wall or ceiling section.
When painting with a roller, always make the first stroke away from you.
◆ To paint a ceiling, begin at a corner, about 3 feet away from one wall and overlapping the cut-in strip on the adjacent wall.
◆ Without lowering the roller from the ceiling, make three more strokes—alternately toward and away from you—to form a letter "W" about 3 feet square *(above, left)*.

On a wall, push the roller upward on the first stroke and then complete an "M" pattern *(above, right)*.

2. Completing the section.
Fill in the "W" or "M" pattern with crisscrossing strokes of the roller without lifting it from the surface. Use even pressure to avoid bubbles and blotches, and stop when the entire section is evenly covered with paint.

Reload the roller with paint, then repeat the preceding two-step sequence in the next section.

SPECIAL EFFECTS WITH PAINT

With a little extra effort and some simple tools, you can give an ordinary painted wall an eye-catching patterned finish. Stippling, ragging, sponging, and streaking, all shown below, are among the most popular methods.

A major appeal of these special finishes is that they draw the eye away from small imperfections in a wall or a ceiling. The thick paint that is used in stippling does even more—it can completely cover minor cracks and bumps.

The paint commonly used for these effects is available at most home-supply stores. Stippling requires a creamy, stucco-like covering known as textured paint, available in alkyd- and latex-base varieties. Sponging works with any type of paint, but a special glossy finish called a glaze is best for ragging and streaking.

Stippling

Since textured paint sets quickly, work in 3- by 3-foot sections. Begin by covering the first section with a $\frac{1}{16}$-inch-thick coat of paint, using a trowel, brush, or wide sponge-rubber applicator. Then pat the flat side of the tool against the wet paint. This raises peaks of paint on the surface, producing a deeply stippled effect.

Ragging

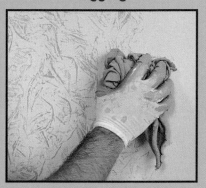

Apply a base color of alkyd semigloss paint to the wall. After the base coat dries completely, dip a clean, dry, crumpled rag into a glaze of the second color and dab it against the wall. Alternatively, you can roll a coat of glaze onto the base coat and dab it with a clean rag to reveal the underlying color.

Sponging

Cover the wall with the base coat, and allow it to dry completely. Then, lightly dip a sponge into the second color and dab it against the surface. The greater the pressure you apply with the sponge, the stronger the second color appears on the wall.

If you wish, you may sponge a second and a third color onto the base coat of paint, using a fresh sponge for each.

Streaking

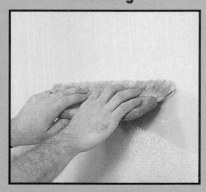

Also called stria, this technique gives the wall a gently striped effect that resembles wallpaper. After applying the glaze, drag a wide wallpapering brush vertically down the wall. If you need help keeping the brush straight, hang a plumb bob from the ceiling to serve as a guide.

To minimize drips and smears, work systematically from the top to the bottom of a room: Paint the ceiling first, then the walls, then windows, doors, and other woodwork, and finally the baseboards.

Ceiling and Walls: Plan on painting the entire ceiling and each wall without stopping. A roller attached to a 4- or 5-foot extension pole is ideal for reaching a ceiling. On a textured surface, be sure to use a roller with a long nap *(page 37)*.

On walls, some people prefer to paint in vertical portions from top to bottom. However, if you are using a roller on an extension pole to reach the top of the wall, you may find it easier to work horizontally, to avoid attaching the roller to—and removing it from—the pole more than once.

Windows and Doors: Painting double-hung windows in the sequence that is shown on the opposite page will solve the tricky problem of your having to move the sashes to paint surfaces that are obstructed by the lower sash. Paint the horizontal parts of the frame with back-and-forth strokes of the brush and the vertical parts with up-and-down strokes.

With doors, follow the techniques that are described on page 46 to achieve best results.

CEILINGS AND WALLS

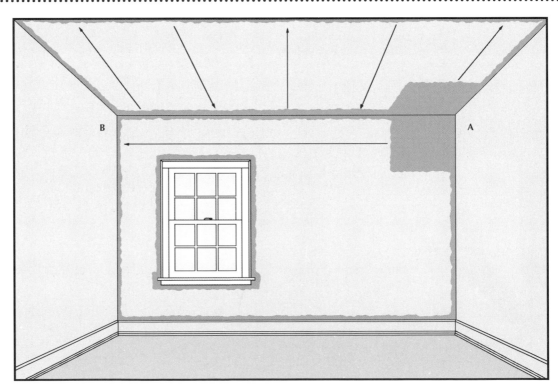

A basic pattern.
Paint a 2-inch-wide strip around the edges of the ceiling using the cutting-in technique described on page 41. Start painting the ceiling at a corner (A or B), then work back and forth across the short dimension of the ceiling in 3-foot-square sections, as indicated by the arrows. To prevent lap marks caused when wet paint is laid over dry, blend the paint at the edges of adjacent sections before the paint on either dries. After coating the entire ceiling, check your work for missed or thin spots, and revisit them with a roller lightly loaded with paint.

Before painting a wall, cut in not only along the edges, but also around the entire frame of any door or window and along baseboards. Apply paint across the wall in tiers, beginning at corner A or B and alternating direction as with the ceiling. Check your work for missed spots.

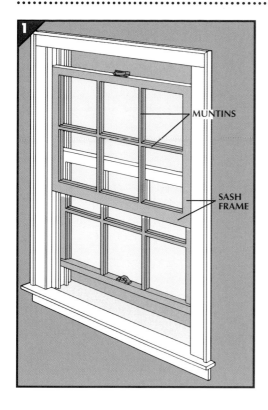

1. Start on the sashes.

◆ Raise the inside sash and lower the outside sash, leaving each open about 6 inches.

◆ Paint the inner sash first, omitting the top edge. Begin with the muntins (horizontals then verticals), followed by the sash frame (horizontals then verticals). Bead the paint onto the wood (page 41), allowing a narrow strip—about $\frac{1}{16}$ inch wide—to flow onto the glass and form a seal between the two materials. This irregular edge of paint is straightened during final cleanup (page 49).

◆ On the outside sash, paint the same parts in the same order as far as they are exposed—but do not paint the bottom edge until you paint the house exterior.

2. Complete the sashes.

◆ Push up on the bottom of the outside sash and down on the unpainted top of the inside sash, positioning them about an inch from their closed positions.

◆ In the same order as in Step 1, paint the surfaces of the outside sash that were obstructed; also paint the top edge of the inside sash.

◆ Proceed to paint the wood framing of the window, starting with the top horizontal. Coat the two side pieces next and finish with the sill.

◆ Wait until all of the paint is thoroughly dry before proceeding to the jambs in Step 3; meanwhile, work on other windows or on doors (page 46).

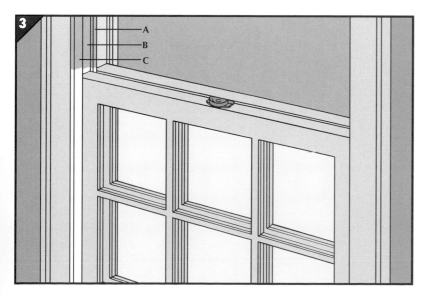

3. Finish with the jambs.

◆ When the paint is dry to the touch, slide both sashes up and down a few times to make sure they do not stick. Then, push both sashes all the way down to expose the upper jambs (left).

◆ Paint the wooden parts of the upper jambs in the order shown by the letters A through C; metal parts are never painted. Avoid overloading the brush to prevent paint from running into the grooves of the lower jambs.

◆ Let the paint dry, then raise both sashes all the way and paint the lower halves of parts A through C.

◆ Wait for the paint to dry, then lubricate parts A and B of the jambs with paraffin or with silicone spray.

CASEMENT WINDOWS

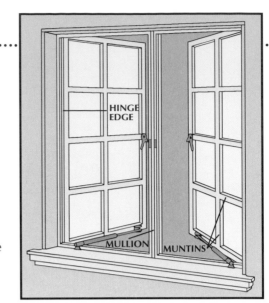

Windows that open outward.

Casement and awning windows may be made of aluminum, steel, or wood. An aluminum window does not need to be painted, but to protect the metal against dirt and pitting, consider coating it with a metal primer or with a transparent polyurethane varnish. Coat a steel casement with both a metal primer and paint, or with a paint especially suitable to metal, such as an epoxy or polyurethane paint. Treat a wood case-ment the way you would any other interior woodwork—unless the wood is clad in vinyl, which requires no paint.

Before painting, open the window. Working from inside outward and always doing horizontals first and then verticals, paint the parts in this order: muntins, sash frame, hinge edge, window frame and mullion, and sill. Leave the window open until all the paint dries.

DOORS, CABINETS, AND LOUVERS

Hinged doors.

◆ Cover metal hinges, knobs, and latches with masking tape to protect them from paint spatters.
◆ Work from top to bottom when painting a door. On a panel door, shown here, paint the panels first, the horizontal rails next, and finally the vertical stiles. The top and bottom edges of a door need be painted only once in its lifetime, to seal the wood and prevent warping.
◆ Paint the latch edge only if the door opens into the room you are painting. The hinge edge of a door is painted the color of the room it faces when the door is open.

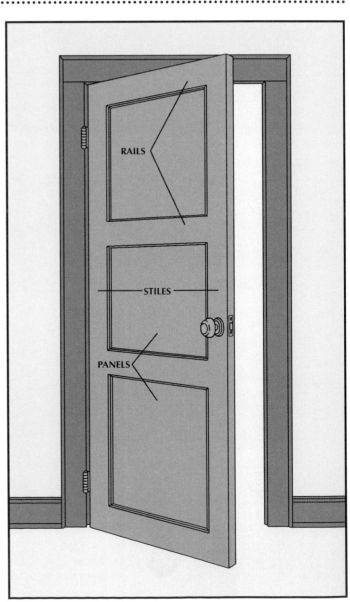

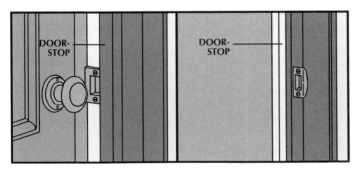

Doorframes and jambs.

◆ Paint the top of the door-frame, then the two sides, followed by the part of the jamb between the frame and the doorstop.
◆ Paint the doorstop as follows: If the door opens into the next room (above, left), paint the side of the door-stop that directly faces you and the broad side that faces into the door opening.
◆ If the door opens into the room you are painting, paint only the edge of the door-stop that the door closes against (above, right).

Painting a built-in cabinet.

◆ Remove all drawers; they will be painted separately.

◆ Work your way systematically from the inside of the cabinet to the outside, excluding the interior spaces where the drawers fit; they receive no paint *(right)*. Paint the walls first. Next, paint shelf bottoms, followed by the tops and edges. Do the insides of the doors before moving to the outside surfaces, painting from top to bottom.

Paint only the fronts of drawers *(inset)*. Do not coat the bottoms or exterior sides—paint there would prevent smooth operation. If you wish to paint the insides of drawers, do the sides first, then the bottoms.

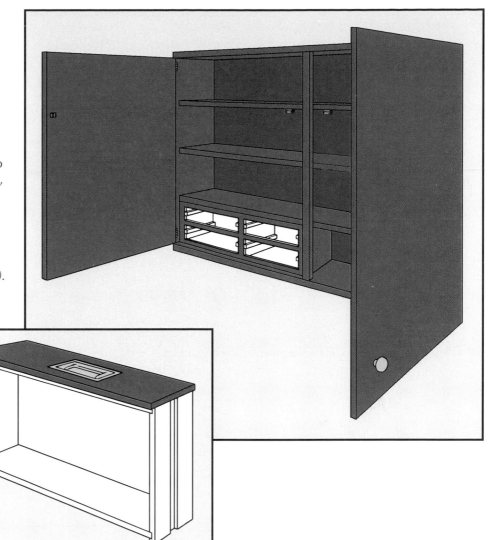

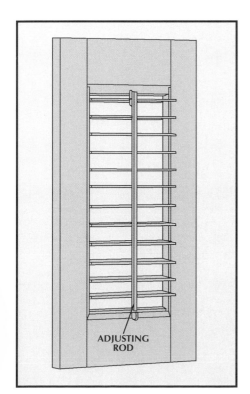

ADJUSTING ROD

Solving the slat problem.

The narrow slats of a louvered shutter or door call for a $\frac{1}{2}$-inch brush and a slow-drying alkyd paint, so you have time to smooth drips on the slats.

◆ For an adjustable louver *(left),* open the louver wide and set the slats to a horizontal position.

◆ Begin with the back of the panel so that you can smooth paint drips from the front.

◆ To avoid paint buildup where slats meet the frame, start painting at one end of a slat, flowing the paint toward the center in a long, smooth stroke. Repeat this technique at the opposite end of the slat.

◆ Cover as much of the slats as you can reach from the back side of the louver, opposite the adjusting rod.

◆ Turning the panel over, paint the inner edge of the adjusting rod, then wedge a matchstick or toothpick through one of its staples to keep the rod clear of the slats.

◆ Finish painting the slats one by one, smoothing out paint drips as you go.

◆ Next, paint the outer edges of the frame, horizontals first, then verticals. Paint the edges of the frame, and complete the job by painting the rest of the adjusting rod.

The slats of a stationary louver are set in a fixed, slanted position. Paint the backs first, from the ends toward the center. On the front, work the brush into the crevices between slats, then smooth out the paint with horizontal strokes.

Begin restoring a painted room to normal by pouring paint from buckets and trays back into the cans. Scrape as much paint as possible from the containers with a brush or roller. Clean the lip of the can and hammer the lid on tight.

Cleaning Your Equipment: Wipe buckets and roller pans clean using paper towels dampened with the appropriate solvent—water for latex- and vinyl-base paints, mineral spirits for alkyd-base products.

If you have been painting with water-base products, simply rinse brushes and rollers with warm running water. Use a paintbrush comb *(below)* to dislodge stubborn paint from brushes. To clean applicators of alkyd paint, fill containers such as coffee cans with enough solvent to cover a roller or the bristles of a brush. Agitate the applicator vigorously, replacing the solvent when it becomes saturated. Continue the process until the solvent is barely discolored, then run a paintbrush comb through the bristles.

Banishing Moisture: Dry brushes and rollers initially with a spin-drier *(opposite)*, then wash them in warm, soapy water. Rinse thoroughly, and use the spin-drier again.

Thoroughly dry brushes, hanging by the handle if possible; stand rollers on end.

Before putting away a brush, return it to its original package or fold it in heavy kraft paper *(opposite, top right)*. Hang it up or lay it flat for storage. Cover a roller with heavy kraft paper or place it in a perforated plastic bag to prevent it from becoming mildewed.

Final Touches: Cap thinners tight to prevent evaporation, and store them with leftover paint out of reach of children and well away from heat sources such as radiators and furnaces. Protect water-base paints from freezing.

Discard disposable dropcloths and paint-spattered newspapers. Check with local authorities as to disposal of used solvents and solvent-soaked paper towels. When the paint on window frames dries, scrape paint overflow from windowpanes as shown at the bottom of the opposite page.

⚠️ **CAUTION** *Provide adequate ventilation to disperse toxic fumes from solvents and thinners. Do not smoke near solvents and thinners or use them near an open flame.*

TOOLS

Paintbrush comb	Utility knife
Spin-drier	Ruler or putty knife
	Window scraper

Taking a Break

For interruptions lasting less than a day take the following precautions:

✔ If you will resume work within 15 minutes or so, simply rest your brush, unwrapped, on a support, never on its bristles. Leave a roller in the roller pan.

✔ For longer breaks, wrap wet brushes or rollers in plastic wrap or aluminum foil. Do not bind the bristles too tight.

✔ Cover paint that is left in a roller tray or pail tightly with plastic, or return the contents to the can and seal it. To avoid splatters, drape a cloth over the lid before tapping it in place.

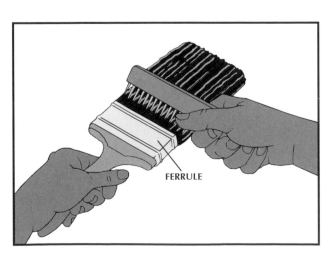

FERRULE

A comb for a brush.

◆ Push the sharp wire teeth of a paintbrush comb into the tightly packed bristles just below the ferrule, then pull the comb toward the tips of the bristles to loosen partially dried paint from the brush.

◆ At a later stage of the cleanup process, just before wrapping the paintbrush for storage, draw the comb through the bristles once more to straighten and untangle them. The brush is then ready for a future paint job.

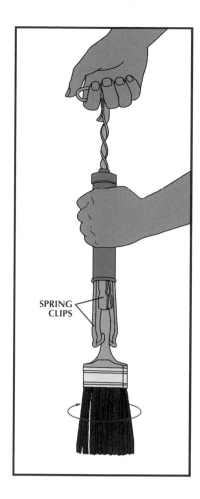

SPRING
CLIPS

A spin-drier for brushes and rollers.

This cleanup aid spins excess solvent or water from paint applicators with a minimum of effort. To avoid spraying nearby objects, keep the brush or roller inside a paper bag, a bucket, or a garbage can with a plastic liner (not shown).

◆ Secure a brush in the drier by pushing the handle into the stiff spring clips *(left),* or slip a roller over them.

◆ Push the handle in and out of the tube to spin the brush or roller at high speed. Doing so throws paint-laden solvent or water from the applicator by centrifugal force.

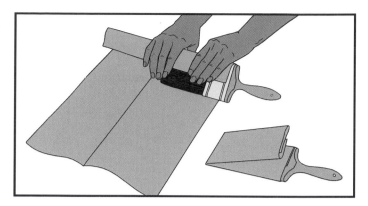

Wrapping a brush.

◆ Cut a rectangle of heavy kraft paper—a section of a grocery bag will do—about twice the combined lengths of the ferrule and bristles and about four times the width of the brush. Crease the paper down the center the long way.

◆ Place the brush on the paper as shown above and roll the brush into the paper.

◆ Fold the rolled-up paper at the crease. Secure it with a rubber band, making a wedge-shaped package that will preserve the bristles' taper.

A NEAT EDGE FOR WINDOWPANES

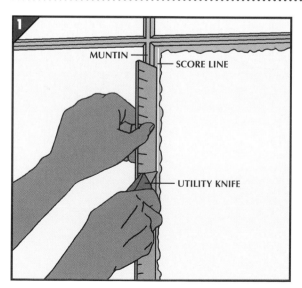

MUNTIN
SCORE LINE
UTILITY KNIFE

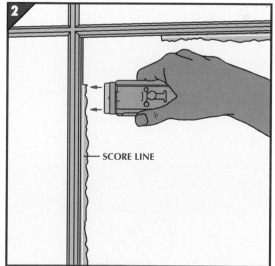

SCORE LINE

1. Scoring the paint.

With a utility knife or single-edged razor blade, score the paint on the glass, using a wide-blade putty knife or ruler as shown above to keep the score line at least $\frac{1}{16}$ inch from both sides of each muntin and from the sash or the casement frame.

2. Removing the paint.

Position a window scraper so that the blade is parallel to the score line, and carefully push the blade under the paint, stopping at the score. The paint will come off easily, leaving a neat, straight edge.

2 WALLPAPERING Techniques

The stunning array of wallpaper on the market suits any decorating mood and budget. Whether you opt for cheerful florals, stately paisley and foulard looks, soft neutral patterns, geometric designs, or traditional stripes, checks, and dots, it's important to apply your wallpaper correctly.

This chapter will help you do that with ease as you learn the basics of preparing walls for new wallpaper. We'll teach you how to remove existing wallcoverings and how to apply new wallpaper over existing paper. We've assembled a comprehensive tool kit for paperhanging. We'll show you how to hang your wallpaper and borders symmetrically and evenly for a professional-looking job. We've included tips on how to recognize and hang straight-match and drop-match patterns to their best advantage.

This chapter also covers types of wallcovering paste and how to apply it. Using time-saving prepasted coverings eliminates this step. You'll master trimming and brushing wallcoverings, as well as the ins and outs of papering around switchplates, doors, windows, slanted walls, and arches. A list of maintenance tips at the end of the chapter will help your finished wall treatment project wear as beautifully as it looks.

A large pattern maintains a spacious look while bringing life to a plain wall. The gentle neutral colors of this wallpaper add sophistication and act as a subtle, unobtrusive backdrop to wall hangings.

Dark, cool patterns are soothing and work well with the stately theme of this study. The vertical pattern below the chair rail stylishly mimics the look of more expensive wood wainscoting.

Brightly colored wallpaper is an inexpensive way to create a cheerful environment for your imaginative child. Here, an array of coordinating wallpapers, fabrics, and borders creates an interesting yet unified decorating theme.

patterns work well in small spaces where the detail ved clearly. Three matching coordinating patterns— l, running border, and small floral—make the walls esting. The soft cream background adds warmth.

Patterns & Materials

Like painting, wallpaper is one of the most cost-effective ways to dress up a room. Wallcoverings come in a myriad of designs and formats, which gives home decorators an endless palette of colors and patterns to work with. Paper patterned with stripes, checks, and plaids can lend a traditional look, while tiny floral patterns can be restful and relaxing. Textured neutrals produce a subtle, sophisticated look. Geometric patterns impart a clean, modern style and are particularly good for bathrooms. Large floral prints can make a room seem larger, and can even make a ceiling seem higher when arranged in vertical rows. To widen a room, try wallcoverings patterned with horizontal stripes.

After you've settled on a certain color scheme or look, purchase fabrics and wallpaper and borders at the same time to give your decorating project a coordinated look. If that's not possible, bring swatches of fabric and wallcoverings along so you can match patterns and motifs from store to store. To keep patterns from "fighting" each other, use only a few patterns in each room. Thin strips of molding such as chair rail can bridge two wallpaper patterns or hide seams.

Select wallcovering types according to durabilty and effect. Washable, scuff-resistant coverings are well suited for kitchens and bathrooms; vinyl-faced treatments backed with cloth or paper are particularly durable. Metallic foil

wallcoverings are embossed with light-reflective inks that produce a sophisticated look, as do wallcoverings flocked with fabric. These patterned coverings often highlight wall imperfections, and may require a base of lining paper beneath them. Burlap wallcoverings can be painted and are particularly good for areas prone to condensation. Heavy, matte textures make burlap, tweeds, and linens absorb light and produce warmer, muted effects. Grasscloth, made of natural grasses woven into cotton and backed with paper, is good for natural, textured looks. It's quite fragile, though, and must be hung carefully. Silk wall treatments are also fragile but are long-lasting and impart a luxurious look. They're usually backed with paper to make them easier to handle.

After you've cut and hung the wallcovering, be sure to save the scraps. They'll come in handy for repairing any future rips or tears and can be used to cover hatboxes, wastepaper baskets, and room screens. Try placing these items in your wallpapered room for a customized, coordinated look. Used in other rooms, the scrap-covered items can subtly and economically extend your decorating scheme throughout the house. Wallpaper also lends itself perfectly to lining drawers and closet shelves. Try using the scraps on kitchen pantry shelves, too, for a lovely and creative way to make the most of your wallcovering dollars.

A Tool Kit for Paperhanging

The paperhanging tools shown here are grouped according to the various stages of preparing a room for a wall covering and hanging the paper.

Not every tool in this collection is necessary for every job. The water box, for example, is needed only for prepasted papers, and the artist's brush is used mostly for small repairs to damaged or peeling wallpaper. Tools like the trimming knife and the utility knife are interchangeable. Some do double duty; a utility knife and the seam roller, for example, are as helpful for minor repairs on previously hung paper as they are in hanging new paper.

All these tools are available at home-improvement and decorating stores; many are packaged as a complete wall-covering tool kit. If you are acquiring tools separately, buy only those you need for your project.

Scraping and repairing.
A wall scraper is the tool used to remove paper without wetting it or to break the surface for soaking. A wide, flexible putty knife helps peel a soaked covering away from a wall. You need a narrower, rigid putty knife if the walls must be repaired before the new covering is applied.

WALL SCRAPER

FLEXIBLE PUTTY KNIFE

RIGID PUTTY KNIFE

PLUMB BOB

Measuring and marking.
A metal straightedge at least 36 inches long takes measurements and guides long cuts. A plumb bob helps you establish a precise vertical line. The chalk line marks a straight line on a wall; the string coats itself with powdered chalk stored in the case.

CHALK LINE

METAL STRAIGHTEDGE

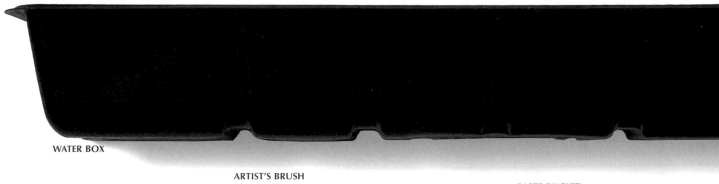
WATER BOX

ARTIST'S BRUSH

PASTE BUCKET

Pasting.

A paste bucket and brush are used to mix and apply adhesive. Water boxes come in several sizes; an extra-long one lets you soak two strips of prepasted paper at a time. The artist's brush is ideal for pasting small tears or peeling corners.

PASTE BRUSH

SEAM ROLLER

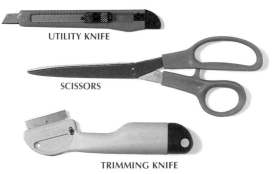
TRIMMING GUIDE

Cutting.

Wallpaper can be cut with scissors, a utility knife, or a trimming knife. This utility knife has a segmented blade; snap off the tip when it dulls. The trimming knife uses a single-edged razor blade.

UTILITY KNIFE

SCISSORS

Edging and rolling.

The metal trimming guide creases paper against the wall at a ceiling or baseboard for cutting. A seam roller gives a final smoothing to edges.

TRIMMING KNIFE

SPONGE

SMOOTHING BRUSH

Smoothing and cleaning.

A smoothing brush fixes the paper firmly on the wall. The sponge is for wiping up stray adhesive. For prepasted papers, a sponge is recommended for smoothing instead of the brush.

Whatever type of surface you are papering over—wood, new wallboard or plaster, paint, a stripped wall, or existing paper—the wall must be properly prepared if the new paper is to adhere well.

Preparing a Painted Surface: Before papering over paint, wash the wall with a household cleaner to remove mildew, dirt, and grease, and rinse well. Lightly push a flexible putty knife along the walls to knock off any loose material and also to help you find popped nails or other imperfections in the wall. Repair damaged surfaces as described on pages 20 through 33, then coat the wall with an opaque all-purpose primer-sealer, which is compatible with all types of papers and adhesives.

Primer-sealer prevents paste from being absorbed into the wall and provides a surface for the new paper to glide onto easily. It binds chalking paint, eliminating the need to remove an old finish, and it roughens semigloss and satin paints for good paper adhesion.

Stripping Paper: Whenever possible, remove old paper; new coverings will always adhere better to a stripped wall. Vinyl or vinyl-coated coverings, which can be identified by their smooth, plastic textures, are called strippable papers because they are easily pulled from a wall. If a test pull at a top corner gets no results, you are probably dealing with a nonstrippable material or a strippable paper applied over unprimed wallboard. Try removing the paper by soaking or steaming *(pages 59-61)*.

If these methods fail—as may happen in a bathroom covered with a vinyl material stuck to the wall with waterproof adhesive—you can dry-scrape the wall *(opposite)*. Once you have stripped the paper, prepare the walls as you would a painted surface.

Papering over Paper: You may decide to apply new paper over an existing wall covering because the wall beneath is too fragile to withstand paper stripping, or because the time you save by leaving the old paper on the wall is more important than the long-term durability of the job.

Applying new wallpaper over old, however, is risky: the water in wallpaper paste can loosen old layers so they pull away from the wall. Make sure the old covering is firmly attached to the wall and as smooth as possible.

Never attempt to paper over more than three layers of paper, no matter how well they seem to be attached. The weight of the additional layer, plus wet wallpaper paste, can pull away the whole sheaf of papers.

Apply spackling compound to smooth the seams, and coat the old paper with opaque all-purpose primer-sealer. If you are applying new paper to vinyl, you must use a vinyl-to-vinyl adhesive, even if the new paper is prepasted.

Final Preparations: Before getting ready to apply new paper, refinish the trim and paint the ceiling if these are part of your redecorating plan. While it is simple to wipe wallpaper paste from woodwork, cleaning paint from new wallpaper is next to impossible.

TOOLS

Flexible putty knife (3" or 4")
Utility knife
Wall scraper
Sponges
Cheesecloth
Wallpaper steamer

MATERIALS

Water
Chemical stripping solution
Primer-sealer

SAFETY TIPS

When you are working with chemical stripping solutions, rubber gloves and goggles are essential. A dust mask prevents droplets of the solution from getting in your mouth and nose.

STRIPPING AND SCRAPING OLD PAPER

Removing strippable wall coverings.
◆ With a fingernail or a utility knife, lift a corner of the covering at the top of a section.
◆ Carefully peel the covering downward, pulling it flat against itself *(left)* to minimize ripping of the paper backing.
◆ Remove any backing that remains stuck to the wall, but leave the fuzzy residue to help the new wall covering adhere.

If the paper surface of wallboard peels off with the wall covering, it was applied without a primer-sealer. Soak the material to remove it *(below)*, or repaste the corner and apply the new wall covering over the old.

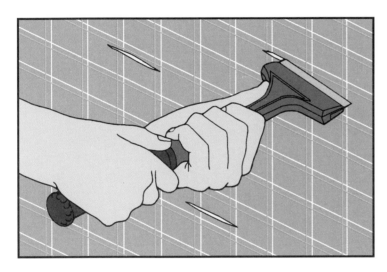

Dry-scraping paper.
Nonstrippable papers that cannot be soaked off because of waterproof adhesives must be removed from the wall using a wall scraper.
◆ Hold the blade of the scraper perpendicular to the wall and slit the paper horizontally. Apply gentle pressure to avoid damaging wallboard behind the paper.
◆ Slide the blade into a slit at an angle and loosen a section of paper at a time. Tear the loosened sections off with your fingers.

SOAKING PAPER TO REMOVE IT

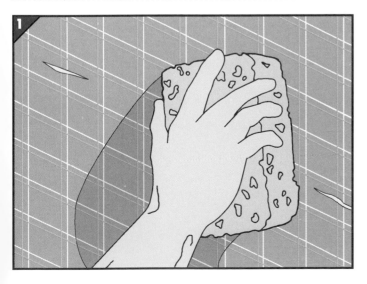

1. Wetting the paper.
A stripping solution of ethyl alcohol and other chemicals or a liquid containing enzymes that break down the organic materials in wallpaper paste works more quickly than plain water.
◆ Spray the paper with a small amount of water. If the water penetrates, there is no need to perforate the paper. Otherwise, you must puncture the paper so that stripping solution can get behind it. Use either the blade of the scraper *(above)* or the perforating tool shown on page 60.
◆ With a large sponge or a garden sprayer set for a fine stream, not a mist, wet all the walls with stripping solution.
◆ Wait 5 to 10 minutes—or the length of time recommended by the manufacturer—then wet the first wall again and proceed to Steps 2 and 3. (Always resoak a wall before beginning to strip paper.)

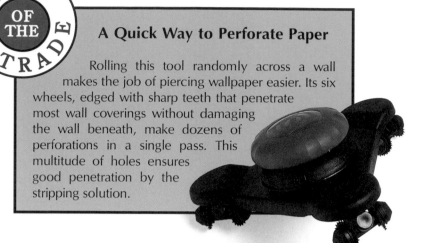

A Quick Way to Perforate Paper

Rolling this tool randomly across a wall makes the job of piercing wallpaper easier. Its six wheels, edged with sharp teeth that penetrate most wall coverings without damaging the wall beneath, make dozens of perforations in a single pass. This multitude of holes ensures good penetration by the stripping solution.

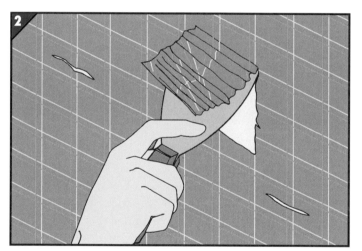

2. Loosening the paper.

Holding a putty knife at about a 30-degree angle, firmly push the wet paper up from one of the perforations in the paper. The paper should come up easily *(left)*. If it does not, resoak and try again. Where the stripping solution fails to soften the paste, you will have to use a steamer *(opposite)*.

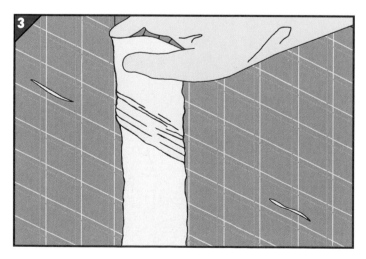

3. Stripping paper away.

◆ Grasp the loosened paper with your fingers and draw upward steadily and firmly *(left)*. To help prevent the paper from ripping, pull it parallel to the wall.
◆ After stripping off all the paper in the room, wash the walls with cheesecloth dipped in the stripping solution to remove any of the remaining scraps of wallpaper and paste.

THE POWER OF STEAM

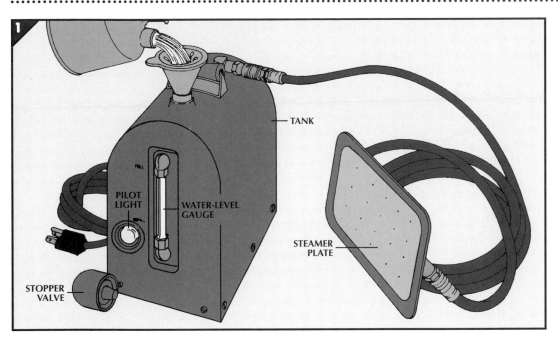

TANK

PILOT LIGHT

WATER-LEVEL GAUGE

STEAMER PLATE

STOPPER VALVE

1. Starting the steamer.

When soaking fails, rent an electric steamer, available at most wallpaper dealers. Typically, the device consists of a boiler and a perforated plate that applies the steam to the wall covering.
◆ To fill the tank, unplug the cord and remove the stopper valve at the top.
◆ Set a funnel in the opening, and pour in boiling water until the water-level gauge indicates full.
◆ Plug in the steamer; a pilot light shows when the unit is on. The steamer is ready to use when vapor comes from the steamer plate.

2. Using the steamer plate.

◆ Hold the plate firmly against the wall without moving it.
◆ When the paper around the plate darkens with moisture or water droplets run down the wall, move the plate onto an ad-jacent area in the same strip of paper and repeat the steaming process.
◆ When you have steamed half a strip, proceed to Steps 2 and 3 on the preceding page to remove the paper.

Wallpaper goes on the wall in consecutive strips, both clockwise and counterclockwise from the first one, with the pattern of each matching the previously completed section. Since the pattern unfolds from the starting point, the placement of the first strip affects the entire wallpapering job. Designs with narrow stripes and small random patterns match easily and can be begun conveniently alongside any door or window. But before you begin to hang a complex pattern, make sure you choose your starting point carefully.

Getting the Pattern Right: Complex patterns usually look best when the overall arrangement is symmetrical and the strips placed so the pattern draws a viewer's attention to a single part of the room—one wall, or the space above a fireplace, or the area surrounding one or more windows. When planning such an arrangement, try to avoid hanging strips whose width is less than

6 inches; they may be difficult to align and to affix.

Before putting up the first strip, inspect the wallpaper and note if the pattern is centered on the roll. If it is not, move the roll to the left or right to center the pattern on the wall rather than the roll.

Ensuring Alignment: When you hang the first strip and periodically thereafter, check to make sure that the paper is going on straight. Use a chalk line, metal straightedge, or carpenter's level to make vertical lines on the walls, and align the paper with them as you proceed *(page 65).*

A Suitable Finish: Unless the room contains an interruption on one wall such as a floor-to-ceiling storage unit or a built-in corner cabinet, a mismatch will occur along one edge of the last strip. Plan ahead to locate the mismatch in an inconspicuous place *(page 64).*

LOCATING THE FIRST STRIP

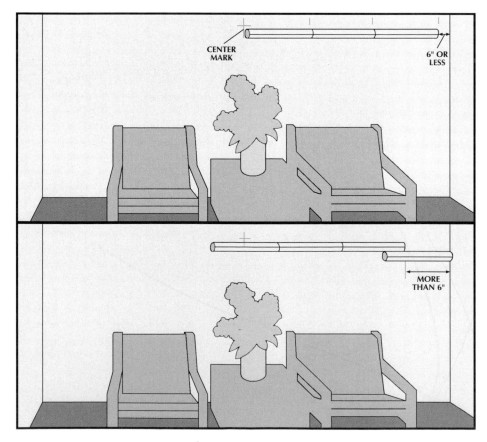

CENTER
MARK

6" OR
LESS

MORE
THAN 6"

To center on a wall.

◆ Locate and mark the center of the wall. Then, using a roll of wallpaper, measure the distance to the nearest corner: place one edge of the roll against the mark and move the roll toward the corner, one width at a time, until less than the width of one roll remains.

◆ If the remaining distance is 6 inches or less *(left, top),* plan to center the first strip of paper over the mark *(left, bottom).* If the remaining distance exceeds 6 inches, hang the first strip of paper where you started measuring— with the left edge of the strip against the pencil mark.

◆ To center the pattern above a fireplace, make the pencil mark above the center of the mantel and proceed as for a wall.

To center between two windows.

The width of the wall between the windows determines the placement of the first strip of wallpaper.

◆ With a pencil, mark a spot that is halfway between the windows and then center a roll of paper on that mark.

◆ If centering the roll on the mark results in narrow strips at each window edge *(above, left)*, you may prefer to hang the first strip alongside the center mark *(above, right)*.

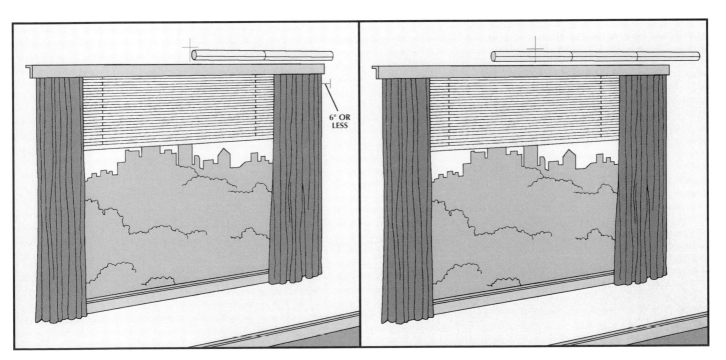

To center above a window.

◆ Mark the center of the wall section above the window and measure as for walls *(opposite)*, moving the roll toward the window's right upper corner.

◆ If the last full roll of wallpaper extends 6 inches or less beyond the corner of the window *(above, left)*, plan to center the first strip on the mark *(above, right)*.

PLANNING THE LAST STRIP

To end at a floor-to-ceiling interruption.
If a wall you plan to paper contains a section of paneling, a fireplace, or a built-in cabinet or bookcase, as in the illustration at left, make this area the target of your final strip. After you choose the location of your first strip *(pages 62-63)*, work from there both clockwise and counterclockwise, ending at the left and right sides of the interrupted area. In this way, there will be no mismatched strip anywhere.

To end in a partly hidden area.
An unobtrusive corner is best for ending in mid-pattern. In the room above, for example, the shallow corner where the fireplace meets the wall gets no direct light from the nearest window and is inconspicuous from most directions. Another option might be a corner of the room that is obscured by furniture.

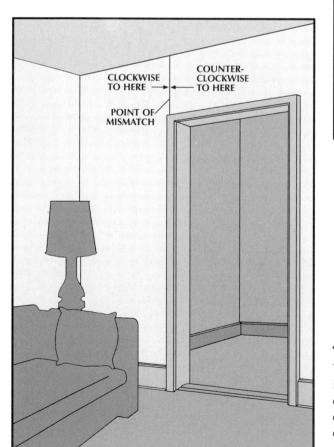

To end above a door.
The narrow strip of wall above a door is a likely place to finish papering. Join the last two strips above the side of the door that is closer to the room's nearest corner *(left)*. If the door is centered on the wall, consider the location of windows and lamps and choose the side of the door that receives less light.

GETTING THE PATTERN STRAIGHT

No house has truly vertical walls. If you hang strips of wallpaper by following the planes of the walls, the paper will be uneven by the time you finish the job.

To avoid slanted strips, draw a true vertical line and align the first strip with it. Recheck the alignment frequently, particularly after turning a corner; doing so enables you to move the paper before the adhesive dries. Two simple tools for marking a vertical line on a wall, a chalk line and a metal straightedge, are illustrated here.

Before putting up chalked lines, test one with your wallpaper; the chalk may show through some translucent or light-colored papers. You can substitute a carpenter's level for the straightedge; read both upper and lower vials to make sure that the level is truly vertical. Then press the level firmly against the wall and draw a pencil line along its side.

CHALK LINE CASE

STRAIGHTEDGE

Chalk line.
◆ Tack the end of a chalk line high on the wall; when the case stops swinging, the string will be vertical.
◆ Without altering the position of the case, pull it slightly downward until the string is taut, press it firmly against the wall, and snap the string with the other hand *(above)*.

Metal straightedge.
◆ Tack a metal straightedge loosely to the wall through the hole in one end.
◆ When the straightedge comes to rest, hold it firmly against the wall and draw a light pencil line along its edge *(above)*.

A Mess-Free Pasting Method

Unless you use prepasted paper and a water box *(opposite, bottom)*, the choice of an adhesive and its correct application have much to do with the success of a wallpapering project. Purchase the one recommended by the wall-covering manufacturer; if no such instructions accompany the wallpaper, follow your dealer's advice.

Types of Adhesive: Whether organic or synthetic, adhesives are available in both liquid and dry form. Pour liquids directly into a

bucket if you plan to apply with a paste brush, or into a roller tray for a paint roller. Dry adhesives must be mixed with water; directions on the package indicate how much. Approximately 30 minutes before use, pour the powder slowly into the water to minimize lumps. Mix thoroughly, making sure that you dissolve all lumps.

Applying the Paste: In order to spread adhesive evenly over the back of a strip of wallpaper, you'll

need a table at least half as long as the strip. Neatness counts in pasting; avoid getting adhesive on the pattern side—or on the table where the next strip of wallpaper would come in contact with it. One way of achieving this is to spread several layers of kraft paper on the table, discarding the top layer after applying the paste to each strip. The method demonstrated here, however, eliminates waste by keeping the brush well away from the table surface during the entire operation.

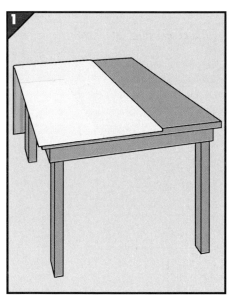

1. Pasting the lower left area.
◆ Measure and cut the wallpaper into strips *(page 68)*, then lay one strip on the table, pattern side down, so that the left and lower edges extend beyond the table a quarter inch or so.
◆ Apply paste to the lower left quarter, covering a little less than half the length of the strip.

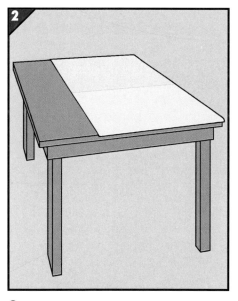

2. Pasting the lower right area.
◆ Shift the strip across the table, allowing the strip's right and lower edges to jut slightly beyond the tabletop.
◆ Paste the lower right quarter.

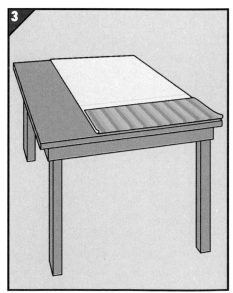

3. Making the lower fold.
Pull the strip toward you, and without creasing the paper, gently fold the pasted section onto itself, pattern side out. Make this fold somewhat shorter than the one you will make at the top *(Step 6)* so you can identify the top when you are ready to hang the strip.

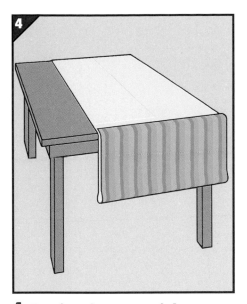

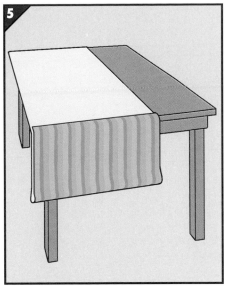

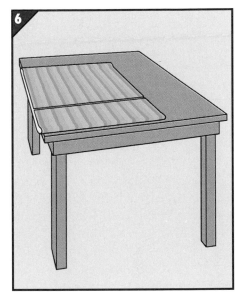

4. Pasting the upper right area.
◆ Slide the strip toward you until the upper edge of the paper barely overlaps the table. Let the folded section hang freely over the edge of the table, and make sure that the right edge of the paper still extends beyond the right edge of the table.
◆ Paste the upper right quarter of the wallpaper strip.

5. Pasting the upper left area.
◆ Shift the strip to the left across the table to position the strip's left and upper edges slightly beyond the edge of the table.
◆ Paste the upper left quarter.

6. Making the top fold.
◆ Fold the upper section onto itself as you did the lower section in Step 3, bringing the top edge just short of the bottom edge. Do not crease the fold.
◆ Set the pasted strip on a clean surface to cure for about 10 minutes; the strip will then be ready to hang *(pages 68-70).* While you are waiting, apply paste to additional strips.

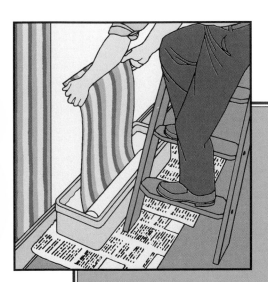

USING A WATER BOX

Before hanging a prepasted paper, buy a special plastic container called a water box from your wallpaper dealer. An inexpensive item, it will simplify your job.

Set the box, two-thirds full of water, on newspaper directly below each section of wall as you work. After cutting a strip of wallpaper to the proper length, roll it loosely from bottom to top, with the pattern inside, then lay it in the box to soak for as long as the manufacturer recommends—usually 10 seconds to 1 minute. If the paper floats to the surface, slip an object without sharp edges—such as a wooden dowel—inside the rolled strip to weight it down.

Next, place a stepladder sideways in front of the water box. With the pattern facing you, draw the paper up as you climb the ladder *(above).* Hang the paper immediately *(pages 68-70).*

After you have decided on a starting point and established a vertical guideline at that location *(pages 62-65)*, cut the first strip—a length of wallpaper at least 4 inches longer than the height of the wall. At the same time, cut as many additional strips as you plan to hang in one session, making sure that the patterns of successive strips will match. To do this for each new strip, unroll the paper alongside the previously cut strip and shift it up and down until the patterns align *(page 72)*. When you cut the new strip, allow an extra 2 inches at each end.

Apply paste to the strips and let it cure *(pages 66-67)*. If the wallpaper has selvages—blank strips along both edges—remove them after pasting *(Step 1, below)*.

On the Wall: Hang the first strip as explained opposite and on the fol-lowing page. As you smooth the paper, eliminate air bubbles, especially large ones. The brush strokes that are diagramed on page 70 will take care of most of them. Any small bubbles that resist smoothing will probably vanish as the paper dries. (If some small bubbles persist, you can get rid of them by the tactics described on page 98.)

Trim the strip. Then, before the paste dries, wring a clean sponge in clear water and remove paste from the ceiling, the baseboard, and the face of the strip itself. Rinse the sponge often.

Making Seams: The usual way to join two strips is with a butted seam *(page 73)*; the edges of the wallcovering meet without any overlap. Only in special situations —such as turning corners or allowing for excessive shrinkage—will an overlap be necessary. In such cases, you can opt for either a lapped seam or a less noticeable wire seam, both of which are described on page 73.

Because a vinyl wallcovering will not adhere to itself, you must apply a vinyl-on-vinyl adhesive in order to make an overlapping seam. Alternatively, you can use a technique that is called double-cutting to create a butted seam from an overlap *(page 75)*.

Bonding the Seams: Avoid stretching edges when you join strips of any kind of material. Except for very fragile coverings, use a seam roller to get a strong bond *(page 74)*. Because seam rolling works best after the adhesive has begun to dry, you will save time if you hang four or five strips before starting to roll the seams.

TOOLS

Straightedge	Scissors
Trimming or utility knife	Trimming guide
Smoothing brush	Seam roller
	Sponge

THE FIRST STRIP

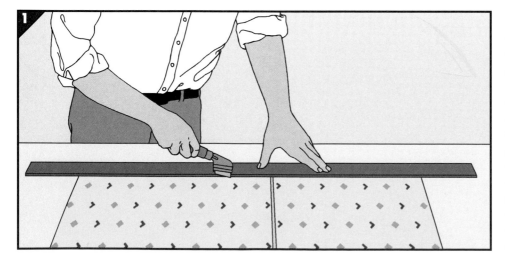

1. Trimming the selvages.

◆ If your paper has selvages, align the side edges of a pasted and fold-ed strip, making sure that the visible portions of the selvages lie precisely over the selvages on the underside of the folds.

◆ Cover the visible selvage on one side with a straightedge. Using the straightedge as a guide, cut off the selvage with a firm, continuous stroke of your trimming knife or any sharp utility knife.

◆ Repeat the procedure on the other side of the strip.

2. Starting the alignment.
◆ Unfold the top section of the strip. Starting at the ceiling line and allowing roughly 2 inches for final trimming along the ceiling, align one of the side edges of the paper with the plumb, or vertical, line.
◆ As you align the paper, pat the top section into place with your hand, just lightly enough to make it hold on the wall. Because pasted wallpaper may stretch, be careful not to pull the edges of the strip.

3. Brushing at the ceiling line.
◆ Brushing with short, upward strokes, press the topmost few inches of paper against the wall, up to—but not beyond—the ceiling line.
◆ Work in this fashion across the entire width of the strip, pressing the paper firmly with the smoothing brush into the angle formed between the ceiling and the wall.

4. Brushing on the top section.
◆ With brisk, light strokes, press the entire top section of the strip against the wall, stopping an inch or so from the upper edge of the lower fold. Do not worry at this stage about occasional air bubbles.
◆ To remove wrinkles, gently pull the lower part of the strip away from the wall up to the point where a wrinkle has formed, then brush the paper smooth.

5. Applying the lower section.

◆ Unfold the lower section of the strip and align it against the plumb line down to the baseboard.

◆ Press this part of the strip to the wall as in Step 4, using light brush strokes and removing wrinkles.

6. Smoothing the strip.

◆ Remove all air bubbles and ensure a firm bond between the paper and the wall with firm brush strokes—using both hands on the brush if necessary. Smooth the paper from the middle of the strip toward its top and bottom edges, following the general direction of the arrows shown at right. Do not move the brush from side to side; this may stretch the paper.

◆ If any wrinkles appear while you are brushing, remove them as you did in Step 4.

◆ Finally, go over the entire surface of the strip with firm, vertical strokes.

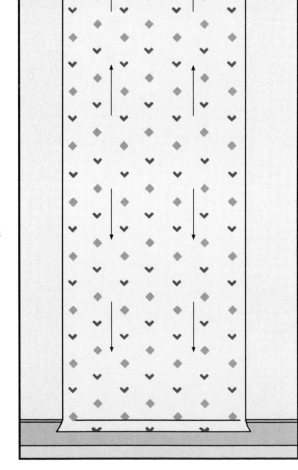

1. Creasing the edges.

Press the wallpaper against the upper edge of the baseboard with the blunt side of a pair of scissors. The scissors will form a crease along the line where the paper is to be trimmed.

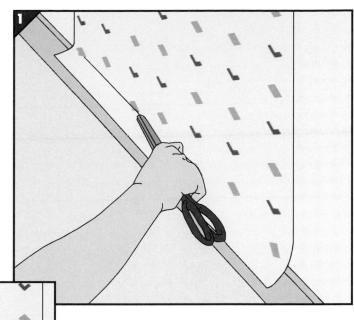

2. Trimming the paper.

◆ Gently lift the strip away from the wall and use scissors to cut off the excess along the crease you made in Step 1 above.

◆ Brush the paper down again with your smoothing brush.

◆ Repeat Steps 1 and 2 along the ceiling line.

Instead of scissors, you can use a trimming knife *(left)* to trim the paper in places where pulling the strip away from the wall would be awkward, such as around windows. Another possibility is a utility knife with snap-off blades *(page 57)*. Be sure to change blades frequently. With either tool, a trimming guide (sold in paint stores) will ensure a straight cutting stroke.

MATCHING PATTERNS

Straight-match pattern.
In this type of pattern, the design stretches across the full width of a strip so that when strips are properly matched the design repeats horizontally from strip to strip. Other designs—such as plaids—may consist of small patterns that repeat horizontally several times between both edges of a strip. In either case, adjacent strips will be identical.

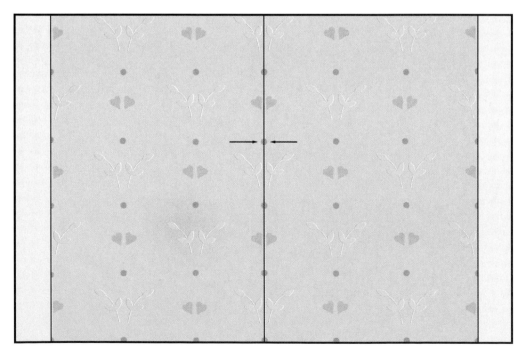

Drop-match pattern.
This type of pattern consists of a design that extends beyond the width of a single strip. The most common variety is drawn in such a way that design elements repeat diagonally on the wall *(left)*. Wallpaper designers usually incorporate a small element of the pattern along the edges of the paper *(arrows)* as a matching guide.

TYPES OF SEAMS

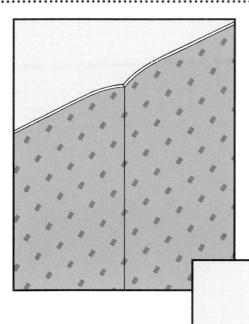

Butted.
For this seam, bring the adjacent edges of two strips of wallpaper firmly against each other until the edges buckle slightly. The buckling eventually flattens out against the wall as the paper dries and shrinks. This is the best-looking seam and the one most frequently employed when papering a flat expanse of wall.

Wire.
The edge of one strip of a wire seam overlaps the adjacent edge by no more than $\frac{1}{16}$ inch, hiding only a tiny portion of the pattern. Use this method if you have trouble butting paper or if the paper shrinks so much that the seams spread open.

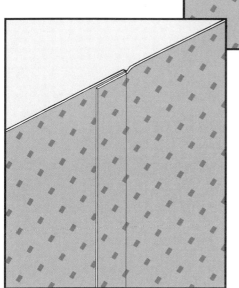

Lapped.
In this type of seam, one strip overlaps the adjacent one by $\frac{1}{4}$ to $\frac{1}{2}$ inch. A lapped seam produces a noticeable ridge and is appropriate only in special cases—near corners, for example, where you must correct the alignment of the paper because the walls are not perfectly vertical, or in preparation for double-cutting *(page 75)*.

JOINING SEAMS

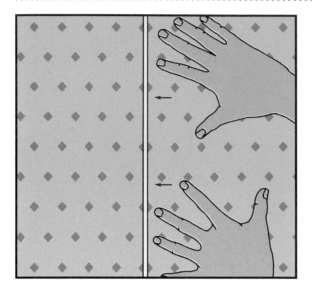

Positioning.

◆ For a butted seam, affix each new strip lightly on the wall about $\frac{1}{4}$ inch away from the previous strip. Keeping your hands flat and well away from the edge of the strip to avoid stretching it, move the strip until the pattern matches and the edges meet and buckle very slightly.

◆ For a lapped seam, affix the strip about $\frac{1}{4}$ inch (or $\frac{1}{16}$ inch for a wire seam) over the previous one instead of away from it. Using the same hand motions, adjust the position of the new strip until the pattern matches.

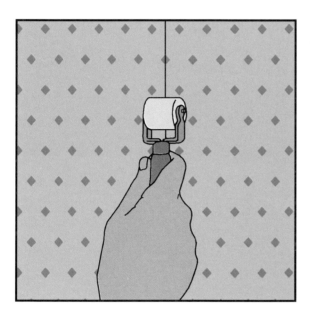

Rolling the seams.

When the adhesive is partly dry—10 to 15 minutes after you have hung a new strip—press the edges of the seam firmly together and against the wall with a seam roller, moving the cylinder against the seam with short up-and-down strokes.

Do not use a seam roller on textured papers, foils, or other fragile coverings; they could be marred by the rolling action. Instead, press the seam with a sponge as shown below.

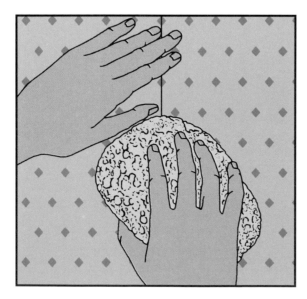

The sponge method.

To join the edges of fragile papers, press each seam gently together with your fingers and a damp sponge.

DOUBLE-CUTTING A LAPPED SEAM

1. Cutting through the seam.
Using a straightedge to guide your trimming knife, slice through both thicknesses of the seam down the middle of the overlap. This will sever two narrow bands of paper, one clearly visible on the outside of the overlap and the other one hidden underneath.

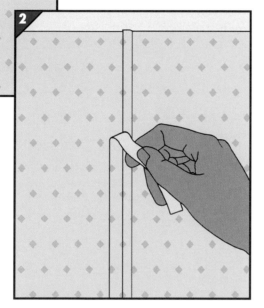

2. Removing the outer band.
Carefully peel off the outer band of the cut overlap. Use your trimming knife to deepen the cut if you find that the separation of the bands is not complete.

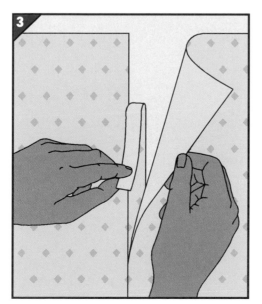

3. Removing the inner band.
◆ Lift the edge of the outer strip and peel off the covered band *(left)*.
◆ Press both of the cut edges together with a sponge, and finish with a seam roller *(opposite)*, unless the paper is of a kind that rolling would damage.

Corners, and the openings and moldings of doors and windows, pose more paperhanging problems than flat walls, but a few simple rules can guide you through the job.

Most corners are at least slightly out of plumb, so a new plumb line is needed on each new stretch of wall *(page 65)*. A less-than-perfect corner can also cause wrinkles if you try to bend more than a few inches of a strip around it. The solution to this and other potential difficulties is to cut the paper lengthwise and hang it in two sections.

Working at Openings: Papering around window moldings *(pages 78-80)*—a technique that you can adapt to doorframes—also requires custom paper-cutting to fit the material to the trim.

A casement window, which is recessed without moldings, is handled by bending the wallpaper into the recess, then finishing with smaller pieces. The exact application method depends on the type of wall covering and the amount of overlap at the opening *(pages 81-85)*. To minimize the effect of unavoidable pattern mismatches, choose a wallcovering with a small overall pattern for a room with casements.

Using a vinyl covering for a casement is trickier than paper, because vinyl cannot adhere to itself in a lapped seam. The seams should be double-cut *(page 75)* and positioned away from casement edges to prevent fraying.

The techniques shown on these and the following pages work from left to right; if you go the other way, simply reverse the directions in the instructions.

TOOLS

Scissors	Sponge	Chalk line
Paste bucket	Water box	Metal straightedge
Paste brush	Trimming knife	Smoothing brushes
	Trimming guide	Seam roller

MATERIALS

Wallcovering
Paste
Water

INNER CORNERS

1. Dividing the strip.
◆ At the top and bottom of the wall, measure the distance between the edge of the last strip and the corner, then add $\frac{1}{2}$ inch to the greater of the two measurements *(right)*.
◆ Use this figure as the width of a partial strip cut from the left side of the paper; save the right-hand section.
◆ Hang the left section next to the last strip, pressing it into the corner and smoothing it onto the adjacent wall. Trim the strip at the top and bottom.

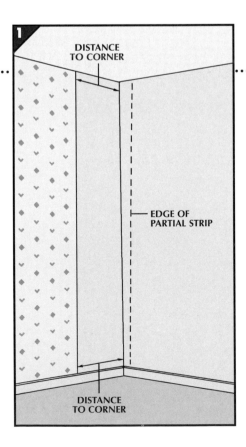

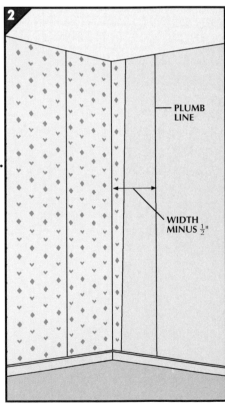

2. Restoring vertical alignment.
◆ Subtract $\frac{1}{2}$ inch from the width of the right-hand section of the strip.
◆ Measuring from the corner, use this figure to mark the unpapered wall *(above)*, then establish a plumb (vertical) line through the mark *(page 65)*.

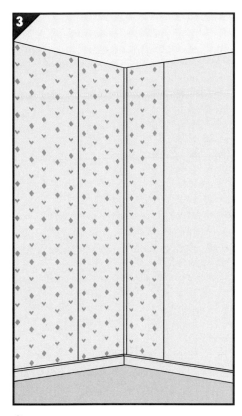

3. Positioning the second piece.

◆ Hang the right-hand section of the split strip with its right edge on the plumb line and its left edge overlapping the first section near the corner.
◆ If you are using a vinyl covering, double-cut the seam *(page 75)*.

The seam or the overlap may slant on the wall because the corner is not plumb (angles exaggerated here for clarity). The resulting visual distortion is usually slight and inconspicuous.

OUTER CORNERS

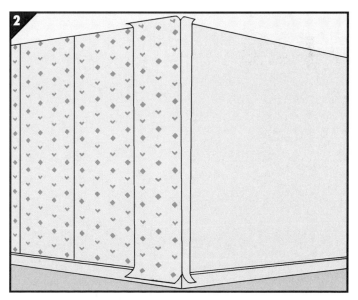

1. Dividing the strip.

◆ At the top and bottom of the wall, measure the distance between the edge of the last strip and the corner, then add 1 inch to the greater of the two measurements *(above)*.
◆ Use the result as the width of a partial strip cut from the left side of the paper; save the right-hand section.

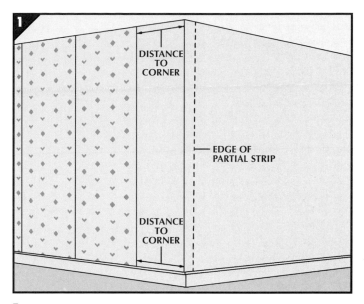

2. Turning the corner.

◆ Hang the left-hand section of the strip, smoothing it on the wall as far as the corner.
◆ Slit the excess paper upward from the ceiling line and downward from the baseboard at the bottom *(above)*.
◆ Fold the paper around the corner and smooth it on the adjacent wall. Trim the strip at the top and at the bottom of both walls.

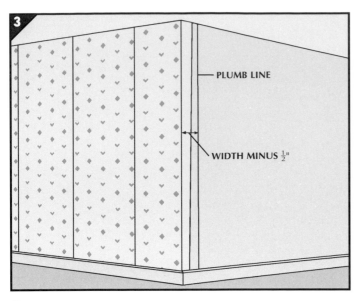

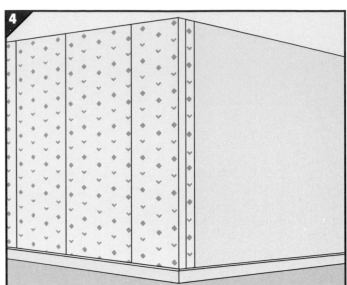

3. Restoring vertical alignment.
◆ Measure the width of the right-hand section of the split strip and subtract $\frac{1}{2}$ inch.
◆ Measuring from the corner, use this figure to mark the unpapered wall *(above)*, then establish a plumb (vertical) line through the mark *(page 65)*.

4. Hanging the right-hand section.
Follow the procedure for an inner corner *(page 77, Step 3)*, double-cutting the seam if you are using a vinyl covering.

DOUBLE-HUNG WINDOWS

1. Approaching the window.
◆ Hang the strip that will overlap the left side of the window as you would the preceding strips, but smooth it onto the wall only as far as the window's vertical molding.
◆ Use scissors to cut away any overlap that exceeds 2 inches *(right)*.

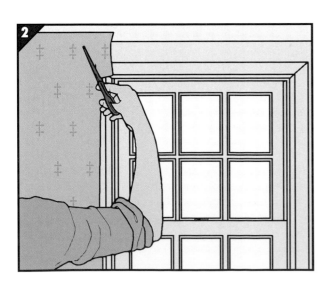

2. Slitting the corners.
Cut the paper diagonally at the top and bottom corners of the window molding *(left)*, ending each cut against the wall, precisely where the outer corner of the molding meets the wall.

3. Smoothing the rest of the strip.
◆ Smooth the paper to the wall above and below the window.
◆ Press the wallpaper firmly against the side of the molding.

4. Trimming the strip.
◆ With a trimming knife and a trimming guide, cut away excess paper at the top, side, and bottom of the molding where it meets the wall *(above)*.
◆ When you reach a corner, especially at the sill, make cuts into the trim allowance to ease the tautness of the paper so it will lie flat against the wall.
◆ Trim at the ceiling and baseboard *(page 71)*.

5. Top and bottom strips.
◆ Hang short, full-width strips above and below the window until the distance to the opposite side of the window frame is less than the full width of a strip, matching the pattern carefully.
◆ Trim the strips at the ceiling, the upper and lower moldings, and the baseboard.

6. Attaching the last window strip.
◆ Hang the top of the long strip that overlaps the right side of the window, matching the pattern precisely along the edge of the last short strip.
◆ Smooth the long strip onto the wall only down to the outer corner of the molding.

7. Papering down the second side.

◆ Use scissors to cut a horizontal slit in the paper about 2 inches below the top of the window frame. Stop cutting about 2 inches from the outer edge of the frame. (This cut relieves the pull of the still-unattached portion of the long strip.)

◆ Slit the strip diagonally at the upper corner as was done in Step 2.

◆ Attach the paper along the right side of the window molding, pressing just enough to hold it in place.

8. Matching the last seam.

◆ Trim excess paper and make a diagonal slit at the lower corner.

◆ Slide the left edge of the strip to the edge of the short strip under the window and check the pattern match at the seam.

◆ If the seam is poorly aligned, lift the strip from around the bottom and the side of the window molding, and ease it back into place until the seam at the bottom matches satisfactorily.

9. Finishing the right-hand strip.

◆ With firm strokes of the smoothing brush, smooth the entire strip on the wall, pressing its edges neatly against the molding.

◆ Finish trimming the paper around the side of the window, the ceiling, and along the baseboard.

CASEMENT WINDOWS AND PAPER WALL COVERINGS

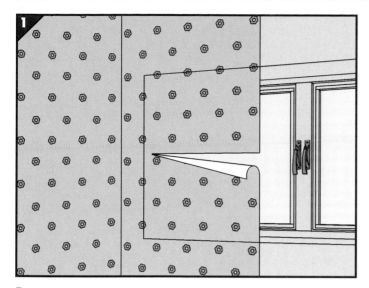

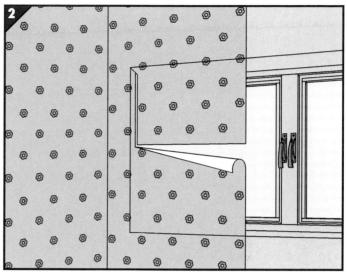

1. The first cut.

◆ Hang the strip of wallpaper that overlaps the casement as you would on a flat wall, pulling it taut and smoothing it on the wall around the recess. Trim excess paper at the ceiling and baseboard.

◆ With scissors, make a horizontal cut in the strip, midway between the top and the bottom of the casement. End the cut about 1 inch from the left side of the casement.

2. Vertical and diagonal cuts.

◆ Cut upward from the end of the horizontal cut, parallel to the casement edge. About 1 inch from the top, cut diagonally to the upper corner of the casement.

◆ Make similar cuts to the lower corner of the casement.

3. Covering the casement.

◆ Brush the upper and lower flaps of wallpaper smoothly onto the top and bottom of the casement recess and trim the paper at the window frame.

◆ Press the paper's narrow vertical flap onto the left edge of the casement.

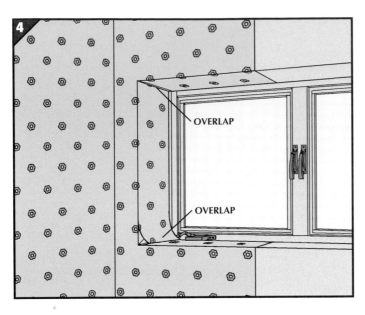

4. Completing the job.

◆ Measure and cut a matching piece as wide as the side of the recess and long enough to overlap the flaps on the top and bottom.

◆ Hang the piece on the side and smooth it against the side, top, and bottom.

To finish papering the casement, hang short full-width strips above and below as needed, then repeat the steps shown here to cover the other side.

OVERLAP

OVERLAP

CASEMENT WINDOWS AND VINYL COVERINGS—LONG OVERLAP

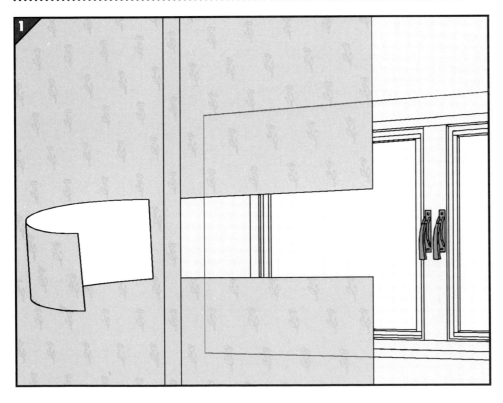

1. The first cut.

◆ When most of a strip of vinyl wallpaper overlaps a casement window, hang it as on a flat wall, smooth it, and trim it at the ceiling and baseboard.

◆ Cut out a full-width section of the strip in the middle of the opening, leaving enough paper above and below to cover the top and bottom of the recess. Make the cuts with scissors over the recess; use a trimming knife over the wall.

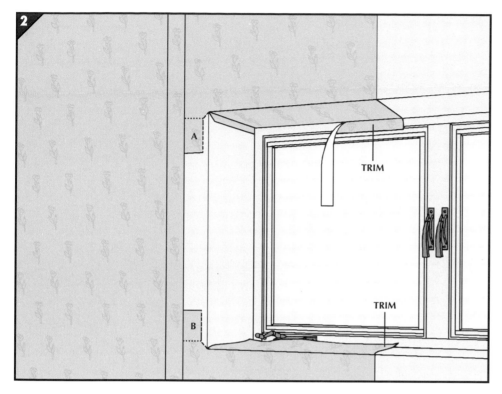

2. Hanging the overlap.

◆ Starting at the top and bottom corners of the casement, slit the vinyl on the wall with a trimming knife, making two cuts, each at a 45-degree angle and about $1\frac{1}{2}$ inches long. Then make two vertical cuts from the ends of these diagonals to the edges of the section you have removed. (These four cuts are indicated by dashed lines in the drawing at left.)

◆ From 1 inch below and above the ends of the diagonal cuts, make two horizontal cuts to the left edge of the strip *(dotted lines)* and pull away the two rectangles of paper marked A and B.

◆ Press and smooth the overlapping flaps onto the top and bottom of the casement, then trim them at the window frame.

3. Completing the job.

◆ Cut a piece of wallpaper as long as the height of the casement and that matches the pattern on the strip to the left of the window. Trim the piece to a width that will reach from the last complete strip around the corner to the window frame—plus a 4-inch allowance for trimming and double-cut joints.

◆ Paste and hang this piece, and trim it at the window frame. Along the left, top, and bottom edges of the piece, double-cut the overlaps *(page 75)*.

Finish papering the casement by hanging short full-width strips above and below as needed, then repeat the steps shown here to cover the other side.

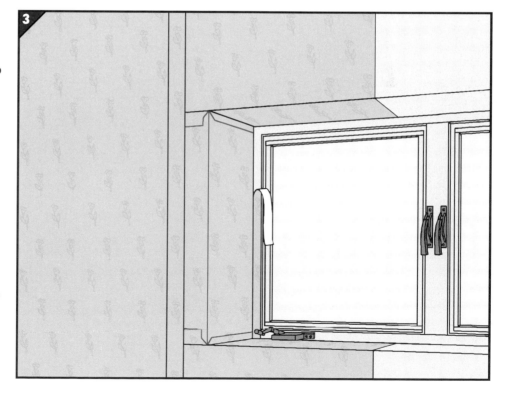

1. The first cuts.

◆ When a strip of vinyl wallpaper overlaps only a few inches of a casement window, hang it as on a flat wall and trim it at the ceiling and the baseboard.

◆ At the top and bottom corners of the casement, use a trimming knife to make two 45-degree cuts along the wall, each about $1\frac{1}{2}$ inches long, above and below the casement *(dashed lines, right)*. Continue the cuts parallel to the top and bottom of the casement.

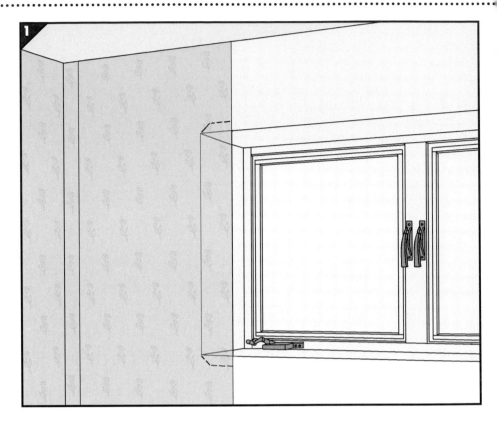

2. Hanging the flap.

◆ Press and smooth the flap onto the side of the casement, pasting the projections at the flap's ends to the top and bottom of the casement recess.

◆ Starting at the ends of the diagonal cuts, make vertical cuts to the ceiling and baseboard. Pull off and discard the narrow lengths of paper above and below the casement.

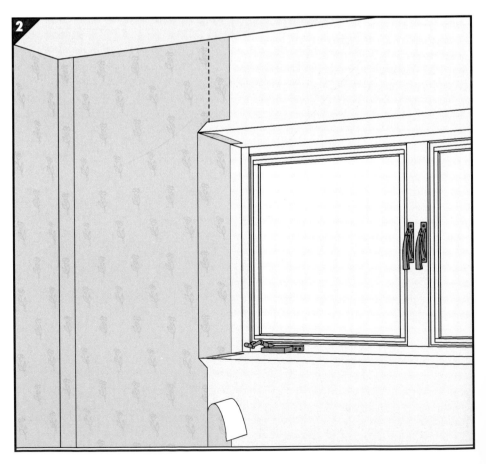

3. Fitting the matching piece.

◆ Measure and cut a piece of wall-paper, matching the pattern of the flap, the same length as the flap and about 1 inch wider than the distance from the edge of the flap to the window frame.

◆ Paste and hang the matching piece flush with the window frame, then double-cut *(page 75)* along the overlap between the flap and the new piece.

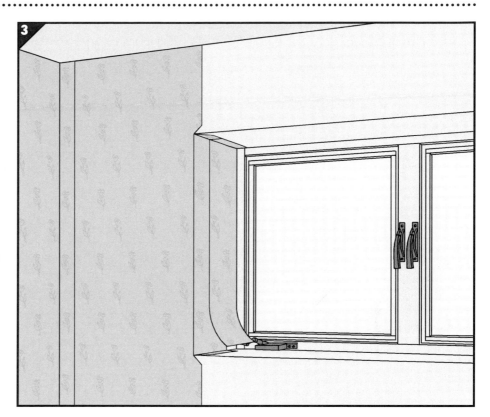

4. Hanging the next strip.

◆ Cut a matching section of wallpaper long enough to cover the wall above the casement and the top surface of the casement recess—plus a 4-inch trim allowance.

◆ Paste and hang the strip flush with the left edge of the casement, and trim it at the ceiling and the window frame.

◆ Cover the area from the bottom of the frame to the baseboard with another matching section.

◆ Double-cut all overlaps between the new strip, the previous strip, and the matching piece on the casement side.

Finish papering the casement by hanging short full-width strips above and below as needed. Repeat the steps shown here to cover the other side.

The high walls of a stairway, the slanted walls of a dormer room, and an arched doorway require special techniques for handling long strips of paper and for papering along angles and around curves.

Planning and Strategy: Prepare all surfaces thoroughly *(pages 58-61)*. Estimate the amount of paper needed for stairwell walls *(page 319)*, and buy at least one extra roll to allow for trimming the slanting bottoms of the strips. Measure and cut the strips for the wall beside the stairs, called the well wall, one by one to be sure that each is the correct length.

Slanted walls and their unusual angles present special problems. Estimate the amount of paper needed by measuring the area of all the surfaces to be covered as accurately as possible, then add at least one extra roll to compensate for the oddly shaped sections you will cut. Paper a recessed, walk-in dormer separately, rather than as part of the main room.

When papering an archway, measure around the opening, floor to floor, with a tape measure, and allow an extra 2 inches to account for overlaps and slight imperfections in the arch that cannot be measured by the tape.

Use vinyl-to-vinyl adhesive when overlapping corners with vinyl wall coverings, or use the double-cutting technique shown on page 75.

Choosing a Paper: For all these jobs, a small, scattered pattern is better than a large, bold design; precise matching is almost impossible with long, cumbersome strips in a stairwell, and with such a pattern slight mismatches are less noticeable. The same is true for slanted walls, where a scattered pattern would help disguise the inevitable mismatches that result where angled walls meet.

When papering an arch choose a pattern without a strong up-and-down orientation. Doing so makes it easier to match the pattern on the inside of the arch and prevents the paper from appearing to be upside down across the top of the arch.

⚠️ **CAUTION** *Be sure to observe the rules of ladder safety described on pages 315 to 318. If the ceiling height of the upper floor is more than 8 feet, do not use the improvised scaffold shown here; instead, rent scaffolding and have it set up by a professional.*

TOOLS

Stepladder	Smoothing brush	Paste brush and bucket
Extension ladder	Seam roller	Water box
Scaffold-grade plank	Tape measure	Plumb bob
(2 x 10)	Utility knife	Trimming knife

HANDLING THE HEIGHTS OF A STAIRWELL

1. Hanging the top of the first strip.

◆ Set up a platform for the stairwell *(page 317)*, then mark a plumb line at the point where the baseboard angles downward *(page 65)*.
◆ Paper the upper-landing wall *(pages 68-71)*, aligning the right side of the first strip on the plumb line.
◆ Mark another plumb line one strip width to the right of the first plumb line. Prepare a strip of paper the length of this line plus 4 inches for top and bottom allowances.
◆ Working from the platform, hang the top of the first well-wall strip. Overlap the strip onto the ceiling about 2 inches, and butt it against the adjacent upper-landing strip.

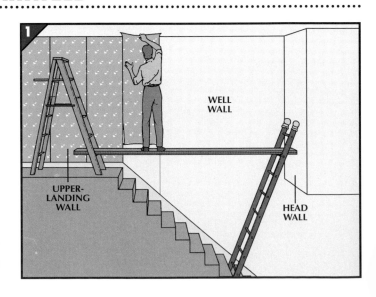

WELL WALL

UPPER-LANDING WALL

HEAD WALL

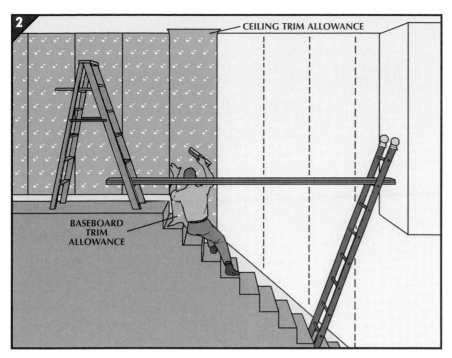

CEILING TRIM ALLOWANCE

BASEBOARD TRIM ALLOWANCE

2. Finishing the bottom of the strip.

◆ Unfold and hang the bottom section of the first well-wall strip.

◆ Finish smoothing the top section. Crease and trim the paper at the ceiling line *(page 71)*, and then roll the seam halfway down the strip.

◆ Smooth the bottom section. Crease and trim the paper along the baseboard; then roll the rest of the seam and smooth the entire strip.

◆ Hang the remaining well-wall strips *(dashed lines)* by the same method until you have hung the last full-width strip before the corner between the well wall and the head wall.

3. Turning the inner corner.

◆ Measure from the edge of the last strip to the head wall and add $\frac{1}{2}$ inch. Cut a strip lengthwise this distance from its left edge.

◆ Hang the top of this section, making a 1-inch slit at the top corner and smoothing the $\frac{1}{2}$-inch overlap onto the head wall.

◆ Crease and trim the paper at the ceiling line and roll the seam as far as you can. If possible, work from the staircase when applying the middle of this long section; otherwise, arrange the platform as shown in Step 5.

◆ Continue applying and smoothing the section downward, and make a $\frac{1}{2}$-inch slit where the bottom of the head wall meets the well wall. Press the paper below the slit against the well wall, and trim it at the bottom.

◆ Measure the width of the remaining section of the strip you cut lengthwise and subtract $\frac{1}{2}$ inch. Mark a plumb line on the head wall that distance from the corner between the well wall and head wall.

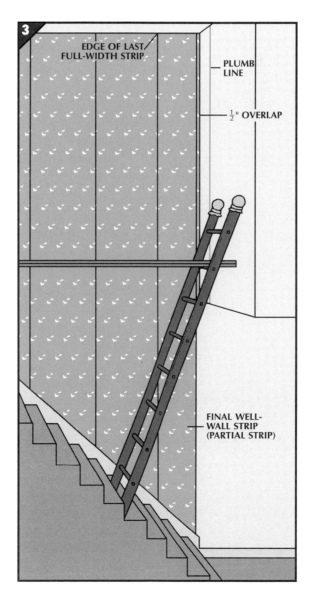

EDGE OF LAST FULL-WIDTH STRIP

PLUMB LINE

$\frac{1}{2}$" OVERLAP

FINAL WELL-WALL STRIP (PARTIAL STRIP)

FIRST HEAD-WALL STRIP (PARTIAL STRIP)

PLUMB LINE

4. Papering the head wall.

◆ Measure the height of the head wall, excluding any moldings. To the height add 4 inches for top and bottom trim allowances; cut both the remaining section of the corner strip and the other full-width strips for the head wall to this length.

◆ Paste and fold the remaining section of the corner strip, hanging the top only and aligning its right edge to the plumb line.

◆ Hang the tops of the remaining strips until you reach the last full-width strip before the far corner.

◆ Cut a partial strip lengthwise for the far corner. The overlap will vary: For an outer corner, as shown in the drawing, add 1 inch; an inner corner requires only $\frac{1}{2}$ inch.

◆ Hang the top of this last strip, slitting the top of the paper so it fits around the corner.

SLIT

OVERLAP AT OUTER CORNER

5. Completing the job.

◆ Arrange the stairwell platform so that you can comfortably reach the bottom of the head wall (right), then hang the bottoms of the strips.

◆ Smooth the overlap around the corner, slitting the paper at the bottom corner. When the strips are in place, press out bubbles and smooth the paper with a clean paint roller on a long handle or with a broom covered with a clean rag.

◆ Trim the bottoms of the strips flush with the bottom of the head wall, treating a molding there as if it were a baseboard.

◆ Reassemble the two-ladder platform and trim the strips at the ceiling line.

◆ If the stairwell has three sides, or another inner corner, go on to paper the second well wall, and then paper the remaining landing walls.

COVERING SLANTED WALLS

1. Hanging the top of the corner.
◆ Hang vertical strips of paper as described on pages 68 to 71.
◆ Where a strip first overlaps the slanted corner, crease the paper along the ceiling line as far as possible, then make a small slit in the paper where the ceiling meets the top of the slanted corner so the paper lies flat. Crease the paper into the corner.
◆ Trim at the ceiling line as far as the corner, then cut the rest of the strip parallel to the corner, leaving a $\frac{1}{2}$-inch overlap.
◆ For the remaining full-width strips, measure the right-hand edge of the preceding strip from corner to baseboard and add 4 inches. Hang the strips, creasing each into the slanted corner before trimming, to leave a $\frac{1}{2}$-inch overlap on the slanted wall.

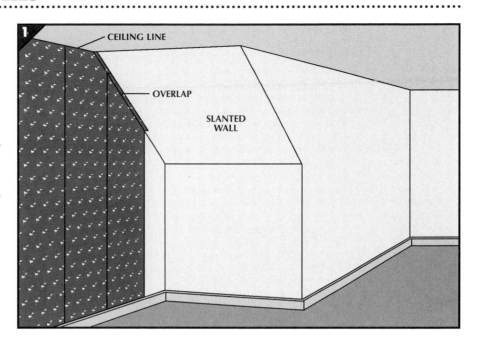

2. Finishing the corner.
◆ Measure the horizontal distance from the edge of the last full-width strip to the corner of the short vertical wall—called a knee wall—and add $\frac{1}{2}$ inch to this measurement. Find the vertical distance from the top of the last full-width strip's right-hand edge to the baseboard, then add 4 inches for trim allowances.
◆ Cut a partial strip as wide as the first figure and as long as the second. Hang the strip, butting its left edge against the last full-width strip.

◆ Crease and trim the top of the strip against the slanted wall, leaving a $\frac{1}{2}$-inch overlap for turning the corner. Make a slit at the angle between the slanted wall and the knee wall, and another slit at the baseboard. Trim all the strips flush to the baseboard.
◆ To mark the position for the first strip on the slanted and knee walls, measure the width of your wallpaper and subtract $\frac{1}{2}$ inch. Mark a plumb line on the knee wall this distance from the corner. Using the same measurement, snap a chalk line on the slanted wall.

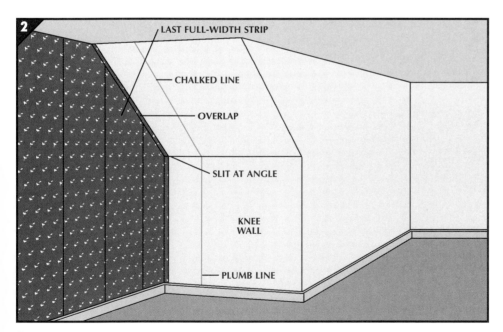

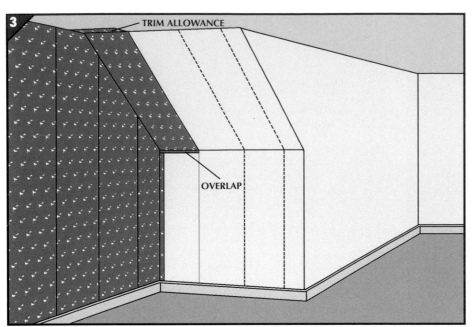

TRIM ALLOWANCE

OVERLAP

3. Covering the slanted and knee walls.

◆ Measure the distance between the ceiling and the joint where the slanted and knee walls meet, and add $2\frac{1}{2}$ inches. Cut a full-width strip to this length.

◆ Measure the height of the knee wall, and add 2 inches. Cut a second full-width strip of paper to this length.

◆ Hang the right edge of the first strip along the chalked line on the slanted wall, with $\frac{1}{2}$ inch of overlap onto the knee wall. Align and hang the second strip along the plumb line of the knee wall, covering the $\frac{1}{2}$-inch overlap.

◆ Smooth the strips, then trim the al-

lowances at the ceiling and baseboard.

◆ Hang full widths of paper *(dashed lines)* up to the last full-width strips before the corner.

◆ If the slanted wall and knee wall end at an outer corner, proceed to Steps 4 and 5.

◆ For an inner corner, such as is found with a walk-in dormer, paper the facing wall using the same techniques that are described in Steps 1 and 2, overlapping the paper onto the slanted and knee walls.

◆ Then measure the distance from the last full-width strip to the corner and hang a strip of that size, covering the overlaps on the slanted and knee walls.

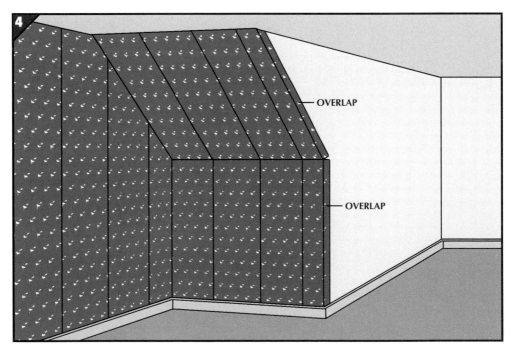

OVERLAP

OVERLAP

4. Turning an outer corner.

◆ Measure the distance from the edge of the last full-width strips to the outer corner, and add 1 inch. Use this figure for the width of partial strips for the slanted and knee walls, making them as long as the strips cut for Step 3.

◆ Cut and hang these final strips separately, and slit the paper at the ceiling and at the baseboard to fit it around the corner.

◆ Before tackling the triangular sections next to the slanted wall, hang the remaining full vertical strips.

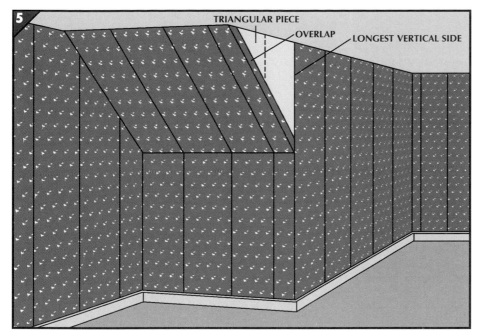

TRIANGULAR PIECE
OVERLAP
LONGEST VERTICAL SIDE

5. Papering leftover triangles.

◆ First measure and cut paper for the longest vertical side of the triangle, including trim allowances and using the full width of the paper if possible. Hang the strip, then trim it to fit—in this case, horizontally at the ceiling and diagonally at the outer corner.

◆ Measure the small triangle to the left of the last strip, then hang a piece of wallpaper cut to this size and shape, plus trim allowances.

PAPERING AN ARCH

Getting around the curve.

◆ Paper the wall in which the arch is built, allowing the wall covering to extend 1 inch into the opening.

◆ Make relief cuts every 3 or 4 inches *(inset)*, stopping $\frac{1}{8}$ inch from the edge of the opening. Wrap the resulting flaps around the corner, rewetting the paste if necessary.

◆ Let the paste dry, then trim the flaps $\frac{1}{8}$ inch from the edge of the opening.

◆ Cut two side strips of wallpaper equal in width to the thickness of the arch wall and long enough to reach from the baseboard to a point where the arch be-

gins to curve. Hang one piece on each side of the archway.

◆ Cut a center strip 2 inches longer than the distance between the tops of the side strips, and hang it, overlapping the side strips.

◆ Double-cut the seams *(page 75)*.

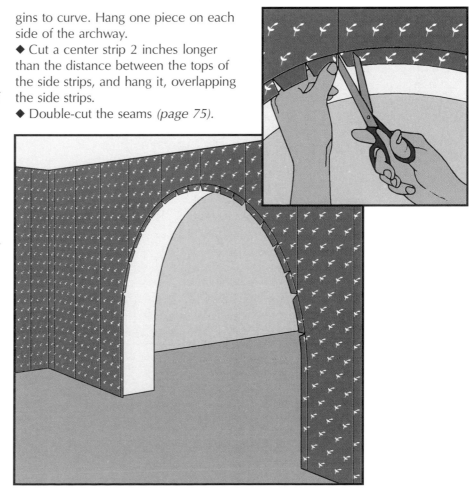

When hanging wallpaper, the best way to deal with a fixture is not to paper around it but to remove the obstacle and paper under it. After the fixture has been restored to its place, it will appear to rest against a surface design unbroken by any seam.

For a receptacle or, as shown here, a light switch, you need only detach a cover plate. For a wall-hung lamp, you must detach the fixture and also disconnect its wires.

 CAUTION *Never dismantle an electrical fix-ture without first removing the fuse or tripping the circuit breaker that controls current to it. This precaution is especially important in paperhanging: Wet wallpaper adhesive is an excellent conductor of electricity and can create a dangerous shock hazard.*

 TOOLS

Voltage tester
Screwdriver
Trimming knife
Scissors

1. Detaching the plate.
◆ Turn off power to the switch.
◆ Undo the screws in the cover plate, and remove the plate.
◆ Check the switch with a voltage tester to make sure it is off.

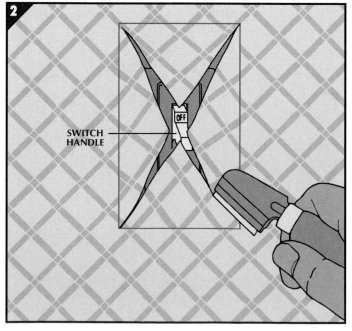

2. Cutting a hole for the switch.
◆ Hang a strip of wallpaper in the usual manner, covering the recessed box.
◆ Split a small opening to uncover the switch handle, and with a trimming knife or scissors, cut diagonally to each corner of the box *(left)*.
◆ Cut the flaps of the X to make a rectangular hole as big as the box, using the inside of the box as a guide.
◆ Screw the plate back on—perhaps first covering it with matching paper *(Steps 3-5)*.

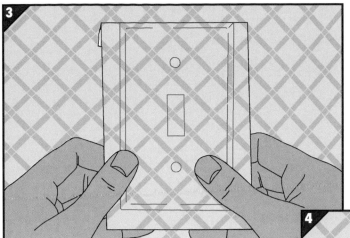

3. Matching the paper for the cover plate.

◆ Cut a piece of paper larger than the plate.
◆ Slip the plate over its switch, ease the plate's top away from the wall, and fold the top of the paper over the plate. Match the upper fold of the paper to the wall above.

4. Allowing for the bevels.

◆ If the paper on the plate matches that on the wall perfectly at the top but poorly at the bottom because of the beveled shape of the plate, create a close match at both edges by moving the paper about $\frac{1}{8}$ inch downward (arrow).
◆ Fold the top and bottom of the paper over the plate, and crease these folds firmly.
◆ To match the side edges, follow the same procedure: Fold one side of the paper over the plate, match the pattern at this edge of the plate, then move the paper about $\frac{1}{8}$ inch away from the edge.
◆ Fold the paper over the left and right edges of the plate, and crease these folds firmly.

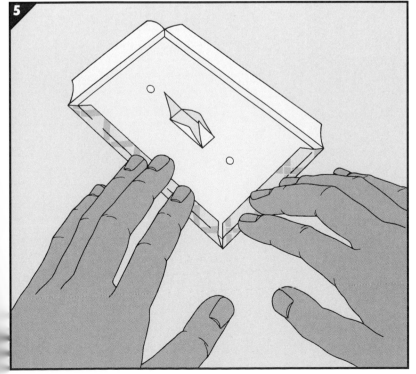

5. Covering the plate.

◆ Apply adhesive to the matching piece of paper, and mount it on the front of the plate, using the creases you have made as a guide for exact placement.
◆ Cut off the corners of the paper diagonally with a pair of scissors, then fold the paper over the back of the plate and press it firmly to both sides of the plate.
◆ Cut a small X over the switch-handle slot of the plate, and fold the flaps through the slot to the back of the plate.
◆ Mark the location of the screw holes, and remount the plate.

Borders are narrow strips of wall covering used to highlight elements of a room. Applied over paint or wallpaper, borders can frame mirrors or pictures and accent the edges of windows and doors. Often, a border circles an entire room, either at chair-rail height—36 to 40 inches above the floor—or along the wall where it meets the ceiling.

Border Basics: Borders are sold prepasted in 5-yard spools or, in some cases, by the yard. Measure the path the border is to cover. Add 10 percent to the total to account for waste resulting from matching the pattern at seams or making miter cuts around corners of doors, windows, and the like *(opposite)*.

When applying a border over paint, follow the wall-preparation techniques described on page 58. If you are pasting the strip to a wall covering, you will need to brush on a vinyl-to-vinyl adhesive after soaking the paper to moisten the paste.

To prevent the pattern of a dark wall covering from showing through a light-colored border, apply an opaque primer-sealer to mask the underlying pattern *(page 58)*. To do so, lightly mark the border area in pencil, then carefully coat the wall covering within the outline.

Begin hanging the border in an inconspicuous corner in case you cannot make a perfect match where the end of the border meets the beginning. Elsewhere, butt border segments together if the pattern match is acceptable. If not, overlap the pieces until you achieve a match, then double-cut the seam *(page 75)*. Turn corners using the techniques for regular wallpaper *(pages 76-78)*.

Other Considerations: Carefully mark with a level guideline the route that the border will follow. A border hung even slightly askew at one end will slant noticeably as it crosses the wall.

Choose a nondirectional pattern if the border will be applied both horizontally and vertically. Make sure that elements such as mirrors or pictures that you want to accent have square corners; if they do not, hanging a border will only emphasize the irregularity.

TOOLS

Tape measure
Carpenter's level
Water box
Paste brush and
  bucket

Smoothing brush
Combination
  square
Utility knife
Straightedge
Seam roller

HORIZONTAL BORDERS

Plotting a level line.
Because floors and ceilings sometimes are not level, do not rely on measurements that use them as reference points. Instead, make a series of horizontal tick marks on the wall for the top edge of the border with a pencil and a carpenter's level to maintain a consistently level line across a wall.

Preparing a border.
◆ Cut the border to manageable lengths—4 to 6 feet—and roll each loosely with the pattern facing inside.
◆ Immerse the rolls in water one at a time for the period recommended by the manufacturer.
◆ Unroll the border and apply vinyl-to-vinyl adhesive. Then fold the paper into a series of 6-inch pleats, paste side to paste side, with the edges aligned and without creasing the folds *(left)*.
◆ Allow the paper to "rest" for the time recommended by the manufacturer before applying the border to the wall.

MITERING CORNERS

1. Applying the first leg.
◆ Paste the first strip along an edge of a window sill—the bottom, in this case—so that the ends extend beyond the corners by at least one full width of the border.
◆ Remove any wrinkles and bubbles from this strip with a smoothing brush before hanging the next section—here, along the side of the window.

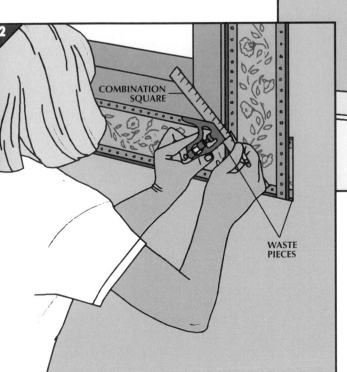

2. Cutting the miter.
◆ Match the pattern of the two strips at the inside of the corner, smoothing the strip as you position it.
◆ Lightly mark a 45-degree line from the corner of the window to the outside edges of the borders, setting a combination square against the window frame as a guide *(left)*.
◆ Cut through both layers of border, and peel away the two waste pieces that result.
◆ Smooth the strips against the wall, and roll the seam.

Wallpaper is vulnerable to a variety of small flaws or injuries, but it is also easily repaired. For example, to secure a loose seam or a tear whose flap is intact, simply paste the paper down again, using a small, long-handled artist's brush to apply the adhesive so that the paper is not stretched. Other fixes are only slightly more complicated.

Patching Holes: The torn-patch method shown below produces an almost invisible repair for holes no larger than about an inch. This technique works best on light paper with a small, busy pattern. The double-cut method described on the opposite page serves for larger holes or dark papers. It must be used for vinyls and foils, which cannot be torn.

Deflating Bubbles: If bubbles are inconspicuous or located out of harm's way, leave them alone. However, if they are located in a place where an accidental puncture could result in a tear, flatten them as explained on pages 98 to 99.

TOOLS

Artist's brush
Metal straightedge
Utility knife
Putty knife
Sponge

MATERIALS

Wallpaper paste
Masking tape

THE TORN-PATCH METHOD

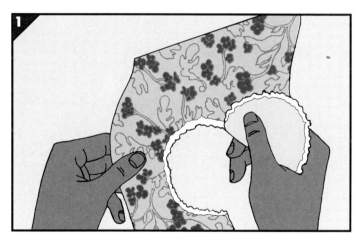

1. Tearing a neat patch.

◆ Practice tearing on a scrap of the same or similar wallpaper before you make the patch. Grasp the paper with the index finger of one hand atop the section that will be the patch, and the thumb of the other hand atop the section that will be discarded.
◆ Rotate the hand holding the patch section gently upward *(above)* and twist it slightly in toward the other hand; at the same time, pull down and toward the patch with the other hand. This should produce a patch with an intact design on top and a feathered edge on the underside. The entire patch should be no more than 3 inches wide.

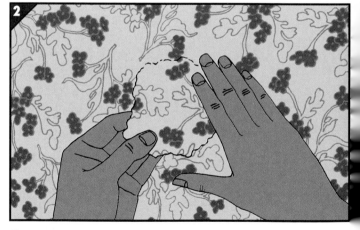

2. Applying the patch.

◆ If you use adhesive, apply a thin layer to the patch with an artist's brush, stroking outward from the center to the feathered edge. For prepasted paper, wet the patch and shake off excess water.
◆ Handle the fragile edge carefully as you position the patch over the damaged paper, and match the top of the patch to the pattern below.
◆ Make the final pattern alignment when the whole piece is in place. The match may not be exact, but the discrepancy is rarely great enough to be noticeable.

THE DOUBLE-CUT METHOD

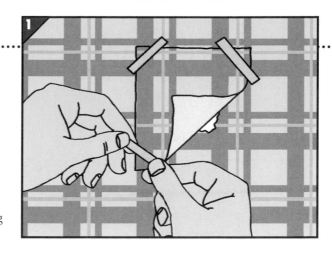

1. Placing the patch.
◆ Cut a scrap that overlaps the damaged area by about 1 inch on all sides. If the damage is located in one corner of a pattern square, as in the example shown, the patch should include the whole square.
◆ Position the wallpaper scrap over the damaged area, align it to the pattern exactly, and secure it with masking tape (right).

2. Making the cut.
◆ Hold a metal straightedge against one side of the scrap piece. With a sharp utility knife, cut cleanly through both layers of paper—along pattern lines, if possible—all around the damaged section (left).
◆ Carefully peel off the masking tape and remove the patch and the scrap that it was cut from. If any part of the patch is still attached to the scrap, place the paper on a work surface and neatly cut the pieces apart with the knife.
◆ Go over the cuts on the damaged section of wallpaper with the utility knife to make sure that the edges have been completely separated.
◆ Pry up one corner of the cut area with the tip of the blade. With vinyls and most heavy papers, it should come out in one piece. If it does not, pry gently all around the edge with a putty knife (inset). Then scrape any glue or lumps of paper off the wall.

3. Inserting the patch.
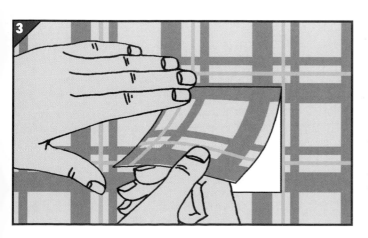
◆ If you use adhesive, apply it to the wall with a small artist's brush in order to avoid smearing any on the undamaged wallpaper. If your paper is prepasted, wet the patch and shake off the excess water.
◆ Hold the patch lightly with the fingers of both hands, taking care not to crease the paper. Insert the top edge into the cleaned-out section (left), pat it down lightly, then let the rest of the patch fall into place and press it gently with a clean, damp sponge.
◆ After a few minutes press again with a clean sponge to be sure the patch is firmly in place and that all corners and edges are down.

CUTTING FLAPS TO FLATTEN A BUBBLE

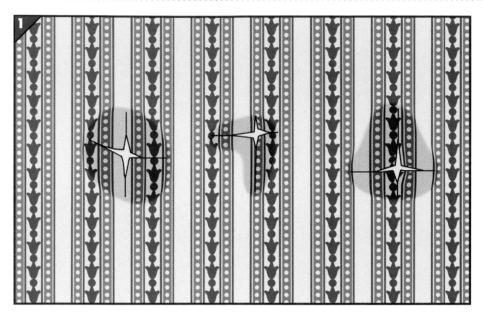

1. Making the cuts.

Most bubbles can be eliminated by making two crosswise cuts, which let air escape and create flaps so that adhesive can be applied to the underside of the paper. Bubbles pop up in a variety of shapes, three of which are shown by shaded areas in the drawing, along with the best configuration of cuts to make for each shape. Slash along a pattern line wherever possible.

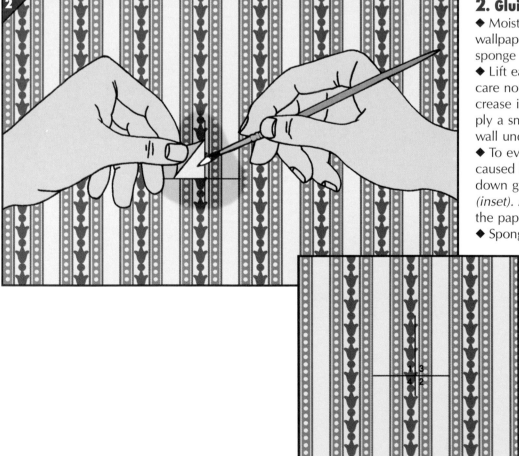

2. Gluing down the flaps.

◆ Moisten the patterned side of the wallpaper flaps with a clean, damp sponge to make them flexible.

◆ Lift each flap in turn, taking special care not to bend it back far enough to crease it. With a thin artist's brush, apply a small amount of adhesive to the wall underneath.

◆ To evenly distribute any slack caused by stretching, pat the flaps down gently in the sequence indicated (inset). Any overlap will disappear as the paper dries and shrinks.

◆ Sponge off excess adhesive after the flaps have been in place for a few minutes, but take care not to raise the flaps with the sponge.

CURVED CUTS INSTEAD OF STRAIGHT

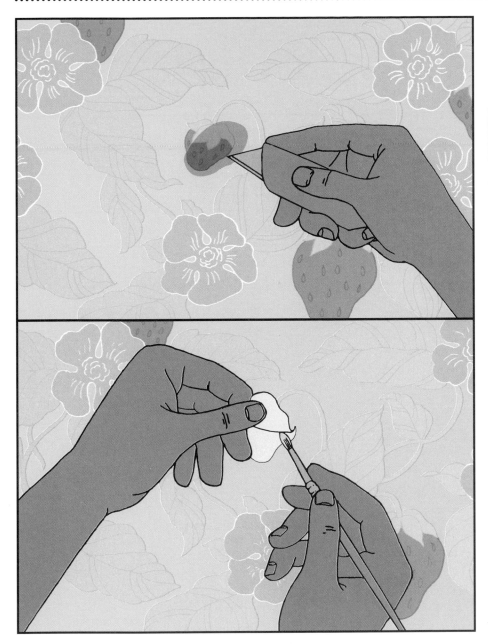

Cutting on a curve.

On some wallpaper patterns, such as the one that is shown above, a bubble can be flattened by making one curved cut instead of two intersecting slashes. The bubble *(shaded area)* in this wallpaper has developed directly under a circular pattern design. When this situation or a similar one occurs, make a single curved cut that is three-quarters of the way around the edge of the design and coinciding with the pattern. Lift, without creasing, the curved flap that you have cut, then paste down the flap as described in Step 2 on page 98.

paste down the flap as described in Step 2 on page 98.

MAINTAINING YOUR WALLPAPER

Most of today's wall coverings can be washed with mild soap and water. Never use abrasive powdered cleansers on wallpaper, even vinyls, and never use household cleaners containing kerosene or other petroleum distillates.

Start at the bottom of a wall and work upward: If you work from the top, the dirty water will flow down onto the dirt-clogged paper, leaving streaks that are very hard to remove. When the dirt is off, rinse the paper with clean water.

The material called cleaning dough, which works like a big eraser, is ideal for surfaces that are not washable. Stubborn spots that will not come off with the dough can often be removed with a paste made from carbon tetrachloride and cornstarch or fuller's earth; when the paste has dried, brush it away. Before using cleaning dough or the paste, make a test application in an inconspicuous area; either cleaner could change the paper's appearance.

Clear protective-spray coatings render any wallpaper washable and add special protection over patched areas. Apply these coatings as soon as the adhesive is dry under the paper and before dust has a chance to build up.

For future repairs, save unused powdered adhesive and wallpaper scraps. Label the adhesive container and put it in a cool, dry place. Store leftover scraps in a sheet of brown wrapping paper sealed in a cardboard mailing tube.

Updates

Besides brightening living spaces and making rooms useful, lighting is an important decorating tool that can produce a range of looks and moods. Today's lucky home decorators have more and more fixtures to choose from as lighting manufacturers continue to design new products to match nearly any taste and budget. To help you choose the right lighting for your home, we'll walk you through the principles of general, task, and accent lighting. We'll show you examples of each, and discuss how to use them in various rooms.

The most difficult electrical installations are best left to a professional electrician, but there are a number of home lighting projects you can take pride in doing yourself. To get you started, we'll show you how to change an incandescent light fixture. You'll also learn how to install fluorescent fixtures and will pick up background information on rapid-start and instant-start fixtures. One of the most versatile fixtures is track lighting, which can function as general, task, or accent lighting. This chapter explains how to purchase and install this fixture as well as recessed lighting. Did you know that ceiling fans are easy to install and use only modest amounts of energy? You'll learn how to install these, with and without combination lighting. We'll even show you how to ensure that the fan is properly supported and how to locate it for optimal safety and cooling efficiency.

These adjustable spotlights accent the owner's flock of shorebird decoys. Flexible fixtures allow lights to be redirected to highlight any interesting feature in a room.

Recessed lighting is perfect for a small bathroom to cut down on clutter. Positioning the lights over the mirror and bath provides perfect task lighting while also accenting the clean white of the tiles and porcelain.

Lamps are the most versatile of all lighting. A bedside lamp is ideal for night reading, and small lamps on either side of a mirror provide a clear, unshadowed reflection.

The sconces in this study add a warm flare to the cool, gray wall and accent the detailed gold molding over the fireplace.

Ceiling fans are easy to install and useful as well as decorative. They help circulate air in a room, carry a breeze from an open window, and keep heat from getting trapped up near the ceiling in winter.

Setting the Mood

Lighting is an integral part of good decorating. Besides brightening living spaces, clever lighting can set certain moods. It can draw attention to cherished pieces of artwork and can be repositioned in a room to create a new look. A basic understanding of lighting types and fixtures will help you choose lighting you'll love.

Incandescent and fluorescent lighting are the two main types of lighting used in homes. Incandescent bulbs have screw-type bases and don't cost very much. They emit quite a bit of heat and produce warm-toned light. Fluorescent bulbs produce cooler-looking light that's available in "warm white," "cool white," and "daylight" tones. Since fluorescent bulbs don't produce much heat, they're especially good for places where air conditioning is heavily used. Fluorescent lighting uses much less electricity than incandescent lighting, which makes it energy-efficient. Halogen bulbs are actually a form of incandescent lighting. They're filled with halogen gas, which produces a very white light that's closer to daylight than incandescent or fluorescent lighting. Halogen shouldn't be handled directly; traces of moisture, dirt, or skin oil can make them shatter when they're turned on. They're more expensive but last a long time.

general lighting

task lighting

accent lighting

The three main ways to light a home are known as general, task, and accent lighting. General lighting provides a background of even illumination. Multiple overhanging lights and recessed lights placed along a ceiling can help create uniform lighting and prevent heavily shadowed areas. Uplights cast light onto the ceiling, where it is reflected off and gives a sense of natural light.

Task lighting focuses light for doing close work. For living rooms and bedrooms, table lamps, pharmacy lamps, and desk lamps provide good light for reading or doing crafts. When selecting table lamps, remember that light shades emit more light while dark ones limit it. In a kitchen, try overhead lighting strategically placed to shine directly on your countertops and work spaces.

Perhaps the most decorative option, accent lighting is used to draw attention to favorite features or add drama to a room. You can highlight a favorite picture with a small spotlight above the frame, or place wall-mounted sconces with lights shining upward to emphasize beautiful crown molding or simply make a plain wall appear more interesting.

TOOLS

Utility knife
Screwdriver
Wire stripper
Adjustable wrench

MATERIALS

Coat hanger wire
Light fixture
Wire caps
Crossbar
Nipple
Reducing nut
Hickey

A new light fixture can both enhance a room's look and save energy. While incandescent bulbs produce softer and more natural light, fluorescents *(pages 110-111)* use less wattage, give off less heat, and last far longer. The following procedures apply to almost any incandescent fixture mounted on a wall or ceiling.

Removing the Old Fixture:
With the power turned off, remove the bulbs or tubes. Free a fixture stuck to the wall or ceiling with paint or caulk by cutting around the decorative cover, or canopy, with a utility knife. Unscrew any mounting screws or cap nuts, then pull the fixture away from the box and hang it from the box with a hook that is made of coat hanger wire. Disconnect the wiring.

If the exposed ends of house wires have cracked insulation, cut them back and strip off $\frac{1}{2}$ inch of insulation to reveal bright, clean wire. If necessary, strip the new fixture wires to the same length.

Mounting a Fixture: Most new fixtures come with mounting hardware and instructions. If not, and if the new fixture is similar in size and weight to the old one, you may be able to reuse some of the old hardware.

Every light fixture must be fastened securely to a ceiling or wall box. Moreover, heavy fixtures such as chandeliers must have additional support and should be attached to a box stud *(opposite)*.

HANGING LIGHTWEIGHT FIXTURES

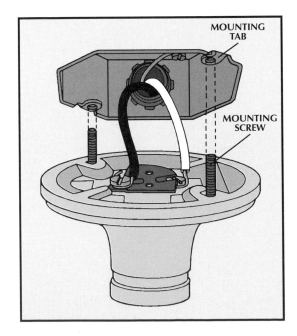

MOUNTING TAB

MOUNTING SCREW

Connecting a simple fixture.
A single-bulb porcelain fixture, typically used in garages and basements, connects to house wiring by means of terminals.
◆ To install this type of fixture, connect the black house wire to the brass-colored terminal and the white house wire to the silver-colored terminal.
◆ Secure the fixture to the threaded mounting tabs of the box with screws. Tighten the mounting screws gingerly; overtightening can crack the ceramic.

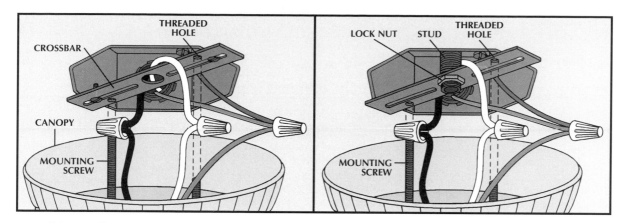

Attaching a fixture with an adapter.

Light fixtures are often fastened to outlet box mounting tabs with screws, typically through holes in the canopy.

◆ Where canopy holes do not align with the tabs, adapt the box with a slotted crossbar. Screw the crossbar to the tabs *(above, left)*, or for box with a stud in the center, slip the crossbar onto the stud and secure it with a lock nut *(above, right)*.

◆ Fasten the canopy to the threaded holes in the crossbar with screws trimmed, if necessary, so they do not press against the back of the box.

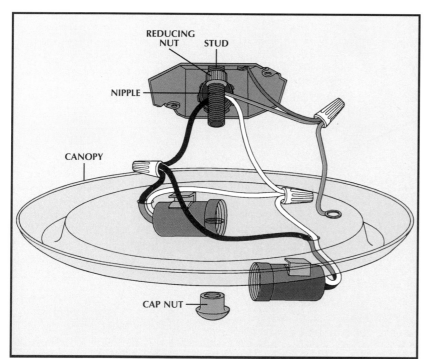

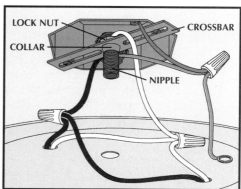

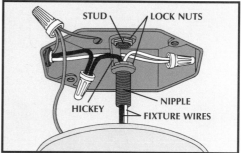

Securing center-mounted fixtures.

If the box has a built-in stud, extend it with a smaller-diameter nipple held to the stud by a reducing nut *(above, left)*.

If the box has no stud, use a crossbar with a threaded collar in the center *(above right, top)*. Screw a nipple into the collar and secure it

with a lock nut so the nipple protrudes through the canopy just far enough to engage the cap nut. Fasten the crossbar to the box tabs.

To hang chandeliers or other fixtures whose wires pass through the canopy *(above right, bottom)*, attach a nipple to the stud with a C-shaped adapter called a hickey. Secure both nipple and hickey with lock nuts.

Pass the fixture wires through the nipple into the box.

◆ With the nipple in place, connect the fixture's white, black, and ground wires to the house circuit's corresponding wires. Fold the wires into the box or under the canopy.
◆ Fasten the fixture to the nipple with the cap nut, drawing the canopy against the wall or ceiling.

Adding a Dimmer Switch

A dimmer switch has a control knob or toggle that not only turns a fixture on and off but also adjusts the lighting level from low to high. These devices provide versatility and can create dramatic effects in home lighting. In a three- or four-way switching scheme—one in which a fixture is controlled by two or three switches—you can replace one of the switches with a three-way dimmer (*opposite*). With this setup, the lights can be turned off at any of the switches, but only the dimmer will control the level of light.

Installation Requirements: In place of the typical screw terminals, dimmers have built-in leads that are connected to the cable wires with wire caps. Replacing an existing switch with a dimmer generally requires only a screwdriver and a voltage tester. Before buying a dimmer switch, measure the depth of the wall box it will occupy and compare it with the manufacturer's specifications for the switch.

⚠ **CAUTION** *Turn off power to the circuit at the service panel and check the switch with a voltage tester.*

A Range of Styles

Dimmers are available in several models and with a variety of control mechanisms (*right*). The single-pole type has two lead wires, which may be black or red; three-way switches have three black or red leads. Depending on its design, a switch may also have a green lead wire, which attaches to the ground screw in the wall box or is joined with a wire cap to the bare copper ground wires.

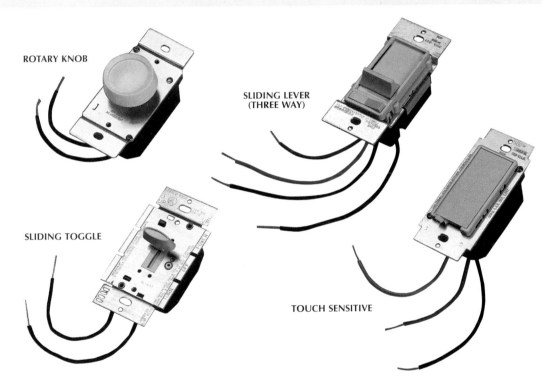

ROTARY KNOB

SLIDING LEVER (THREE WAY)

SLIDING TOGGLE

TOUCH SENSITIVE

REPLACING A WALL SWITCH

1. Removing the old switch.
◆ Unscrew the cover plate and confirm that the power is off. To do so, touch one probe of a voltage tester to the metal outlet box—or to the bare copper ground wire if the box is plastic—then touch the other probe in turn to each of the terminals of the switch. With push-in terminals, insert the probe into the release slot of each terminal. If the tester's light does not glow on contact, power to the switch is off.
◆ Remove the screws from the mounting strap (*right*).

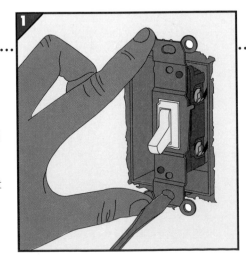

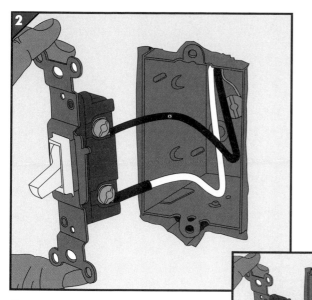

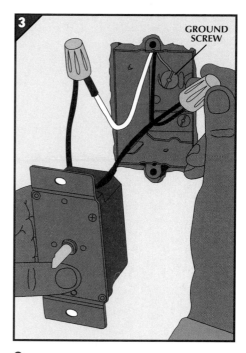

GROUND
SCREW

2. Checking the cables.

◆ Pull the switch from the wall and count the cables entering the box. If there is one cable with a black and a white wire, the white wire may be recoded with black electrical tape *(above)*. Where there are two cables, two black wires are secured to the switch and the white wires are joined with a wire cap *(inset)*.

◆ Remove the wires from the switch by loosening the terminal screws with a screwdriver.

3. Attaching the dimmer.

◆ With wire caps, join the leads of the dimmer switch to the wires that you detached in Step 2; tug each connection gently to make sure it is secure *(above)*. If the dimmer has a green lead wire, attach it to the ground screw of the box or join it with a wire cap to the bare copper wires.

◆ Screw the switch to the box and reattach the cover plate.

A THREE-WAY SWITCH

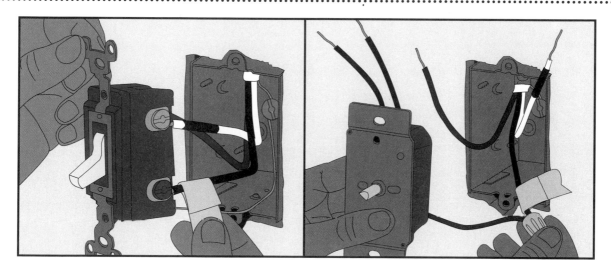

Installing the switch.

One three-way switch in a three- or four-way switching arrangement may be replaced by a three-way dimmer switch. Before removing the wires from the existing switch, mark the common wire—secured to the black or darkest terminal—with masking tape *(above, left)*. Join the common lead of the dimmer switch to the taped wire *(above, right)*, then connect each of the other leads to any of the remaining wires in the box.

Installing Fluorescent Fixtures

Although the cost of bulbs and installation may be greater, fluorescent lighting gives more uniform illumination than incandescent lighting and is more efficient in its use of energy. Using the hardware that comes with a new fixture, you can mount fluorescents quite easily with an electric drill and spade bit. Follow the procedures on page 106 to remove old incandescent or fluorescent fixtures.

The heart of every fluorescent fixture is the ballast, a device that provides a quick surge of voltage to start the tube, then limits the current while the tube is lit. After 10 or more years, a ballast will wear out, but often it is more economical to install a new fixture than to replace a ballast.

Types of Fixtures: Fluorescents come in a variety of shapes and sizes, but most of them fall into three categories:

Rapid-start fixtures, which light after a few seconds' delay, often are used in home workshops and laundry rooms. These fixtures may malfunction if turned on and off frequently in a brief period of time.

Instant-start fixtures turn on at the flick of a switch but wear out quickly because of the high-voltage surge when switched on.

Compact fluorescent bulbs are self-contained fixtures that have the ballast or an adapter in the base. More efficient and versatile than fluorescent tubes, compact fluorescents screw into ordinary incandescent bulb sockets.

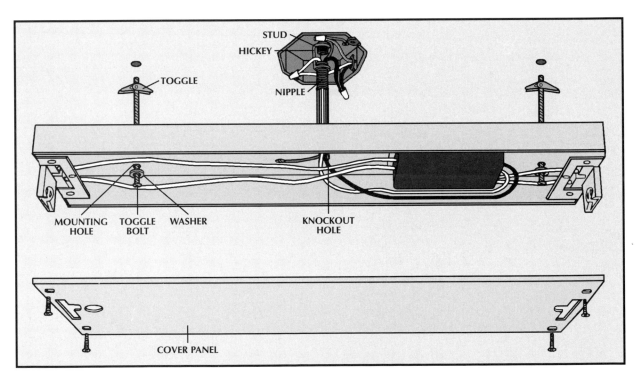

Mounting a one-tube ceiling fixture.

◆ Position the fixture with the knockout hole for the wires centered on the ceiling box, and mark the ceiling through the fixture-mounting holes. Lower the fixture and, with a spade bit, drill $\frac{5}{8}$-inch holes at the marks.

◆ Slip a toggle bolt and washer through the fixture-mounting holes and screw a toggle onto the end of each of the bolts.

◆ Thread a hickey to the stud and a nipple to the hickey; if there is no stud, attach a crossbar to the box tabs and a nipple to the crossbar (page 107).

◆ Have a helper support the fixture or hang it from the box with a wire hanger, then lead the fixture wires through the nipple and connect them to those that are in the box, black to black and white to white. Connect the ground wires from the fixture and the house circuit to each other and to the grounding jumper in the box if it is metal.

◆ Raise the fixture. While folding the wires into the box, push the toggles through the ceiling holes and guide the fixture onto the nipple. Tighten the toggle bolts.

◆ Finally, install the cover panel and the tube.

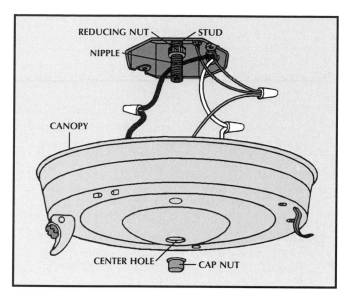

REDUCING NUT — STUD
NIPPLE
CANOPY
CENTER HOLE — CAP NUT

Hanging a circular fixture.

◆ Thread a reducing nut onto the stud and screw a nipple into the nut.

◆ Connect the fixture wires to the house wires—black to black and white to white. Join the ground wire in the fixture to the circuit grounding wire and to a jumper in the box if it is metal. Fold the wires into the box.

◆ Raise the fixture to the box so that the nipple protrudes through the center hole of the canopy. Thread the cap nut onto the nipple and tighten to secure the fixture against the ceiling.

Troubleshooting Guide

PROBLEM	REMEDY
Tube will not light.	Replace fuse or reset circuit breaker. Replace tube. Rapid-start: Rotate tube on holder. Instant-start: Make sure pins are fully seated in sockets. Check that tube wattage equals that shown on ballast.
Ends of tube glow but center does not light.	Check attachment of fixture's ground wire and circuit ground.
Tube flickers, blinks, or spirals.	Normal with new tube. Should improve with use. Rapid-start: Rotate tube on holder. Instant-start: Make sure pins are fully seated in sockets. Replace tube.
Fixture hums or buzzes.	Tighten ballast connections.
Blackening at end of tube.	Tube worn out. Replace tube.

For concentrated illumination from above, nothing surpasses a track light system and recessed fixtures. Track lighting, shown on these pages, is the more flexible of the two, but recessed units are a less obtrusive option.

Purchasing: Both types of equipment are sold in kits or as separate components. Track is available in 2-, 4-, and 8-foot sections that can be snapped together with connectors to form straight, right-angled, T-shaped, or X-shaped arrangements. Installation methods vary, and units from one manufacturer may not fit those of another.

Some recessed fixtures are designed specifically for finished or unfinished ceilings; others, like the unit shown on pages 98-99, can be adapted to either situation. For insulated ceilings, choose fixtures with an IC rating; these may be safely buried in insulation.

Wiring Requirements: A 15-amp circuit with a wall switch is adequate. A track system can be wired to a ceiling box at any point along its length by means of a special connector called a canopy. Recessed fixtures come with their own wiring boxes attached. When installing several such units on a single circuit, make sure that all but one are rated for "through-wiring" with two cables; the last fixture needs only a single cable.

TOOLS

Nail set
Hammer
Screwdriver

Drill with $\frac{3}{4}$-inch bit
Tin snips
Electronic stud
 finder
Dry-wall saw
Fish tape

MATERIALS

Track lighting kit
Canopy kit
Light fixtures for
 track
Electrician's tape
Wire caps
Bulbs

Recessed lighting
 kits
Cardboard
Plastic-sheathed
 cable
Patching materials
 for ceiling

WIRING TRACK LIGHTS TO A CEILING BOX

1. Removing the knockouts.
◆ Holding a length of track against the ceiling box, mark the large circular knockout nearest the center of the box *(right)*.
◆ Lay the track section upside down across two lengths of scrap lumber. With a nail set and hammer, remove the marked knockout and the small circular knockout next to it.
◆ In the same manner, remove a keyhole-shaped mounting knockout near each end of the track section.
◆ If you plan to install a single section, install the plastic end caps provided with the kit; otherwise, place caps on end sections before installing them.

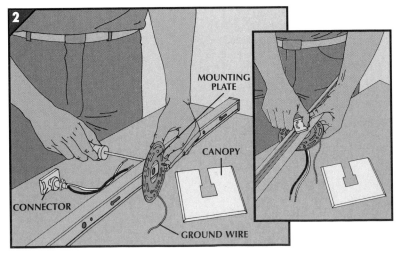

2. Attaching the mounting plate.
◆ Hold the plate against the ceiling side of the track, ground wire on top. Position the center hole at the large knockout opening, and align one of the threaded holes in the plate with the smaller knockout. Fasten the pieces together loosely with the screw provided *(far left)*, leaving a $\frac{1}{8}$-inch space between plate and track for the canopy.
◆ Thread the connector wires through the large track knockout and mounting plate. Lock the connector to the track by turning it clockwise *(inset)*.

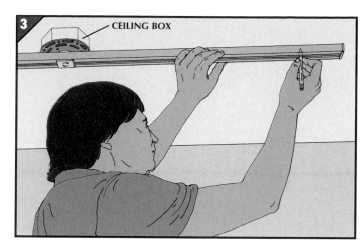

CEILING BOX

3. Marking the ceiling.

◆ Fasten the plate to the ceiling-box mounting tabs temporarily, using the screws provided with the box.

◆ Pivot the track on the loosely fastened mounting plate screw to align the track parallel to a nearby wall, and mark the ceiling at the midpoint of each keyhole slot *(right)*.

◆ Unscrew the mounting plate from the ceiling box and drill holes for toggle bolts at the marks. Assemble two bolts and push their toggles into the holes.

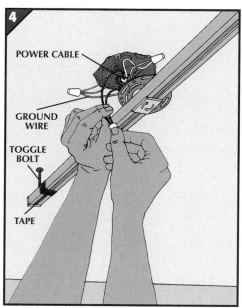

POWER CABLE

GROUND WIRE

TOGGLE BOLT

TAPE

4. Wiring the track.

◆ Suspend the track from the toggle-bolt heads. Wrap tape around the track to prevent it from accidentally slipping off the boltheads.

◆ Connect the connector wires to the wires of the cable entering the ceiling box, black to black and white to white *(left)*.

◆ Connect the ground wire from the mounting plate to the ground wire in the power cable and to the ceiling box, if it is metal.

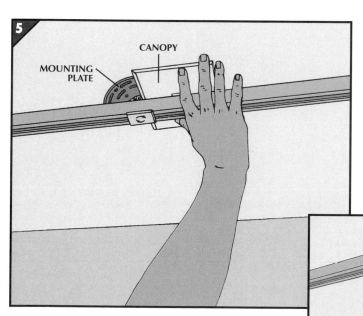

MOUNTING PLATE

CANOPY

5. Adding the canopy.

◆ Tuck all wiring connections into the ceiling box, and screw the mounting plate securely to the box.

◆ Slide the canopy between the mounting plate and the track to conceal the plate and ceiling box *(left)*. Tighten the mounting plate screw.

◆ Unwrap the tape from the ends of the track and tighten the toggle bolts to hold the track against the ceiling.

◆ Extend the track as desired, using toggle bolts to secure each section of it to the ceiling.

◆ Fit light fixtures to the track *(inset)*, and then lock them in place.

TECHNIQUES FOR RECESSED LIGHTING

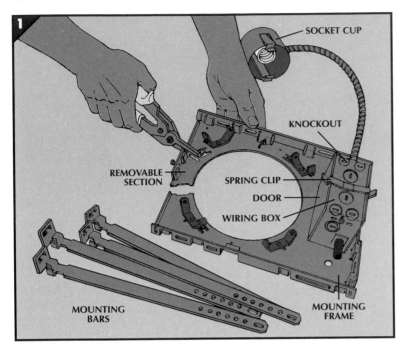

1. Preparing the mounting frame.

◆ Remove the frame's mounting bars and place the frame on a piece of cardboard. Outline the frame and circular opening with a pencil, then cut along the lines to create a template.

◆ With tin snips, cut out the removable section of the frame opposite the wiring box *(left)*.

◆ Lift the spring clip on top of the wiring box and remove one of its two detachable doors. Unscrew the two cable clamps that are inside and modify them for use with plastic-sheathed cable.

◆ Reinstall the clamps and remove one knockout above each clamp.

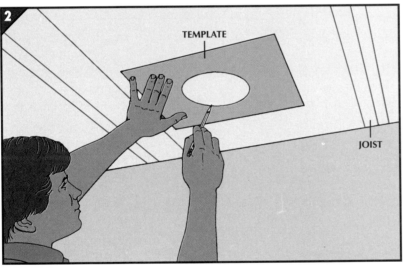

2. Cutting a ceiling opening.

◆ With a stud finder, locate the ceiling joists. Using the template, mark fixture locations on the ceiling between joists.

◆ Drill a small hole in the center of each circular mark. Bend hanger wire to a 90-degree angle, insert one end through the hole, and rotate the wire to check for obstructions. If you find any, relocate the fixtures. Otherwise, cut openings.

◆ At each joist running between fixtures, cut an access opening in the ceiling . Drill a $\frac{3}{4}$-inch hole through the center of each joist.

3. Wiring connections.

◆ Fish a two-conductor cable from a junction box to the first fixture opening, followed by another cable from the second fixture opening to the first—and so on downstream.

◆ At the first ceiling opening, rest a fixture-mounting frame atop a stepladder, and clamp the cable ends to opposite sides of the box.

◆ Red wire caps *(right)* indicate the connections to be made between the cable and fixture wires. Connect black to black, white to white, and the ground wires.

◆ Reattach the box door.

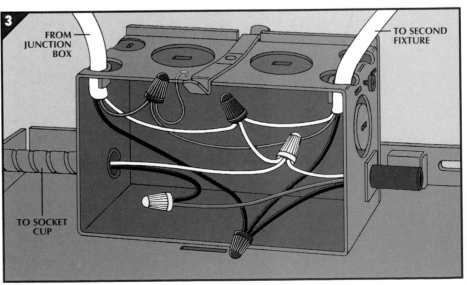

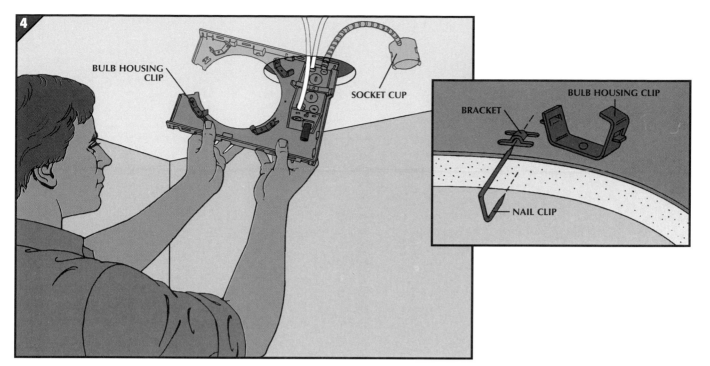

BULB HOUSING CLIP

SOCKET CUP

BRACKET

BULB HOUSING CLIP

NAIL CLIP

4. Securing the mounting frame.

◆ Push the socket cup through the ceiling opening and set it beside the lip of the hole.

◆ Beginning at the opening cut in the frame in Step 1, work the frame through the hole *(above),* and rest it on the ceiling with the opening in the frame aligned with the ceiling hole.

◆ Slide the long ends of the four nail clips provided with the fixture partway into the brackets at the frame's edge *(inset).* Align the short ends of the nail clips with the center of the ceiling material, then tap them into the ceiling with a hammer.

5. Installing the bulb housing.

◆ Bring the socket cup back through the opening. Rotate the bulb housing clips inward.

◆ Insert the socket cup into the top of the bulb housing so that tabs in the cup snap into slots in the housing.

◆ Push the assembly into the frame *(right)* until the bulb housing flange rests against the ceiling, completing the installation.

◆ At the second fixture opening, connect cables from the first and third fixture openings to the second fixture in its wiring box, and complete the installation as described above.

◆ When all fixtures are in place, patch the access holes at each joist.

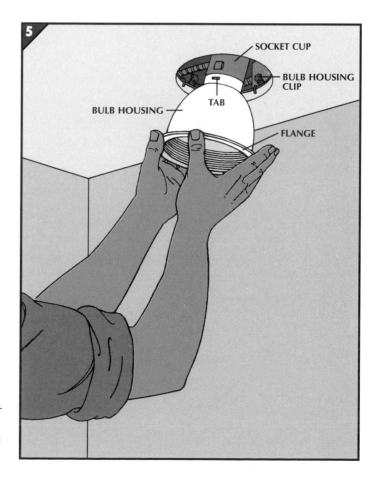

SOCKET CUP

BULB HOUSING CLIP

BULB HOUSING

TAB

FLANGE

Hanging a Ceiling Fan

Easy to install and modest in electricity consumption, a ceiling fan can be useful all year round. Most fans have reversible action to draw cool air upward in the summer and send warm air downward in the winter, abetting the work of your heating and cooling system. Some ceiling fans, such as the one shown here, can also accommodate a light fixture.

Proper Support: Because ceiling fans may weigh anywhere from 35 to 50 pounds, sturdy mounting is essential. The outlet box that the fan will be hung from must be metal—

and it should be secured directly to a joist or suspended between joists by a crosspiece known as a bar hanger.

Placement Considerations: Fan blades must be at least 7 feet from the floor and 24 inches from the nearest obstruction. Where there is only a small amount of vertical room, choose a fan that mounts against the ceiling. For a higher ceiling or one that is angled or vaulted, hang the fan from an extension called a downpipe, available in several lengths. Never mount a fan

where it may become wet—on an open porch, for example.

Installation: Fans are sold in kits, which include all the necessary parts. Before beginning work, turn off the electricity to the outlet at the service panel, and check that it is off with a voltage tester. Although the fan is heavy, it can be installed by one person: A hook on the plate attached to the outlet box serves to support the fan while you connect the wires. Do not operate the fan motor until the blades have been attached.

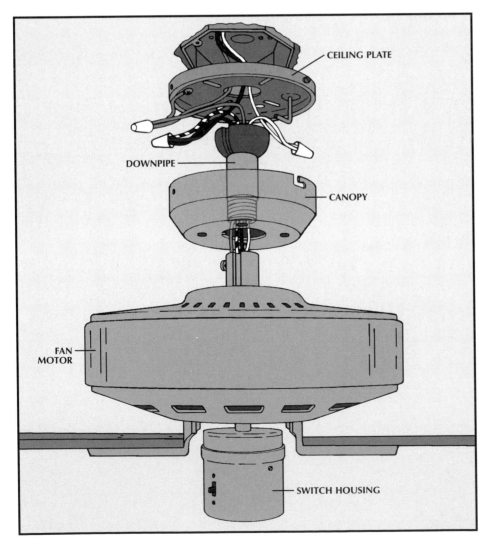

Labels: CEILING PLATE, DOWNPIPE, CANOPY, FAN MOTOR, SWITCH HOUSING

Anatomy of a ceiling fan.

Electricity for the ceiling fan at left is supplied through an outlet box that is braced above the ceiling to support the weight of the fan motor. The fan hangs from a ceiling plate that is fastened to the outlet box. Often, a downpipe is used to lower a fan for better air circulation. A light kit *(next page)* that works independently of the fan motor can be attached to the switch housing so that a ceiling fan can double as a light source.

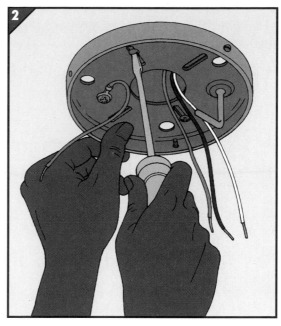

1. Assembling the fan.

◆ Insert the downpipe in the canopy, and feed the fan wires through the pipe.

◆ Screw the downpipe into the fan, and tighten the setscrew securing the fan to the pipe.

To omit the downpipe, feed the wires through the canopy and fasten it to the fan motor with the screws provided.

2. Attaching the ceiling plate.

◆ Feed the electrical wires from the outlet box through the ceiling plate.

◆ Position the plate on the outlet box and fasten it to the ears of the box with the screws that come with the box.

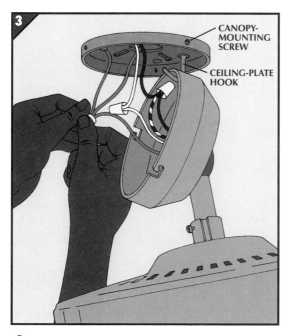

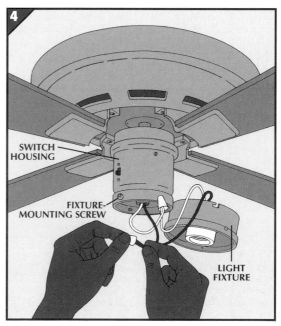

3. Connecting the wires.

◆ To support the fan, hang the canopy from the hook in the ceiling plate.

◆ Connect the black and black-and-white fan motor wires to the black ceiling-box wire.

◆ Join the two white wires, then connect the three ground wires *(above)*.

◆ Hook the canopy onto mounting screws in the ceiling plate and tighten them.

4. Attaching a light fixture.

◆ Remove the cover plate from the bottom of the switch housing.

◆ Connect the wires in the switch housing to those of the light fixture, black to black and white to white.

◆ Mount the fixture to the switch housing with the screws provided.

Treatments

Whether you're fixing up a spare bedroom as a nursery, revamping a basement into a family room, remodeling your kitchen, or turning your living room into a gallery for a treasured art collection, think of your home as a bare canvas that's just brimming with decorating possibilities.

This chapter contains a variety of projects you'll take pride in completing to change the look of one room or your entire house. To start, you'll learn how to make walls and ceilings as uniform as possible. This process, called "truing," is the basis for applying new wallboard or paneling. You'll also learn how to work with wallboard like a pro. Next, you'll learn how to install decorative moldings and medallions to give your project a period look. A sure-fire way to brighten a room is to install mirrored panels and tiles, and you'll find step-by-step methods to achieve this luxurious and contemporary effect. Try using brick veneer on a wall if you want the warm beauty of brick but not the headache of building a true brick wall. To subdivide a large area into separate spaces, you'll learn how to form and install dividers. This chapter also includes information on working with prefabricated ceilings and simulating beamed ceilings, plus installing soundproofing.

Mirrored walls are ideal for opening up small spaces. The stylish mirrors in this bathroom also reflect the overhead lighting and brighten the room.

Exposed ceiling beams are ideal for setting a cozy, country atmosphere. Avoid the expensive, more labor-intensive work of adding real beams by installing simulated beams that achieve the same rustic effect.

The warm red tones of the exposed
brick combined with white ceilings
and a sturdy hardwood floor give this
room the perfect studio charm.

Decorative and versatile, a folding screen can conceal clutter, hide an awkward feature, or provide
an area of privacy in a room. Cover the screen with
your favorite fabrics to add a decorator's touch.

Inspired
Accents

If you're looking for a quick, inexpensive way to punch up a room, molding is a terrific option. These long, decorative bands are usually made of wood, plaster, or plastic formed into cornices, picture rails, chair rails, and trim. Molding also shows up as molded-plaster friezes, plaques, and other fancy items that can be used to inspire period looks. Whether you opt for linear bands or fancy plaster shapes, molding enhances any room by adding dimension to otherwise flat surfaces and creating highlights and shadows.

Cornice moldings are placed at the very top of walls against the ceiling to draw the eye upward. Their cousins, friezes, are placed just below the ceiling and are heavily textured with patterns that stick out from the wall. Friezes were especially popular in the 18th century but became less popular when home-owners realized that the patterned designs and high placement near the ceiling made them difficult to keep clean. Like friezes, ornamental plaster plaques are not as popular as they once were but still appear in very formal decorating schemes. Plaques are placed flat against walls and project out to add interest. As their name suggests, picture rails were originally used to hang pictures. These long strips of molding are placed about a third of the way down from the top of the wall. Special picture hooks fit in the

cornice molding

frieze

grooves or channels along the upper edge. Chair rails, placed one-third of the way up a wall, were originally intended to protect walls from being scuffed by the backs of chairs. Today they're often used as decorative elements to separate paint from wallpaper or other interior finishes used on the same wall. Molding placed around doors and windows is known as trim. When it's placed very low on a wall against the floor, it's called baseboard molding.

Besides its good looks, molding is a practical way to change a room's atmosphere. Cornice moldings used with wallpaper make rooms seem loftier. Picture rails partnered with wallpaper are a good way to add style to a wall. A chair rail placed about 3 feet above a baseboard gives a wall dimension. If you decide to use baseboard and cornice moldings on the same wall, make sure they're the same width to balance each other and to beautifully "bookend" the wall.

cornice molding

ornate friezes

picture rail

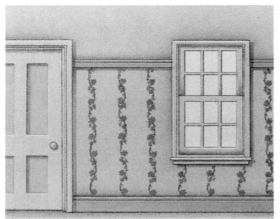

chair rail

When you refurbish a room with new wallboard or paneling, first-class results depend on a uniform underlying surface. If walls are not flat—without noticeable ridges and valleys—it will be difficult to apply the new covering satisfactorily.

Checking for Defects: A long, straight board will help you assess the condition of a wall or ceiling. Slide the board across the surface and look for gaps larger than $\frac{1}{4}$ inch between the two.

Small areas of imperfection can be rebuilt with plywood or wallboard patches, shimmed to bring them flush with the surrounding surface.

Redeeming a surface with more extensive flaws requires adding a grid of boards called furring strips or building a false wall in front of the old one.

A Furring-Strip Grid: Before laying out a grid for the strips *(opposite)*, remove moldings and trim, and adjust the depth of door and window jambs to suit the new wall thickness *(page 130)*. You may also have to reposition electrical outlet boxes or adjust their depth *(page 131)*. Plan vertical strips to coincide with the edges of the panels to be applied over them. In a wood-frame wall, nail the strips to studs where possible; between

studs, secure them using the method described on page 217.

Working over Masonry: Fasten the strips with case-hardened cut nails supplemented by construction adhesive. On any masonry wall below ground level, apply a coat of waterproof masonry sealer before attaching the furring strips.

If driving nails into masonry will compromise its watertightness, erect a false wall in front of it *(page 128)*. A false wall may also be needed if you plan new electrical junction boxes or switches, since the holes they require could create leaks in the masonry or violate local fire codes.

TOOLS

Pry bar	Carpenter's level
Utility knife	Straightedge
Hammer	Chalk line
Nail set	Plumb bob
Pin punch	Ladder
Nail puller	Tape measure
Electronic stud	Saw
finder	Framing square
	Screwdrivers
	Caulking gun

MATERIALS

Furring strips (1 x 2 and 1 x 4)	Finishing nails
	Common nails
2 x 4s	($3\frac{1}{4}$" and $3\frac{1}{2}$")
2 x 4s (pressure-treated)	Wood shims
	Construction adhesive
	Acrylic latex caulk

SAFETY TIPS

Goggles protect your eyes when you are driving nails.

PRYING OFF MOLDING AND TRIM

BASEBOARD

SHOE MOLDING

Removing a length of molding.
◆ If you plan to salvage shoe molding, cut the paint between the molding and the baseboard with a utility knife.
◆ Drive a thin pry bar into the seam near an end of the molding. Place a wood block behind the pry bar to protect the baseboard and slowly pry the molding loose.
◆ Work along the seam, using wedges

to hold the seam open as you go *(above)*, until the whole length of molding is loose enough to remove in one piece.
◆ Apply the same technique to remove baseboards and other moldings.
◆ If you plan to reuse the molding, pull out the old nails from the rear with a nail puller to avoid splintering the face of the molding.

Removing window or door trim.

◆ To avoid splitting window or door casings as you pry them loose, use a pin punch to drive the existing nails completely through one section of each mitered corner, as shown here. A standard nail set is too thick for this task and will split the wood.

◆ Pry off the casing, using the technique described on the previous page.

A GRID OF FURRING STRIPS

A framework for plywood paneling.

Furring strips on this wall, backed by wood shims where needed (page 127), make a flat base for vertical 4- by 8-foot sheets of wallboard or plywood paneling. Space horizontal 1-by-2 strips 16 inches apart from center to center. Place vertical 1-by-2 strips across the wall at 48-inch intervals, center to center.

Leave small gaps between vertical and horizontal furring strips to allow air to circulate behind the paneling. Place additional furring along corners and windows to support panel edges, and span the studs alongside an electrical outlet with a small 1-by-2. Horizontal 1-by-4 furring strips at the top and bottom of the wall serve as backing for cove and base moldings installed after the paneling is in place (page 202).

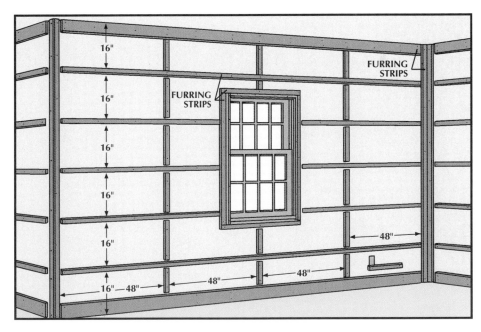

Fast Cuts with a Power Miter Saw

To speed the cutting of furring strips, consider renting a power miter saw, which slices through 1-by-2s with a single stroke. To minimize measuring, rent a model with an extension support on which you can set a stop block, then butt furring stock against the stop for cutting. The saw also pivots for angled cuts, making quick work of mitering moldings for a paneled wall (page 218).

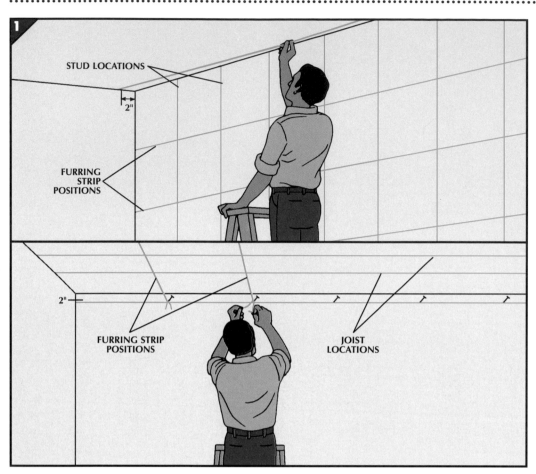

STUD LOCATIONS

2"

FURRING
STRIP
POSITIONS

2"

FURRING STRIP
POSITIONS

JOIST
LOCATIONS

1. Setting up reference lines.

◆ With a pencil and straightedge, rule the wall with vertical lines marking the locations of wall studs.
◆ In the same way, mark the horizontal positions where furring strips will be installed on the wall.
◆ Snap a chalk line against the ceiling, 2 inches from the wall *(left, top)*.

◆ On a ceiling, mark the locations of ceiling joists with a chalk line.
◆ Snap the chalk line 2 inches below the ceiling along the two walls that parallel the joists.
◆ Along each chalked line on the walls, drive nails every 16 inches for furring strips, and run taut strings across the joists between opposing nails *(left, bottom)*.

2. Positioning the first strips.

◆ Cut furring strips $3\frac{1}{2}$ inches shorter than the length of the wall or ceiling; make the top and bottom strips from 1-by-4s and the rest from 1-by-2s.
◆ For a wall, hang a plumb bob from the chalked line on the ceiling, opposite a line marking a stud.
◆ Measure the distance from the plumb line to the wall at each intersection of stud and furring strip line. Record each measurement on the wall.
◆ At the point with the smallest measurement—the highest spot along the

wall—secure a horizontal, 1-by-2 furring strip with a single nail. Then nail the strip to the wall at any other line intersection marked with the smallest distance from the plumb line.

On a ceiling, use the same procedure to locate the lowest point, measuring from the joist lines vertically to the strings. Slip a furring strip under the string that crosses the lowest point and nail the strip to the ceiling wherever it crosses a joist line marked with the smallest ceiling-to-string distance.

3. Shimming the strip.

◆ At the first nail driven into the furring strip, hang a plumb bob from the chalked line on the ceiling and note the distance from the plumb line to the face of the furring strip.

◆ Reposition the plumb bob in front of the stud nearest one end of the furring strip.

◆ At the stud, place wood shims behind the strip until the distance between its face and the plumb line equals the measurement taken at the first nail. Drive a nail through the furring strip and shim into the stud. There is no need to glue or nail the portion of strip that extends from the stud toward the corner.

◆ Shim the other end of the furring strip in the same way.

On a ceiling, measure and make a note of the distance between the string and the furring strip at the first nail. Shim out one end of the furring strip until the distance from the string to the face of the furring strip is the same as at the first nailing point. Nail the strip to the joist nearest the end of the strip. Repeat at the opposite end.

4. Truing a furring strip.

◆ Press the edge of a long, straight board against the furring strip, spanning two nailed points.

◆ Note any gaps between the board and the furring strip or the strip and the wall, and build out these points with shims at each stud as you nail the furring strip in place.

On a ceiling, use the same technique to true and nail the first furring strip.

5. Installing the remaining strips.

◆ Install and true a 1-by-4 furring strip at the top of the wall and fasten it with two nails at each stud.

◆ Span the two trued furring strips with a long, straight board as an aid to fitting the remaining horizontal strips *(left)*, including the 1-by-4 strip at the base of the wall.

◆ At each corner, install two 1-by-2 vertical strips. Elsewhere on the wall, install vertical strips to fit between the horizontal ones and shim them flush with the horizontal strips. If a horizontal strip does not intersect a single high spot on the wall, shim the strip where it passes close to the wall and nail it there. Proceed as described in Steps 1 through 4.

On a ceiling, install and true two 1-by-4 strips along opposite edges, parallel to the reference strings and the same distance from them as the first strip, using the same techniques you employed on the wall. Install and shim a 1-by-2 under each string and at the two unfurred ceiling edges, with short cross strips where needed to support panel edges.

A FALSE WALL OVER MASONRY

1. Making the frame.

◆ For the top and sole plates of a false wall, cut two 2-by-4s the length of the wall. On a concrete floor, make the sole plate from pressure-treated lumber.

◆ Lay the plates side by side on the floor, with their ends aligned. With the aid of a square, mark the stud positions across both plates simultaneously, beginning flush with one end of the plates *(left)*.

◆ Mark additional stud positions at 16-inch intervals. Finish with marks for studs flush with the other end of the plates.

◆ Turn the plates on edge, the marked faces toward each other, and position 2-by-4 studs cut $4\frac{1}{8}$ inches shorter than the height of the ceiling or joists.

◆ Fasten each stud with two $3\frac{1}{4}$-inch nails driven through the plate and into the stud, top and bottom.

2. Erecting the framing.

◆ Raise the wall framing into position about an inch away from the masonry wall. Plumb the framing at several points with a carpenter's level.

◆ Cut strips of $\frac{1}{2}$-inch wallboard $4\frac{1}{2}$ inches wide. Insert them between the top plate and the ceiling or joists; push them into position against the masonry wall and flush with the edge of the plate, to act as firestops. Shim as necessary for a snug fit.

◆ Nail the bottom and top plates to the floor and the ceiling with $3\frac{1}{2}$-inch nails.

◆ In cases where panels will be installed horizontally, toenail 2-by-4 supports *(inset)* between studs at 24-inch intervals to provide additional nailing surfaces for the paneling.

◆ Install similar nailing surfaces around electrical boxes or access doors *(page 197)*.

ENCLOSURES TO CONCEAL PIPES AND DUCTS

A vertical enclosure.

Most pipes, ducts, and girders can be enclosed with smaller, modified versions of a false stud wall *(above)*. There is no need to add a dry-wall firestop above such a small enclosure.

◆ Construct two narrow vertical walls reinforced with horizontal supports.

◆ Nail the top plate of one wall to a ceiling joist; fasten the top plate of the adjoining wall to 2-by-4 blocking installed between joists.

◆ Nail adjoining end studs of the two walls together at the corner; secure the bottom plates of each wall to the floor.

◆ For three-sided enclosures, either vertical or horizontal *(page 130)*, first construct and install two stud walls for the parallel sides of the enclosure. Then install horizontal supports to form the third side.

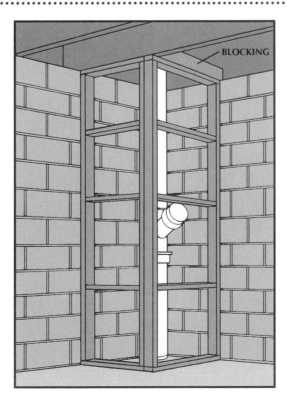

BLOCKING

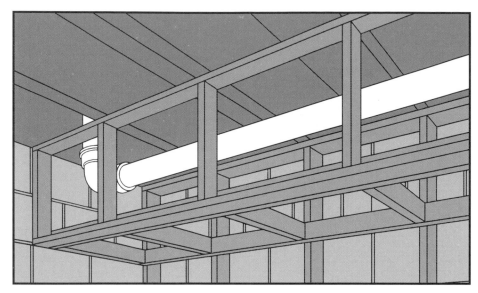

A horizontal enclosure.

◆ Construct two stud assemblies, one to be hung vertically from the ceiling and the other to fit horizontally between it and the adjacent wall *(left)*.

◆ Nail the vertical assembly through the top plate to ceiling joists or to horizontal blocking between them.

◆ Fasten the other assembly to wall studs, then nail together the top plates of the two assemblies.

DEEPENING WINDOW JAMBS

1. Removing a window stool.

To account for the additional thickness of a new wall surface and associated furring strips, add wood extensions to window jambs. Begin by removing the inner sill, called a stool.

◆ Drive all of the existing nails through the horn of the stool into the jamb *(page 125, top)*.

◆ Pry up the stool *(right)* and use it as a pattern for cutting a new one from stool stock *(inset)*, extending the back edge of the stool an amount equal to the thickness of the furring strips and new wall surface together.

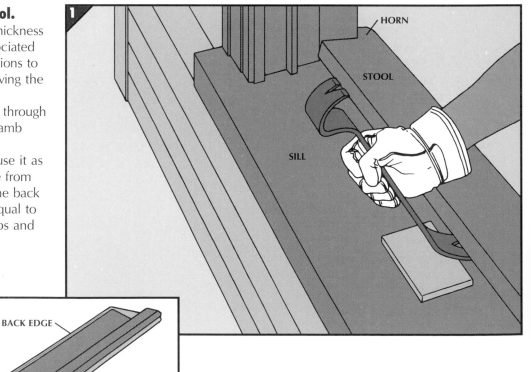

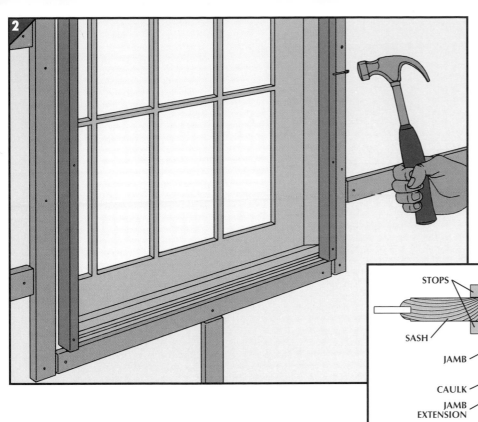

2. Attaching jamb extensions.

◆ From $\frac{3}{4}$-inch-thick stock, cut three jamb extensions—two for the sides, one for the top. Make the depth of the extensions equal to the combined thicknesses of the furring strips and the new wall surface.

◆ Nail the extensions to the edges of the jambs with finishing nails whose tips have been blunted to avoid splitting the thin wood, offsetting the extensions about $\frac{1}{8}$ inch from the face of the jamb (inset).

◆ Lay a bead of acrylic latex caulk in the corners formed by the extensions and the jambs.

If $\frac{1}{4}$-inch-thick paneling has been applied directly to a wall without furring strips, extend jambs with $\frac{1}{4}$- by $\frac{3}{4}$-inch lattice. This narrow stock lets you avoid the tricky job of sawing long, thin strips from wider boards.

STOPS
SASH
JAMB
CAULK
JAMB EXTENSION

EXTENDING AN ELECTRICAL OUTLET BOX

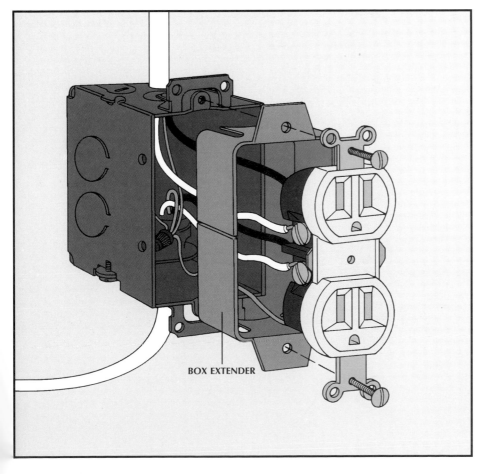

BOX EXTENDER

Attaching a box extender.

◆ Cut off the electricity at the main service panel and remove the fixture faceplate. Unscrew the fixture from the box, leaving the wires connected.

◆ Slide a collarlike extender over the fixture and its wiring and into the box.

◆ With the long bolts supplied with the extender, reattach the fixture to the box, adjusting the position of the extender so that the fixture will lie flush with the new wall surface.

How to Hang Wallboard

Wallboard, the material most commonly used to finish walls and ceilings, is simply a sheet of chalklike gypsum wrapped in heavy paper *(below)*. Easy to cut and somewhat flexible, wallboard can be fastened to a variety of supporting structures: joists, furring strips, or studs of wood or metal. The joints where panels meet are concealed with either adhesive-backed fiberglass mesh or paper tape and covered with pastelike joint compound *(pages 138-141)*.

Dimensions of Wallboard: Generally made in 4- and $4\frac{1}{2}$-foot widths, wallboard comes in 8-, 10-, and 12-foot lengths and in thicknesses of $\frac{3}{8}$, $\frac{1}{2}$, and $\frac{5}{8}$ inch; $\frac{1}{2}$-inch wallboard is considered standard. Using 12-foot sheets will save time, reducing the number of joints to be finished. But if such sheets are too heavy and unwieldy to handle, use shorter ones.

Before You Begin: To determine how many sheets of wallboard you need, calculate the square footage of each wall, ignoring all openings except the largest, such as archways or picture windows. Do the same for the ceiling. To convert this figure into sheets, divide it by the area of the panels you intend to buy. A 4- by 8-foot sheet is 32 square feet; a 4- by 12-foot sheet is 48 square feet.

Plan to hang panels horizontally rather than vertically on walls, unless the wall is very narrow. In rooms with ceilings higher than 8 feet, use sheets of wallboard $4\frac{1}{2}$ feet wide, trimmed to fit. If the ceiling is taller than 9 feet, you'll need a filler strip. Place it at the bottom of the wall, cut edge down.

You will also need fasteners—either nails or screws *(below)*—and adhesive, which reduces the number of screws or nails required while greatly increasing the strength of the attachment.

Prior to hanging the panels, make sure the walls have sufficient insulation. If necessary, add insulating batts. Fasten them to the sides of the wall studs, with the vapor barrier facing into the room.

Hanging the Wallboard: Install the ceiling first, then the walls, always beginning in a corner. Measure and cut wallboard so that end-to-end joints fall at joists or studs and are staggered by at least 16 inches in adjacent rows.

Installing wallboard horizontally on walls results in fewer joints and fewer dips and bows. To further reduce the number of joints, wherever possible arrange wallboard sections so that joints fall along the frames of doors and windows.

 TOOLS

Dry-wall T square	Tape measure
Utility knife	Chalk line
Wallboard saw or	Caulking gun
keyhole saw	Dry-wall hammer
	Electronic stud
	finder

Screw gun or electric
  drill with screwdriver
  bit
Pry bar
Tin snips

 **MATERIALS**

Wallboard
Wallboard adhesive
Dry-wall nails or
  screws
Corner bead

 **SAFETY TIPS**

Protect your eyes with goggles when driving nails or screws.

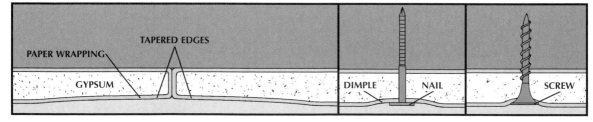

Wallboard and its fasteners.

The long edges of the wallboard panel are slightly tapered *(above, left)* starting 2 inches from the edge. When two sheets are butted side by side, they form a shallow trough for joint tape, making the seam easier to conceal.

Dry-wall nails *(above, center)* have broad heads and unusually sharp points. Buy nails with ringed shanks for extra grip in wood framing or furring strips. Drive the nails to a depth slightly below the wallboard surface, and fill the resulting hammerhead dimple with joint compound. Neither the nailhead nor the dimple should break the paper wrapping.

Dry-wall screws *(above, right)* can be used in metal or wood framing. Sink screwheads to just below the wallboard surface, leaving the paper intact.

NAILS VERSUS SCREWS FOR HANGING WALLBOARD

A dry-wall hammer *(photograph)* is the tool of choice for nailing wallboard in place. It has a rounded head that reduces the risk of tearing the wallboard paper and leaves a dimple in the surface of the wallboard for easy filling. A sharpened edge opposite the head is useful for tucking excess paper on a trimmed edge into a joint for a neater seam.

But a misplaced hammer blow can damage wallboard, and nailing overhead is tiring, increasing the risk of error. Furthermore, a nail may eventually pop out of its dimple—especially on ceilings—if the wood in studs or furring strips is green.

For easier installation and a tighter attachment, use dry-wall screws. This thin, sharply pointed fastener requires no pilot hole and is easily driven through wallboard into either wooden or metal framing members with a screw gun *(below)* or an electric drill. A funnel-shaped head allows the screw to sink slightly below the wallboard surface without breaking the paper.

ELECTRIC MUSCLE FOR DRY-WALL SCREWS

If you decide to secure wallboard with dry-wall screws, you can use an electric drill equipped with a screwdriving bit, but a screw gun *(photograph)* will make the job easier. This tool has an adjustable depth gauge and a built-in clutch that stops the drill once the screw is driven the desired depth, greatly reducing the risk of tearing the wallboard's paper wrapping.

To set the depth gauge, rotate the collar on the nosepiece until the drill bit extends beyond the depth stop just enough for the screw to sink slightly below the wallboard surface. Test the setting by placing a screw on the end of the screwdriver bit. Then hold the screw gun to position the screw against the wallboard and squeeze the trigger while applying forward pressure. (The bit will not rotate unless pressure is applied.) When the depth gauge meets the wall, the clutch disengages and the bit stops rotating. If necessary, readjust the depth gauge to seat the screw properly.

DEPTH GAUGE

COLLAR

Shortening a panel.

◆ Position a dry-wall T square on a wallboard panel as shown at right and cut through the paper wrapping with a utility knife.

◆ Grasp the edge of the panel on both sides of the cut and snap the short section of wallboard away from you, breaking the panel along the cut.

◆ Cock the short section back slightly, then reach behind the panel with a utility knife to make a foot-long slit in the paper along the bend.

◆ Snap the short section forward to break it off.

DRY-WALL T SQUARE

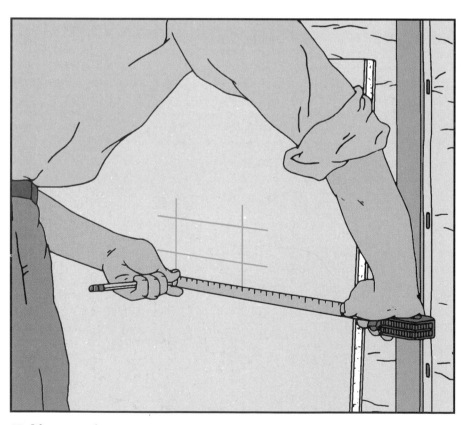

Making openings.

◆ To mark a panel for a small opening such as the hole for an electrical box,

measure from the point on the wall where the edge of the sheet will rest to the near and far sides of the box.

◆ Similarly, measure from the point where the top or the bottom edge of the panel will fall to the top and bottom of the box.

◆ Transfer these measurements to the sheet: Hold the tape measure between your thumb and forefinger at the first measurement as shown at left. Rest the side of your forefinger against the edge of the panel and hold a pencil against the end of the tape with the other hand, then move both hands down the panel simultaneously to mark the first of the four edges of the opening.

◆ Repeat this procedure for each of the other three measurements.

◆ Cut the opening with a wallboard saw or a keyhole saw (pages 25-26).

For a larger opening, such as a window, mark the wallboard the same way. Cut all four sides with a saw, or saw three sides, then score and break the fourth.

HANGING A CEILING

1. Applying the adhesive.
◆ Measure and trim the first panel so the end not butted against the wall will coincide with the center of a joist edge.
◆ Mark joist locations on the panel with a chalk line.
◆ Apply a $\frac{3}{8}$-inch-thick bead of wallboard adhesive to the underside of each ceiling joist to be covered by the first panel. So adhesive will not ooze out between sheets, start and stop each bead about 6 inches from the point where the sides of the panel will fall.
◆ Also apply adhesive to the edges of the joists to which you will attach the ends of the panel.

2. Attaching the wallboard.
◆ With a helper or two, lift the panel into position against the adhesive-coated joists and drive a nail or screw into each joist at the center of the sheet. If using dry-wall nails, double-nail at each joist, except at the ends, driving a second nail 2 inches apart from the first.
◆ Fasten the tapered sides of the panel to each joist, 1 inch from the panel edges.
◆ Secure the ends with nails or screws spaced 16 inches apart and $\frac{1}{2}$ inch from the edge.
◆ Continue in this fashion until the entire ceiling is covered. If you find there will be a gap along the wall running parallel to the joists, trim panels to ensure that the filler strip *(page 136, Step 3)* will span at least two joists.

GIVING DRY WALL A LIFT

You can install wallboard without enlisting friends or neighbors as helpers by renting a dry-wall lift. This handy tool raises a wallboard panel to the desired height and holds it in position while you secure it to the wall or ceiling. Casters make the lift easy to position, and a brake keeps it from moving once it is in place.

To use the lift, rest one edge of a wallboard panel on a pair of metal hooks attached to a frame with adjustable arms that together form a cradle for the sheet. Angle the cradle for a ceiling or wall, then turn the wheel to raise the sheet of wallboard to the correct height.

Devising a Tapered Joint

The ends of wallboard panels, unlike the sides, are untapered. As a result, no shallow, joint-tape trough *(page 132)* is formed between sheets butted end to end, making the seam difficult to conceal. One remedy is to staple cardboard shims, $\frac{1}{16}$ inch thick, along the edges of the joists or studs on either side of the joint. The shims cause the wallboard to slope toward the joist or stud behind the joint, creating a slight depression for the joint tape.

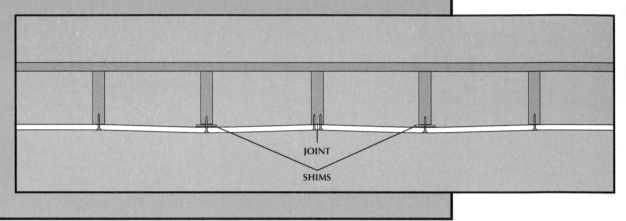

JOINT

SHIMS

FILLER STRIP

3. Adding a filler strip.

Fill gaps in the ceiling with wallboard strips cut to fit.
◆ Cut a strip from the side of a sheet and butt it against the adjoining panel so the tapered edges meet, ensuring a smooth joint.

◆ Secure the filler strip with adhesive and fasteners driven into the joists.
◆ Use a utility knife or the blade at the back of a drywall hammer *(page 133, photograph)* to trim away small amounts of excess gypsum.

SECURING WALL PANELS

1. Installing wallboard horizontally.

◆ On the ceiling and the floor, mark the centers of wall studs as a guide to fastening the sheets of wallboard.

◆ Trim the first panel to end at the center of a stud. Shim the adjacent studs if you choose *(opposite, top)*.

◆ As for ceiling joists *(page 135, Step 1)*, apply adhesive to the studs that will be covered by the first sheet.

◆ With a helper, lift the panel into place, tight against the ceiling. Secure it with three rows of fasteners driven into each stud an inch from the bottom edge of the panel, then across the middle, then an inch from the top edge. If using dry-wall nails, double-nail the midsection of the sheet *(page 135, Step 2)*.

◆ Finish attaching the sheet with fasteners spaced every 8 inches across the ends, $\frac{1}{2}$ inch from the edge—except where an end falls at an inside corner. In that case, leave the end unfastened, butt the next panel against it, and fasten the end of the second sheet to a stud. At an outside corner, lap the end of the second sheet over the end of the first, and nail the ends of both panels to their common stud.

After the upper course, install a lower course, trimming the

panels lengthwise to leave a $\frac{1}{2}$-inch gap at the floor. Arrange the panels so that joints in the lower course do not align with those in the upper one. With a helper, use foot levers *(Step 2, below)* to raise the panel off the floor while securing it.

2. Installing vertical panels.

For narrow sections of wall, install panels vertically, joining them at the midpoint of studs.

◆ Apply adhesive in the pattern for horizontal panels. Lift the panel into place against the ceiling, using a pry

bar on a scrap of wood as a foot lever.

◆ Secure the panel to each stud with fasteners spaced about 2 feet apart, starting 1 inch from the top and ending 1 inch from the bottom. If using dry-wall nails, double-nail the midsection *(Step 1, above)*.

3. Attaching a corner bead.

◆ To protect an outside corner, trim a metal corner-bead strip to the correct length by cutting through the flanges with tin snips, one flange at a time.

◆ Position the corner bead over the wallboard joint and fasten it to the stud beneath with nails or screws driven through holes in the bead.

Hiding Wallboard Seams

All that remains after installing wallboard *(pages 132-137)* is to conceal fastener heads, corner bead, and the seams between dry-wall sheets. Joint compound is an essential element in all three tasks. Buy a 5-gallon drum of joint compound for every ten 4- by 8-foot sheets of wallboard you have installed.

Taping and Feathering: Covering fastener heads and corner bead requires only the application of joint compound. To hide and strengthen a seam between wallboard sheets, however, precede the joint compound with joint tape made of paper or fiberglass mesh.

Paper joint tape is stuck to the wall with an underlying layer of joint compound *(opposite)*, whereas fiberglass tape has an adhesive backing to make the work go more quickly. Either tape is then covered with two layers of compound in a process known as feathering *(page 141)*.

A Final Smoothing: After joint compound dries, you must sand or sponge away grooves and ridges. Sand with 120-grit, open-coat paper wrapped around a sanding block; a sanding plate on a pole lets you reach high areas. A light back-and-forth motion works best except for rubbing down a high spot, where a circular motion is preferable.

Sponging avoids both the dust made by sanding and the risk of scratching the wallboard's paper surface. Saturate a wallboard sponge with water, wring it dry, then gently rub it across the joint compound with a smooth, sweeping motion.

TOOLS

Wallboard knives
  (5", 8", 12")
Joint compound
  pan
Sanding plate
  and pole
Sandpaper (120-grit,
  open-coat)
Wallboard sponge
Corner trowel
Crown trowel

MATERIALS

Joint compound
Wire coat hanger
Paper or fiberglass
  joint tape

SAFETY TIPS

Goggles shield your eyes from dripping joint compound when you are working overhead. Always wear a dust mask when sanding joint compound.

HIDING FASTENERS AND CORNER BEAD

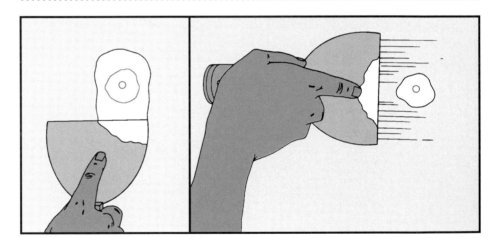

Covering a nail- or screwhead.
◆ Load half the width of a 5-inch knife blade with joint compound.
◆ Holding the blade nearly parallel to the wallboard, draw the compound across the nail- or screwhead so that it fills the dimple completely *(above, left)*.
◆ Raise the knife blade to a more up-right position and scrape off excess compound with a stroke at right angles to the first *(above, right)*.
◆ Apply two additional coats in the same fashion, allowing the compound to dry between coats.
◆ After the third coat dries, lightly sand or sponge the patch smooth.

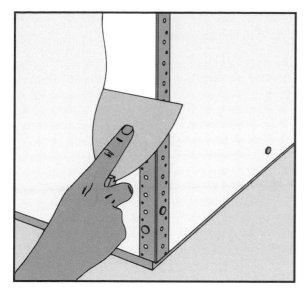

Covering a corner bead.

◆ Load the left two-thirds of a 5-inch knife with joint compound.
◆ With the right 2 inches of the knife overhanging the corner, run the knife down the left side of the bead *(left)*.
◆ Load the right side of the knife and run it down the right side of the bead.
◆ Scrape the knife across the edge of a scrap of wood to clean it, then remove excess compound and smooth the joint by running the knife alternately down the left and right faces of the bead.
◆ Apply and smooth a second coat without letting the knife overhang the corner, feathering this layer about $1\frac{1}{2}$ inches beyond the first.
◆ Apply a third coat using an 8-inch knife to feather the compound an additional 2 inches on each side.
◆ Once the compound dries, sand or sponge it smooth.

APPLYING TAPE TO A FLAT JOINT

1. Applying joint compound.

When using fiberglass tape *(photograph)*, skip this step and adapt the knife technique shown in Step 2 to stick the tape along the bare joint. A coat-hanger spindle, hooked to your belt, holds a roll of joint tape at the ready.
◆ Thin a batch of joint compound with a pint of water for every 5 gallons of compound, then load half the width of a 5-inch knife with the mix.
◆ Center the blade over the joint, cock-ing it slightly so the blade's loaded side is the leading edge, and smoothly run the knife along the joint *(right)*. Hold the knife almost perpendicular to the wallboard at the start, but gradually angle it closer to the board as you draw it along the seam to fill the depression at the wallboard's tapered edges.

For an end-to-end joint, where the sheets do not have tapered edges, apply a $\frac{1}{8}$-inch-thick layer of compound.

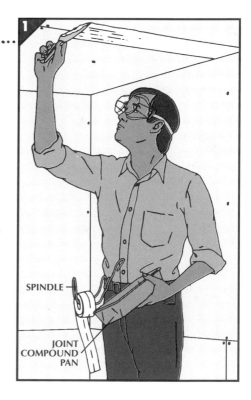

SPINDLE

JOINT COMPOUND PAN

FIBERGLASS TAPE

2. Embedding paper tape.

◆ Press the end of the tape into the wet compound at one end of the joint.
◆ As you hold the tape over the joint with one hand, run the blade of a 5-inch knife along the joint with the other to force the tape into the compound *(left)*. At the far end of the joint, use the knife as a straightedge in order to tear the tape.
◆ Run the knife along the joint a sec-ond time, pressing firmly to push the tape into the compound and to scrape off most of the excess compound.
◆ Then go over the tape a third time, pushing down on the knife to eliminate any air bubbles, and return the excess compound to the pan.

At an end-to-end joint, where the paper tape rides on the surface, do not scrape off excess compound completely. Leave a combined tape-and-compound thickness of about $\frac{1}{8}$ inch.

TAPING AN INSIDE CORNER

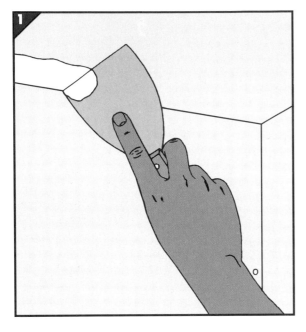

1. Applying the compound.

Fiberglass tape requires no initial application of compound; simply crease the tape down the center and press it into the corner. To apply paper tape:
◆ Load half the width of a 5-inch knife with joint compound.
◆ Run the knife along one side of the corner joint, then the other, lifting the inside of the blade slightly to create a thicker layer of compound at the joint. Do not be concerned if you scrape off some of the compound on the first side while coating the second.

A corner trowel (photograph) has angled faces for applying joint compound to both sides of a corner at once.

CORNER TROWEL

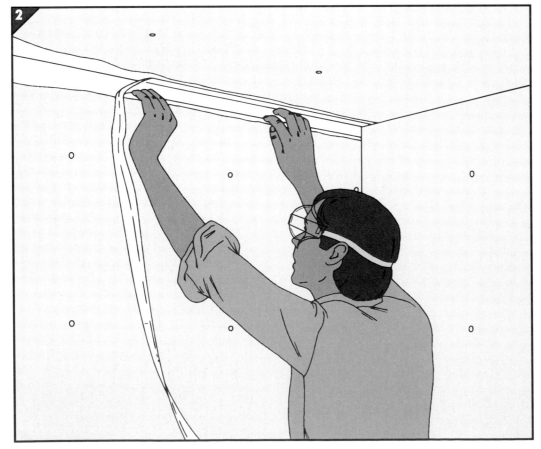

2. Embedding the tape.

◆ Fold the tape along its lengthwise crease line and press it lightly into the joint compound with your fingers.
◆ Run a 5-inch knife or corner trowel lightly along both sides of the crease, applying just enough pressure to make the tape stick to the compound. Then repeat, using more force to squeeze out excess compound.
◆ Finally, coat the tape lightly with some of the excess, and run the knife or trowel over it one last time, leaving a film of compound on the tape.

Completing a flat seam.

◆ For paper tape, thin the compound as described in Step 1 on page 139. With fiberglass tape, use the compound as it comes from the can.

◆ Load the full width of an 8-inch knife with joint compound and cover the tape with an even layer of the material.

◆ Clean the knife and draw it over this layer, holding the blade slightly off center and lifting the edge nearer the joint about $\frac{1}{8}$ inch. Do likewise on the other side of the joint to create a slight ridge that feathers out evenly on both sides.

◆ Let the compound dry and lightly sand or sponge it (page 138).

◆ For paper tape, thin the compound with a quart of water for every 5 gallons and apply a final layer with two passes of a 12-inch knife: On the first pass, rest one edge of the knife blade on the center ridge and bear down on the other edge; on the second pass, repeat this procedure on the other side of the ridge.

◆ Let the compound dry and give it a final sanding or sponging.

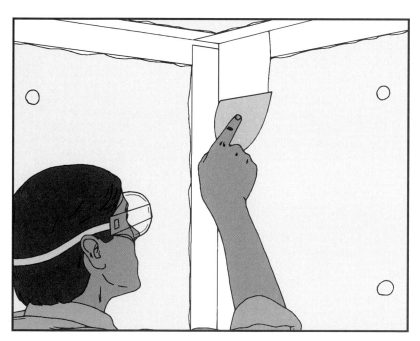

Feathering an inside corner.

For this procedure, thin the joint compound as you would for a flat seam (above).

◆ Load the full width of a 5-inch knife with joint compound and spread an even layer of compound over one side of the corner.

◆ Scrape off any compound that laps onto the corner's second side, then draw the knife down the first side again, bearing down on the outside edge of the knife in order to feather the compound.

◆ Smooth this layer one more time, removing any excess and scraping off any compound that was left on the wall beyond the feathered edge.

◆ After the first side of the corner has finished drying, apply joint compound to the second side in the same fashion.

◆ Then repeat this procedure on both sides with an 8-inch wallboard knife.

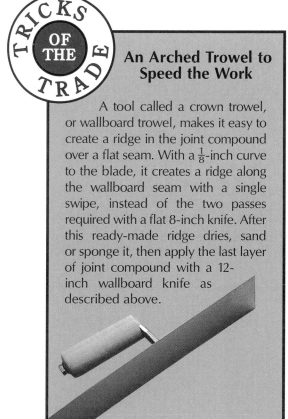

TRICKS OF THE TRADE

An Arched Trowel to Speed the Work

A tool called a crown trowel, or wallboard trowel, makes it easy to create a ridge in the joint compound over a flat seam. With a $\frac{1}{8}$-inch curve to the blade, it creates a ridge along the wallboard seam with a single swipe, instead of the two passes required with a flat 8-inch knife. After this ready-made ridge dries, sand or sponge it, then apply the last layer of joint compound with a 12-inch wallboard knife as described above.

Decorative Moldings for Walls

Artisans have been affixing decorative moldings to walls for hundreds of years. Such ornaments remain popular today, either to give authenticity to a restoration or to add interest to a flat surface. Lumberyards stock some styles, but many of the more elaborate patterns must be ordered from craft studios or manufacturers.

Bottom, Middle, and Top: The walls of most houses are finished with baseboard and shoe molding at the floor. Normally plain in contour, these moldings can be replaced with some with more interesting shapes. Or you can dress up a room by adding chair rail or crown molding to the walls.

Chair rail lines the wall about 3 feet above the floor. Originally used simply to prevent chair backs from marring walls or paneling, chair rail has assumed a more purely decorative role. Today it often serves as a divider between wall elements, with paneling or wallpaper installed between the chair rail and the floor or ceiling.

Crown molding fits at the top of the wall. Some styles lie flat against the wall; others fit at an angle, bridging the corner between wall and ceiling. The latter style has flat surfaces at the top and bottom that rest against the ceiling and wall.

Three Kinds of Joints: As indicated in the diagram below, different joints are used for inside corners, outside corners, and where a wall is too long for a single length of molding. The techniques that follow are used with chair rail, crown molding, and baseboard but fit crown or baseboard molding at the junction of the ceiling or floor instead of along a level line on the wall as for chair rail. Trim all the molding $\frac{1}{16}$ inch longer than needed to allow it to "snap" into place.

 TOOLS

Caulking gun
Tape measure
Carpenter's level
Chalk line
Miter box
Backsaw
Nail set
Electronic stud finder
Coping saw
Combination square
T-bevel

 MATERIALS

Wire caps
Panel adhesive
Wallboard screws or flat-head wood screws
Spackling compound
Latex caulk
Finishing nails (2", $3\frac{1}{4}$")
Wood putty
Baseboard
Shoe molding
Chair rail
Crown molding
Wood glue

SAFETY TIPS

Protect your eyes with goggles when nailing molding.

Planning the installation.

Depending on the shape and size of a room, adding chair rail or other moldings may require as many as four different joints. The most common are the coped joint, intended for inside corners, and the butt joint at door casings. A room with an alcove or with facing walls of different lengths *(right)* contains at least one outside corner, where a miter joint is the most appropriate. For a wall longer than a single length of molding—or for greatest economy of materials—use a scarf joint to fasten molding pieces end to end.

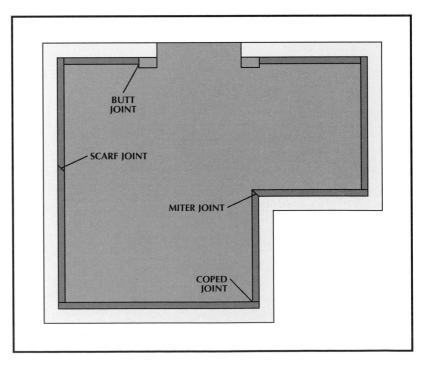

HANGING CHAIR RAIL

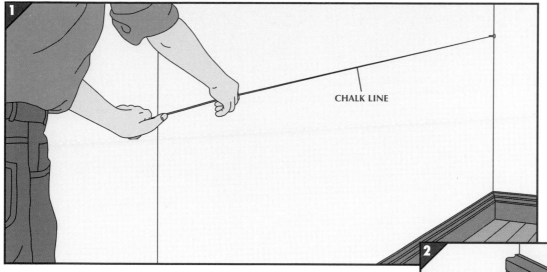

CHALK LINE

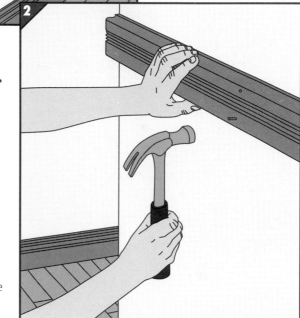

1. Determining the height.

◆ Make a mark at one end of one wall, typically 36 inches from the floor.
◆ Use a level and a long, straight board to make a second mark at the other end of the wall.
◆ Drive a finishing nail into the wall at one of the marks and hook a chalk line on the nail. Align the chalk line with the second height mark and snap it against the wall *(above)*.
◆ Repeat the procedure for the other walls in the room.

2. Affixing the molding.

◆ With an electronic stud finder, locate and mark the positions of the wall studs.
◆ Align the chair rail with the chalked line, cutting special joints for corners and extensions *(below and opposite)*.
◆ With 2-inch finishing nails, secure the chair rail to the wall studs *(right)*.
◆ Countersink all the nails with a nail set and cover the holes with spackling compound or wood filler.

CUTTING SPECIAL JOINTS

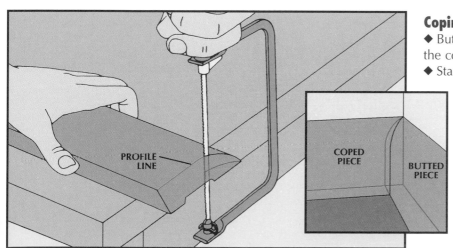

PROFILE LINE

COPED PIECE

BUTTED PIECE

Coping an inside corner.

◆ Butt the square end of a piece of molding into the corner and nail it in place.
◆ Stand the adjoining piece on edge in a miter box and cut the end at a 45-degree angle. Run a pencil along the curved edge of the cut to make it more visible.
◆ With a coping saw, cut vertically along the pencil mark *(left)*, and fit the molding against the end of the piece already in the corner *(inset)*.

Fashioning a scarf joint.

◆ Butt one end of a piece of molding into the corner and mark the other end at a wall stud.

◆ Stand the molding on edge in a miter box, and trim the marked end at a 45-degree angle *(right)*.

◆ Secure the molding to the wall studs with 2-inch finishing nails.

◆ Miter one end of the next piece to slip under the miter on the preceding piece. Cut a parallel miter on the other end, unless the chair rail reaches a corner with an adjacent wall. In that situation, cut only one end of the piece at a 45-degree angle, then square cut the other end to fit an inside corner or miter it for an outside corner.

◆ Glue the mitered ends together, and drive a nail through the overlapping miters into the stud *(inset)*.

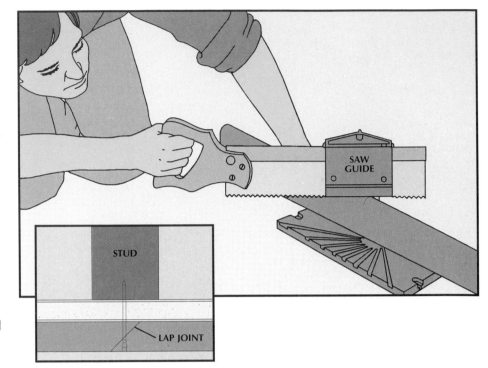

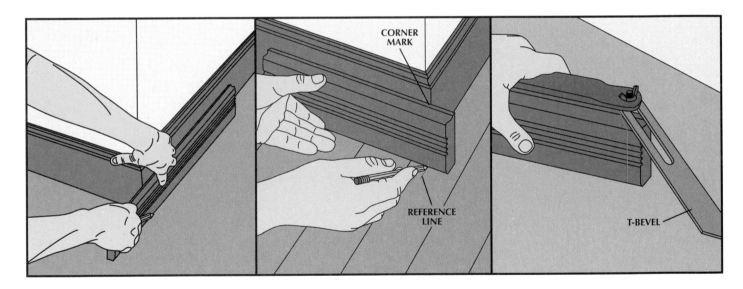

Fitting an outside corner.

If the corner is 90 degrees, simply cut both pieces of molding at 45 degrees in a miter box.

◆ Otherwise, hold a piece of molding against one wall and use its outside face to mark a reference line on the floor *(above, left)*.

◆ Next, place the molding against the adjoining wall and make two marks on it: one on its top edge in line with the corner, and another on its front face at the reference mark on the floor *(above, center)*.

◆ Use a combination square to extend the mark on the face of the molding to the top edge.

◆ Adjust a T-bevel to the angle formed by the end of this line and the corner mark on the top edge of the molding *(above, right)*.

◆ Use the T-bevel to adjust the saw in the miter box to that angle and cut the molding. If the molding doesn't fit the corner exactly, pare down the front or the back of the cut to accommodate the difference.

PUTTING UP CROWN MOLDING

WASTE PIECE

1. Cutting the molding.

◆ Set the molding upside down and face outward in the miter box, as if the bottom of the box were the ceiling *(inset)*.

◆ For an outside corner, angle the saw as shown at left for molding on the right-hand side of the corner; move the saw to the corresponding angle on the other side of the miter box for the left side, with the waste piece to the left of the blade. If the joint gaps when you put the pieces in place, pare down the front or back of the miters to fit.

◆ For a coped inside corner, cut the molding so that the shorter edge fits against the ceiling.

A Shortcut for Nailing

For easier and faster installation of ceiling molding, first attach 1-inch triangular wood nailers called chamfer strips at the junction of the ceiling and wall. Secure them to the top plate with 2-inch dry-wall screws in plaster, or 2-inch finishing nails in wallboard. Space the fasteners at 2-foot intervals. Nail the crown molding into the chamfer strip as in Step 2 at right.

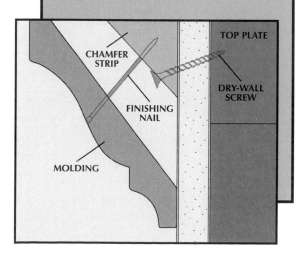

CHAMFER STRIP

TOP PLATE

DRY-WALL SCREW

FINISHING NAIL

MOLDING

CROWN MOLDING

2. Installing the molding.

◆ Begin at a corner and work across the room, enlisting a helper if necessary. Hammer $3\frac{1}{4}$-inch finishing nails through the convex section near the center of the molding and into the top plate at approximately 16-inch intervals *(above)*. To ensure hitting the plate, hold the nails at about a 45-degree angle.

◆ Countersink the nailheads with a nail set.

Mirrored Walls to Brighten a Room

Strategically hung mirrors have long been used to create a feeling of spaciousness in small rooms. Covering an entire wall with mirror tiles or panels can amplify that result, making such a room seem even lighter, larger, and more open.

Mirror tiles are made of thin glass that makes them lightweight but also tends to lessen their reflective quality. For a more distortion-free reflection, install mirror panels, which are made of thicker glass.

Mirror tiles attached to a wall with tape may be removed fairly easily; wear work gloves to protect your hands in case glass breaks. Installation with mastic, however, makes the mirrors a permanent part of the wall. Removing the glass panels is impossible without breaking them and seriously damaging the wall.

Installing Mirror Tiles: Available as 1-foot squares, mirror tiles are attached with a double-faced tape that is sold both in rolls and in pre-cut squares. The tape works well on most smooth, very clean surfaces but will not adhere to vinyl wall coverings. Once you peel the protective cover from the tape, hold it only by the edges; skin oils can cause this tape to fail.

Mounting Mirror Panels: Heavier mirrors require supporting hardware, as well as the use of a mastic adhesive compounded specifically for mirrors. These mastics do not react with the silver on the mirror and are applied in thick pats that never harden. Because of this resilience, mastic can withstand sudden jolts—even a minor earthquake—that might otherwise jar the mirror loose.

When you buy mastic, ask the mirror dealer to recommend the one that is most suitable for the surface you intend to stick the mirror to. Some require covering the back of the mirror with a special bonding coat; read label directions carefully.

Planning the Layout: Although mirrors may be mounted wall to wall and floor to ceiling, walls frequently are not square. You can simplify your installation if you leave at least a narrow border of uncovered wall.

Tailoring mirrors to fit irregularities can be difficult. If you need smaller pieces of mirror to cover the desired area, the thin glass tiles are the only type that you can cut yourself *(opposite)*. Thicker mirrors require professional cutting.

Handling Mirrors

✔ A square foot of $\frac{1}{4}$-inch mirror panel may weigh more than 3 pounds. Work with a helper if the panels are larger than 12 square feet.

✔ If mirror panels do not come with protective wrapping, safeguard the silvered backing from scratches by placing sheets of paper between the panels. Drape a towel or blanket over the back of a larger mirror until it is ready to be mounted.

✔ When carrying a mirror more than 3 feet long, hold it vertically so it will not sag and break of its own weight.

✔ If you and a helper will be navigating stairs while carrying a heavy mirror, post the stronger person at the lower end.

✔ Always store mirrors on edge.

⚠ **CAUTION** *If a mirror starts to fall while you are carrying or mounting it, do not try to catch it. Get out of the way—quickly.*

 TOOLS

Carpenter's level
Chalk line
Glass cutter
Drop cloth
Hacksaw
Screwdriver

 **MATERIALS**

Mirror tiles or panels
Mirror tile adhesive tape
Black plastic tape ($\frac{1}{2}$")
Masking tape
J molding
Escutcheon nails ($\frac{3}{4}$")
Felt
Mirror mastic
Screws and plastic anchors
J clips
Adjustable top clips

 SAFETY TIPS

Work gloves not only protect your hands from the sharp edges of mirror tiles and panels but also shield the mirror backing from harmful salts and oils from human skin. Wear goggles when trimming thin mirror tiles.

MIRROR TILES: LOW-COST AND EASY TO INSTALL

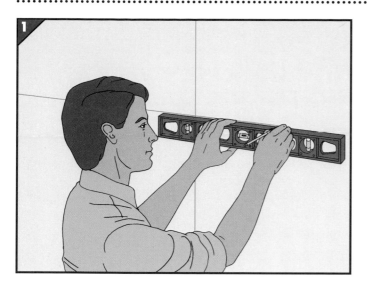

1. Laying out the tiles.

◆ Using a carpenter's level as a straightedge, mark a light pencil line around the perimeter of the area to be tiled.

◆ Using a chalk line as a plumb bob, snap a vertical guideline through the center of this area, between the upper and lower edges.

◆ Measuring down from the top of the vertical line, make a mark at the 1-foot measure closest to your eye level. Draw a level horizontal line through this mark to the ends of the tile area *(left)*.

◆ Peel off the protective cover from one side of a square of mirror tile adhesive tape. Press the tape firmly to the back of a tile $\frac{3}{4}$ inch from a corner; repeat at the other corners. Attach tape to the other tiles.

2. Setting the tiles.

◆ Strip the outer paper from the tape on the first tile, place the tile in one corner formed by the guidelines, and press the corners of the mirror against the wall.

◆ Set tiles in rows, working outward from the center. Before sticking each tile to the wall, test it for fit against its neighbors, without uncovering its adhesive tape. Where the edges of an imperfect tile do not align exactly with the edges of adjoining tiles, place a strip of black plastic tape on the wall, butted against one of the adjacent tiles, to camouflage the misfit. Then stick the imperfect tile in place, leaving a slight gap along the edge that coincides with the tape.

◆ Install all of the full mirror tiles, leaving until last any area that requires cut tiles.

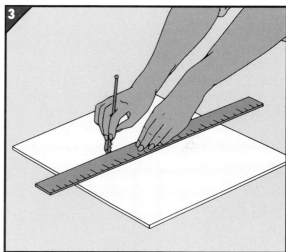

3. Cutting border tiles.

◆ Measure the gap to be filled by a partial tile, and mark a cutting line on the face of a tile with a felt-tip pen.

◆ Score along the cutting line with a glass cutter, using a straightedge as a guide. For best results, hold the cutter as shown above, start the scoring wheel $\frac{1}{16}$ inch in from one edge of the tile, and apply even pressure as you draw the wheel across the glass in one smooth motion.

◆ Wearing work gloves and goggles, align the scored line of the tile with the edge of a workbench. Break the tile by giving the protruding side a sharp downward snap.

◆ Affix adhesive tape in the corners of the cut tile and press it firmly against the wall.

MOUNTING BEVELED REFLECTING PANELS

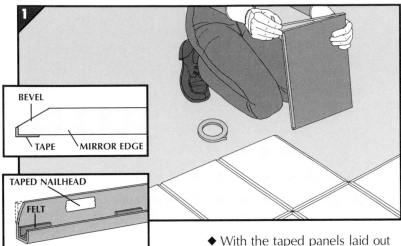

BEVEL

TAPE   MIRROR EDGE

TAPED NAILHEAD

FELT

1. A dry run on the floor.

◆ On a carpet or drop cloth, lay out all of the panels as they will be placed on the wall.

◆ Pad each joint between panels with a single thickness of $\frac{1}{2}$-inch masking tape, cushioning the edges as shown above. Wearing work gloves, affix a strip of tape below the bevel and fold the excess onto the back of the mirror (upper inset).

◆ With the taped panels laid out on the floor, measure the bottom edge of the array. With a hacksaw, cut a section of metal J molding to this length, shaping the ends as shown in the lower inset.

◆ Draw a level guideline for the molding and then fasten it to the wall with $\frac{3}{4}$-inch escutcheon nails. Cover the nailheads with masking tape to keep them from scratching the mirror backing, and pad the bottom of the molding channel with squares of felt.

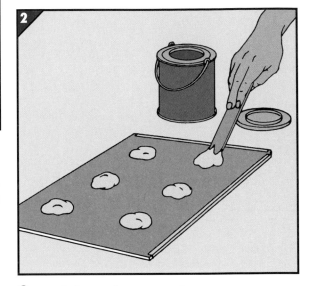

2. Applying mirror mastic.

With a wood paint paddle or a scrap of wood with a smooth end, daub pats of mastic onto the back of the mirror. For every square foot of mirror, apply four pats of mastic roughly $1\frac{1}{2}$ inches square and $\frac{7}{8}$ inch thick. Keep the mastic at least $2\frac{1}{2}$ inches from the edges of the mirror. If mastic begins to harden on the daubing stick, discard the stick and use a clean one.

3. Installing the panels.

◆ Set the first mirror panel into the channel at one end of the J molding, then press the panel against the wall. Apply uniform pressure to the mirror surface until the mastic flattens and the back of the tile is approximately $\frac{1}{4}$ inch from the wall.

◆ Repeat this procedure to install a second panel against the edge of the first.

◆ Complete the bottom row of panels before you begin installing the rows above.

◆ After all the panels are on the wall, run a carpet- or foam-rubber-covered straightedge over the mirrors to correct their alignment and produce a flat plane.

SECURING MIRRORS WITH MASTIC AND J CLIPS

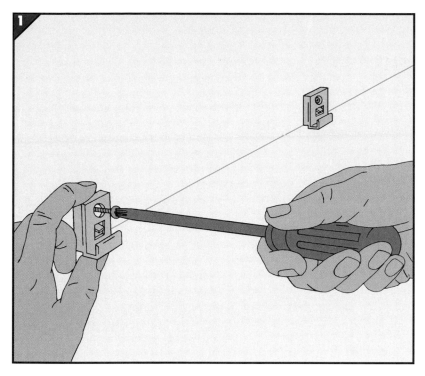

1. Bottom supports for big mirrors.

◆ Draw a level guideline along the wall to establish the position of the lower edge of the mirrors. Mark the locations of mirror-panel edges along this line.

◆ Measure from the bottom guideline to mark a line for the tops of the mirrors, checking it with a carpenter's level.

◆ With screws and plastic anchors, install two J clips for the bottom of each mirror, spacing one-third and two-thirds of the distance between panel-edge marks. If you use metal J clips, pad the clips *(page 148, Step 1)*.

◆ Cover all screwheads with masking tape.

2. Finishing the job.

◆ Above each clip on the bottom line, screw an adjustable clip *(photograph)* at the top line. Tape the screwheads.

◆ For every square foot of mirror, apply four pats of mastic as described on the facing page.

◆ With a helper holding the panel to prevent it from falling, tilt the top of the mirror away from the wall and lift the bottom into the J clips. Lift the tops of the adjustable clips and fit the mirror into them.

◆ Starting at the bottom, apply even pressure over the entire mirror surface, forcing it against the mastic until the panel is a uniform $\frac{1}{4}$ inch away from the wall.

◆ Install subsequent mirror panels edge to edge in the J clips. Press the panels evenly into the mastic so their reflecting surfaces form a perfectly flat plane *(page 148, Step 3)*.

The Rustic Flavor of Brick Veneer

Brick veneer is an artful illusion. Composed of $\frac{1}{2}$-inch-thick slabs of real brick, this surfacing material offers all the warmth and charm of a solid brick wall at a fraction of the cost and weight.

Veneer Options: Two forms of brick veneer are available: individual bricks and preassembled brick panels. Loose bricks, glued to the wall with a special adhesive, come in a wide variety of colors, finishes, and textures. Panels contain about 36 bricks glued to a fiberboard backing that usually measures $16\frac{1}{2}$ by 48 inches. Fastened to the wall with nails, panels are easier to install than individual bricks, although obstacles pose more difficulties. Panels are also heavier and more expensive.

Preparation: Any wall used as a backing for individual bricks must be clean and free of wallpaper. If it is painted, score it with a pointed tool to roughen the surface for the adhesive. Baseboards must be removed, but you can leave window and door trim in place. The faceplates of electrical outlets and switches should be removed and their outlet boxes extended with special collars *(page 131)*.

Before installing either individual bricks or panels near a stove or fireplace, check with local authorities. Although the bricks themselves are fireproof, some fire codes require that they be backed with a fireproof material such as metal or cement-base panels.

Filling the Joints: The gaps between bricks—whether set individually or in panels—are filled with mortar. To mix the mortar from scratch, combine $2\frac{1}{2}$ parts sand, 1 part Portland cement, and enough water to thin the mixture to the consistency of applesauce. This is thinner than for conventional bricklaying because the mortar does not have to support the weight of the bricks. If you prefer to use a ready-mix mortar, add a tablespoon or 2 of liquid detergent to keep the mixture flowing smoothly.

Apply the mortar with a mortar bag *(page 153)* fitted with a nozzle equal in diameter to the space between bricks—usually $\frac{1}{2}$ inch. Before the mortar dries, smooth it with a tool called a jointer, which has a convex surface for pressing the mortar in against the edges of the bricks.

 TOOLS

Chalk line
Level (4')
Tile nippers
Putty knife
Mortar bag
Ruler
Hammer

Jointer ($\frac{1}{2}$")
Wire brush
Electronic stud
   finder
Nail set
Utility knife
Cold chisel
Notched trowel

 **MATERIALS**

Nails ($1\frac{1}{2}$" finishing,
  $1\frac{1}{2}$" roofing, $1\frac{1}{2}$"
  fluted-shank
  masonry)
Brick veneer

Veneer adhesive
Mortar
Fiberboard
  ($\frac{1}{2}$" thick)

 **SAFETY TIPS**

Wear goggles when cutting bricks, hammering, and chiseling.

Components of brick veneer.

You can refinish any wall with the brick types shown at right. Flat bricks, called stretchers, are used to cover most of the wall's surface. Half-sized stretchers, called headers, give the appearance of a brick seen end-on and serve to vary the pattern. Two-sided bricks wrap around wall edges, and three-sided bricks cover corners.

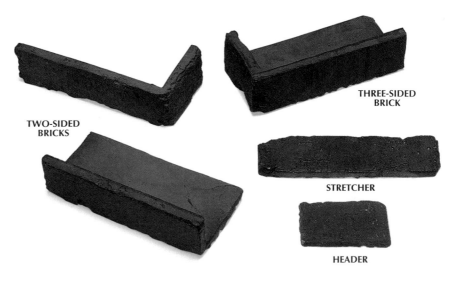

TWO-SIDED
BRICKS

THREE-SIDED
BRICK

STRETCHER

HEADER

MIMICKING THE LOOK OF REAL BRICK

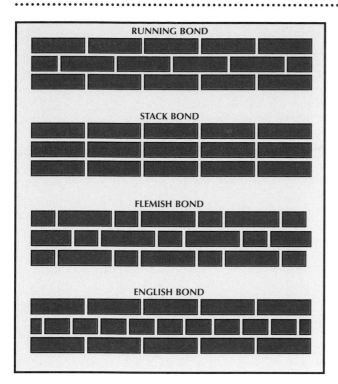

RUNNING BOND

STACK BOND

FLEMISH BOND

ENGLISH BOND

Choosing a pattern.

Veneer bricks can be arranged in any of the patterns used for structural brick walls *(left)*. Most common is the traditional running-bond pattern, in which stretcher bricks are set in staggered rows, or courses. Also popular is stack bond, although this pattern is difficult to align perfectly over large spaces. Flemish and English bond, combining stretchers and headers, are derived from Colonial houses in which header bricks joined the two layers of a double brick wall.

The number of bricks needed for each pattern varies but is generally six or seven bricks per square foot. To estimate how much you will need more precisely, lay out your pattern on the floor next to the wall for which it is intended, leaving about $\frac{1}{2}$ inch between the bricks for mortar.

SETTING INDIVIDUAL BRICKS

1. Measuring and marking courses.

Use this procedure for a wall without windows or other interruptions.

◆ At one end of the wall, make a vertical series of marks, spaced $2\frac{3}{4}$ inches apart, beginning at a point $2\frac{3}{4}$ inches above the floor. If the floor is not level, mark the wall at the higher end.

◆ Tap a nail into the first mark and tie a chalk line around it. Have a helper hold the line taut against the far end of the wall while you level it with a 4-foot level. When the chalk line is level, snap it; the mark left on the wall establishes the top of the first course, with room for a mortar joint below.

◆ Repeat for each mark along the wall.

If a window or door interrupts the wall, use the top of the window or doorframe, or the bottom of the window frame, as a starting point.

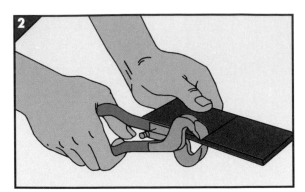

2. Cutting bricks to fit the pattern.
◆ Draw a pencil line across the back of the brick where the cut will be.
◆ Align the blades of the tile nippers with the pencil line and cut through the brick along the line.
◆ Smooth the cut by chipping away rough edges with the nippers.

3. Establishing the pattern.
◆ Start by installing a column of bricks up an inside or outside corner. On an inside corner, use header and stretcher bricks, alternating them as the pattern requires; wrap outside corners with two-sided bricks *(inset)*.
◆ With a putty knife, apply adhesive to the back of each brick in $\frac{3}{4}$-inch daubs, about $\frac{1}{2}$ inch thick and 2 inches apart.
◆ Line the top of the brick against the chalked guideline and press it against the wall with a slight twisting motion to spread the adhesive, which will ooze out around the edges of the brick.
◆ Tap $1\frac{1}{2}$-inch finishing nails partway into the wall beneath two-sided bricks to hold them in place until the adhesive sets—from 48 to 72 hours; then remove the nails.

VENEERING IRREGULAR AREAS

Outlining an arch.
For this situation, use two-sided bricks with either the long or short ends facing out. Apply adhesive to each brick as in Step 3 above.
◆ Find the center of the arch and set a brick there, holding it in place with $1\frac{1}{2}$-inch finishing nails tapped partway in at an angle.

◆ Set a brick at each end of the arch and secure it with nails in the same fashion.
◆ Measure the distance between the center brick and each end to determine the spacing of the remaining bricks. Then, working on one half of the arch at a time, set the rest of the bricks *(left)*.

Framing a raised hearth apron.

◆ Cap the corners of the hearth with three-sided corner bricks, then set two-sided bricks along the hearth edges. Space the bricks evenly across the edge, adjusting the distance between them as necessary to avoid cutting any bricks.

◆ Set bricks along the side edges in the same way.

◆ Then fill in the top of the apron with bricks in the pattern of your choice.

◆ Start veneering the apron sides by setting two-sided bricks down the vertical edges of the hearth apron, securing them with $1\frac{1}{2}$-inch finishing nails until the adhesive sets.

◆ Finally, fill in the sides of the apron with the pattern of your choice, securing these bricks with nails also.

FILLING JOINTS WITH MORTAR

1. Applying the mortar.

◆ After the adhesive has set, remove the supporting nails.

◆ Using a mortar bag equipped with a $\frac{1}{2}$-inch nozzle, fill the horizontal joints and then the vertical joints with enough mortar so that it bulges out slightly beyond the face of the brick *(right)*. To prevent dried mortar from clogging the nozzle, rinse out the mortar bag between fillings.

2. Tooling the joints.

◆ When the mortar is dry and crumbly to the touch—in about 20 minutes—smooth and flatten it with a $\frac{1}{2}$-inch jointer. Work the vertical joints first, pushing the mortar surface about $\frac{1}{8}$ inch be- low the face of the brick.

◆ When the mortar is completely dry, usually within 1 or 2 hours, rub the bricks and joints vigorously with a stiff-bristle or wire brush to clean them of mortar remnants.

MOUNTING BRICK VENEER PANELS

1. A base for corner bricks.

Each corner requires a pair of $\frac{1}{2}$-inch plywood or fiberboard framing strips. The exact width will be specified by the manufacturer, but in any case, one strip must be $\frac{1}{2}$ inch wider than the other to provide an even framing surface.

Nail the framing strips to each corner: For an outside corner, lap the wider strip over the narrower one; for an inside corner, set the wider one flush with the corner and lap the narrower one over it.

2. Nailing the panels.

◆ Using a stud finder, locate the wall's studs and mark them at approximately $16\frac{1}{2}$-inch intervals up the wall. If the floor is not level, snap a level chalk line across the wall $16\frac{1}{2}$ inches above the highest point of the floor.
◆ Butt a panel against the corner framing strip. Keeping its top edge against the chalked line, nail the panel to the wall stud nearest the corner *(right)*. For wallboard or plaster walls, use $1\frac{1}{2}$-inch roofing nails driven through the panels, between bricks, into the studs. For cinder block walls, use $1\frac{1}{2}$-inch fluted-shank masonry nails. Use a nail set to get the nails flush with the backing.

3. Interlocking the panels.

◆ Have a helper pull the unattached end of the first panel away from the wall just enough to let you slide the adjoining panel into it until the two backing boards meet; then push both panels against the wall.
◆ Nail the second panel to the stud nearest the joining edge, then finish nailing the first panel to the wall; each panel should be anchored by at least 12 nails.
◆ Continue adding and interlocking the panels until you have installed the last full panel that fits across the wall.
◆ Then install panels in parallel rows above the one already in place.

To fill in gaps, measure the remaining spaces. Mark and score the back of a panel to fit each space, and cut through the board with a utility knife along the scored line. If you need to remove an entire brick that overlaps the cut, pry it off; to trim an overlapping brick flush with the cut, use a hammer and cold chisel.

4. The finishing touches.

Any remaining spaces must be filled with individual bricks; use the adhesive recommended by the manufacturer.

◆ Cover outside corners with two-sided bricks, supported with $1\frac{1}{2}$-inch finishing nails until the adhesive sets.

◆ Cover inside corners with flat bricks cut to size and temporarily supported by nails in the same manner.

◆ After the adhesive has set, remove the support nails and fill the mortar joints as shown in Steps 1 and 2 on page 153.

PLASTIC OR PLASTER MASONRY

Veneer bricks made of plastic or plaster can be almost as convincing as real brick veneer—and they are easier to install because you can cut them with a utility knife. The adhesive is applied to both the wall and the brick. Since it has a mortarlike texture and color, there is no need to fill joints with mortar.

Another veneering option is plaster stone (right). Purchased in boxed sets, these facsimile stones have subtle variations in color and texture and are cut to fit together well.

Exposing a Brick Wall

Many houses built before 1940 have interior walls made of brick covered by a layer of plaster. Stripping away the plaster to expose the brick often adds color, texture, and rustic charm to a room. Before beginning the job, however, remove a square foot of plaster in a lower corner to determine whether the brick is attractive enough to reward the work.

Preliminary Preparations: Although exposing brick involves few steps, the job takes at least 10 days and is dusty work. Remove from the room all furnishings and the contents of closets or cabinets. With masking tape, seal closet and cabinet doors, heat returns and registers, and all doors leading to other parts of the house. Archways and similar openings can be sealed with a dust curtain of plastic sheeting taped to ceiling and floor. Overlap the sheets about 8 inches.

Cover the floor with hardboard $\frac{1}{8}$ inch or more thick, followed by plastic sheeting at least 4 mils thick. Seal the plastic to the bottoms of the walls with duct tape.

Turn off the power to the wall and remove the cover plates, switches and receptacles, and outlet boxes. Also remove the wood trim along the wall except doorframes and window frames; leave these intact unless you plan to trim the jambs to match the exposed wall.

Sprucing Up the Wall: To match the color of the existing mortar when patching crumbling mortar joints, take a sample to a masonry supplier for help in custom-tinting a mortar mix. Muriatic acid for cleaning bricks is available at paint stores, as are a variety of masonry sealers in flat or glossy finishes.

 TOOLS

Bricklayer's hammer (18-oz.)	Hammer
	Pointing trowel
Wire brush with medium bristles	Stiff-bristled brush
	Caulking gun
Cold chisel	Paintbrush

 **MATERIALS**

Masking tape	Flexible metal conduit
Duct tape	
Plastic sheeting (4-mil)	Muriatic acid
	Masonry sealer
Hardboard ($\frac{1}{8}$")	Latex or silicone caulk
Mortar	

 SAFETY TIPS

Goggles and a dual-cartridge respirator protect eyes, nose, and mouth from plaster dust and acid fumes. Work gloves keep hands safe from jagged plaster, while rubber gloves help prevent acid burns.

1. Breaking away plaster.

◆ Open windows in the work area for ventilation.
◆ Starting at the bottom of the wall, strike the plaster surface with a bricklayer's hammer at a 45-degree angle *(left)*. Pull cracked plaster away from the wall and strike succeeding hammer blows about 6 inches above the broken edge of the plaster.
◆ With the chisel end of the hammer, chip off stubborn clumps of plaster and pry plaster out of tight spots, as in corners and under doorframes and window frames.
◆ If the plaster has been laid over metal or wood lath, pry it loose and pull it off the wall with gloved hands.

2. Repointing the wall.

◆ Clean any remaining plaster off bricks with a wire brush.

◆ With a cold chisel and hammer, remove loose mortar around bricks and deepen the recesses for outlet boxes so that outlets and switches will be flush with the wall.

◆ If wiring has been exposed by the removal of the plaster, clear out mortar joints to a depth of 1 inch in a stepped path leading to the box. Slip a narrow, flexible metal conduit over cloth-covered cable. Without cutting the cable, fit it into the opened joints.

◆ Mix mortar and press it into gaps in the mortar joints with a pointing trowel, covering conduit where necessary. Fill in spaces around door and window frames.

◆ Allow new mortar to set for at least 48 hours.

3. Cleaning the wall.

◆ With windows wide open, pour 1 part muriatic acid into a plastic bucket containing 3 parts water.

◆ Wash the wall with the acid mixture and a stiff-bristled brush. Try to avoid spattering; if acid spills on the drop sheet, blot it with newspaper.

◆ Rinse the wall by scrubbing it twice with water.

◆ Let the wall dry for at least a week before proceeding.

⚠ **CAUTION** *Handle muriatic acid with care. If some splashes on your skin, flush it away with water, then apply a burn ointment. A stinging sensation in your nose or eyes is a signal to leave the room immediately. Flush the affected area thoroughly with water, and take a rest from the work until the stinging subsides.*

4. Rewiring and sealing the wall.

◆ Mortar all the surfaces inside an electrical-box recess.

◆ Slip the supply wire into the box and push it into the recess.

◆ Scrape away excess mortar, then press a board against the box to make it flush with the wall.

◆ Repeat for other outlets and switches.

◆ Let the mortar dry 48 hours.

◆ Brush a coat of masonry sealer over the entire wall.

◆ When the sealer is dry, reconnect switches and receptacles and replace the cover plates.

◆ Restore the baseboards and any other wood trim that was removed, refitting them at the corners if necessary.

◆ Caulk the joints between adjoining sections of brick and plaster wall, around doorframes and window frames, and between the baseboard and the brick wall.

Wall Panels that Divide and Decorate

Instead of building a solid wall to split up a room, you can often achieve the same result with a strategically placed divider that is lightweight and easy to build. The simplest dividers consist of a wood frame around a panel made of any material you like, from opaque plastic to latticework interlaced with a vine.

Building the Frame: The type of wood used for the frame is up to you, though the size of the lumber depends on the panel. Frames for light, thin panel materials like plastic can be built from 1-by-3s; for heavier panel materials you might use 2-by-3s or 2-by-4s.

In the dividers illustrated here, the panels are no more than $\frac{1}{4}$ inch thick and are sandwiched between a continuous strip of lattice attached to one side of the frame, and a continuous strip of quarter-round molding *(page 160)*. For panels thicker than $\frac{1}{4}$ inch, it is customary to use quarter-round molding on both sides of a thicker frame *(page 160)*, resulting in a stronger divider whose two sides are identical.

Floor-to-ceiling dividers are held in place with a channel of decorative molding nailed to the ceiling *(page 161)*, while H-style dividers are secured to the ceiling with angle irons *(page 161)*. Either frame should be $\frac{1}{4}$ inch shorter than the ceiling, so that its top edge will not catch against the ceiling when you are raising the divider into place.

TOOLS

Hammer
Corner clamps
Carpenter's level
Straightedge

Circular saw, or
  handsaw and
  miter box
Tape measure
Scriber

MATERIALS

Frame lumber
Carpenter's glue
Finishing nails (2")
Lattice strips
Panel material

Brads ($\frac{3}{4}$")
Quarter-round
  molding
Angle-iron braces
Hollow-wall anchors
Decorative molding
Wood screws

SAFETY TIPS

Goggles protect your eyes when you are hammering, sawing, and working with power tools.

Ways to divide a room.

Wood-framed divider walls commonly take one of two basic forms that offer varying degrees of privacy. One is a single rectangle extending from floor to ceiling *(above, left)*; the other, with air space above and below, is mounted in an H-shaped frame *(above, center)*. Either can be used in multiples to stretch farther or to accommodate narrow panels *(above, right)*.

DIVIDERS THAT FOLD

A popular alternative to permanent wall dividers is the folding screen. Easily moved or set aside depending on the occasion, a folding screen consists of three narrow dividers built according to the instructions seen on this page and the next and linked with hinges. In order to achieve the accordion-fold effect shown here, mount the hinges on alternating sides of the dividers.

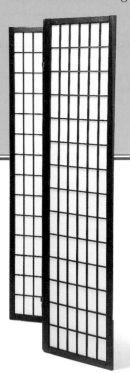

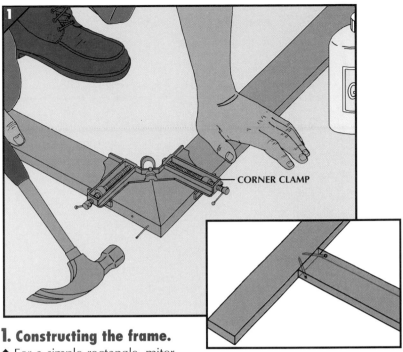

CORNER CLAMP

1. Constructing the frame.

◆ For a simple rectangle, miter four lengths of 1-by-3 lumber so that the inner edges are $\frac{1}{8}$ inch longer than the panel dimensions.
◆ Working corner by corner, apply glue to the mitered ends, then secure the frame pieces in a corner clamp.
◆ Drive 2-inch finishing nails into the joint from each direction (above).

For an H-style frame, glue and toenail the top and bottom of the frame to the sides (inset). Use a corner clamp to secure each joint while driving the first nail.

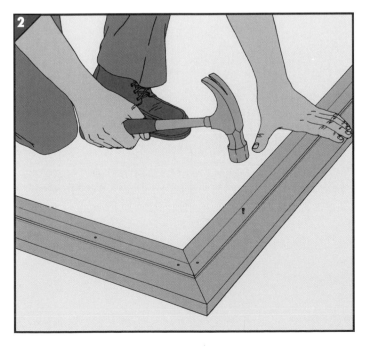

2. Tacking lattice to the frame.

If the difference between panel and frame thicknesses is an inch or more, secure the panel on both sides with quarter-round molding as described in Step 3. Otherwise, proceed as follows:
◆ Scribe a guideline around the back of the frame, $\frac{7}{8}$ inch from the inner edge.
◆ Miter cut four $1\frac{3}{4}$-inch lattice strips so their outer edges are the same length as the scribed lines.
◆ Apply glue to the back of the frame between the inner edge and the scribed line.
◆ Lay the lattice strips along the line and fasten them to the frame with $\frac{3}{4}$-inch brads at 6-inch intervals (left).
◆ Turn the frame over and insert the panel, resting it on the lattice strips.

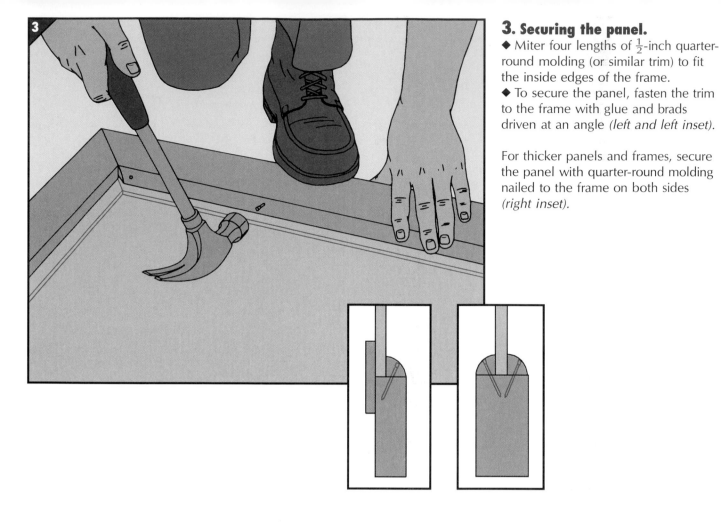

3. Securing the panel.
◆ Miter four lengths of $\frac{1}{2}$-inch quarter-round molding (or similar trim) to fit the inside edges of the frame.
◆ To secure the panel, fasten the trim to the frame with glue and brads driven at an angle *(left and left inset)*.

For thicker panels and frames, secure the panel with quarter-round molding nailed to the frame on both sides *(right inset)*.

LINKING FRAMES WITH LATTICE STRIPS

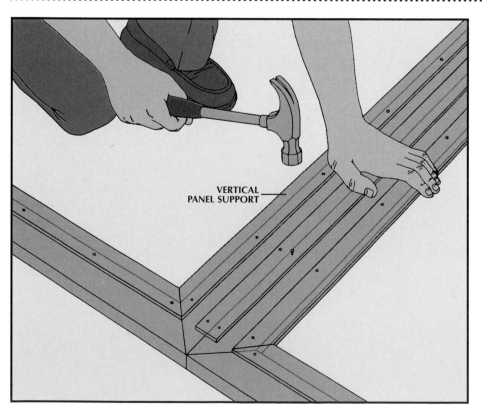

VERTICAL PANEL SUPPORT

Connecting divider panels.
◆ Cut a lattice strip to the same length as the vertical panel supports.
◆ Butt two panels together side by side, and fasten the strip evenly over the seam with glue and $\frac{3}{4}$-inch brads spaced 6 inches apart *(left)*.
◆ Carefully turn the frame over and fasten an identical strip of lattice to the other side.

ERECTING A DIVIDER

Bracing an H frame.
◆ Hold the divider in place and mark guidelines on the ceiling for two angle-iron braces.
◆ Then fasten angle irons to the ceiling, using expansion shields in plaster and hollow-wall anchors in wallboard.
◆ Raise the divider and attach the free leg of the angle iron to the frame (inset).
◆ Check the panel with a level to make sure it is plumb, then toenail the bottom of the frame to the floor.

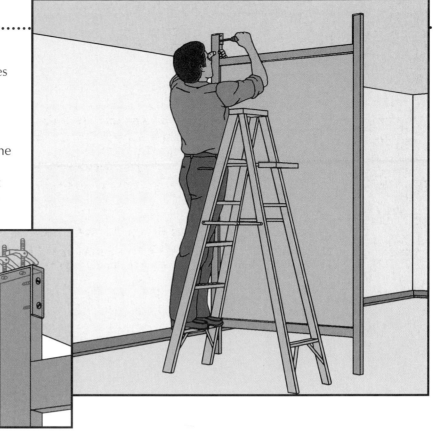

Securing a rectangular divider.
A three-sided, mitered channel anchors the divider to the ceiling and may serve the same purpose at the floor. For a ceiling channel, place the molding in the miter box upside down (page 202). To fit the divider snugly against the wall, notch either the base-board and its shoe molding or a corner of the divider frame.
◆ For the ceiling, cut two pieces of molding that are equal in length to the width of the divider plus the thickness of its frame; miter one end of each piece. Miter a third piece on both ends so that the inside edge equals the thickness of the divider frame.
◆ Glue and nail one of the long pieces of molding to the ceiling at the panel location.
◆ Raise the divider against the molding (left), and nail through the molding into the divider frame.
◆ Place the second long piece of molding against the other side of the divider and fasten it to the ceiling.
◆ Fit the short piece of molding between the ends of the longer ones (inset).

At the floor, adapt the foregoing procedure or anchor the frame with nails or screws driven at an angle into the floor.

Building a Wall with Metal Framing

Sturdier than a wall divider but quicker and easier to install than a wall framed with wood 2-by-4s, a metal-stud wall is a convenient way to partition a room. When covered with gypsum wallboard the finished wall is almost as rigid as the same material supported by wood studs; however, it is not as strong. Heavy items such as cabinets and bookshelves must be supported by additional wood framing.

The Components of the System: Metal framing, available from many building-supply distributors, consists of three-sided tracks, the sides of which angle slightly inward, and studs that fit into the tracks. The back—or spine—of each stud is stiffened with ribbing and has holes to accommodate electrical or plumbing lines.

Constructing the Wall: Assembly of metal framing begins with installing floor and ceiling tracks, which correspond to the sole and top plates of a wood-frame wall. In a doorway, the doorjambs are attached to wood studs screwed to metal ones.

When securing studs to the tracks, drive the screws with a screw gun or with a variable-speed drill fitted with a screwdriver bit. Metal studs cannot support the weight of wallboard panels installed horizontally. To finish the wall, arrange the panels vertically, as described on page 137, and fasten them with fine-threaded dry-wall screws.

TOOLS

Tin snips
Chalk line
Plumb bob

Caulking gun
Level
Electric drill with
  screwdriver bit or
  a screw gun

MATERIALS

Steel tracks and
  studs
Wallboard adhesive
2 x 4s

Plastic grommets
Fine-threaded dry-
  wall screws ($1\frac{1}{4}$")
Self-tapping pan-
  head sheet-metal
  screws ($\frac{1}{2}$" No. 8)

SAFETY TIPS

The edges of the metal framing are very sharp; wear work gloves when handling it. Protect your eyes with goggles when using the drill.

FRAMING A PARTITION WALL WITH STEEL

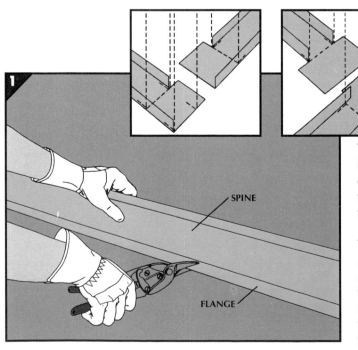

1. Preparing the tracks.

Trim tracks for the top and bottom plates with straight-cutting tin snips, severing the flanges first and then the spine.

To make a corner *(inset, above, left)*, transfer the inside width of the spine to the flanges that will form the inside of the corner. Cut the flanges, flatten them outward, then overlap the two sections of track. When installing the studs *(Step 4, opposite)*, frame the corner with three studs *(dashed lines)* to support the wallboard.

Where one wall intersects another, cut and flatten the flanges as shown in the right-hand inset, then overlap the tracks. As with a corner, three studs are required. The two on the intersected track must be placed within 3 inches of the intersection.

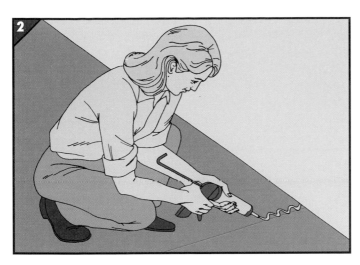

2. Laying the floor track.
◆ Snap a chalk line on the floor to mark the location of one edge of the track.
◆ With a plumb bob, mark two points on the ceiling directly above the ends of the floor line as a guide for the ceiling track.
◆ On the floor, apply a $\frac{3}{8}$-inch-wide bead of wallboard adhesive along the track side of the chalked line in a serpentine pattern.
◆ Press the track firmly into the adhesive, making sure the edge of the track is aligned with the chalked line.
◆ Secure the track to a wood floor with $1\frac{1}{4}$-inch dry-wall screws, 2 feet apart. Substitute fluted masonry nails if the floor is concrete.

3. Fastening the ceiling track.
Align the ceiling track with the two marks made in Step 2 and fasten it. If the track crosses ceiling joists as shown here, attach it to each one with a dry-wall screw.

If the track runs directly under a joist, fasten it with dry-wall screws, 16 inches apart. To install a track between joists, use hollow-wall anchors if the ceiling is finished. Otherwise, bridge the joists with 2-by-4 blocks nailed at 2-foot intervals. Screw the track to the blocks.

4. Erecting the studs.
◆ Cut studs $\frac{1}{4}$ inch shorter than the height of the new wall, trimming them at the top to keep the prepunched holes aligned.
◆ To preserve working space for attaching wallboard, place the end studs 2 inches from the existing walls. Set each stud edgewise into the floor and ceiling tracks, then turn it.
◆ Working from either end, install studs with their centers 16 inches apart, then plumb each one with a level.
◆ Fasten floor- and ceiling-track flanges to stud flanges with $\frac{1}{2}$-inch No. 8 self-tapping sheet-metal screws. To do so, clamp the track and stud flanges together with locking C-clamp pliers (photograph). Unless you have access to only one side of the tracks, place a fastener on both sides.

MAKING WAY FOR A DOOR

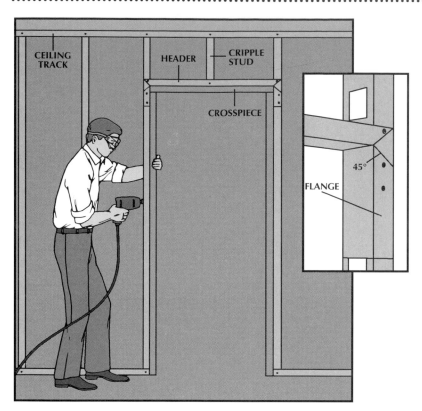

A frame within a frame.

◆ Determine the size of the rough opening required for the door.

◆ Install two metal studs—spines toward the door opening—3 inches farther apart than the width of the rough opening.

◆ Make a header from a piece of track 12 inches longer than the width of the opening. To do so, first mark the spine 6 inches from each end. Cut the flanges at a 45-degree angle, beginning about 5 inches from the ends, then bend down the ends to form right angles *(inset)*.

◆ Position the header 1½ inches above the height of the rough opening and screw it to the studs.

◆ Attach an interior frame of 2-by-4s to the metal frame with 1¼-inch dry-wall screws driven through the studs and into the wood at 2-foot intervals. Be sure to rest the 2-by-4 crosspiece on the uprights.

◆ Cut a short cripple stud to fit between the header and the ceiling track and install it at the center of the door opening.

ROUTES FOR WIRING AND PLUMBING

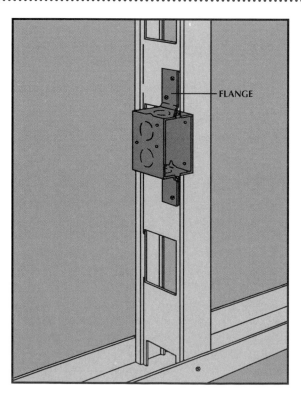

Installing an electrical box.

An electrical box that has flanges on one side is the easiest type to install in a new metal-stud wall. To mount the flanges on a stud, position the face of the box so that it will be flush with the wall surface; then secure the box with ½-inch self-tapping sheet-metal screws.

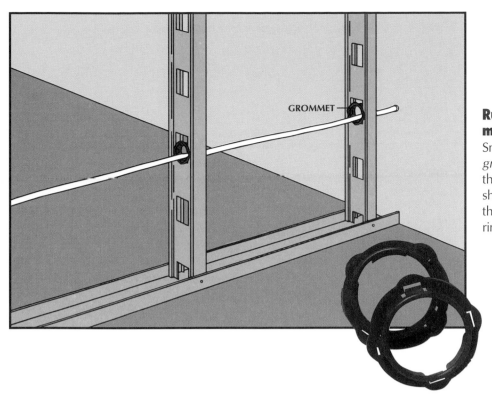

Running cable through metal studs.

Snap round plastic grommets *(photograph)* into the holes through which the cable will pass to protect it from sharp sheet-metal edges. Then thread the cable through the grommet-rimmed openings to the electrical box.

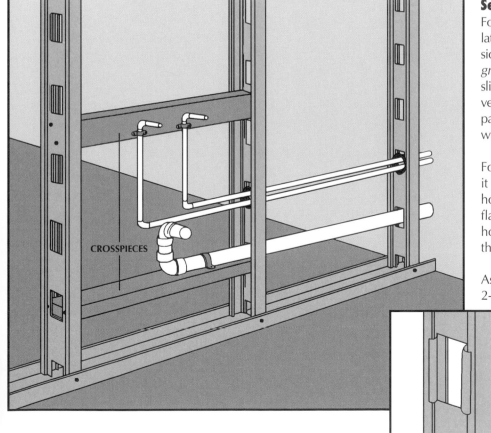

Securing pipes to metal studs.

For copper pipes, which must be insulated from steel studs to prevent corrosion, snap plastic grommets *(photograph, above)* into stud holes before slipping the pipes through them. To prevent the pipes from rattling where they pass through the studs, you can also wrap them with pipe insulation.

For drainpipes to fit through the studs, it may be necessary to enlarge the holes. With tin snips, cut toward the flanges at the top and bottom of each hole and bend the resulting tabs out of the way *(inset)*.

As support for the ends of pipes, cut 2-by-4 crosspieces to fit between studs. Install the crosspieces—either faceup or on edge, depending on the kind of support needed—and fasten them with $1\frac{1}{4}$-inch dry-wall screws driven through the studs and into the wood. Clamp the pipes to the crosspieces with pipe straps.

A prefabricated ceiling, easy to install and designed to absorb sound, can be an appealing alternative to plaster or wallboard. Two basic structural systems are used for such ceilings: interlocking tiles that are attached to the old ceiling *(right and pages 167-169)* or floating panels suspended from the old ceiling on a lightweight metal grid *(pages 170-173)*. Because the tiles or panels of a prefabricated ceiling are precut and already embossed with a decorative finish, they dispense with such plaster or wallboard preliminaries as mortar mixing or joint taping as well as a final application of paint or wallpaper. As for their acoustic benefits, they can absorb 50 to 80 percent of the sound that would otherwise reverberate in a room.

Tile Ceilings: The installation method for tiles depends on the condition of the existing ceiling. If your ceiling is level and free of cracks, you can fasten tiles directly to the existing surface with brush-on adhesive and staples (first removing any loose paint or wallpaper). If, however, the ceiling is cracked or uneven, an intermediate buffer of furring strips *(right)* will be needed.

You can hide obstructions, such as a pipe or duct, by building a wood frame around the obstacle *(pages 129-130)*, then fastening tiles to the frames.

Suspended Ceilings: When a number of overhead pipes or ducts must be concealed—as in an unfinished basement, for instance—a ceiling made of suspended panels is the logical choice. Better lighting may be another reason: Fluorescent-light fixtures set into the grid flush with the ceiling provide a more even light than narrow surface-mounted fixtures. To provide the maximum amount of light reflection, paint the existing ceiling structure above the fixtures—including any exposed joists—with two coats of vinyl-base, nonyellowing white paint.

First Steps: Acoustic tiles and panels should be unpacked and allowed to stand for at least 24 hours in the room where they are to be installed. This allows them to become acclimated to the temperature and humidity. You should also complete electrical wiring for the ceiling before installing tiles or panel grids *(pages 131 and 172)*.

CLIP-ON TILES

In the case of a cracked or uneven ceiling, tiles must be attached to furring strips for support. The strips can be made either of wood *(pages 125-128)* or of metal. Wood is less expensive, but the metal system eliminates the need to staple each tile in place. Instead, tiles are secured with metal clips, which come in a kit with the furring strips. The clips snap onto each strip and hook over one of the tile's flange edges *(above)*.

Metal strips are laid out in the same way as wood strips *(opposite)*, except that a final strip is placed an inch from the edge of each wall that runs perpendicular to the joists. Several strips compose one row, with a slight gap, no wider than $\frac{1}{4}$ inch, between each strip. The strips must be perfectly aligned in case a clip needs to straddle two of them. If a full-length strip is too long to finish a row, cut it to size.

 TOOLS

Steel rule
Chalk line
Hammer
Staple gun
Utility knife
Compass
L square
Line level
Saw (keyhole or saber-saw blade)
Hacksaw
Tin snips
Pop riveter
Punch or drill

 MATERIALS

Acoustic ceiling tiles
Acoustic ceiling panels
Luminous panel
Furring strips
Cove molding
L-shaped wall angles
Runners
Cross Ts
Channel molding
Vertical cross Ts
Hanger wires
Ceiling staples
Common nails ($1\frac{1}{2}$")
Finishing nails ($2\frac{1}{2}$")
Dry-wall nails or screws ($1\frac{1}{4}$")
Screw eyes
Rivets
Cable connector
Lock nut
Wire caps

 SAFETY TIPS

Protect your eyes with goggles when stapling, sawing, hammering, and riveting. Wear both goggles and gloves when cutting metal.

1. Laying out the work.

The following method of planning the installation of 1-foot-square ceiling tiles ensures borders of equal and visually pleasing width. A graph paper map of the layout can be useful.

◆ Find the midpoint of a wall and measure from there to the corner. If the distance is an even number of feet plus 3 inches or more, use the midpoint as the starting point in marking off 1-foot intervals along the top of the wall *(left)*. If less than 3 inches, move the starting point 6 inches to the left or right of the midpoint. Mark all walls in this way, and mark the location of any concealed joists *(page 326)*.

◆ To calculate the quantity of tiles needed, count the 1-foot intervals along two adjacent walls; add 1 to each number, then multiply the two numbers.

◆ To determine the quantity of furring strips, count the 1-foot intervals along one of the walls that parallel the joists, and add 2 to this number.

◆ Snap a chalk line across the ceiling between corresponding marks on the two walls running parallel to the joists.

◆ Center furring strips over these lines, and nail them to the joists they cross, leveling them as shown on page 127, Step 3.

◆ Attach furring strips to the two ceiling edges that abut the joists.

2. Installing full tiles.

Use a hand or power stapler *(photograph)* for installation.

◆ Start the tiling in one corner, using two chalk lines as guides. Snap one down the center of the next-to-last furring strip from the corner. Snap the other at a right angle to it, connecting the last pair of 1-foot marks on the walls that parallel the furring strips.

◆ Align the first full tile with the intersection of these lines, tongued edges facing the corner and grooved edges facing the center of the room.

◆ Staple through the flanges on the grooved edges and into the furring strips *(right)*.

◆ Slide two additional tiles into place, fitting their tongued edges into the grooved edges of the first tile *(inset)*. Make sure the grooved sides of each new tile face toward the positions of the next tiles.

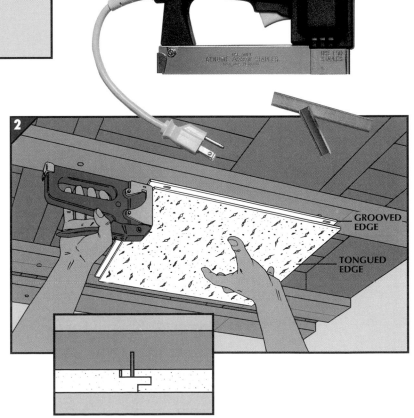

GROOVED EDGE

TONGUED EDGE

3. Adding border tiles.

To cut a border tile to size, measure the distance from both ends of the nearest full tile to the wall, transfer these measurements to a tile, and cut the tile with a utility knife and a straightedge guide *(left)*. Start a border at a corner as follows:

◆ Temporarily slide the border tiles on either side of a corner into place, with their cut edges against the wall.

◆ Using the two border tiles as a guide, measure and cut the corner tile. Then remove the adjacent border tiles and insert the corner tile.

◆ Staple the flange edges of the corner tile to furring strips. Replace and staple the adjacent border tiles.

◆ Along the edges against the walls, fasten all the tiles with $1\frac{1}{2}$-inch common nails, which will be covered later by molding.

◆ Continue working outward in both directions from the corner, alternately installing full tiles and border tiles.

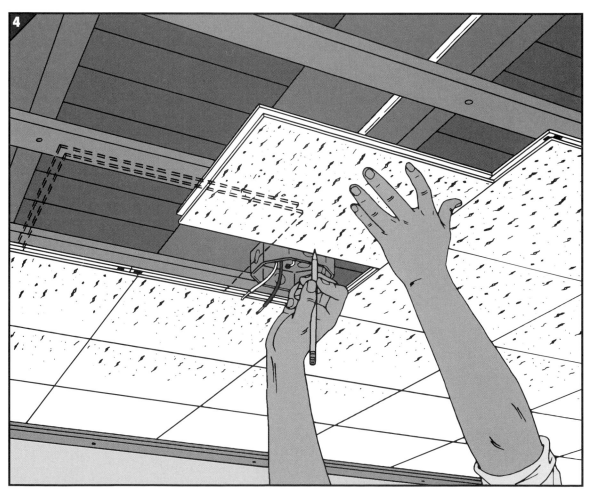

4. Marking an opening for an outlet box.

◆ Tile as closely as possible to two adjacent sides of an octagonal outlet or junction box.

◆ Slip the tongue of a free tile into the groove of an installed tile.

◆ Slide the free tile toward the outlet box until it butts against the edge. Lightly mark where the midpoint of the box meets the tile, then repeat the process on the adjacent side *(above)*.

◆ With a small L square, indicate the point where lines aligned with the two edge marks intersect; this marks the box's center.

◆ Use a compass to swing from this center a circle slightly smaller than the size of the box.

5. Cutting the box opening.

◆ With a keyhole or saber-saw blade angled slightly outward, cut a beveled edge around the marked circle.

◆ Slide the tile over the outlet box and staple it to the furring strips.

◆ Continue tiling outward until the entire ceiling is covered.

6. Attaching ceiling molding.

Cover the edges of the tile and the nailheads along the wall with $1\frac{1}{2}$-inch cove molding. For long strips of molding, have a helper steady one end while you attach the other *(left)*.

◆ Drive finishing nails through the center of the molding into the wall studs—$2\frac{1}{2}$-inch nails are generally sufficient, but use longer nails for heavier molding.

◆ Trim the molding so it will join snugly at the corners, using the techniques shown on page 203.

1. Installing the edge framing.

The framing at the edge of a suspended ceiling of 2- by 4-inch acoustic panels must be perfectly level; one leveling method uses chalk lines:

◆ Mark a corner at the desired ceiling height—at least 3 inches below any obstructions—and drive a nail in halfway. Stretch a chalk line from the nail to the next corner, hook a line level over it, and fasten the other end of the line in the corner when it is level. Remove the line level and snap the line against the wall. Repeat the process around the room.

◆ Secure L-shaped edge-framing strips to each wall with $1\frac{1}{4}$-inch dry-wall nails or screws driven into the studs. Position this framing with the long leg of the L against the wall and the other flush with the chalked line (left).

◆ Lap the ends of adjoining sections over one another (inset).

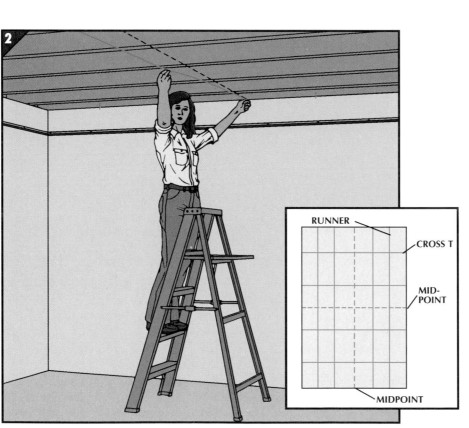

RUNNER
CROSS T
MID-POINT
MIDPOINT

2. Laying out the grid.

To establish the positions of runners and cross Ts (inset) supporting the panels, first mark the locations of any concealed joists (page 326), then proceed as follows:

◆ On walls parallel to the joists, mark the midpoint at joist level. On walls that run perpendicular to the joists, mark the midpoint just below the edge framing.

◆ Indicate positions for runners by snapping chalk lines at 2-foot intervals across the ceiling or exposed joists, at right angles to the joists. To determine the first runner position, calculate the overage by measuring the number of full feet from the midpoint of the wall to a corner (page 167, Step 1). If the overage is 6 inches or more, use the midpoint for the first runner position. If it is less than 6 inches, place the first runner 1 foot on either side of the midpoint, and use this position as a reference point for the other chalked lines.

◆ To lay out the positions for cross Ts, stretch strings across the ceiling at 4-foot intervals, parallel to the joists and attached just below the edge framing; check strings with a line level. Determine the position for the first cross T by measuring from a midpoint to a corner to find the overage, but this time note that the overage is calculated from the last foot mark divisible by 4. If the overage is 6 inches or more, stretch the first string between the midpoints; if it is less than 6 inches, offset the first string 2 feet to one side of the midpoints and use this string as a reference for the remaining strings.

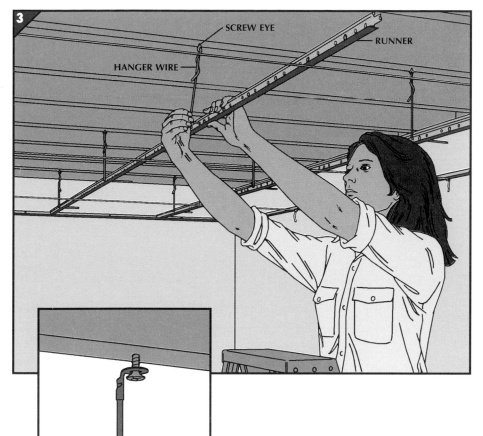

SCREW EYE

RUNNER

HANGER WIRE

3. Attaching the runners.

Use the stretched strings as guides to the height of the runners, checking frequently to make sure they are level.

◆ Position the runners so a slotted hole falls at every string line; trim the runners with a hacksaw when necessary.

◆ Working along the chalked lines, drive a screw eye into every fourth joist and suspend a hanger wire from it, allowing the wire to extend at least 6 inches below final ceiling height. Slip the wire through the nearest round hole of a runner, then twist it closed.

◆ To join sections of runners, butt or snap their ends together, according to their design. Make sure that slots in the added section align with the strings.

◆ Trim the runner ends to rest on the edge framing.

Some hanger wires are made with eyelets that loop over screws (inset). To level the runner, simply adjust the screws.

4. Connecting the cross Ts.

◆ Hook the cross Ts into the runner slots every 2 feet at the locations marked by the strings.

◆ Trim the wall ends of the cross Ts with tin snips to rest squarely on the edge framing.

CROSS T

5. Installing a luminous panel.

◆ With the power turned off, run an electric cable from a junction box to where you will install the luminous panel.

◆ Insert four screw eyes into the joists above the location chosen for the luminous panel. Set the screws so the wire hangers will be angled slightly inward when attached to the panel.

◆ With a helper, angle the panel into position *(left)*, resting it on the flanged edges of the runners and the crossed Ts.

◆ Attach the top of the luminous panel to the four screw eyes with hanger wire threaded through prepunched holes in the panel.

◆ Once the panel is attached to the ceiling, follow the manufacturer's instructions to connect the wiring.

◆ Insert fluorescent tubes, close the outside cover, and turn on the power.

◆ Surround the luminous panel with acoustic panels, angled into position in the same way.

◆ At the edges of the ceiling, trim border panels to fit.

BOXING IN OBSTRUCTIONS

MAIN RUNNER

MAIN RUNNER

DROPPED RUNNER

DROPPED RUNNER

EDGE FRAMING

1. Installing a dropped runner.

When an obstruction runs parallel to the runners on the main part of the ceiling, install the main grid *(pages 170-171 and above)* as close as possible to both sides.

◆ Attach hanger wires directly beneath the last main runner on both sides of the obstruction, cutting the wires so the dropped runners will lie at least 3 inches below the obstruction. If the dropped runners butt against a wall, attach a piece of edge framing to the wall for support.

◆ Attach the runners to the hanger wires *(page 171, Step 3)*, aligning the slots for the cross Ts *(left)*.

If an obstruction runs perpendicular to the runners on the main ceiling, cut the main runners on both sides of the obstruction, leaving a 2-foot gap between them for cross Ts. Then install dropped runners as described above.

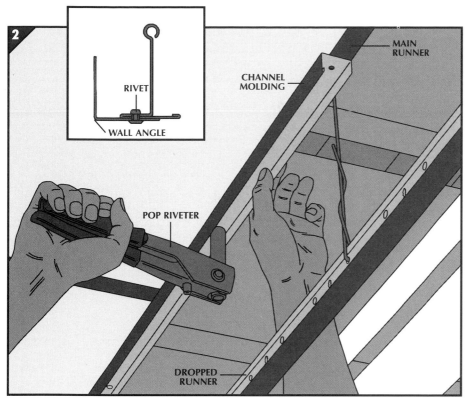

2. Attaching side-panel supports.

◆ Hold a piece of U-shaped channel molding against the bottom of the main runner nearest the obstruction and drill $\frac{3}{16}$-inch holes through both the molding and the runner's inner edge. Space the holes about 18 to 24 inches apart.

◆ Use a pop riveter to fasten the molding to the runner (left).

◆ Fashion a support for the bottom of the side panels by fastening an L-shaped wall angle to the dropped runners, positioning it so that the space between the runner and the angle is just wide enough to accommodate the panel—usually $\frac{1}{2}$ to $\frac{3}{4}$ inch (inset).

◆ If the enclosure does not extend all the way across the room, provide similar top and bottom supports for the panel that frames the end of the enclosure.

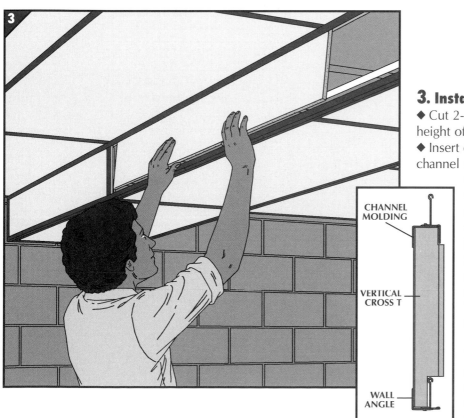

3. Installing side panels.

◆ Cut 2- by 4-foot acoustic panels to fit the height of the enclosure.

◆ Insert each panel by angling it up into the channel molding then letting it drop into the wall angle.

◆ As each panel is installed, add a vertical cross T to fit snugly between the wall angle on the dropped runner and the channel molding on the ceiling runner (inset). Then insert another panel and continue in this way until the obstruction is enclosed. If the vertical cross Ts need steadying, you can pop rivet or screw them to the runners.

To provide a neat corner trim on an enclosure that does not extend across the room, fit sections of wall angle over the corner and attach the molding to the upper and lower runners.

Exposed ceiling beams lend a room the aura of antiquity, but adding such beams requires major structural changes and the chore of hoisting heavy timbers. You can achieve the same look by creating lightweight, hollow "beams" out of 1-by-4s or 1-by-6s as shown here. Assemble beams longer than 12 feet from multiple sections. Once assembled, the simulated beams can be finished in any number of decorative styles, from delicate hand-painted designs to a deliberately roughened surface.

Most simulated beams parallel each other across the width of a room and are hung from the existing joists. For a look that is more elaborate, add crossbeams at right angles between long beams. You can even erect posts along the walls beneath the ends of the beams and, as a final touch, attach bracing beams at 45-degree angles, running them from the posts to the ceiling beams.

TOOLS

Circular saw
Hammer
Nail set
Block plane
Rasp
Electric drill with wire-brush attachment
Paintbrush
Electronic stud finder

MATERIALS

Lumber (1 x 4s, 1 x 6s, 2 x 4s, 2 x 6s)
Carpenter's glue
Finishing nails (2")
Wood stain
Wood putty
Polyurethane finish
Sandpaper
Common nails ($3\frac{1}{2}$")
Toggle bolts

SAFETY TIPS

Put on goggles when using a hammer. A hard hat offers good protection whenever there are unsecured boards overhead.

1. Building the beam.

◆ To make a hollow U-shaped beam, first measure and cut three 1-by-4s or 1-by-6s to the same length.
◆ Glue and nail the boards together with 2-inch finishing nails *(above),* positioning the side pieces so that their edges overhang the bottom piece by no more than $\frac{1}{16}$ inch.
◆ Countersink the nails. Then plane the beam to make the bottom and lower edges of the sides flush with each other.
◆ Hold the beam temporarily in place against the ceiling to check its length before proceeding to Step 2.

2. Applying the finish.

To create a rough-hewn look, scrape the beam with a rasp *(left)*, scar it using a drill with a wire-brush attachment, or hit it with a chain or old keys; make sure to round and gouge the edges of the side pieces as you work. Apply a stain, then fill gaps and cover nailheads with matching wood putty.

To simulate a Tudor or Early American beam, bevel the edges of the side pieces and apply mahogany or walnut stain. Fill with matching wood putty and finish with polyurethane varnish.

For a beam with painted decorations, cover nailheads and fill gaps with wood putty. Sand the wood and add the design, with a stencil or freehand. Finish with polyurethane varnish.

3. Installing mounting tracks.
◆ For each beam made of 1-by-4s, cut a 2-by-4 of equal length. Use 2-by-6s for 1-by-6 beams.
◆ Locate ceiling joists with an electronic stud finder.
◆ With a helper, position each 2-by-4 or 2-by-6 as a mounting track across the joists and fasten it to each with two $3\frac{1}{2}$-inch common nails *(above)*.

If the beams run parallel to and between joists, fasten the tracks to the ceiling with a toggle bolt every 2 feet.

4. Mounting a beam.
◆ With a helper, slide the beam onto its mounting track.
◆ Pressing the beam firmly against the ceiling, drive 2-inch finishing nails at 1-foot intervals through the sides of the beam and into the track. Countersink the nailheads.
◆ Cover the nailheads with matching wood putty and touch up the finish as needed.

Soundproofing a room can be tricky, because noise not only travels through air—directly and around corners—but also penetrates ordinary hollow walls with little loss of intensity.

Any vibrating surface—such as a loudspeaker cone or human vocal cords—starts air molecules moving in a wavelike pattern, transmitting acoustic energy to the eardrums. To be effective, a sound barrier must block airborne sound waves, interrupt acoustic energy transmitted through solids, and plug acoustic leaks. A solid brick wall is a good sound barrier, but the thin, flat surface of stud-and-wallboard construction is not. The flexible wallboard picks up sound vibrations and transmits them through the studs, setting in motion the wallboard on the other side.

The Tactic of Isolation: One way to weaken sound waves is to isolate a wall or ceiling surface from its supporting studs or joists, leaving at least 2 inches of space between surfaces. You can accomplish this when in-

stalling new walls by mounting wallboard on resilient $\frac{1}{2}$-inch metal furring channels *(opposite)*. To add a sound-deadening layer over an existing wall, use 2-inch Z-shaped channels *(page 179)*.

Vibration is further reduced by leaving narrow gaps between adjacent wall surfaces and filling the gaps with flexible acoustic caulking compound that does not harden over time. You can suppress sound even more by filling the wall with fiberglass insulation; the fibers act like tiny springs to damp acoustic energy.

Sealing the Gaps: Holes and cracks in the wall can leak a surprising amount of noise. Plugging an opening $\frac{1}{8}$ inch wide around an electrical outlet box, for example, can improve the soundproofing effectiveness of a wall by as much as 10 percent. Other ways to suppress noise include damping vibrations in heating ducts and sealing gaps around doors *(page 183)*. Some central heating systems, however, may depend on gaps under interior doors for adequate air circulation.

 TOOLS

Tape measure
Plumb bob
Chalk line
Combination square
Power screwdriver
Staple gun
Framing hammer
Caulking gun
Electronic stud finder

 **MATERIALS**

Resilient furring channels
Z channels
Studs (2 x 4 and 2 x 6)
Fiberglass insulation
Outlet box extender
Wallboard ($\frac{1}{2}$" and $\frac{5}{8}$")
Shims
Acoustic sealant
Nails (3" and $3\frac{1}{2}$")
Staples ($\frac{1}{2}$")
Neoprene-coated duct liner
Duct-liner adhesive
Door gasket
Threshold gasket
Dry-wall screws (1", $1\frac{1}{4}$", $1\frac{1}{2}$", and $1\frac{5}{8}$")
Brads
Wood screws (1")

 SAFETY TIPS

Wear a respirator, goggles, and gloves when removing plaster or wallboard and when handling fiberglass. Gloves are a must when handling resilient furring channels and Z channels, which are made of sheet metal.

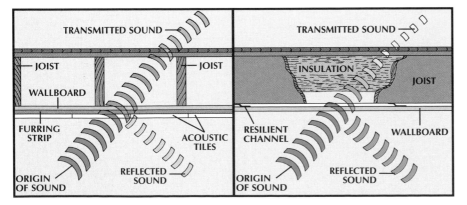

Sound absorption and transmission.
Porous acoustic tiles covering a wallboard ceiling *(far left)* reduce noise within a room by absorbing airborne sound waves, but they do a poor job of blocking sound transmission between rooms, since sound waves pass through their lightweight, porous composition. A wallboard ceiling that is mounted on resilient channels and that has insulation between the joists *(near left)* does little to suppress sound within a room, but it significantly reduces sound transmitted to the room above.

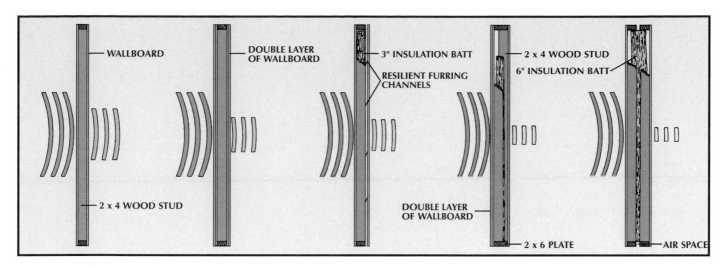

WALLBOARD

DOUBLE LAYER OF WALLBOARD

3" INSULATION BATT

RESILIENT FURRING CHANNELS

2 x 4 WOOD STUD

6" INSULATION BATT

2 x 4 WOOD STUD

DOUBLE LAYER OF WALLBOARD

2 x 6 PLATE

AIR SPACE

A variety of sound barriers.

The sound-reducing capabilities of the five walls diagramed above are determined by the thickness of the wall, the density and rigidity of the surface, and the nature of the contact between the surface and its support.

A standard 2-by-4 stud wall *(far left)* that is covered with one layer of wallboard renders conversation in the next room audible but indistinct.

A second layer of wallboard on each surface *(near left)* transmits only loud speech, but not clearly.

Mounting one layer of wallboard on resilient channels and adding a layer of insulation between studs *(center)* reduces sound transmission significantly.

Offsetting 2-by-4 studs on 2-by-6 plates, adding an insulation layer, and doubling one wallboard surface *(near right)* blocks both structural and airborne sound transmission dramatically.

Still more effective is the hollow double wall *(far right)*. With two pairs of 2-by-4 sole and top plates set 1 inch apart, a 6-inch layer of insulation, and a layer of wallboard on each side, this double wall stops sound better than a 4-inch solid brick wall.

SOUNDPROOFING AN EXISTING WALL

1. Attaching resilient furring channels.

◆ Remove the existing wall surface and pry out any nails.
◆ Add box extenders to electrical outlet boxes *(page 131)*, bringing their openings out $1\frac{1}{2}$ inches—$\frac{1}{2}$ inch for the channels and 1 inch for a double layer of $\frac{1}{2}$-inch wallboard.
◆ Staple $3\frac{1}{2}$-inch-thick batts of fiberglass insulation between studs.
◆ Snap a chalk line across the studs 6 inches below the ceiling and 2 inches above the floor. Between the lines, mark the studs for evenly spaced rows of channel 20 to 24 inches apart.
◆ Fasten the channel to the studs, mounting flange down, with $1\frac{1}{4}$-inch dry-wall screws driven through the holes provided in the flange. Position channel joints at studs, overlapping the channel sections at least 2 inches *(photograph)*.

⚠ **CAUTION** *When removing plaster or wallboard and when handling fiberglass, keep the room well ventilated. If you are demolishing a wall built before 1978, test for asbestos and lead (page 15).*

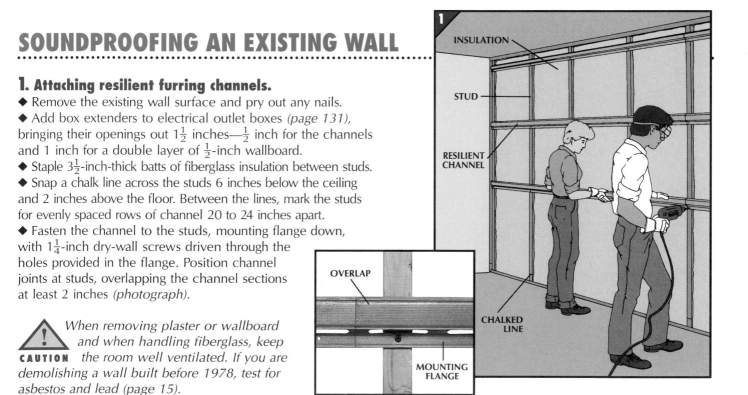

INSULATION

STUD

RESILIENT CHANNEL

CHALKED LINE

OVERLAP

MOUNTING FLANGE

2. Attaching the wallboard.

Install one layer of $\frac{1}{2}$-inch wallboard panels vertically, the second horizontally.

◆ Trim panels for the first layer $\frac{1}{4}$ inch shorter than the ceiling height.

◆ Shim the first panel to support it $\frac{1}{8}$ inch above the floor, then fasten it to the channels with 1-inch, fine-threaded dry-wall screws at 24-inch intervals.

◆ Remove the shims and use them to install the rest of the first layer, leaving a $\frac{1}{8}$-inch gap between panels.

◆ Caulk the gaps between panels and at the floor and ceiling with acoustic sealant *(inset)*.

◆ Install the second layer of wallboard, duplicating the $\frac{1}{8}$-inch gaps of the first. Use $1\frac{5}{8}$-inch dry-wall screws spaced 16 inches apart. Caulk the gaps with acoustic sealant.

◆ Complete the joints between panels and at the corners and ceiling with tape and joint compound, as shown on pages 138 to 141.

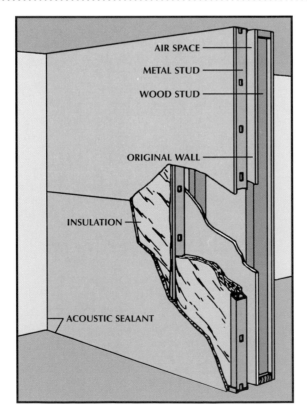

A FREESTANDING SOUND BUFFER

Cross section of a double wall.

A metal-stud wall constructed 2 inches away from an existing wall utilizes the space between walls and the inherent resiliency of metal studs as dual barriers to structure-borne sound. The wall is assembled as shown on pages 162 to 165 and covered with a single layer of $\frac{5}{8}$-inch wallboard. Spaces between studs are filled with $3\frac{1}{2}$-inch batts of fiberglass insulation to reduce airborne sound. Each panel of wallboard is installed $\frac{1}{8}$ inch away from adjacent surfaces, and the gaps are caulked with acoustic sealant.

This freestanding wall effectively suppresses the transmission of even low-pitched sounds, such as those produced by an electric bass guitar. You can further reduce noise transmission by removing the wallboard from the original wall to make room for additional insulation.

ADDING A CEILING LAYER

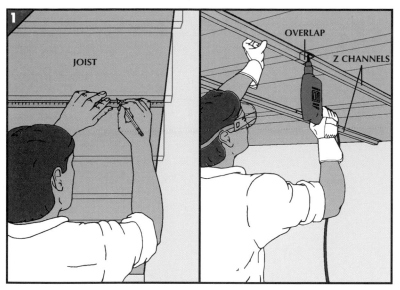

1. Attaching Z-shaped furring channels.

◆ Locate and mark joist positions as shown on page 126.

◆ Mark the ceiling 6 inches from both ends of the joists *(far left),* then divide the space between the marks into equal intervals of 20 to 24 inches.

◆ Use the divisions to snap a series of chalked lines on the ceiling, perpendicular to the joists.

◆ Fasten the Z channels along the chalked lines with a $1\frac{1}{2}$-inch dry-wall screw at each joist *(near left),* making sure that all the flanged edges face in the same direction. When joining lengths of channel, overlap the ends 2 inches and fasten them to the joist with a single screw.

2. Adding wallboard and insulation.

Start mounting the wallboard panels at the side of the room opposite to the direction the open flange is pointing.

◆ Mount the first row of wallboard to the Z channels, using 1-inch, fine-threaded dry-wall screws at 12-inch intervals and leaving a $\frac{1}{8}$-inch gap between the panel edges and adjacent walls. If more than one panel is needed to span the ceiling, center the joint between panels on the lower flange of the metal channel *(inset).* Drive the screw nearest the flange corner first, to prevent the flange from sagging and ensure a smooth seam between panels.

◆ After installing the first row of panels, insert 2-inch-thick batts of fiberglass insulation on top of the wallboard between the joists.

◆ Install additional rows of wallboard and insulation as above, with the exception of the last row. There, glue the insulation batt to the back of the panel before fastening it to the channels.

◆ Caulk all of the $\frac{1}{8}$-inch gaps with acoustic sealant. Finish the seams between panels with tape and joint compound, as shown on pages 138 to 141.

REBUILDING A CEILING

1. Creating space for insulation.

◆ Uncover the ceiling joists, observing the same precautions as in removing a wall *(page 15)*. Pry out any nails that remain in the joists.

◆ If the room has a ceiling light fixture, extend the electrical outlet box *(page 131, bottom)*.

◆ Install 6-inch-thick batts of fiberglass insulation between the exposed joists and against the subfloor above. Staple the batts to the sides of the joists at 2- to 3-inch intervals.

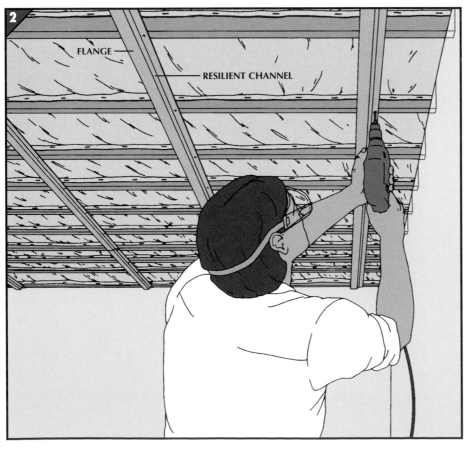

FLANGE

RESILIENT CHANNEL

2. Attaching resilient channels.

Install resilient furring channels across the exposed joists, following the method for Z channels shown on page 179, Step 1. Make sure all the flanges face the same direction. Plan channel joints to fall at joists and overlap the sections at least 2 inches.

◆ Fasten wallboard panels across the resilient channels using 1-inch drywall screws, leaving a $\frac{1}{8}$-inch gap around the perimeter of the ceiling. Center joints between panels on channel flanges and fasten the panels as shown on page 178, Step 2.

◆ Caulk all the gaps with an acoustic sealant, and finish the seams between panels as described on pages 138 to 141.

OFFSET STUDS TO MUFFLE SOUND

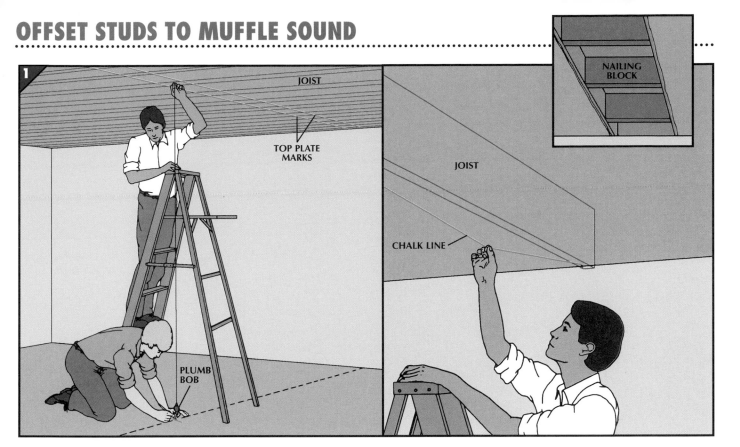

JOIST

TOP PLATE MARKS

NAILING BLOCK

CHALK LINE

PLUMB BOB

JOIST

1. Locating the top and sole plates.
This sound-resistant wall requires top and bottom plates of 2-by-6s instead of the 2-by-4s used for most walls. For a wall running perpendicular to joists *(above, left)*, snap two parallel chalked lines across the ceiling $5\frac{1}{2}$ inches apart. Drop a plumb bob near the ends of each line, mark the floor, and snap guidelines for the sole plate.

To build a wall parallel to joists, center

the top plate directly under a joist if possible *(above, right)*.
◆ Locate the joist with a stud finder *(page 326)*. Then, at each side of the room, drive a nail partway into the joist at the centerline.
◆ Snap a chalk line between the two nails to mark the centerline of the top plate, then snap the chalk line $2\frac{3}{4}$ inches from the centerline on either side to outline the top plate.
◆ Duplicate the lines on the floor for

the sole plate, as described above.

If the wall must stand between joists, expose the two joists that will flank the new wall, and install nailing blocks of joist lumber between them *(inset)*. Toenail a block every 2 feet and fill between them with insulation. Then patch the ceiling *(pages 138-141)* and snap chalked lines for the plates as if the wall were running perpendicular to the joists.

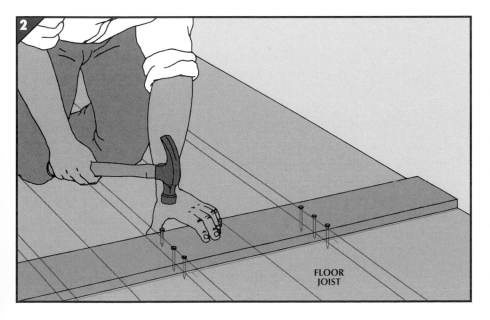

FLOOR JOIST

2. Installing the sole plate.
◆ Cut 2-by-6 lumber to the length of the wall for both the sole plate and the top plate.
◆ For a wall perpendicular to joists, find the joists with a stud finder and mark their centers along one side of the outline.
◆ Set the 2-by-6 sole plate within the outline and fasten it to the underlying joists with $3\frac{1}{2}$-inch nails *(left)*.

If the new wall runs parallel to the joists, simply nail the sole plate to the floor, driving $3\frac{1}{2}$-inch nails at 16-inch intervals.

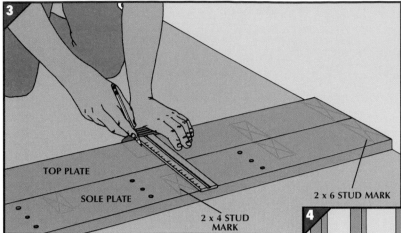

3. Marking the plates for studs.

◆ Mark each end of the sole plate for a 2-by-6 stud.

◆ Next, mark the sole plate every 12 inches for a 2-by-4 stud. Align the first stud with one edge of the sole plate, the second stud with the other edge, and so on.

◆ Lay the top plate beside the sole plate and, using a combination square, transfer the marks to the top plate as shown at left.

4. Assembling the framework.

◆ With one or more helpers, fasten the top plate to the ceiling as planned in Step 1 on page 181. Use $3\frac{1}{2}$-inch nails.

◆ Measure the distance between the sole and top plates, and cut two 2-by-6 studs to this length. Nail them to the ends of the plates—and to the adjacent walls, but only if there is a stud in the existing wall to nail to.

◆ Cut 2-by-4 studs to fit between the plates and align them with the marks on the top and sole plate. Toenail them in place with 3-inch nails, two nails on one side, a third on the other.

5. Completing the wall.

◆ Fasten batts of fiberglass insulation, $3\frac{1}{2}$ inches thick and 24 inches wide, between the studs, using $\frac{1}{2}$-inch staples to hold the batts in place.

◆ Cover both sides of the wall with a double layer of $\frac{1}{2}$-inch wallboard, staggering joints and leaving a $\frac{1}{8}$-inch gap around the edges of the wall.

◆ Caulk the $\frac{1}{8}$-inch gaps on both sides of the wall with acoustic sealant. Finish wallboard joints with tape and joint compound as shown on pages 138 to 141.

A DOUBLE WALL TO STOP LOW-PITCHED SOUND

Constructing the two walls.
◆ Mark the floor and ceiling for two 2-by-4 sole plates and two top plates, 1 inch apart. Cut the plates, set them side by side, and mark them for 2-by-4 studs, 16 inches on center.
◆ Assemble the frames as shown at left, toenailing the studs to the plates.
◆ Staple 6-inch-thick batts of fiberglass insulation between the studs.
◆ Cover the outer wall surfaces with a double layer of $\frac{1}{2}$-inch wallboard, staggering joints and leaving $\frac{1}{8}$-inch gaps around the edges.
◆ Caulk perimeter gaps with acoustic sealant and finish seams with tape and joint compound *(pages 138-141)*.

PLUGGING ACOUSTIC LEAKS

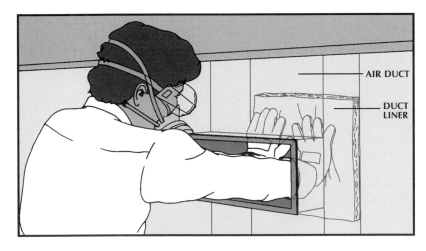

AIR DUCT

DUCT LINER

Muffling an air duct.
◆ Remove the register and measure as far into the duct as your arms will reach in both directions.
◆ Cut three pieces of 1-inch-thick neoprene-coated fiberglass duct liner to this length and wide enough to fit snugly along the back and sides of the duct, without blocking the register.
◆ Seal the cut edges of the pieces with duct-liner adhesive to prevent glass fibers from being released into the air.
◆ Working with one piece of liner at a time, spread duct-liner adhesive on the rough, uncoated side of each piece and press it into place on the duct wall.
◆ Replace the register.

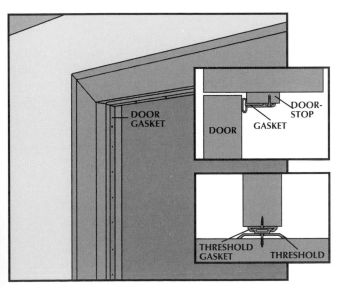

DOOR GASKET

DOOR-STOP

DOOR

GASKET

THRESHOLD GASKET

THRESHOLD

Sealing interior doors.
◆ Cut lengths of vinyl weatherproofing gasket to fit along the stops at the top and sides of the doorframe *(upper inset)*. Test-fit the gasket by holding it against the frame and closing the door; the gasket should compress slightly without interfering with the latch.
◆ Attach the gasket to the stops with 1-inch brads at 3-inch intervals. If the gasket has a metal mounting strip, you may substitute 1-inch wood screws for the brads.
◆ Measure the gap between the bottom of the door and the threshold; if the doorframe has no threshold, install one made of either aluminum or wood.
◆ Remove the door from the frame and trim the bottom of the door to accommodate a threshold gasket mounted in a metal strip *(lower inset)*. Install the gasket with 1-inch wood screws.
◆ Rehang the door and test the gasket fit by sliding a credit card between the gasket and the threshold; the card should meet slight resistance.

Options

There's nothing like paneling to bring wood's classic warmth and beauty to a room. Wood paneling is versatile, too; it acts as a natural sound and heat insulator. It's also a good way to disguise less-than-perfect walls, too. This chapter discusses how to install wood-veneer paneling, including estimating the number of sheets you need, cutting the sheets, and securing them to the wall. You'll find out how to plot curves for rounded windows, and how to panel oddly shaped openings. We'll show you the best way to stack panels for extra height, how to make herringbone patterns from vertical grooves, and how to miter moldings to hide edges.

Next, you'll learn the fine points of solid-wood paneling. Included here is a primer on various types of milled edges and on installation patterns. Because they're more complicated, diagonal and herringbone patterns are best on walls with few doors or windows.

Most wood paneling requires some sort of stain or protective finish. Near the end of the chapter you'll find a special box on finishes for fine wood that will help you select and apply water-based stains, polyurethane, and oil-based finishes. And finally, you'll learn how to cut and install traditional raised paneling and wainscoting.

The most elegant style of wood paneling, traditional raised paneling, adds a rich, formal tone to this exquisite dining room.

Wood paneling is not limited to stained finishes; most softwoods take well to paint, too. The pink-painted wood paneling strikes the perfect balance between rustic and comfy in this bedroom.

The casual, country look of white-painted wainscoting coordinates with the wallpaper to bring an outdoor, garden feel to this kitchen.

Different colors of wood paneling work well together here to divide the first and second floors. The use of the darker paneling below with the lighter cream above accents the spacious dimensions from floor to ceiling.

Surface Interest

prairie-stained

light-stained

W arm and elegant, wood paneling is a classic decorating option. Its cost can rival that of wallpaper as an economical wall treatment. If your walls are less than perfect, wood paneling is a good way to disguise pitted, peeling, and otherwise damaged surfaces. It acts as a natural sound and heat insulator, too.

Wood paneling made of boards is traditionally installed vertically but also can be installed horizontally, diagonally, and in interlocking herringbone patterns to lend visual interest to a room. The most common softwood paneling species is pine, which is relatively inexpensive and readily accepts a variety of stains and paints that give your paneling a new look. Rich dark stains work well in dens for a cozy effect. Create an outdoor feel with white or soft gray stains. Left "natural" and merely coated with protective clear varnish, light and lovely pine will make any room seem brighter and sunnier.

If money is no object, look into maple, walnut, redwood, and cedar paneling. These hardwoods are more durable than pine and have naturally richer tones. Aromatic cedar gives off a spicy scent that repels moths and makes it particularly useful for paneling closets. Wood from salvage yards is often a good source for paneling. Using recycled board not only helps protect new- and

light-stained birch

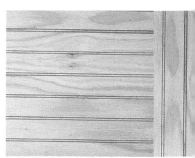
clear-stained

honey-stained

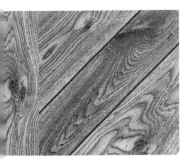

old-growth forests, but also ensures that the wood you choose will be full of historic character from use in old barns and other structures.

Handsome plywood paneling can bring the warmth of wood to a room for a much lower cost than solid-wood boards. Plywood panels come in large 4-by-8-foot and 4-by-10-foot boards, which makes them a snap to install. If your walls are in good shape you can attach the paneling directly to them; you'll need only paneling adhesive and special nails colored to match the finish. Damaged walls need a grid of furring strips to provide a base for the paneling. The finest—and most expensive—plywood paneling consists of real-wood veneers bonded to plywood and protected with a clear finish. Veneered-wood panels provide the beauty of redwood, maple, birch, teak, redwood, and other species at a fraction of the cost of solid wood.

Another wood paneling choice is wainscoting, which covers the lower third to bottom half of a wall. Wainscoting consisting of vertically installed solid-wood boards lends a charming country look to a room; more formal wainscoting made of standard dimensional lumber trimmed with inset molding is right at home in a traditional decorating scheme.

Panels of Wood Veneer

Nothing brings the warmth of wood to a room as quickly as paneling for the walls. Sheet paneling, whose installation is shown on the following pages, is far less costly than solid-wood boards *(page 204)* and easier to install.

Paneling comes in 4- by 8-foot sheets from $\frac{5}{32}$ inch to $\frac{1}{4}$ inch thick. It may be surfaced with real wood veneer or, at less expense and some loss of ambience, with simulated woodgrain printed on paper or vinyl *(chart below)*. Most styles have a vertical groove pattern, giving the appearance of individual boards.

Before You Start: To estimate how many panels you need for a room with 8-foot ceilings, measure the width of the walls in feet and divide by 4. Store the panels for 48 hours in the room where they will be used, stacked one atop another with small wood blocks between them. Remove any floor and ceiling molding in the room, as well as wall-mounted light fixtures and cover plates for outlets and switches.

Cutting and Securing the Sheets: Mark paneling on the back for trimming. To make a long, straight cut, use a circular saw; a saber saw is best for curved and short, straight cuts. Buy blades suitable for paneling: a plywood blade with 6 teeth per inch (TPI) for a circular saw, a blade with 10 TPI for a saber saw.

Paneling is best attached directly to existing wallboard or plaster if the wall is free of valleys deeper than $\frac{1}{4}$ inch. As a starting point, choose a corner of the room that allows paneling and wallboard joints to be staggered. Fasten panels to the wall first with panel adhesive—one 11-ounce tube for every three panels. Follow with paneling nails colored to match the finish and long enough to reach the studs in the wall.

To smooth out an uneven wall—or if working over a masonry wall—build a framework of furring strips *(pages 124-131)*. When paneling is attached to furring strips or to exposed studs in fire-prone areas such as halls, stairways, kitchens, and utility rooms, many fire codes require a layer of $\frac{1}{2}$-inch wallboard under the paneling.

 TOOLS

Electronic stud finder	Saber saw
Chalk line	Caulking gun
Carpenter's level (4')	Nail set
Tape measure	Block plane
Straight scrap wood	Plumb bob
Circular saw	Electric drill
	Hole saw

 MATERIALS

Scrap plywood	Wood blocks (8")
C-clamps	Paint thinner
Panel adhesive	Parting bead ($\frac{1}{4}$")
Shims	Chalk
Paneling nails ($1\frac{5}{8}$")	

1 x 2 strips
Wood glue
Hinges
Doorknob
Catch

 **SAFETY TIPS**

Protect your eyes with goggles when hammering, drilling, or cutting with a power saw. Ventilate the room when applying paneling adhesive.

TYPES OF SHEET PANELING

Panel	Composition	Pros and Cons
Simulated pattern on hardboard	Heated and compressed wood fiber covered with paper- or wood-printed finish; $\frac{5}{32}$ or $\frac{3}{16}$ inch thick.	Great variety of styles; dulls saw blades quickly.
Simulated pattern on plywood	Plywood covered with a paper-, vinyl- or wood-printed finish; $\frac{5}{32}$ or $\frac{3}{16}$ inch thick.	Stronger and more flexible than hardboard; can be bent to fit curved walls; less costly than real wood veneer, but often thinner and less solid.
Wood veneer on plywood	Real wood veneer over a plywood backing; veneer can be hardwood or softwood; usually $\frac{1}{4}$ inch thick.	Texture and patina of real wood; best resistance to moisture, sound, and impact; each panel unique; more expensive than printed panels.

FITTING AND CUTTING PANELS

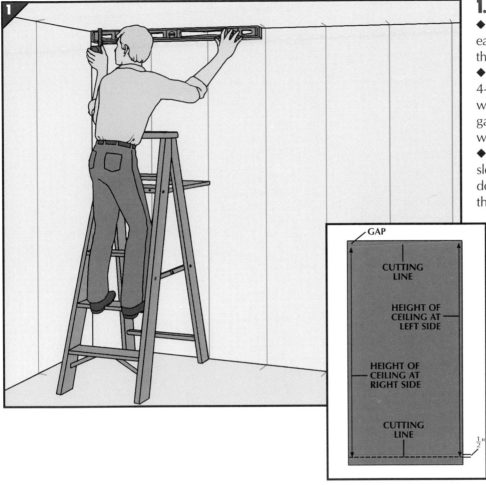

1. Establishing cutting lines.

◆ Locate studs *(page 326)* and mark each center with a chalk line. Extend the lines onto the ceiling and floor.

◆ At the corner of the room, position a 4-foot level horizontally against the wall, touching the ceiling. Measure any gap between the level and the ceiling where the gap is widest *(left)*.

◆ To mark a cutting line to match a sloping ceiling, turn the panel face-down. If the ceiling slants downward to the right as shown, mark the left edge of the panel with the width of the gap; otherwise mark the right edge. Draw a line from that point across the top of the panel to the opposite corner *(inset)*.

◆ Measure the distance from floor to ceiling at the corner of the room and 4 feet away from the corner.

◆ Subtract $\frac{1}{2}$ inch from both measurements and mark the distances on the sides of the panel, measuring from the top cutting line—or from the top edge of the panel if the ceiling is level.

◆ Draw a cutting line *(blue)* between the marks.

GAP

CUTTING LINE

HEIGHT OF CEILING AT LEFT SIDE

HEIGHT OF CEILING AT RIGHT SIDE

CUTTING LINE

$\frac{1}{2}$"

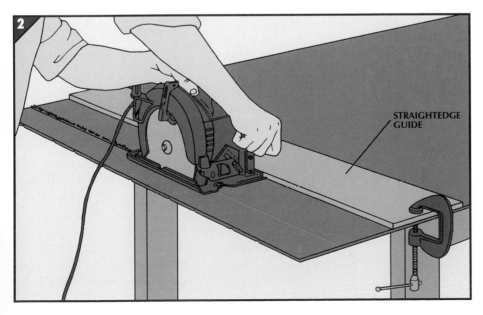

STRAIGHTEDGE GUIDE

2. Sawing the panels.

◆ Clamp a guide—the factory-cut edge of a sheet of plywood works well—to a scrap piece of wood, and make a short cut. Measure the distance from the guide to the cut.

◆ Use this measurement to position the guide parallel to the bottom cutting line. Clamp the guide securely and trim the panel *(left)*.

◆ Trim the top of the panel as marked to match the ceiling slope.

3. Applying panel adhesive.

◆ Spread adhesive in a continuous $\frac{1}{8}$-inch-wide serpentine bead on the wall surfaces that will underlie panel edges.

◆ Apply a similar bead of adhesive along the chalked lines marking the studs behind the panel *(left)*.

When fastening panels to studs or furring strips, apply adhesive where panel edges will fall as described above, but on intermediate studs or furring strips, apply the adhesive in 3-inch-long beads 6 inches apart.

4. Plumbing the first panel.

◆ Press the panel lightly against the adhesive, and wedge shims beneath it to lift it $\frac{1}{4}$ inch off the floor.

◆ Check that the panel is plumb with a 4-foot level held against the panel edge. Adjust the shims as needed to make the edge vertical.

◆ Secure the panel along the top edge with four $1\frac{5}{8}$-inch-long paneling nails. You may need longer nails if fastening through plaster and lath.

⚠ **CAUTION** *For a satisfactory paneling job, plumb this first panel precisely. If the grooves are not vertical, they will converge at corners, making it necessary to remove the paneling and start over with new panels.*

5. Securing the panel.

◆ Press the panel against the wall to compress the adhesive. If the adhesive manufacturer requires it, pull out the bottom of the panel and insert an 8-inch wood block at each end, between the panel and the wall *(left)*. Let the adhesive dry according to the manufacturer's recommendation, then remove the blocks and push the panel against the wall again, tapping it with your fist to make a tight seal.

◆ With a rag dipped in paint thinner, wipe away any adhesive on the finished face of the panel.

◆ Nail the edges of the panel to the wall, spacing the nails 1 foot apart, then nail along the intermediate studs or furring strips at 2-foot intervals, placing the nails either in the grooves or $\frac{1}{8}$ inch from their edges.

◆ Set all paneling nails with a nail set.

WOOD BLOCK

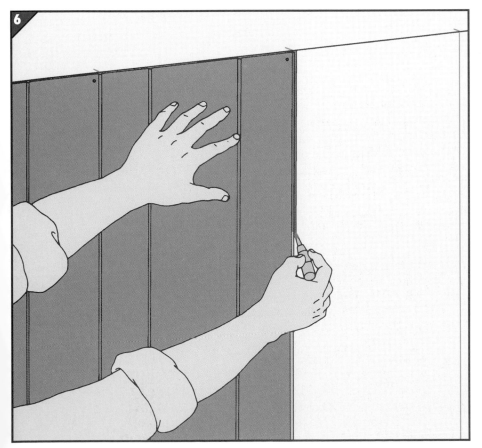

6. Setting adjoining panels.

◆ Stain the edge of the panel and the wall with a felt-tip pen the color of the grooves. Doing so keeps the joint between panels inconspicuous, even if the panels shrink.

◆ Tap paneling nails into the wall at the edge of the panel, top and bottom, to serve as spacers between panels.

◆ Install the next panel the same way as the first. To plumb it, butt it against the spacer nails, then remove them.

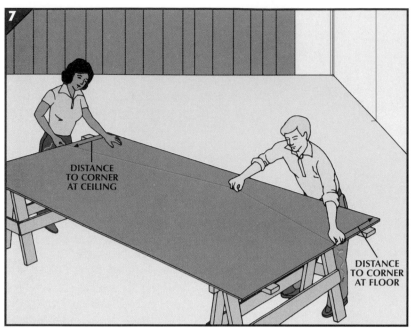

DISTANCE TO CORNER AT CEILING

DISTANCE TO CORNER AT FLOOR

7. Fitting a panel to a corner.

◆ Cut the corner panel to the proper height *(page 191, Steps 1-2)*.

◆ Measure the distance from the corner of the room to the edge of the last panel installed, at both ceiling and floor. Mark these distances on the back of the corner panel so that the factory-cut edge will fall against the panel already in place.

◆ Snap a chalk line between the two marks *(left)* and cut along the line with a circular saw. Save the waste piece for possible use in another corner.

◆ Install the panel as you would a full-width panel, shaving the cut edge, if necessary, with a block plane for a perfect fit.

◆ Continue to panel around the corner by installing the first panel of the next wall as in Steps 1 through 5, using a level to plumb the panel. If this wall is less than the width of one panel, place the trimmed edge in the corner so you can use the factory-cut edge to plumb it.

PLOTTING CURVES FOR ROUNDED WINDOWS

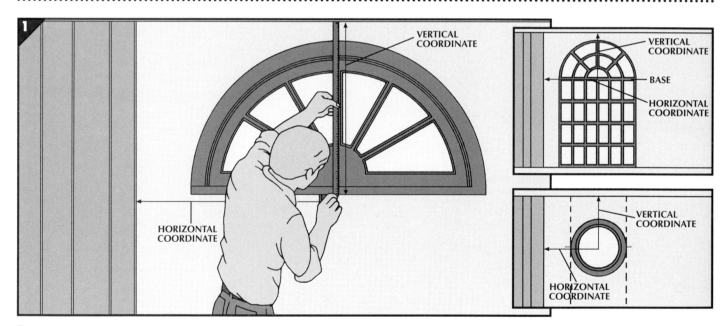

VERTICAL COORDINATE

HORIZONTAL COORDINATE

VERTICAL COORDINATE

BASE

HORIZONTAL COORDINATE

VERTICAL COORDINATE

HORIZONTAL COORDINATE

1. Locating the center.

◆ Trim the panel *(page 191, Steps 1-2)*.

◆ Remove any window moldings and mark the midpoint of the base of the semicircular window.

◆ Measure the distance from the ceiling to the midpoint of the base *(above)*. Subtract $\frac{1}{4}$ inch for the clearance at the top of the panel.

◆ Measure from the center of the base to the edge of the last panel installed.

◆ Using these two distances as vertical and horizontal coordinates, plot the center of the semicircle's base on the back of the panel so that the mark coincides with the center of the base when the panel is turned faceup.

If the semicircle is an arch framing the top of a door or window *(inset, top)*, use the top of the rectangular section of windows as the base of the semicircle in the method described above.

For a circular window *(inset, bottom)*, mark one side of the window where a plumb bob from the ceiling just touches the frame, then mark the other side of the window in the same way. Measure the width of the window at these points and halve it to find the center of the window. From the center, find the vertical and horizontal coordinates as above and plot the center of the circle on the back of the trimmed panel.

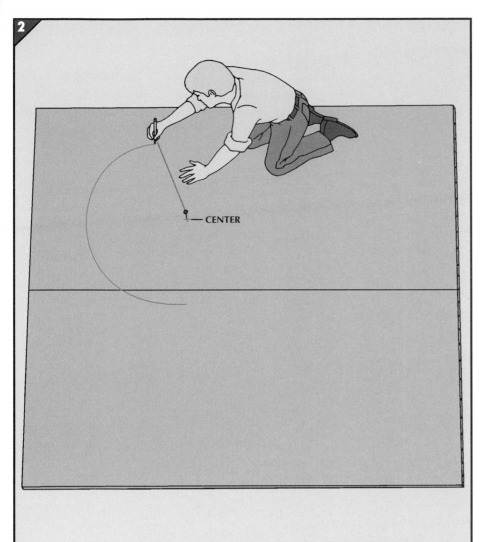

CENTER

2. Drawing the curve.

◆ Tack a small nail or brad at the center point plotted on the back of the panel, taking care that the nail does not pierce the front of the panel.

◆ Tie one end of a string to the brad and attach a pencil to the other so the distance between the brad and the pencil point equals half the width of the base—plus $\frac{1}{4}$ inch for ease of fitting.

◆ Swing the pencil in an arc to draw the curve of the window frame. If the window falls at the joint between two panels, lay them facedown and side by side, reversed left to right from the order in which you will install them *(left)*.

◆ Draw any straight portions of the window outline, then cut out the opening and mount the panels.

◆ Before replacing window molding, cut a thin strip of $\frac{1}{4}$-inch parting bead and tack it to the edge of the window frame to serve as filler under the molding edge.

PANELING ODDLY SHAPED OPENINGS

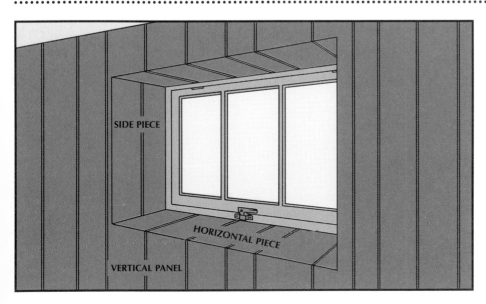

SIDE PIECE

HORIZONTAL PIECE

VERTICAL PANEL

Making grooves turn a corner.

◆ When paneling a corner with horizontal surfaces, as found at a recessed window *(left)*, first cut paneling for the horizontal surfaces. If the opening falls within a single vertical panel, use the waste piece cut from it; vertical and horizontal grooves will align automatically. For an opening at a joint between panels, take care in trimming horizontal pieces so that grooves align. Install the horizontal pieces.

◆ Measure the sides of the window recess, cut waste pieces of paneling to fit, and install them.

◆ For a finished look, trim the opening with outside corner molding.

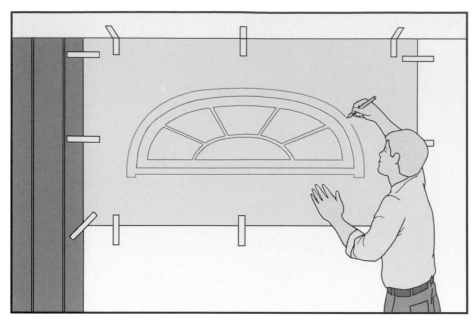

A pattern for an irregular shape.
◆ Tape paper over the opening, butting the sheet against the last panel installed and the ceiling. Outline the shape with a pencil (left).
◆ Remove the paper, then cut out the shape with scissors and discard it.
◆ Turn the resulting pattern over and place it on the back of a trimmed panel. Align the side of the paper with the appropriate panel edge and the top of the paper $\frac{1}{4}$ inch below the panel's top edge to account for the space between the panel bottom and the floor.
◆ Mark the outline on the panel, then cut out the shape $\frac{1}{4}$ inch outside the line for ease of fitting.
◆ Install the panel.

ACCOMMODATING AN ELECTRICAL BOX

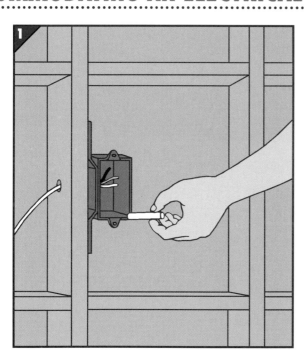

1. Chalking the edges.
To mark the location of an electrical box on paneling for a new wall, as in a false wall built over masonry (pages 128-129), rub the front edge of the box, which typically protrudes beyond the studs, with a piece of chalk.

2. Transferring the shape.
Set the trimmed panel in its exact position over the box, and strike the face of the panel with a padded wood block to transfer the chalked outline onto the back of the panel. If the outline is not completely clear, use a spare electrical box as a pattern to fill in the missing sections with a pencil.

If paneling directly over an existing wall, a protruding switch or receptacle will prevent you from using the edges of the electrical box to mark the panel. Instead, plot the location of the box with coordinates, as described on page 134, and use a $\frac{1}{4}$-inch box extender (page 131) to make it flush with the paneling.

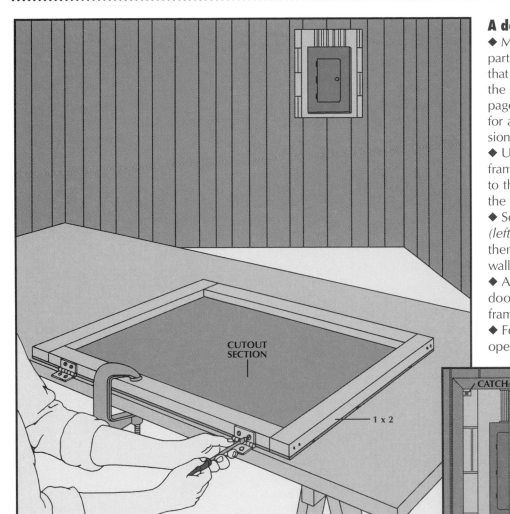

A door for a service panel.
◆ Measure the distances between the parts of the false wall *(page 129, inset)* that frame the service panel and use the system of coordinates shown on page 134 to mark the back of a panel for an opening of the same dimensions. Cut out the opening.
◆ Use the cutout section for a door, framing it with 1-by-2 strips glued to the back and screwed together at the corners.
◆ Screw hinges to one door edge *(left)*, set the door into the opening, then screw the hinges to the false-wall framing.
◆ Attach a knob to the front of the door, and a catch to the back and to a framing stud.
◆ For a more finished look, frame the opening with mitered molding *(inset)*.

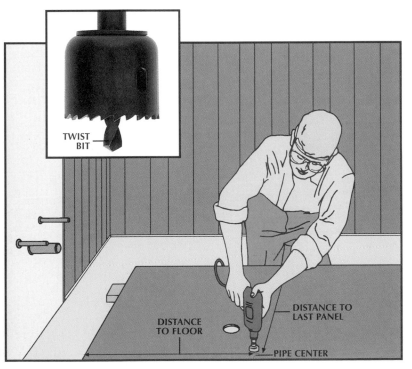

Perfect holes for protruding pipes.
◆ Establish the center of each pipe using the method for finding the center of a circular window *(page 194)*.
◆ Determine the vertical and horizontal coordinates, then transfer them to the back of a trimmed panel. Indent the points that represent the centers of the pipes.
◆ Cut a hole for each pipe, using a hole saw *(photograph)* $\frac{1}{2}$ inch larger than the pipe diameter. Drill only until the twist bit of the saw breaks through the face of the panel.
◆ Remove the saw, turn the panel over, and finish cutting the hole from the face side to avoid splintering it.

Not all walls are rectangular or 8 feet tall, and some have irregular edges or other unusual features. For such situations, you will need to cut panels in special ways.

Stairs: On stairway walls, you must trim the panels to match the diagonal of the stringers—the boards that frame the steps. In many cases only one end of the panel is involved—the bottom edge above the stringer or the top edge below the staircase. But if the stairwell has a slanted ceiling, both the top and the bottom of the panel must be angled. On a finished wall, you must transfer the stringer angle to the panel *(below and opposite, top)*.

High Walls: When a wall is taller than your panels you have several options. You can special-order extra-tall panels, or you can leave a gap along the bottom of the paneling and cover the gap with baseboard, but this extends the paneling only a few inches.

A third option is to put up panels one atop the other until they reach the ceiling. They can be stacked vertically, horizontally, or in a herringbone pattern *(page 201)*. This zigzag design will extend the height 6 inches, but the assembled pieces will be 34 inches wide instead of 48.

A herringbone wall looks best when all the panels are the same width. Divide the wall into equal sections of 34 inches or less and trim panel pieces to that width. Since the edges no longer fall at studs, panels or furring strips *(pages 125-128)* must be attached to walls using the technique in Step 2 on page 217.

 TOOLS

Tape measure
Framing square
Chalk line
Plumb line

Scriber or compass
Coping saw
Long, straight board

 **MATERIALS**

Wood paneling
Cap molding
Flat molding

 SAFETY TIPS

Goggles and earplugs will guard your eyes and ears while you are running a power saw. Wear goggles when hammering nails as well.

SHAPING PANELS TO A STAIRCASE

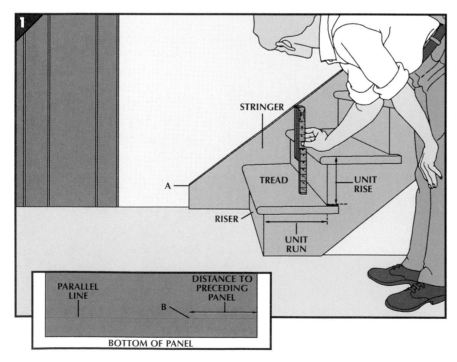

1. Finding the stringer angle.

◆ Measure the unit rise—the distance from the top of one tread to the top of the next.
◆ Find the unit run—the distance between the front of one riser to the front of the next.
◆ From the point where the stringer begins to slope upward (A), measure both to the floor and to the edge of the panel most recently installed.
◆ Transfer these dimensions to the back of the panel to be installed at the bottom of the stairway *(inset)*. The point where they intersect (B) corresponds to A.
◆ Draw a line through B, parallel to the bottom of the panel across its entire width.

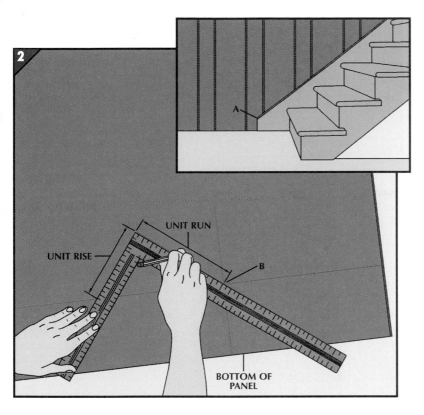

2. Marking the angle.

◆ Place a framing square on the back of the panel as shown at left, with one leg passing through B.

◆ Adjust the square so that the unit-run measurement, read on the outer scale of the square, rests at B while the unit-rise measurement intersects the line drawn parallel to the bottom of the panel.

◆ Draw the unit run on the back of the panel, then extend this line—which corresponds to the top edge of the stringer—across the panel.

◆ Place the remaining panels to be installed face-down alongside the first one, top edge and bottom edges even.

◆ Use a chalk line to continue the slanted line across the panels until it crosses the top edge of a panel.

◆ Cut the panels along this line (page 191) and along the line that runs from B to the bottom of the first panel.

◆ Install the panels (inset) as shown on page 192. Where the top edges do not abut the ceiling, conceal the gaps with cap molding (page 203, top).

CONTOURING AROUND AN IRREGULAR SHAPE

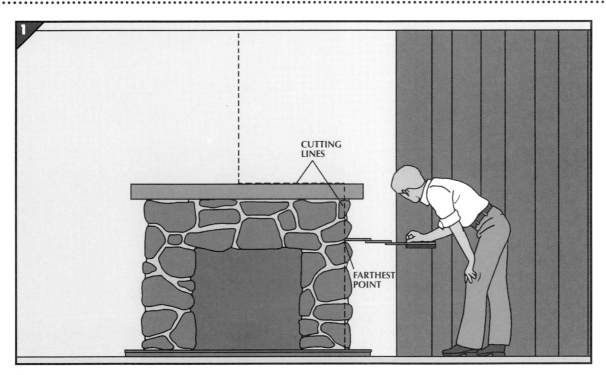

1. Measuring for a fireplace cutout.

◆ Install paneling, as shown on pages 190-193, to within 4 feet of the irregular edge of the fireplace.

◆ For a vertical cutting line at the corner of the panel that will meet the fireplace, measure the distance from the panel last installed to the farthest point on the fireplace edge (above) and mark the back of the panel accordingly.

◆ For a horizontal cutting line, measure from the ceiling to the mantel top, subtracting $\frac{1}{4}$ inch for clearance at the ceiling line and taking into consideration any ceiling irregularities (page 191, top, inset). Mark this distance on the panel, measuring from the top.

◆ Cut out the waste rectangle defined by the vertical and horizontal lines.

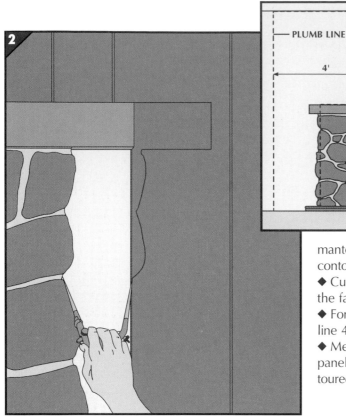

2. Scribing the panel.

◆ Set the newly cut panel against the end of the mantel, keeping the grooves plumb.

◆ Open a scriber or compass to span the distance between the panel edge and the point on the fireplace farthest from it, identified in Step 1. For best results, use a scriber or compass having a clamp to hold the setting.

◆ Starting at the top corner of the mantel and keeping the legs of the compass horizontal, transfer the contour of the fireplace edge onto the panel (left).

◆ Cut out the fireplace shape with a coping saw to avoid splintering the face of the panel, then fit the panel to the fireplace.

◆ For the other side of the fireplace, have a helper hold a plumb line 4 feet from the edge of the panel you just installed (inset).

◆ Measure from the plumb line to the most distant point on the un-paneled edge of the fireplace, then mark and cut a second contoured panel as you did the first.

STACKING PANELS FOR EXTRA HEIGHT

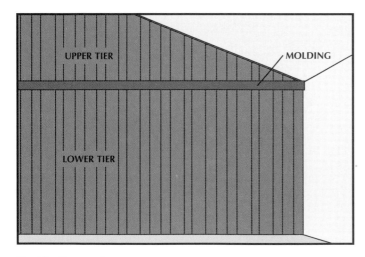

Vertical panels.

To cover a wall up to a high ceiling, install panels vertically in two tiers—the first extending from the floor up 8 feet, the second butted against the first and continuing to the ceiling. Make sure the grooves of both tiers are aligned. Cover the horizontal joint between tiers with flat molding.

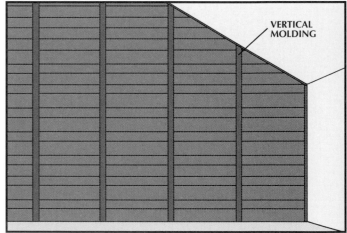

Horizontal panels.

A second way to cover a wall up to a high ceiling is to stack panels horizontally, aligning the grooves of abutting panels. Cover the vertical joints with flat molding. As shown here, additional molding strips reestablish a vertical orientation for the paneling by interrupting the strong horizontal pattern of grooves.

A HERRINGBONE PATTERN FROM VERTICAL GROOVES

1. Marking the panels.

◆ On the back of a panel, mark the midpoint of both sides.

◆ Draw a cutting line from each midpoint to the diagonally opposite corner using a straight board.

◆ From the midpoint of each diagonal line, draw a second cutting line to the nearest corner.

◆ Label the panel edges SIDE A and SIDE B as shown at right.

◆ Similarly mark a second panel, but reverse the direction of the diagonals and label the sides C and D.

◆ Cut both panels facedown with a circular saw guided by a straight board, and discard the top and bottom triangles as waste *(inset)*.

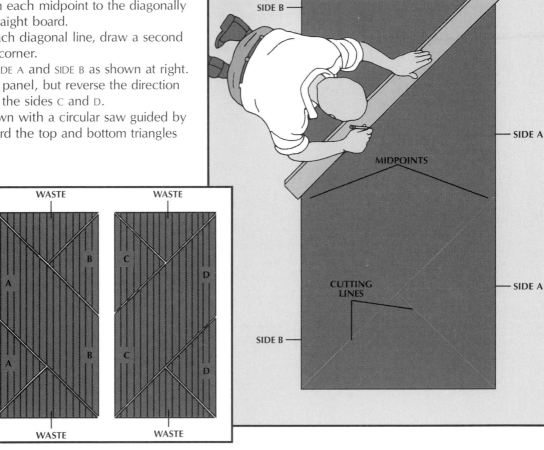

2. Fitting the pieces.

◆ Lay the pieces flat on the floor, butting together two A sides to form the top of a new rectangle and two B sides to form the bottom.

◆ Repeat this procedure for the C and D sides to form the adjoining rectangle, with the grooves running in the opposite direction.

◆ Using the measurements you obtained from dividing the wall into equal sections, mark the assembled panels to that width and cut them at the marks.

◆ Attach the first two sections of paneling to the wall, then cut and install subsequent sections, aligning the grooves to form a continuous herringbone pattern.

Moldings to Hide Edges

When panels are installed professionally, every exposed edge except the inconspicuous vertical joint between panels is covered by a molding. Typically the moldings hide gaps or unfinished edges at the floor *(right)*, ceiling, corners, and tops of paneling that extends only partway up a wall *(opposite)*. As a bonus, moldings speed installation by making precise measuring, scribing, and cutting less essential.

Fine Points of Nailing: To fasten panel moldings, use the same colored paneling nails that are supplied by the manufacturer for fastening the panels. Space the nails at 16-inch intervals, starting at a stud or furring strip, and drive the nailheads below the surface with a nail set.

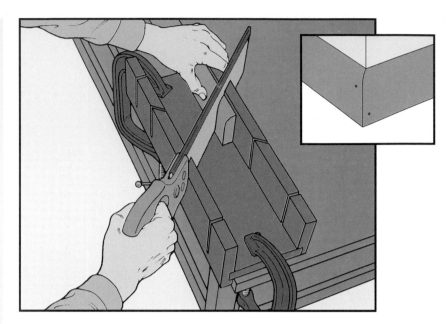

Mitering an outside corner.

◆ Miter both pieces of molding outward at a 45-degree angle, making the front face of the molding longer than the back face.

◆ Test-fit the pieces. If the joint has a gap at the front, sand the back edges of the boards to make them meet satisfactorily. For a gap at the back of the joint, sand the front edges.

◆ Drive a finishing nail through each side of the corner to pull the joint tight *(inset)*.

TOOLS

Coping saw	Sanding block
Backsaw	Hammer
Miter box	Nail set
	T bevel

SAFETY TIPS

Goggles protect your eyes when you are driving nails into molding or paneling.

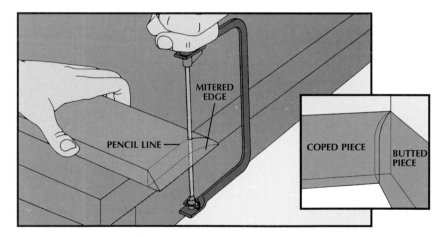

PENCIL LINE

MITERED EDGE

COPED PIECE   BUTTED PIECE

Dealing with an inside corner.

A coped joint permits molding to expand and contract with changes in temperature and humidity without opening a gap where molding pieces meet.

◆ Make a square cut at the end of one piece of molding for a corner. Butt it against the corner and nail it in place.

◆ Miter the end of the other piece at a 45-degree angle, cutting it so that the back face is longer than the front.

◆ With a pencil, highlight the curved edge of the miter cut, then cut along the curve with a coping saw. For a snug fit, angle the blade to back-cut the piece a few degrees, making the front face slightly longer than the back.

◆ Push the shaped end against the face of the butted molding already on the wall *(inset)* and nail in place.

Molding at the ceiling.

◆ To cut cove molding for ceiling corners, place the pieces upside down in the rear corner of a miter box.

◆ For an outside corner, position the left-hand molding to the right of the 45-degree cutting slot that angles the saw to the left, and make the cut as shown here. Place the right-hand piece to the left of the slot that angles the blade to the right.

◆ Test-fit the joint at the corner with the pieces placed correctly between wall and ceiling *(inset),* and adjust for gaps as described *(opposite).*

When coping an inside corner *(opposite),* angle the saw to the right when mitering a left-hand piece, to the left for a right-hand piece. Slant the coping saw for a 30-degree back cut.

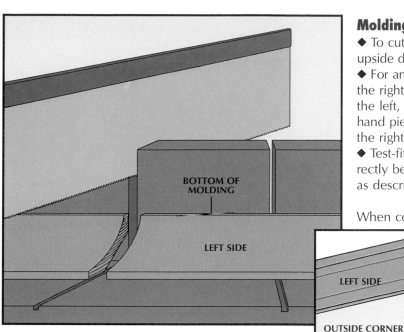

BOTTOM OF MOLDING

LEFT SIDE

LEFT SIDE

OUTSIDE CORNER

Hiding corner joints.

◆ Cut corner molding to fit snugly between baseboard and ceiling molding, At an inside corner, use concave molding; outside corners require convex molding.

◆ Fasten the molding to the wall, nailing concave molding in the center *(inset)* and convex molding through alternate sides.

INSIDE CORNER MOLDING

OUTSIDE CORNER MOLDING

Cap molding for panel edges.

Cover the top edges of panels that end partway up the wall with cap molding.

◆ Fit the molding's lip over the top edges of the panels, then nail it through the paneling and into the wall.

◆ Set a T bevel *(photograph)* to the angle where the cap molding meets a stairway, then transfer that angle to the molding and cut it.

◆ At an outside corner, miter the molding; at an inside corner, use the coping technique shown on page 225.

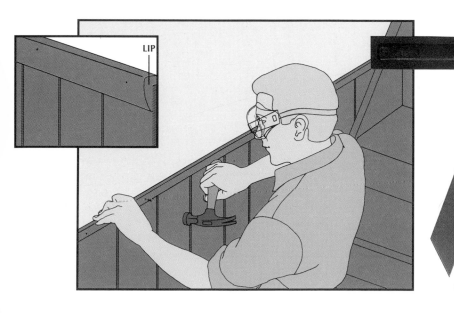

LIP

Solid-wood paneling can bring formal elegance or rustic warmth to a room, depending on the choice of wood (such as rich mahogany or casual pine), the grade—which indicates the degree of knottiness—surface texture (smooth or rough-sawn), and pattern *(below)*.

Buying Panels: Calculating amounts depends on installation pattern, average width of boards, and in some cases whether they are hard- or softwood. Ask a lumber dealer for help.

Preparing for Installation: So the boards will adjust to the temperature and humidity of the room to be paneled, store them there for at least 2 days before you start installation. To reduce warping, stack the boards in layers separated by scrap wood strips. If staining later, stain tongues or overlapped edges before installation.

While the boards acclimate, prepare the wall with furring strips unless you are using a diagonal pattern *(page 210)*. Horizontal strips *(page 206)* are adequate for vertical (and diagonal) installation; furring for a herringbone pattern is shown on page 214. Attach the furring strips using the techniques on pages 124 to 128, but leave a $\frac{3}{4}$-inch space all around the opening for a door or window.

Adding Trim: After installing all the wall panels, add jamb extensions *(page 131, Step 2)* for the door and window trim. Cut trim strips from the same wood as the paneling and miter the corners to form a simple frame. Elsewhere, molding is optional, but base, ceiling, and corner molding can accent the room and cover inconsistencies in measuring and cutting *(pages 202-203)*.

 TOOLS

Tape measure	Nail set
Carpenter's level	Electric drill
Torpedo level	Saber saw
Scriber	Circular saw
Block plane	Chalk line
Hammer	Steel square
	Combination square
	Paintbrush

 MATERIALS

Solid-wood paneling	Finishing nails (2")
1 x 4 furring strips	Wood glue
1 x 2 battens	Brads
Common nails ($3\frac{1}{4}$")	Wood filler
	Wood stain
	Polyurethane finish
	Construction adhesive

CHOOSING PATTERNS AND EDGES

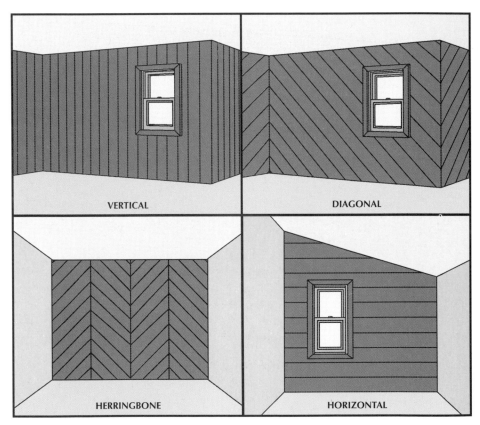

VERTICAL

DIAGONAL

HERRINGBONE

HORIZONTAL

Patterns for every purpose.
Installing boards vertically is most versatile. Smooth, polished woods and elaborate trim give a traditional, formal look. Choose rougher woods and a minimum of trim for a contemporary look.

Diagonal and herringbone patterns are best in a modern setting and on walls with few doors or windows. Diagonal boards on adjoining walls can be placed for a chevron effect as shown here or to continue the same slope.

Horizontal paneling reduces apparent ceiling height. Stagger the joints in each course to avoid unsightly vertical seams.

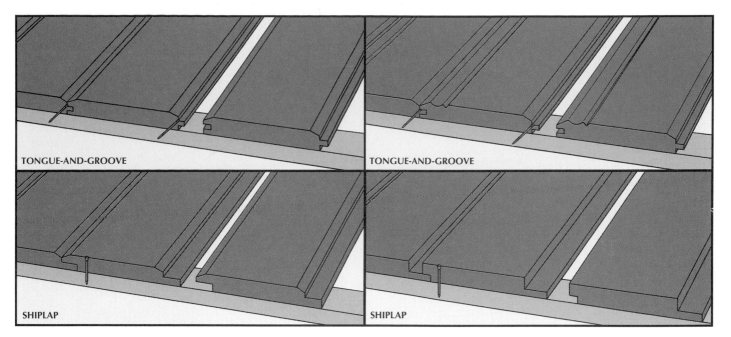

TONGUE-AND-GROOVE

TONGUE-AND-GROOVE

SHIPLAP

SHIPLAP

Milled edges for tight joints.

Solid-wood paneling has characteristic overlapping edges to prevent gaps between boards as they contract with atmospheric changes. A single row of nails per board keeps forces of expansion from loosening the boards.

Tongue-and-groove boards are easy to install in any pattern. Edges can be milled to create V-shaped seams between boards *(top left)* or more elaborate joints *(top right)*. The boards are blind-nailed to furring strips through the base of the tongue; nails are hidden by the next board.

Shiplap boards, which simply overlap each other, are best suited to vertical or horizontal patterns. The boards typically come beveled to form V-shaped seams *(bottom left)* or come with square edges *(bottom right),* which produce a gapped joint. Shiplap boards are nailed through the face.

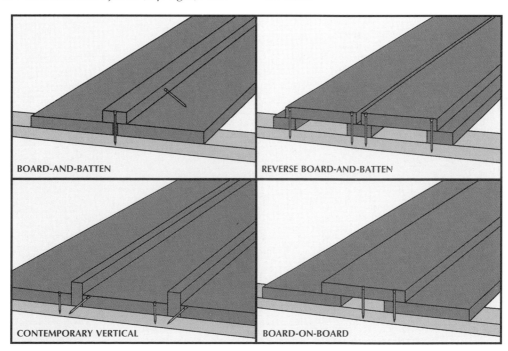

BOARD-AND-BATTEN

REVERSE BOARD-AND-BATTEN

CONTEMPORARY VERTICAL

BOARD-ON-BOARD

Edges for a modern look.

Straight-edged boards and battens installed vertically or horizontally produce a casual, contemporary effect.

Board-and-batten and reverse board-and-batten patterns are made of wide boards set about $\frac{1}{2}$ inch apart with a narrower batten—generally a 1-by-2—nailed either over or under the gap. The contemporary-vertical pattern uses battens set on edge between the wider boards.

Board-on-board paneling is similar to board-and-batten, except all the boards are the same width and the gap between boards in the first layer is about half the width of the boards.

With any of these patterns, when face-nailing is necessary, forestall splitting by blunting the nails and placing them as far as possible from board edges.

CLASSIC VERTICAL PANELING

1. Planning the layout.

To avoid a narrow strip as the last board on a wall, proceed as follows:

◆ After attaching furring strips to the walls, measure the length of the wall between corners formed by the strips *(left);* if the wall has an outside corner, add $\frac{3}{4}$ inch. Divide this measurement by the width of a board measured from the top of the groove on one edge to the base of the tongue on the other.

◆ If the result ends in a fraction smaller than $\frac{1}{2}$, begin paneling the wall with a board cut in half lengthwise.

TRICKS OF THE TRADE

Easy Scriber

A carpenter's pencil can act as a scriber in an uneven corner. Stand a panel board in the corner, against the adjoining furring strip. Use a level to move the board into a plumb position, then press one side of the carpenter's pencil against the furring strip, and run the lead carefully down the board to mark it for trimming *(below).*

2. Starting off plumb.

◆ Measure the starting corner from floor to ceiling and use a circular saw to cut a board to that length.

◆ Stand the board in the corner as shown at left, with the grooved edge abutting the furring strip on the adjoining wall, and check for plumb with a carpenter's level.

◆ If the grooved edge does not fit uniformly against the strip—and if the gap will not be covered by the edge of a panel board or corner mold-

ing—scribe the board to match the corner. Use the technique on page 200, Step 2, or a carpenter's pencil *(above).* Trim the edge to the mark with a block plane.

If you install the first board at an outside corner, where the adjoining wall will not be paneled, trim $\frac{1}{2}$ inch from the grooved edge of the board and place that cut edge plumb and flush with the corner. Plane as necessary for a precise fit.

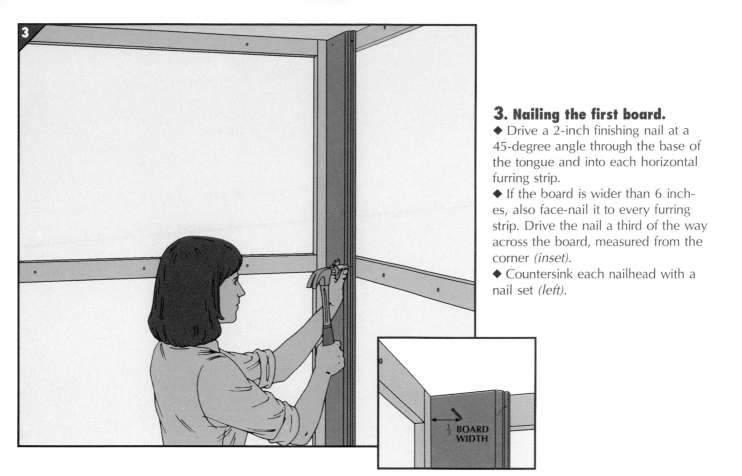

3. Nailing the first board.

◆ Drive a 2-inch finishing nail at a 45-degree angle through the base of the tongue and into each horizontal furring strip.

◆ If the board is wider than 6 inches, also face-nail it to every furring strip. Drive the nail a third of the way across the board, measured from the corner *(inset)*.

◆ Countersink each nailhead with a nail set *(left)*.

BOARD WIDTH

4. Fitting individual boards.

◆ To adjust each paneling board to slight variations in ceiling height, cut a piece of scrap lumber 3 inches shorter than the average ceiling height to use as a measuring template.

◆ Place the template where the next board will go, rest it on the floor, and measure from the top of the template to the ceiling *(above, left)*.

◆ Lay the template on the board to be cut, bottom ends flush, and transfer this measurement to it *(above, right)*.

◆ Cut the board at this point and slide it into place on the wall, grooved edge over the tongue of the previous board.

5. Locking the joints.

◆ To tighten the joint between two boards, cut a scrap of paneling about a foot long and use it as a hammering block.

◆ Slip its groove over the tongue of the outer board and gently tap the edge of the block until the joint is tight *(right)*. Then move the block along the board, closing the entire joint.

◆ Check the board for plumb, re-adjusting the joint at top or bottom if necessary, and nail the board in place.

6. Paneling around an opening.

◆ When you reach an opening such as a window, tap a full-length board in place.

◆ Mark the horizontal furring strips at the top and bottom of the opening where the tip of the board's tongue crosses them.

◆ Reach behind the board and mark the back along the inside edge of the same strips *(left)*. Then ease the board off the wall.

◆ Measure from the marks on the top and bottom furring strips to the inside edge of the vertical furring strip.

◆ With this measurement, mark a notch on the back of the board to fit around the window *(inset)*. Next, drill a $\frac{1}{4}$-inch hole in each corner of the notch to help a saber saw make the turn, and cut out the notch and install the board.

◆ Measure and cut paneling to fit above and below the opening.

◆ Finally, cut a board to fit the other side of the opening as above.

TOP STRIP
INSIDE EDGE
VERTICAL STRIP
BOTTOM STRIP

MAKING NEAT, TIGHT CORNERS

Mitering for an outside corner.

◆ Tap the corner board onto the tongue of the preceding board and mark the corner line on the back of the corner board *(right)*.

◆ Remove the board and clamp it facedown on two sawhorses with a straight 1-by-2 on top to guide a saw.

◆ Set the blade of a circular saw at a 45-degree angle and, with the blade pointing toward the tongue, cut along the corner line.

◆ Lock the board in place, with the beveled edge extending beyond the corner *(inset)*, and nail it to the furring strips.

◆ To miter the adjoining corner board, draw a guideline on the back of the board at the width determined by the procedure described in Step 1 on page 206, measured from the base of the tongue.

◆ Clamp the board facedown and cut along the line, with the saw blade angled toward the board's grooved edge.

◆ Before setting the board in place, spread wood glue on both beveled edges. Pin the boards together with brads, then

set the brads. Let the glue dry.

◆ If you do not plan to install corner molding, trim the sharp corner with a block plane to prevent chipping.

Fitting to an inside corner.

This technique is particularly helpful in a corner where no adjoining paneling or corner molding will cover the edge of the final board.

◆ Cut the final board exactly to width, scribing the cut edge, if necessary, to conform to the corner. Then use a block plane to bevel the corner edge about 5 degrees *(inset)*.

◆ After locking the next-to-last board in place, pull its tongue edge slightly away from the wall, slip on the grooved edge of the final board, and push both boards against the wall at once *(left)*.

◆ Nail the boards as shown in Step 3 on page 207.

DIAGONALS FOR DRAMATIC FLAIR

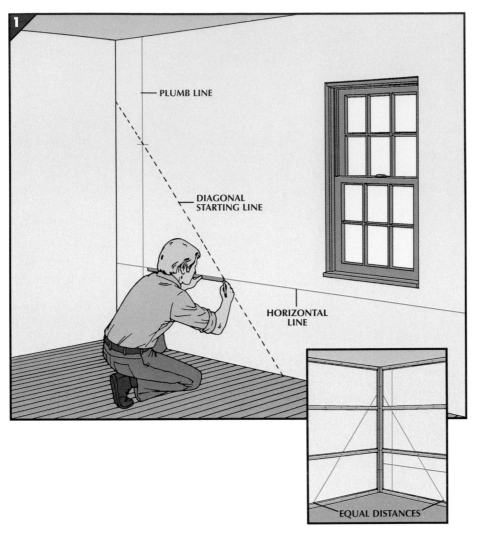

1. Laying out a 45-degree starting line.

Furring strips for a diagonal pattern are installed wall by wall, after each is marked with a diagonal starting line. Construct the line in the direction you want the boards to run, making sure it does not lap over a door or window.

◆ To begin, snap a plumb chalk line from ceiling to floor about 16 inches from the corner of the room, then snap a horizontal line across it about 2 feet from the floor.

◆ Mark each of the lines 3 feet from their intersection, and connect these points with a diagonal line. Extend the line to the corner and floor.

◆ Install furring strips on the wall *(page 204)*.

If the projected paneling reverses direction at a corner, forming an inverted V pattern, construct a second starting line based on the first.

◆ Measure from the corner to the bottom of the first starting line; then mark off this distance along the bottom of the adjoining wall.

◆ Snap a diagonal line between this mark and the top of the first starting line, then install furring strips *(inset)*.

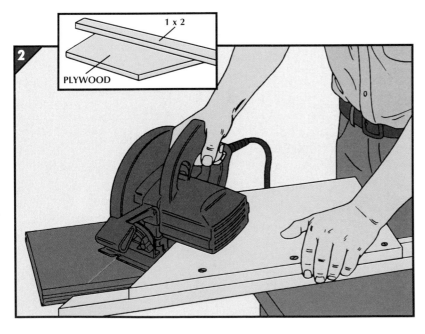

2. Cutting boards to fit.

Use a circular saw and a 45-degree jig that you can make from plywood and a 1-by-2 *(inset)* to miter each end of the board. Make sure that the miters match the surfaces that the board will abut—the floor, wall, ceiling, door, or window.

◆ To cut the first board, measure the length of the starting line.

◆ Transfer the measurement to the grooved edge of the board, then start the cuts at that edge *(left)*.

◆ To cut consecutive boards above the first, measure the length of the tongue edge on the previous board.

When more than one board length is needed for a long diagonal, cut the two board ends square. Apply glue and butt them together. Stagger these butted joints as you go up the wall so that they will not form a diagonal line across the wall.

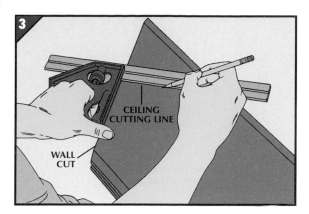

3. Measuring double-angle cuts.
◆ When the end of a board hits two surfaces perpendicular to each other—such as a wall and the ceiling *(below, middle board)*—first miter the end to fit against one of the surfaces (in this example, the wall).
◆ Measure how much of the wall corner remains to be covered by paneling, and mark off this distance on the mitered end, measuring from the grooved edge.
◆ Use a combination square to draw a perpendicular line from the mark to the tongue edge of the board *(left)*, and make the second cut—here, the ceiling cut—along that line.

4. Maintaining a 45-degree angle.
Check the angle of the first three boards after you position each one.
◆ Hold a steel square against the board, lining up the two 12-inch marks on the square with the tongue edge of the board.
◆ Now place a carpenter's level on the horizontal arm of the square and adjust the board until the arm is level.
◆ Nail the board in place.

TONGUE

5. Flanking an opening with a diagonal.
◆ Where a board overlaps the corner of the window or door opening, tap it in place and check its angle *(Step 4, above)*.
◆ Reach behind the board and mark the tongue edge at the inside edges of the furring strips that frame the corner.
◆ Remove the board, lay it facedown, and use a combination square to draw a 45-degree line across the board at each mark *(inset)*.
◆ Cut out the resulting triangle with a saber saw, then nail the board in place.

COMPOUND MITER

WASTE END

◆ Remove the board and then clamp it, facedown, across two sawhorses. Set the blade of a circular saw at a 45-degree angle.

◆ Using a diagonal jig to guide the saw, cut along the marked line with the blade pointing toward the waste end of the board. Doing so creates a compound miter—an edge that is both mitered and beveled.

◆ Tap the board in place, with the compound miter extending beyond the corner *(inset),* and nail it.

6. Fitting an outside corner.

◆ To install the first board that meets the corner of the wall, miter both ends and tap the board in place.

◆ At the bottom of the board, mark the part that extends beyond the corner by drawing a line across the back of the board *(above).*

On subsequent boards, miter the top but leave the bottom end temporarily unmitered. Tap the board in place, mark the part that extends beyond the corner, then cut a compound miter along this line. At the top of the wall, where the last board is simply a small triangle, use wood glue as well as nails to help anchor the board to the furring.

7. Trimming lower boards for fit.

◆ Working down from the starting board, miter the boards to fit, but here use the grooved edge of the previous board as a measure.

◆ Before installing a shorter board near the bottom corner, chisel off the backside of the grooved edge to facilitate fitting the next board.

◆ Check the angle and nail the board in place.

◆ Anchor the triangular board at the base of the wall with wood glue as well as nails.

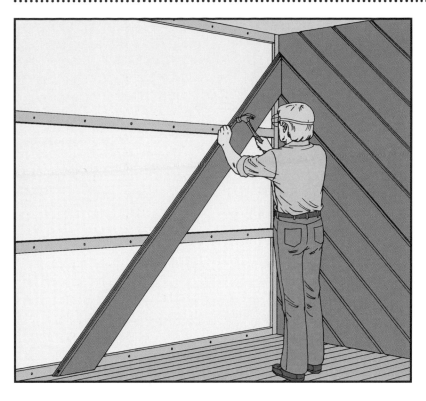

Turning an inside corner.
◆ Cut the first board for the second wall as in Step 2 on page 210, using the previously drawn starting line as a measure.
◆ Position the board so that it forms an inverted V with its mate.
◆ Cut and install succeeding boards, always taking care to match each board to its mate on the adjoining wall.

REFERENCE BOARD   EQUAL DISTANCES

WASTE END

Joining boards at an outside corner.
◆ Where a diagonal forms a V at an outside corner, choose a reference board on the paneled wall. Measure along the ceiling from the lower edge of the reference board to the corner of the room, and transfer the measurement to the adjacent wall. Then draw a starting line from that point to where the lower edge of the reference board meets the corner *(inset)*.
◆ Install furring strips on this wall.
◆ Miter the ceiling end of a panel board that is a little longer than the reference board.
◆ Butt the board against the ceiling, and line up the other end with its mate on the adjoining wall. Have a helper hold the board at the starting line but slightly away from the wall—to allow for the protruding miter of its mate—and mark a cutting line on the back of the board *(left)*. Transfer the cutting line to the front of the board.
◆ Clamp the board, faceup, across two sawhorses and set the circular saw at a 45-degree angle. Pointing the blade away from the waste end, use a diagonal jig to guide the saw one blade thickness outside the marked line to allow for trimming the final joint between the two boards.
◆ Once the joint fits, spread wood glue on the mitered end, and when the board is nailed in place, fasten the mitered ends together with brads.
◆ Mark, cut, and attach all the remaining boards as shown on pages 210 to 212.
◆ When all the boards are in place, use a block plane to smooth the sharp corner. You may omit this detail if you plan to install corner molding.

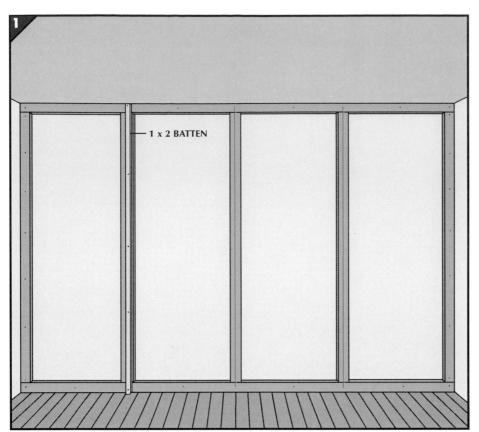

1. Installing the furring strips.

◆ With baseboard and ceiling molding removed, divide the wall vertically into equal parts, marking each division with a plumb chalk line.

◆ Frame the perimeter of the wall with 1-by-4 furring strips, then center and nail a furring strip over each chalked line. If vertical strips are not positioned over studs, attach the strips to the wallboard with construction adhesive. To hold a strip in place while the glue dries, drive two angled nails through it and into the wallboard every 16 inches or so *(page 217, inset)*.

◆ Snap a chalk line down the center of each strip.

◆ At the chalked line on the first furring strip, tack a temporary 1-by-2 batten as a guide for the mitered ends of the first section of boards. A straight batten works best, but you can bend a slightly curved batten to the chalked line as you tack it.

2. Attaching the first board.

◆ With the technique shown in the inset to Step 5 on page 211, mark cutting lines for a right triangle on a panel board, placing the right angle where the milling begins on the grooved edge of the board *(inset)*.

◆ Glue and nail the board in the corner formed by the floor and the batten.

Measure, cut, and install diagonal boards to complete the first wall section, using the methods described on pages 210 and 211.

3. Completing the herringbone.

◆ Remove the batten from the first furring strip, and tack it along the chalked line on the second furring strip.

◆ Install the next section of diagonal boards, beginning with a triangle as before but working from the opposite corner so the boards slope in the opposite direction. Make sure each board aligns perfectly against the corresponding board in the first section, to form a V.

◆ Move the batten to the third furring strip.

◆ Since the next section slopes upward, choose a reference board *(page 213, bottom)* in the second section to guide installation.

◆ Continue across the wall, using the methods on pages 212 to 214.

A CHOICE OF FINISHES FOR FINE WOOD

After filling nail holes, lightly sanding the wood, and cleaning away the dust with a damp cloth, you are ready to finish the walls. Most woods require some sort of finish to protect them from dirt and scratches. The materials you choose to finish the paneling depend on the time you wish to invest and the appearance you wish to achieve. Staining the wood before applying a finish, for example, is not necessary, but it enhances natural color and emphasizes grain. Choose a stain and a finish that are both either water-base or oil-base.

Water-base stains and polyurethane (the most durable) finishes are good for quick application and easy soap-and-water cleanup and are less toxic than oil-base products. Extra sanding is required (since the water in the stain tends to raise the woodgrain), but the finish is crystal clear. Oil-base staining is more time consuming but will dye the wood more deeply than most water-base products. Oil-base finish is also more toxic than water-base and will tend to yellow over time.

Apply water-base stain with a brush having nylon bristles, a foam brush, a pad applicator, or a rag. Allow the liquid to penetrate the wood for about 5 minutes, then wipe off the excess in the direction of the grain with a clean rag. Let the wood dry for about 2 hours before finishing.

When applying the finish, use the same brush or a pad applicator. Since water-base finishes dry quickly, it is important not to overbrush the finish; doing so leaves brush marks on the wood. After 3 to 4 hours, burnish the finish with plastic wool, then wipe with a dampened cloth. Apply at least one more coat.

To apply an oil-base stain, use a brush or pad applicator and leave the stain on the wood no more than 30 minutes. Wipe excess with a rag and let the wood dry for 12 hours before finishing. Oil-base polyurethane finishes, applied with a varnish brush, must dry for 12 to 24 hours between coats. Smooth with plastic wool between coats. Tools can be cleaned with turpentine or mineral spirits.

⚠️ **CAUTION** *Make sure the room is well ventilated when applying oil-base stains and finishes and extinguish any nearby flames. Enclose oily rags in an airtight, flameproof can for disposal.*

Raised paneling, perfected in Colonial times, will lend elegance to any room. With the proper tools, you can make and install the traditional solid-wood version. Or, to save time and money, you can create a facsimile by adding stiles, rails, and other embellishments to plywood panels.

Making a Pattern: Planning is crucial with either type. First make a scale drawing of the existing walls, showing door and window openings, electric switches and outlets, and any other protruding fixtures. Then superimpose a sketch of the paneling on this drawing.

Panel widths should not exceed 24 inches, except at doors and windows, where they should be wide enough to span the opening. Plan the layout so each hole for an electric switch or outlet will fall on a flat surface, rather than on a joint or a section of molding; you may have to move electrical elements. For frame-on-plywood paneling, position stiles to cover the joints between plywood panels.

The width of stiles, rails, and moldings depends on the proportions of the wall but should fall within a general range—stiles, 4 to 6 inches; rails, $2\frac{1}{2}$ to $3\frac{1}{2}$ inches; base moldings, $3\frac{1}{2}$ to 5 inches; crown moldings, 3 inches; door and window casings, 3 inches. Refine your sketch to include these dimensions, then transfer your pattern directly to the wall.

Construction: For frame-on-plywood paneling, use furniture-grade $\frac{1}{4}$-inch plywood, and assemble the paneling directly on the wall. Finishing or painting the paneling and the rails, stiles, and embellishments before installing usually produces a neater finished product. If you are attaching the pieces to the wall with adhesive, however, leave bare all the areas to be glued for better adhesion, and touch up the finish after installation.

For solid-wood raised paneling, softwoods work best. Assemble cut pieces and fasten them to the wall in completed upper-and-lower sections *(page 223)*, applying the finish after installation. See page 215 for suggested finishes for solid-wood paneling. You can also finish solid-wood paneling with paint.

TOOLS

	Router
	Combination square
Table saw	Dovetail saw
Carpenter's level	Wood chisel
Miter box	Doweling jig
Mallet	Electric drill
Nail set	Dowel centers
Dado head	Pipe clamps
C-clamps	Block plane

MATERIALS

	Wood putty
	Hardboard ($\frac{1}{8}$")
Boards ($\frac{3}{4}$")	2 x 4s, 1 x 6s,
Plywood ($\frac{1}{4}$")	1 x 2s
Finishing nails	Carpenter's glue
($2\frac{1}{2}$", 3")	Sandpaper
Construction	Flat-head stove
adhesive	bolts
Moldings	Fluted dowels
Brads ($\frac{3}{4}$" and 1")	

SAFETY TIPS

When hammering or drilling, wear safety glasses to protect your eyes from flying nails or woodchips.

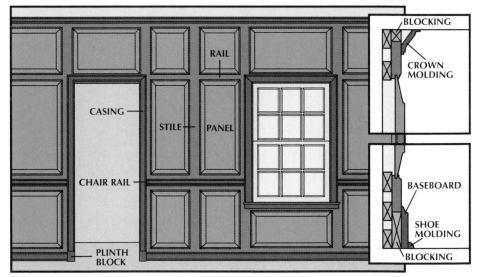

The parts of a raised panel wall.

Vertical stiles and horizontal rails, made of $\frac{3}{4}$-inch boards and joined together with glued dowels, hold the panels inside grooved edges. The top and bottom rails rest against blocking made of inexpensive $\frac{3}{4}$-inch lumber that is slightly narrower than the molding that covers it *(insets)*. Each assembled section is nailed to furring strips behind the edges of every rail and the blocking.

Crown molding trims the wall at the ceiling; casings border the doors and windows. Chair-rail molding covers a joint between upper and lower frame sections, and baseboard and shoe molding separates wall and floor. On both sides of the door, rectangular plinth blocks fill the corner between the casing and base molding.

A FACSIMILE WITH PLYWOOD

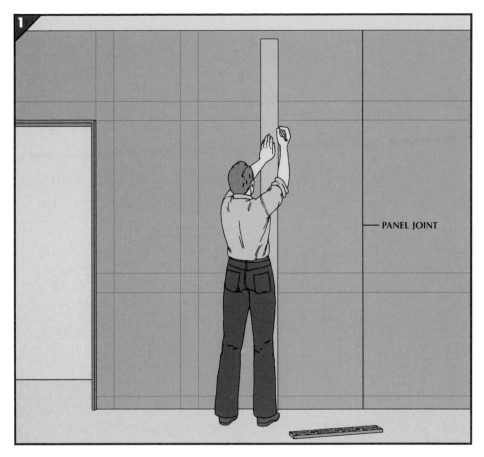

PANEL JOINT

1. Laying out the frame.

◆ Panel the walls with $\frac{1}{4}$-inch plywood as shown on pages 190 to 197; if you are using furring strips, add horizontal ones at the rail heights.

◆ With a pencil and a long straight-edged board, mark positions for the edges of stiles and rails on the plywood-paneled wall. Make sure that all joints between the plywood panels will be covered by stiles and that no stile or rail edge will cross an electrical outlet or switch.

◆ Mark the location of the bottom edge of the bottom rail; it should be 1 inch lower than the top edge of the planned base molding.

◆ Finally, cut all of the stiles, making them $\frac{1}{2}$ inch shorter than the overall wall height for ease in installation.

2. Attaching the stiles and rails.

◆ Line up a stile with one set of stile-edge marks; check it with a carpenter's level for plumb.

◆ If the paneling is installed over furring strips, nail the stile through the paneling to the strips with 3-inch finishing nails; use two at each strip *(left)*.

◆ Position, level, and nail the rest.

◆ Measure and cut rails for a snug fit between stiles, using a miter box to ensure perfectly square ends.

◆ Line up the rails with the pencil marks and tap them into position with a mallet, placing a wood block between mallet and rail.

◆ Nail the rails in place.

If the paneling is installed on wallboard, attach the stiles to the paneling with construction adhesive. Then angle two $2\frac{1}{2}$-inch finishing nails through the stiles into the wall at each rail height to keep stiles in place until the adhesive sets *(inset)*. Measure and cut the rails as above, then glue and nail them into place.

3. Adding mitered molding.

◆ To finish the edges of stiles and rails with quarter-round or patterned molding, cut molding to the length of the rail or stile edge to be covered, and miter each molding end inward at a 45-degree angle *(page 143)*.

◆ Nail the molding in place with 1-inch brads, starting with a stile and working clockwise around to the remaining three sides of the rectangle.

◆ Repeat for each frame, then fill any cracks at miter joints with wood putty.

4. Adding embellishments.

◆ For a raised-panel effect in the rectangle *(below, left)*, cut a piece of $\frac{1}{8}$-inch hardboard 2 inches shorter and narrower than the inside measure of the rectangle.

◆ Bevel the panel's edges with a table saw, then center it in the rectangle and attach it with glue and $\frac{3}{4}$-inch brads.

◆ Repeat for the other rectangles.

Alternatively, add a molding rectangle of the same dimensions as the raised panel described above *(below, right)*.

◆ Outline its location in pencil, then use the technique described in Step 3 to nail the mitered molding along the outline.

◆ Repeat for the other rectangles.

◆ Countersink all nails and fill holes with wood putty.

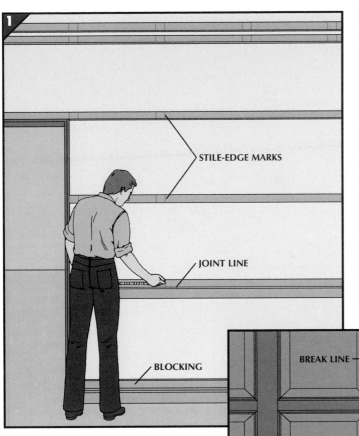

1. Laying out the frame.

◆ Nail furring strips to the wall along the floor and the ceiling, at each rail level, and at the midpoint between any rails that will be more than 2 feet apart *(pages 125-128)*. Determine the location of the joint between the upper and lower sections of the wall. (It will be concealed by the chair rail.) The furring strip there must be doubled or wide enough that each rail edge is backed by furring.

◆ Nail blocking over the furring strip at floor level *(page 216)*.

◆ Mark the exact positions of stile edges on all the strips.

◆ Calculate the exact stile, rail, and panel dimensions using the stile-edge marks. Stiles for the lower section of panels reach from the top of the blocking to the joint line; stiles for the upper section reach from the joint line to 2 inches below the ceiling. Measure the distance between stile edges to determine rail lengths. If you plan to shape the edges of stiles and rails, allow for the decorative edge in calculating the length of the rail, which must meet the stile at the break line *(inset)* where the shaped edge begins.

◆ Cut the stiles and rails, lay them facedown on the floor in the relative positions they will occupy on the wall, and mark them with matching numbers at each joint to speed later assembly.

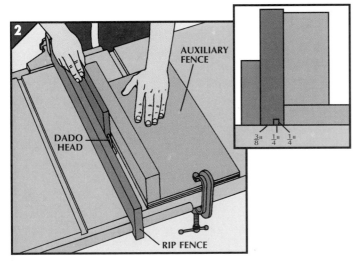

2. Cutting grooves in rails and stiles.

◆ Install a $\frac{1}{4}$-inch dado head on the table saw and lock the rip fence $\frac{3}{8}$ inch from the blade.

◆ Clamp an auxiliary fence—a 2-by-4 nailed to a piece of plywood—to the saw table on the other side of the blade, separated from the rip fence by the thickness of the lumber used for stiles and rails.

◆ Set the dado head to cut $\frac{1}{4}$ inch above the table. With the power on, feed rails and stiles—one edge down and the outside face against the rip fence—over the dado head.

MAKING SKILLFUL CUTS

A featherboard serves as an excellent alternative to the auxiliary fence shown at left, especially when you are working with flawed wood. Not only does the featherboard keep your workpiece from shifting or kicking back as it moves over the table-saw blade, its springy feathers also flex with any warps or imperfections in the wood.

To make a featherboard, miter-cut a 60-degree angle at the end of a 1-by-3 hardwood board. Then make parallel cuts about 5 inches long and $\frac{1}{4}$ inch apart into the mitered end. To use the featherboard, clamp it to the saw table with the feathers touching the workpiece, keeping the wood pressed snugly against the fence.

FEATHERBOARD

3. Shaping stile and rail edges.

◆ Clamp a stile, faceup, on a worktable and put the desired edge-forming bit in the router.

◆ Rest the router base on the stile with the bit an inch or so in from one end; turn on the router and push it toward the stile until the pilot comes into contact with the edge of the wood *(inset)*.

◆ Slowly move the router to the near end of the stile until the bit clears the corner, then move it in the opposite direction, shaping the entire edge of the stile.

◆ If the clamp blocks the path of the router, switch off the motor, reposition the clamp, and restart the cut an inch away from the stopping point, bringing the pilot against the still-uncut edge of the stile.

◆ Shape the stile's opposite edge in the same way; repeat the shaping process on all the remaining stiles and rails except along those edges that are going to be covered by chair-rail molding, door casing, or base molding.

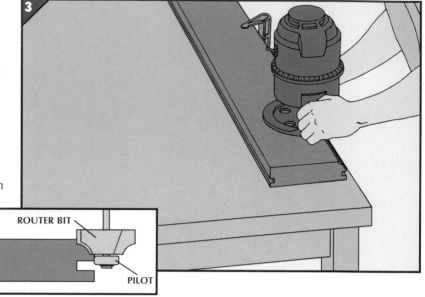

ROUTER BIT

PILOT

4. Preparing a shaped stile for joints.

◆ On the back of a stile that has a shaped edge, mark the points where the rail edges will intersect the stile.

◆ Use a combination square to mark the converging lines of a 45-degree angle from these points *(below, left)*.

◆ With a dovetail saw or other fine-tooth saw, cut along the lines down to the break line of the shaped edge *(below, right)*.

◆ Using a wood chisel with the beveled edge facing down, remove the wood between the saw cuts. Chisel off chips about $\frac{3}{4}$ inch long and $\frac{1}{16}$ inch thick until you have a flat surface at the level of the break line.

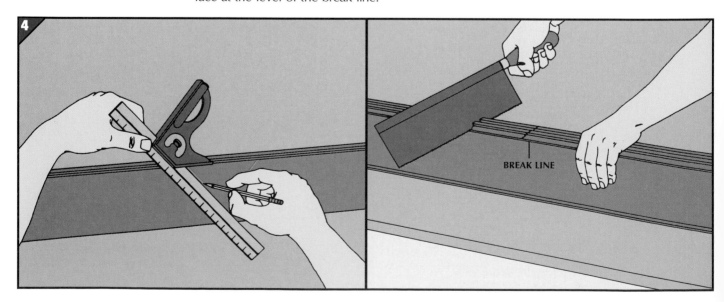

BREAK LINE

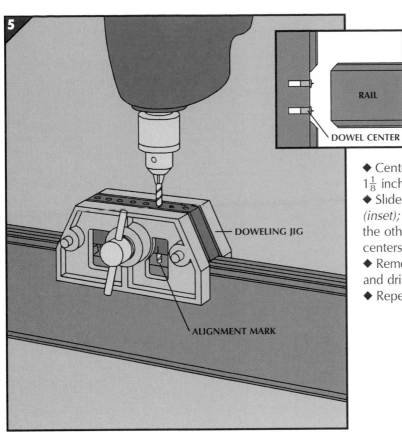

RAIL

DOWEL CENTER

DOWELING JIG

ALIGNMENT MARK

5. Drilling holes for dowels.

◆ Using a miter box, cut a 45-degree angle across each corner of the matching rail. Position the rail for the cut by aligning the saw blade over the point where the break line intersects the rail end.

◆ Mark guidelines for a doweling jig by drawing lines across both ends of the cutout section of a stile, $\frac{1}{2}$ inch in from the bottom of the bevel.

◆ Center the jig over each line and drill a $\frac{5}{16}$-inch hole, $1\frac{1}{8}$ inches deep.

◆ Slide a $\frac{5}{16}$-inch metal dowel center into each of the holes *(inset);* fit the matching rail into the cutout section and tap the other end of the rail to force the points of the dowel centers into the wood.

◆ Remove the rail, align the jig over the dowel-center marks, and drill holes in the rail end to match those in the stile.

◆ Repeat Steps 4 and 5 wherever rails and stiles intersect.

MAKING THE RAISED PANELS

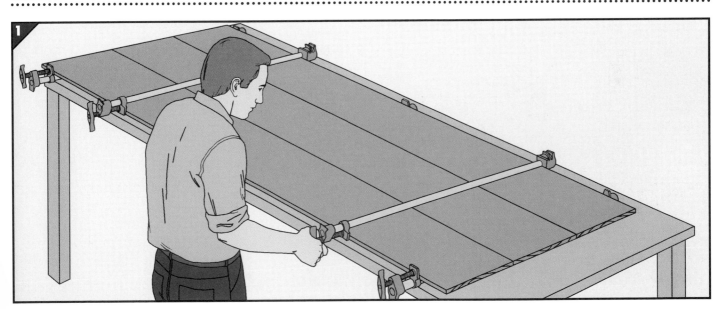

1. Joining boards edge-to-edge.

◆ Select several $\frac{3}{4}$-inch-thick boards that are long enough to make one or two raised panel sections and have a combined width that is greater than the planned width of one panel.

◆ Alternating the direction of the grain to prevent warping, lay the boards edge-to-edge across pipe clamps posi-

tioned near the board ends and at 2- to 3-foot intervals in between.

◆ Place additional clamps across the tops of the boards parallel to and midway between those on the bottom.

◆ Tighten all the clamps, increasing the pressure evenly until the seams between boards are nearly invisible hairlines.

◆ If there are gaps between the boards, remove the clamps and shave the board edges with a block plane.

◆ When board edges meet evenly, spread carpenter's glue on each board edge and reclamp the boards.

◆ After the glue is dry, remove the clamps, cut the panels to size, and sand the faces.

2. Outlining the bevel.

◆ Set the cutting height of a table-saw blade at $\frac{1}{16}$ inch and position the rip fence 2 inches from the blade.

◆ Hold a panel facedown, one edge against the rip fence, and make a $\frac{1}{16}$-inch-deep cut down the length of the panel face. Repeat the same cut on the other three edges of the panel.

◆ Outline the bevels for all the panels, and make similar cuts on a piece of scrap wood the same thickness as the panels, to use in setting the saw blade for the bevel cut.

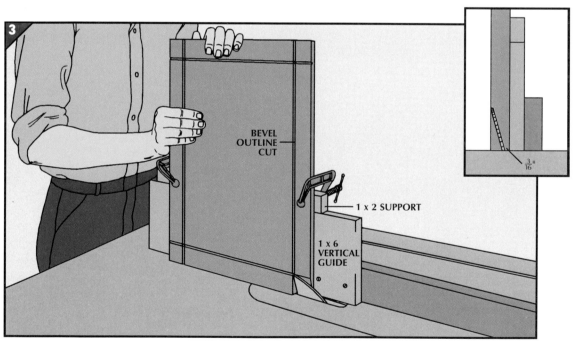

BEVEL OUTLINE CUT

1 x 2 SUPPORT

1 x 6 VERTICAL GUIDE

$\frac{3}{16}$"

3. Cutting the bevel.

◆ Tilt the saw blade away from the rip fence at a 15-degree angle, and fasten a 1-by-6 board to the rip fence as a guide. Anchor the guide to the fence with countersunk flat-head stove bolts.

◆ Position the guide so that its face is $\frac{3}{16}$ inch away from the saw blade at table level, and adjust the cutting height of the blade so that its highest part reaches exactly to the bevel outline you have cut on the piece of scrap lumber (inset).

◆ Slide a panel into the space between the blade and the guide, with the back of the panel against the guide and the end grain down.

◆ To steady the panel, rest a length of 1-by-2 on top of the guide and clamp the panel and the 1-by-2 together.

◆ Turn on the saw and, keeping your hands well above the table, push the panel over the blade.

◆ Repeat this procedure on each side of the panel, repositioning and reclamping the 1-by-2 support before each cut.

◆ Repeat for each panel.

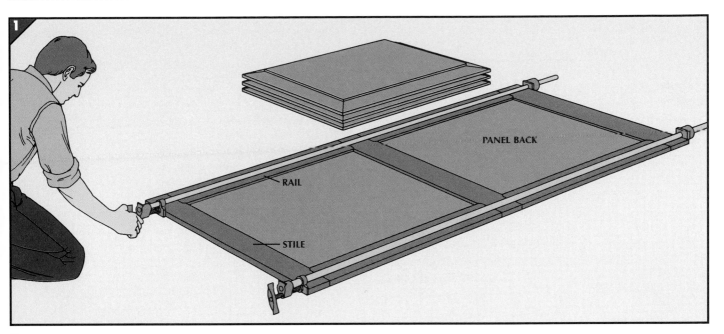

1. Joining the parts.

◆ Place the panels, rails, and stiles of the lower paneling section facedown on the floor, with the adjoining edges facing each other and the bottom edge toward the wall.

◆ Using a wood mallet, tap 2-inch-long fluted dowels into all of the rail holes; then tap the panels into the rail grooves; finally, tap the stiles onto the dowels protruding from the rails.

◆ After successfully test-fitting the pieces, disassemble them and spread a thin film of carpenter's glue inside the dowel holes and on all the facing edges of the joints, but not in the grooves.

◆ Reassemble the parts, using pipe clamps stretched from stile to stile to close the joints.

◆ Let the glue dry, remove the clamps, and assemble the remaining sections in the same way.

2. Raising the paneling.

◆ With helpers providing support at each stile, tilt the lower paneling section against the wall, then lift it and set the bottom rail on the blocking.

◆ Slide a level along the top of the paneling while a helper wedges thin wood shims between the blocking and the bottom rail to level the section.

◆ Fasten the stiles to the wall at each furring strip with pairs of $2\frac{1}{2}$ inch finishing nails.

◆ Raise the upper paneling section into position on top of the lower one, aligning the stiles exactly, and nail the upper stiles to the furring strips.

◆ Nail blocking between the top rail and the ceiling.

◆ When all of the sections are in place, cover the joint between the upper and lower sections with chair rail, and add ceiling, corner, and base moldings (pages 202-203 and 216).

◆ Frame the door and window openings with casings that match the wood of the stiles and rails.

◆ Countersink all nails with a nail set, and fill the holes with wood putty.

Not all wall paneling rises from floor to ceiling; a traditional variety known as wainscoting stops at about hip level. Wainscot paneling can vary in height from 30 to 36 inches, but it generally looks best when it is no more than one-third the height of the wall.

Wainscoting can be made from any of the materials—and in any of the styles—described earlier in this chapter. Wainscoting kits are also available at home centers and lumberyards.

Molding for a Neat Finish: As with floor-to-ceiling paneling, regular baseboard and shoe molding serve as trim at the floor. Wainscoting differs from full-height

panels only in the molding that covers the upper edge. You can employ one-piece cap molding as the top trim for thin wainscoting *(below, left)*. Thicker panels, or ones nailed to furring strips, require wider and more elaborate assemblies of three different pieces of molding *(below, right)*.

Outside corners of the trim are ordinarily mitered or square cut. At inside corners, you can ensure a better fit with a coping cut *(opposite)*. If you plan to set the top molding at the same height as the window stool (the inside extension of the window sill), you will need to scribe and then cut the top molding in much the same fashion as that outlined on page 200.

 TOOLS

Hammer
Miter box and backsaw
Coping saw

 **MATERIALS**

Plywood (interior, $\frac{1}{4}$")
Wood panels
Cap molding
Window-stool stock

Cove molding
Base-cap molding
Baseboard
Shoe molding
Bright finishing nails

SUITING THE MOLDING TO THE PANELS

Top trim for thin wainscoting.
For $\frac{1}{4}$-inch plywood or sheet paneling fastened directly to the wall, the easiest trim to apply is cap molding, already factory cut to lap over the panel edge.

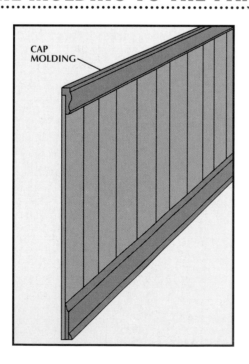

CAP MOLDING

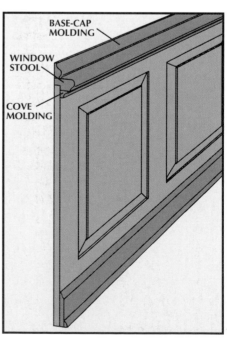

BASE-CAP MOLDING

WINDOW STOOL

COVE MOLDING

Complex molding for thicker panels.
If paneling protrudes farther than the depth of the cap molding—generally $\frac{1}{4}$ inch—you can use window-stool stock, rip cut to the desired width. Trim the stool stock with base-cap molding above and cove molding below.

A COPED JOINT FOR CAP MOLDING

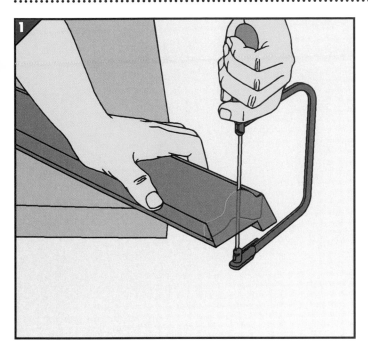

1. Shaping the first piece.
◆ When two pieces of cap molding meet at an inside corner, miter the end of the first piece.
◆ Outline the contoured edge in pencil as shown on page 202, then continue the pencil line across the top of the molding at right angles to the back edge.
◆ With a coping saw, make a vertical cut through the molding along this line *(left)*.

2. Cutting the second piece.
◆ Notch another piece of molding *(right)* to the depth of the wainscot paneling.
◆ Nail that piece to the wall.
◆ Slide the first piece against it *(inset)* and nail it in place.

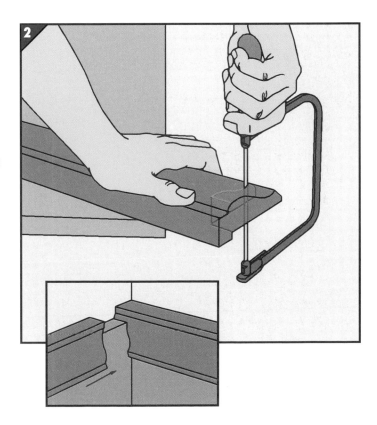

6 FLOORING

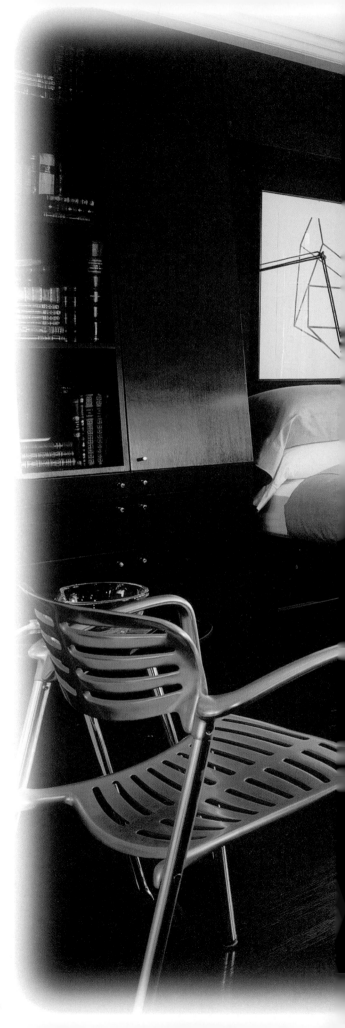

Don't forget the floor when you're planning a decorating or remodeling project. Available in a broad range of materials and looks, flooring offers great opportunities to enhance any decor. Wood is warm and inviting and tile can look rustic or contemporary, but if neither fits into your budget it's nice to know that today's vinyl flooring now resembles wood, tile, stone, and other materials.

You can save a lot of money by installing a floor yourself. We'll first help you fix any existing problems quickly, such as sagging floor, weak framing, old girders, and failing foundations. If you opt for wood, you'll find information on how much to buy, preparing the room, trimming boards, using a power nailer, and gluing wood flooring down as an alternative installation method. You'll also find steps for laying down wood or vinyl tiles. If you choose to work with sheet vinyl, this chapter will teach you how to buy it, how to make a template of the area to be covered, and how to cut and glue the vinyl and adhere seams. If you use tile, you'll learn how to build up the subfloor, cut tiles and lay them in mortar, and add grout. Want to spruce up an existing floor? We'll show you how to refinish wood flooring, remove stains from vinyl, and replace damaged vinyl and tile to keep your floor looking its best.

A less expensive option than tile but still resilient to water damage, vinyl works well in the bathroom. This pale square pattern keeps the room feeling bright and clean.

These vinyl tiles are stylish as well as hard-wearing, and they are impervious to messy kitchen spills. The dark marble pattern contrasts nicely with the neutral tones of the cabinets and appliances.

Tiles come in many sizes and colors, which may be combined for an interesting effect—as with the pattern of this floor framing the room. The earth tone color works well for such a heavily trafficked area.

Easy to keep clean, tile is ideal for kitchens. A classic checkered pattern will draw attention away from a cluttered kitchen and add a sense of order.

Functional Beauty

strip floor

Flooring is more than just a convenient surface to walk on—it can be patterned to become a separate decorating element or can be muted to blend into the background and let a beautiful wall treatment or handsome furniture take center stage. Vinyl, wood, and tile are particularly good flooring materials for decorating.

Vinyl is still the cheapest flooring option, and a wealth of patterns, customizing options, and tough finishes make it very popular. Available in tiles or rolls, it's the easiest type of flooring for a home decorator to install. Because it stands up to a lot of scrubbing, vinyl is particularly good for kitchens and children's playrooms. It comes in lots of floral, calico, plaid, and checked patterns, which can give a kitchen a traditional look, as well as jaunty dots and graphic motifs that work well with a country decor. Vinyl flooring also is available in designs that closely resemble wood, tile, stone, metal, and other materials, as well as vinyl that mimics marble, granite, and terra cotta.

parquet floor

Wood flooring costs more than vinyl flooring but gives rooms a rich, warm look. Red oak is the favorite species in most areas of the country, but light-colored maple is becoming more popular because it blends well with contemporary decors. Save money by using plywood panels. Strip flooring, which consists of boards less than 3 inches wide, is suitable for casual and formal rooms. Boards come up to 8 feet long, but using short boards tends to make a room look larger. Plank flooring, the most expensive option, consists of boards wider than 3 inches. This type of wood flooring shows off a wood's grain and is good for traditional or Early American decors, especially when

plank floor

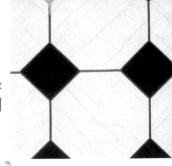

diamonds &
square vinyl

floral vinyl

used with wood dowel plugs or decorative nails. Parquet flooring, the least expensive wood flooring, is sold in custom-designed pieces or prefabricated tiles that form basketweave, herringbone, and other popular patterns when installed. Parquet flooring's multi-directional patterns make it a good choice for rooms with irregular dimensions. To add interest to a wood floor, try using two different wood species or stain colors.

Tile used for flooring is less glossy and much thicker than tile used on walls. It's often textured to provide a no-skid surface, which makes it an especially good option for bathrooms and kitchens. Unglazed Mediterranean clay and terra-cotta tiles give rooms a rustic charm. Ceramic tiles provide an elegant look, and the most popular ceramic flooring consists of large 12- and 16-inch squares that look like slate, limestone, granite, and marble. These big tiles provide the luxurious look of natural stone flooring for just a fraction of the cost. For a fanciful, artistic look, try tiny mosaic tiles, which lend themselves to intricate patterns. Another colorful option is terrazzo tile, which consists of marble chips held together with a cement-type adhesive. It's expensive but lends itself beautifully to borders and intricate patterns.

blu-square
vinyl

combination
ceramic tiles

terra-cotta
tiles

slate-style
tiles

231

A small dip in a floor is irritating but not necessarily dangerous. If less than $\frac{3}{4}$ inch deep and 30 inches long, the dip can be repaired with hardwood wedges driven between a joist and the subfloor *(page 267)*.

A larger sag, in conjunction with other symptoms such as a sticking door, cracked plaster, or leaky plumbing, may indicate structural damage in the supporting framework of joists, girders, and posts.

Pinpointing the Problem: Inspect the framework underneath the floor *(below)* for structural members that are defective. If you have a second-story sag, an entire floor or ceiling may have to be torn out before you can get at the trouble and repair it.

Test for rot and insect damage by stabbing the wood with an awl. Rotted wood feels spongy and does not splinter. A honeycomb of small holes signals termites or carpenter ants; if you find such holes, call an exterminator at once.

A sound joist can be straightened permanently by having a new joist nailed to its side, a technique called doubling *(page 234)*. A slightly rotted joist can also be doubled if it will hold a nail—and if you first coat it liberally with a penetrating wood preservative. Always replace a joist that is thoroughly rotten or insect infested *(pages 235-236)*.

Where a drooping girder is the cause of a sagging floor, the repair may entail the substitution of a steel column for a wood post *(pages 237-239)*, the installation of a new girder *(pages 240-245)*, or both.

Jacking Up the Floor: In order to make any of these repairs, you'll need to jack up the joists or girder under the sag. The jacking techniques shown here for an unfinished basement also apply to finished areas of the house, once you have exposed the supporting framework of the floor.

Always use a screw jack; the hydraulic type is neither as strong nor as reliable. If you are working in a basement, rent a house jack; in a crawlspace, use a contractor's jack. In either case, grease the jack threads before you begin.

 TOOLS

Straightedge (8')
Telescoping house jack
Contractor's jack

 **MATERIALS**

Pad (4 x 8)
Beam (4 x 6)
Blocks (2 x 6)
Timbers (6 x 6)

 SAFETY TIPS

A hard hat guards against painful encounters with joists, girders, and exposed flooring nails.

What holds up a floor.

At the ground floor of a typical house, joists are laid across the shorter dimension of the foundation. Outer joist ends rest on the foundation sills; inner ends rest on a girder supported by posts anchored in concrete footings that may include raised piers. The built-up girder shown here, made of lengths of lumber cut to overlap atop a post, rests in pockets in the foundation wall. Cross members called bridging strengthen the joists and keep them in alignment. Other elements called trimmer joists and headers frame a stairwell opening. Trimmers and headers consist of two boards nailed together to carry the extra weight of the stair and of joists cut short of the foundation sill.

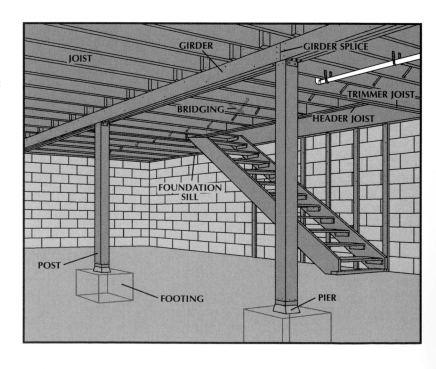

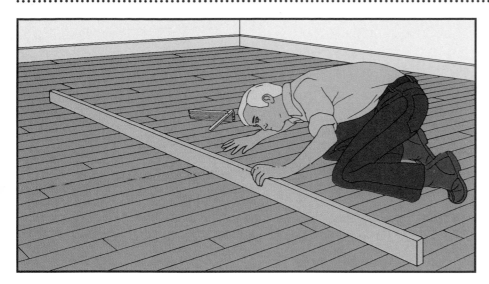

Measuring a sag.
◆ Lay an 8-foot straightedge—either a 2-by-4 or the factory edge trimmed from a sheet of plywood—across the sagging area. Measure the gap between straightedge and floor and mark the floor where the sag is deepest.
◆ Measure from the mark on the floor to two different reference points— walls or stairways, for example—that lie at right angles to each other and that are visible in the basement. There, take measurements from the reference points to position the jack.

STEEL PINS

PAD

PIPE

Jacking from a basement.
◆ Extend the jack to fit between the joist and the floor with about 12 inches to spare, and lock the tube at that length with the steel pins provided.
◆ Set the bottom plate on a length of 4-by-8 lumber. While a helper steadies a 4-by-6 beam at least 4 feet long between the joists and the jack's top plate, screw the jack until the beam presses against the joists. Plumb the jack with a level, then nail the plates to the beam and pad.
◆ Remove the bridging between a joist to be doubled or replaced and its neighbors. To keep the joists parallel, cut 2-by-6 spacers to fit snugly between them and insert as shown on page 234.
◆ Once a day raise the jack no more than $\frac{1}{16}$ inch, about a half-turn. If necessary, slip an 18-inch pipe over the jack handle for leverage. Because the floor will settle after the jacks are removed, raise it $\frac{1}{4}$ inch higher than level.

Jacking from a crawlspace.
◆ Assemble a pyramidal framework, called cribbing, from hardwood 6-by-6 timbers, available from dealers in structural timber. Stack the timbers as shown at right, placing the ones at the top of the structure about 18 inches apart.

◆ Atop the cribbing, set a 4-by-8 pad for the jack, then raise the jack to meet a 4-by-6 beam held across the joists.
◆ Install spacers as described above, then raise the jack $\frac{1}{16}$ inch a day—one-eighth turn on most contractor's jacks—until the floor is $\frac{1}{4}$ inch above level.

Once you have decided whether to double a joist or replace it *(page 232)*, proceed as described on these pages. In either case, electrical cables, pipes, and ventilating ducts that run perpendicular to joists can be substantial hurdles.

Circumventing Obstacles: You can get around one or two such roadblocks when doubling a joist by using the technique shown at the top of the next page. But in some instances of doubling—and often when replacing a joist—it may be more practical to temporarily remove a section of ductwork or to unstaple electrical cables from joists to improve access. When a pipe intrudes, the simplest solution is to notch the joist to fit around it.

One-for-one replacement of an unsalvageable joist is usually suffi-cient. However, if the old joist has sagged badly enough that the sub-floor above it has split or broken, you'll need to install a second new joist for added support.

Choosing Lumber: Buy doublers and replacement joists to match the old joist in every dimension. The single exception is the height of doublers that you plan to use for reinforcing a notched joist. All of the boards should be straight and free of cracks or large knots; if rot has been a problem, use pressure-treated lumber. Before you install a doubler or a new joist, find the crown, an edge with a slightly out-ward, or convex, curve. Install the board with the crown facing up-ward, against the subfloor; the joist will be forced straight by the weight that it bears.

TOOLS

Floor jack
Plane
Pry bar
Reciprocating saw

Saber saw with
   flush-cutting
   blade
Carpenter's nippers
Wood chisel
Cat's paw

MATERIALS

2 x 4s
2 x 6s
Joist lumber
Steel bridging

Construction
   adhesive
Common nails
   ($2\frac{1}{2}$" and $3\frac{1}{2}$")
Finishing nails (3")

SAFETY TIPS

Protect your eyes with goggles when hammering or pulling nails, using a hammer and chisel, or sawing wood with a power saw. Add a dust mask when cutting pressure-treated lumber, and wash hands thoroughly after han-dling it. Wear a hard hat when han-dling heavy objects overhead.

DOUBLING A JOIST

Attaching the new joist.

◆ Remove bridging, insert spacing blocks, and jack up the floor *(page 233)*.
◆ Plane a $\frac{1}{4}$-inch-deep, 18-inch-long notch in the new joist's ends *(inset)*. Remove a spacer and test-fit the joist. Deepen the notches as needed.
◆ Lay a bead of construction adhesive on the top edge of the new joist. While a helper holds it tight against both the old one and the subfloor, fas-ten the doubler to the joist with $3\frac{1}{2}$-inch common nails, staggered top and bottom every 12 inches. Hammer the protruding nail points flat.
◆ Trim $1\frac{1}{2}$ inches from the spacer removed earli-er, and toenail it between the doubler and the neighboring joist.
◆ Remove the other spacing block and install new bridging *(page 268)*.

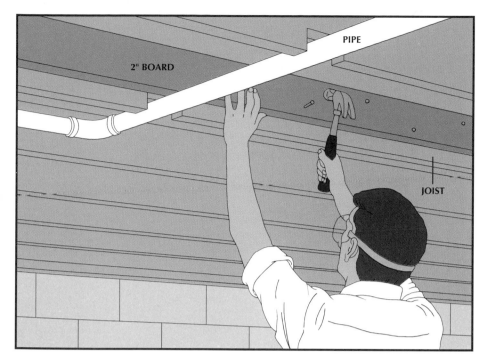

Doubling a notched joist.

◆ To reinforce a joist notched to make way for a pipe, measure the distance between the top of the obstacle and the subflooring.

◆ From the widest 2-inch lumber that will fit in the space, cut two pieces the same length as the weak joist.

◆ With a helper to hold the boards against the subflooring, fasten one of them to each side of the weak joist with $2\frac{1}{2}$-inch nails. If no helper is available, support the boards on nails driven partway into the old joist.

REPLACING A JOIST

1. Mounting a new joist.

◆ Plane or chisel the ends of the new joist to make notches *(inset, opposite)*.

◆ Remove bridging, insert spacing blocks, and then jack up the floor *(page 233)*.

◆ Take out any nails and blocks holding the old, weak joist to the girder and the sill plate. Remove the spacing blocks that are next to the weak joist.

◆ Apply construction adhesive to the new joist's top, then position it so the weak joist is sandwiched between the new one and the sound existing joist that extends to the opposite sill plate.

◆ Force the new joist tightly against the subfloor by driving hardwood shims at the notches *(above)*.

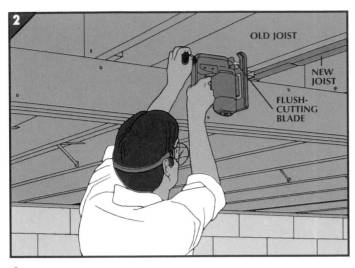

2. Removing the old joist.

◆ Cut through the weak joist at points near the girder and the sill plate with a reciprocating saw or a saber saw fitted with a flush-cutting blade.
◆ With a pry bar, lever the joist away from the nails that hold it to the subfloor.
◆ Trim protruding nail points with a plierslike cutter called a carpenter's nippers.

THE RECIPROCATING SAW
....

With a fast, pistonlike motion, a reciprocating saw can rough-cut wood, metal, plaster, and PVC pipe. When fitted with a long wood-cutting blade, this heavy-duty tool is ideal for cutting out old floor joists. Some models allow you to mount the blade teeth up, a feature that makes for easy overhead cutting and allows you to cut a joist all the way to the subflooring.

3. Splitting out the joist ends.

◆ With a wood chisel, split the ends of the joist that remain on the girder and sill plate (right). Remove the pieces and protruding nails with a pry bar. Drive the claw of a cat's paw beneath any embedded nailheads with a hammer, and then pull on the bar to withdraw the nail.
◆ If there are breaks in the subfloor, install and shim a second new joist in the old one's place (see Step 1).

4. Nailing the joists.

◆ With $3\frac{1}{2}$-inch common nails, nail the new joists to the one they sandwich at the girder.
◆ Then nail 2-by-4 spacers every 3 feet between the new joists (left).
◆ Toenail the new joists to the girder and sill plate.
◆ Trim the spacing blocks (page 234) to fit in the space that lies between each new joist and its neighbor, then toenail the spacers in place.
◆ Drive 3-inch finishing nails, spaced 8 inches apart, through the finish floor and into each joist.

A Stand-In for a Failing Post

When a girder sags at the top of a wood post, the trouble is in the post, not the girder. Either the post's concrete footing has sunk or the post itself has been attacked by rot or termites. Both problems have the same solution: Replace the post with a steel column that is supported by a new footing.

You will need a building permit, and some of the work involved is strenuous: removing the old wood post, breaking through the basement slab with a rented electric jackhammer, digging a hole, and pouring a new footing.

If your house is built on fill or if the span between posts is more than 12 feet, consult an architect or a civil engineer before undertaking this project.

A Steel Replacement: Adjustable steel columns, available at lumberyards and building-materials dealers, are made of 11-gauge, 3-inch

pipe fitted with a threaded base like that of a telescoping jack. Get a column 4 inches longer than the distance between the basement slab and the bottom of the girder, so the base will be anchored in concrete when you patch the slab.

The Key to a Sturdy Post: A post is only as strong as its footing. The size and depth of the footing depend on the load it must bear, on soil conditions and, in unheated basements or crawlspaces, on the depth of the frostline—the point of deepest penetration of frost below ground level.

A footing that is 2 feet square and 22 inches deep is typical, but check your local building code for the required dimensions and whether steel reinforcement is mandatory. Either rent a concrete mixer or, if you are pouring more than one footing, have concrete delivered in a ready-mix truck.

 TOOLS

House jacks
Hacksaw
Electric jack-
  hammer

Masonry trowel
Shovel
Electric drill with
  $\frac{3}{8}$" bit
Carpenter's level

 **MATERIALS**

Plywood ($\frac{1}{2}$")
Common nails
  ($2\frac{1}{2}$")
Adjustable steel
  column

Lag screws (3" x $\frac{3}{8}$")
  and washers
Epoxy bonding
  agent
Concrete

SAFETY TIPS

When operating a jackhammer, wear goggles, gloves, ear protection, and a dust mask.

1. Removing the old post.

◆ To make way for the new column, set up telescoping house jacks *(page 233)* 3 feet to either side of the post. Raise the girder $\frac{1}{16}$ inch a day until the post no longer supports any weight.
◆ Remove the nails or lag screws that fasten the post to the girder. With a helper, tilt the top of the post clear of the girder and lift the post off the vertical steel dowel that connects it to the concrete *(right)*.

If the girder is spliced over the post, reinforce the splice before jacking the girder. Using a hacksaw, cut away any metal splice reinforcement, and nail a 3-foot length of $\frac{1}{2}$-inch plywood across the splice, on both sides of the girder. Secure each plywood piece with 30 $2\frac{1}{2}$-inch common nails.

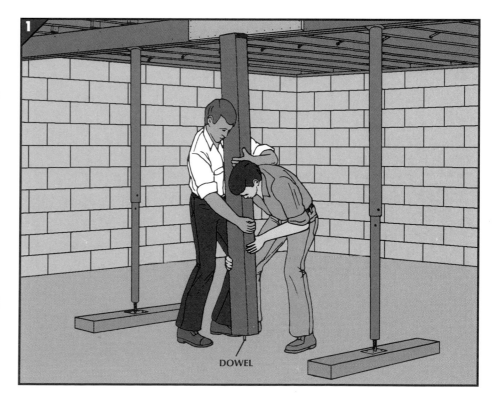

DOWEL

2. Digging the footing.

◆ On the basement floor, mark off a footing of the size that is required by your building code. Rent an electric jackhammer to break through the concrete slab.

◆ Beginning inside one of the footing marks and working toward the line, break out easy-to-handle chunks of concrete with a series of cuts. Hold the jackhammer perpendicular to the slab at the start of each cut; then, when you have chiseled out a groove, tilt the handles slightly toward yourself and lean firmly.

◆ When you have broken up the slab and the old concrete footing within the marks, dig a hole of the depth required by the code.

3. Pouring the footing.

◆ Clean out all loose dirt from the hole and spray it with a hose.

◆ While the hole is still wet, fill it with concrete to a point 4 inches below floor level. Drive a shovel into the wet concrete several times to eliminate air bubbles, then level the surface with a masonry trowel.

◆ The concrete must cure for about 2 weeks: Cover it with polyethylene sheeting, and keep the surface wet by sprinkling it with water twice a day.

4. Bolting the column.
◆ Set the steel column on the new footing. Holding the bottom plate with your toe, turn the column on its threaded base to raise the top plate tightly against the girder.

◆ Center the plate at the marks left by the old post. Using the holes in the plate as a guide, drill $\frac{3}{8}$-inch pilot holes into the girder *(above)*.
◆ Attach the plate loosely to the girder with 3-inch lag screws and washers.

5. Making the column fast.
◆ Tap the base of the column with a hammer as needed to make the column plumb, checking all sides with a level *(left)*, then tighten the lag screws.
◆ Lower the temporary jacks $\frac{1}{16}$ inch a day until they can be removed.
◆ To finish the floor around the column, coat the footing and the edges of the slab with an epoxy bonding agent. Then fill the hole with concrete to the level of the surrounding floor, and trowel it smooth.

Replacing a Girder

A wood girder that sags in one place can be jacked straight and supported with a new steel post *(pages 237-239)*. Several sags, however, are a sign of a weak girder. Since girders must support all the floors above them and part of the roof, multiple sags are serious indeed. The most practical remedy is to replace the weakened girder with one made from laminated veneer lumber, or LVL *(box, below)*.

Maneuvering Girder Boards: Continuous boards make the strongest girder but may be impossible to get into the basement without your making a hole in the foundation. For a basement less than 20 feet wide, however, cutting the boards as shown on page 242 may permit you to carry them through doorways and down stairs.

Building the New Girder: Measure the width of the basement and add 4 to 6 inches for the ends to rest in the foundation wall. Take your measurements to a lumberyard, and they will calculate how many LVL boards you need to build your beam, usually three.

Before beginning work, obtain a building permit. Thereafter, the first step is to support the floor, sag and all, with a framework of 4-by-4 shoring on both sides of the weakened girder *(opposite)*. After cutting out the old girder, bring the new boards inside and assemble the replacement girder. Finally, rebuild the foundation wall under the girder to support it.

 TOOLS

Hammer
Combination square
Saw
Tape measure
Cold chisel
Circular saw
House jacks
Mason's trowel
Joint filler
Mason's hammer
Brick set
Mason's hawk

 MATERIALS

2 x 6s
2 x 4s
4 x 4s
LVL boards
Double-headed
nails ($2\frac{1}{2}$")
Common nails ($3\frac{1}{2}$")
Wood screws ($2\frac{1}{2}$")
Pine shims
Steel or slate shims
Rafter ties
Flashing
Concrete block
(8 x 8)
Mortar
Bricks

 SAFETY TIPS

Wear goggles when hammering, sawing, using a chisel, mixing mortar, or cutting brick. Leather-palmed work gloves protect your hands from rough edges of brick or stone. Irritants in mortar call for a dust mask when mixing it, as well as gloves when applying it. Wear a dust mask when chiseling concrete block. Protect your head with a hard hat when working near joists or with heavy objects overhead.

LAMINATED VENEER LUMBER

Nowadays, many builders make girders, beams, and headers from laminated veneer lumber (LVL) instead of ordinary lumber or steel I-beams. As shown in the photograph at right, LVL is a form of plywood manufactured by gluing sheets of thin veneer together under heat and pressure. Colored wax applied to edges keeps out moisture.

LVL boards have the same thickness as 2-inch lumber and can be ordered up to 16 inches wide and 80 feet long. Lighter than steel and stronger than regular lumber, this material can be cut, nailed, drilled, and shaped with common woodworking tools and is light enough that two people can handle most boards.

PUTTING UP SHORING

1. Building the shoring.

◆ Lay straight 4-by-4s end to end across the floor to form a top plate as long as the girder. Place several shorter 4-by-4s nearby to serve as bottom plates.

◆ Mark post positions every 4 feet along the top plate *(Xs)*, beginning 2 feet from the wall. Mark corresponding positions on the bottom plates.

◆ Find the lowest point of the sag *(page 233)*. Measure from the bottom of the joists to the floor at that point, then cut 4-by-4 posts 7 inches shorter than this distance, to fit between the top and bottom plates.

◆ Toenail the posts to the top plate at the marks you have made, using four $2\frac{1}{2}$-inch double-headed nails per post. Or drive $2\frac{1}{2}$-inch dry-wall screws with an electric drill.

◆ Build a second framework in the same way.

2. Nailing the shoring in place.

◆ Set the bottom plates on the floor, parallel to the girder and 3 feet to either side of it.

◆ Have two helpers set the first section of top plate and posts on the bottom plate at the marks made in Step 1.

◆ Make sure the posts are plumb—if necessary, tap them into position with a hammer—then nail or screw the posts to the bottom plate.

3. Shimming the framework tight.

◆ Insert wedge-shaped pine shims under each joist *(inset)* from both sides of the top plate. Then hammer the wedges so they are tight *(right)*.

◆ Erect additional sections of shoring to create a wall-to-wall framework on each side of the girder.

4. Fastening the joints.
◆ Toenail or screw top-plate sections together *(left)*, and add a post under each joint, fastening it to both sections of the top plate.
◆ Tighten shims that have worked loose.
◆ Pull out the nails that fasten the joists to the old girder, then saw the girder into pieces, cutting it 1 foot from both foundation walls and each post. To prevent pieces of girder from falling on you, have helpers support each piece as you complete the saw cuts.
◆ Pull the end pieces out of the girder pockets, then remove the posts and the 2-foot sections of girder still attached to them *(page 237)*.

INSTALLING THE NEW GIRDER

1. Chiseling out the block.
◆ Outline girder pockets enlarged to accept the LVL boards if you can bring them into the basement through existing openings. Otherwise, substitute for one pocket an access hole two courses (16 inches) tall and 8 inches wide.
◆ For both girder pockets and access holes, chip at the block with hammer and cold chisel to a depth of 4 to 6 inches *(right)*. Punch a hole through the wall at the center of the access hole. Redraw the outline on the outside, using the hole as a reference point.
◆ Complete chiseling from outside. Work behind the siding if necessary, and excavate if the second course of block is below ground level.
◆ If the blocks are hollow, fill the cores at the bottoms of girder pockets and the access hole with mortar.

A GIRDER FROM STAGGERED BOARDS

You may be able to cut girder boards into segments that are small enough to maneuver into position without chipping a hole through your foundation wall. For this technique to work, at least two supporting posts are required. If you have more than two posts, select the the two that result in the shortest boards. In basements with only one post or none, you might find the idea of adding posts more appealing than breaking through the foundation wall *(page 238)*.

The key to a strong girder is to cut the LVL boards so that the joints fall atop posts, staggered as illustrated below. Note that one post supports a single joint; the other post supports two. Also, each board is cut into two pieces, not more.

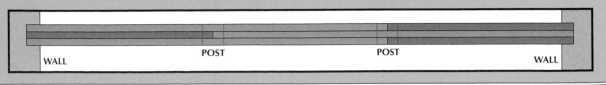

WALL   POST   POST   WALL

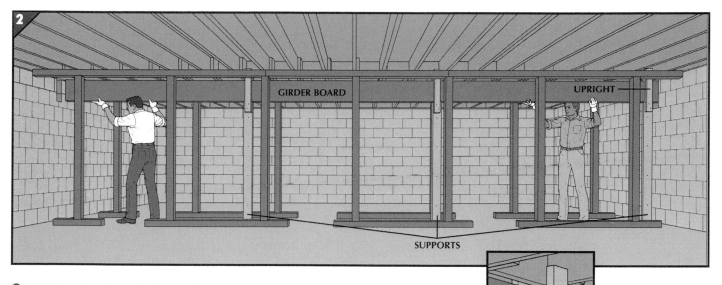

GIRDER BOARD   UPRIGHT

SUPPORTS

2. Sliding the boards into place.

◆ First construct three temporary supports to hold the boards while you slide them into position and nail them together. Each support consists of two 2-by-6s cut 1 inch shorter than the distance between the floor and the bottom of the girder, then nailed together to form a T *(inset)*. Two $2\frac{1}{2}$-foot lengths of 2-by-4 nailed to one end of the T hold the LVL boards on edge.

◆ Stand one support near the hole in the wall, and the others near, but not at, the post locations *(above)*.

◆ Slide the first board through the wall from outside, and place it on the supports and the far sill. Tack the board to the supports to hold it in place.

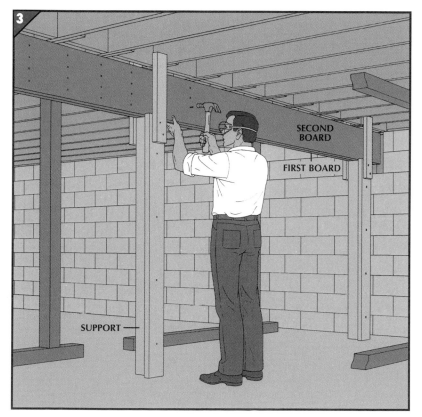

SECOND BOARD

FIRST BOARD

SUPPORT

3. Nailing the boards together.

◆ Slide the second board onto the supports and the far sill, even with the ends of the first board.

◆ Nail the two boards to each other from each side with four $3\frac{1}{2}$-inch nails per foot *(left)*.

◆ Position the third board alongside the first two, and nail it to the second board using the same pattern.

4. Nailing on the flashing.

Wrap aluminum flashing around each end of the girder where it will come in contact with wet mortar.

◆ First bend the flashing so it covers the bottom of the girder and both sides. Use two pieces if necessary.

◆ Next slide on the flashing, either from the basement or from outside the house. Also, cover the exposed end of the girder if you made a hole in the wall.

◆ Tack or nail the flashing on both sides and the end to secure it *(left)*.

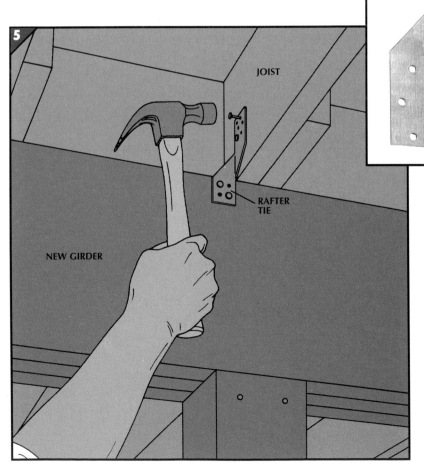

5. Nailing hangers to the joists.

◆ Jack up the girder with telescoping house jacks until it touches most of the joists. Shim beneath the joists that are not touching the girder, as shown on page 241.

◆ Reinstall the posts you removed in Step 4 on page 242.

◆ At every other joist, nail a rafter tie *(photograph)* to the girder and joist that crosses it *(left)*, hammering a nail into each hole in the tie.

SUPPORTING GIRDER ENDS

1. Blocking the hole from outside.

◆ Spread mortar on top of the exposed block.
◆ Butter one side of the 8-by-8 block with mortar, and place it onto the exposed block.
◆ Wedge the two outside corners of the block upward with brick chips to keep the block even with the others.
◆ Fill the other side joint with mortar using a joint filler. Smooth the joints with a trowel.
◆ Lay the second 8-by-8 block on top of the first in the same way.

NEW BLOCK

TRICKS OF THE TRADE

Wedging with Dowels

To make mortar joints around a new block match the thickness of the joints in the rest of the wall, buy a length of dowel that is equal in diameter to the height of the mortar joints. Cut two short pieces and arrange them as shown at right, set back from the face of the wall. Place the block on top of the dowels, then fill the gaps around the block with mortar using a joint filler and mason's hawk *(below)*.

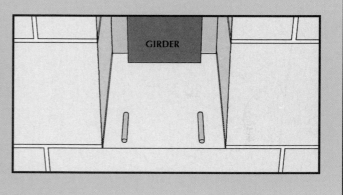

GIRDER

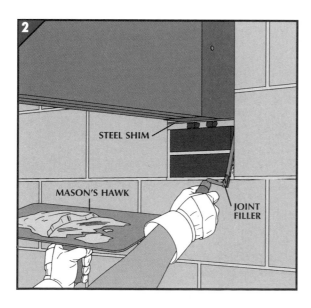

STEEL SHIM

MASON'S HAWK

JOINT FILLER

2. Bricking up the inside.

◆ With a mason's hammer and a brick set, trim bricks about 1 inch shorter than the width of the space below the girder.
◆ Lay mortar on the sill, and center the first brick in the hole. Tap it down with the trowel handle.
◆ Push mortar from a mason's hawk with a joint filler into the spaces on either side of the brick.
◆ Butter the top of the first brick, place a second brick on the mortar, then fill the side gaps with mortar *(left)*.
◆ When the gap under the girder is less than 1 inch, wedge a steel or slate shim up against the girder with brick chips. Then pack mortar under the shim.

The amount of work involved in laying a new wood floor depends on the material of your old floor. The boards of an existing wood floor must be removed. Ceramic tile floors also must be removed—and a new subfloor installed *(below)*—before laying the new boards. Old resilient sheet or tile flooring demands less work; simply re-cement loose flooring *(page 276)*. The preliminaries are even more involved, however, if the subfloor is in poor condition or if you are laying the boards over a concrete slab.

Handling a Damaged Subfloor: Pulling up an old wood floor will expose any ruined subflooring, but resilient flooring can hide damage that would undermine a new wood floor. If the old floor feels soft, peel back the flooring to check the plywood underneath, observing the asbestos precautions on page 278. Cut out the damage and patch the hole with plywood of the same thickness. In severe cases, remove the entire subfloor, repair any structural damage *(page 232)*, then lay a new subfloor *(below)*.

A New Subfloor: Check the joists before installing a subfloor. If they are more than 16 inches apart or are smaller than 2-by-8s, reinforce them *(pages 234-235)*, or install additional joists between the old ones. In attics built for light storage, it may be necessary to use $\frac{3}{4}$-inch plywood for the subfloor instead of the customary $\frac{5}{8}$-inch material.

Concrete Floors: Before trying to floor a concrete slab, check it for excess dampness by laying a 16-inch-square piece of plastic trash bag on the slab and sealing the edges with tape. If condensation occurs after several days, the concrete is a poor choice for a wood floor. Even a dry slab, however, needs a moisture barrier *(opposite)* under a new subfloor, unless you plan to glue the boards to the concrete *(page 253)*.

TOOLS

Caulk gun
Chalk line

Maul (2 pound)

MATERIALS

Construction adhesive
C-D grade plywood ($\frac{5}{8}$")
Dry-wall screws
2 x 4s
Lag screws ($\frac{3}{8}$") and washers
Masonry primer

Wood-to-concrete adhesive
Pressure-treated boards (1 x 2)
Masonry nails ($1\frac{1}{2}$")
Polyethylene film (4 mil)
Ring underlay nails (2")

SAFETY TIPS

Pressure-treated wood contains arsenic compounds as preservatives. Wash your hands thoroughly after handling this wood, and wear a dust mask when sawing it.

Laying a new subfloor.

◆ Make a dry run, staggering joints and leaving $\frac{1}{8}$ inch between sheets and along walls. Where sheets meet at a joist, make sure there is a bearing surface for both.

◆ Apply enough construction adhesive to the joists or sleepers for a single sheet *(right)*, then lay the sheet down.

◆ Secure each sheet with dry-wall screws driven into the joists every 10 inches, except at the edges that run along joists. There, drive the screws $\frac{3}{8}$ inch from the edges, 6 inches apart, and stagger them with those in the adjacent sheet.

◆ To support the subfloor's outer edges, add cleats as necessary to joists hidden beneath walls; nail one or more 2-by-4s to each concealed joist *(inset)* to provide a $\frac{1}{2}$-inch bearing surface. Secure the boards to the joist at 16-inch intervals with lag screws fitted with washers.

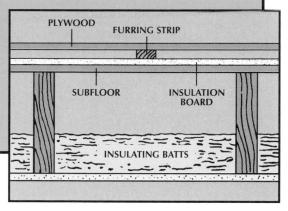

Floating a Floor to Reduce Noise

To help muffle the sounds of footsteps on a floor overhead, you can adapt the "floating floor" techniques used to soundproof apartment buildings.

Glue $\frac{1}{2}$-inch insulation board, available from lumberyards in 4- by 8-foot sheets, to the existing floor or subfloor with clear silicone caulk. Attach 1-by-3 furring strips to the board with construction adhesive, placing the strips between joists. Then fasten a $\frac{1}{2}$-inch plywood subfloor to the furring strips *(right)* and install the finish flooring. If you are planning to replace the subfloor and wish to subdue noise further, lay insulating batts between the exposed joists.

PLYWOOD   FURRING STRIP

SUBFLOOR   INSULATION BOARD

INSULATING BATTS

A MOISTURE BARRIER

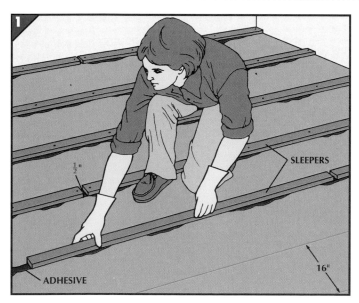

SLEEPERS

$\frac{1}{2}$"

16"

ADHESIVE

1. Laying bottom sleepers.

◆ Sweep the floor clean and apply a coat of masonry primer.

◆ When the primer dries, snap chalked lines 16 inches apart across the short dimension of the room.

◆ Cover each line with a 2-inch-wide ribbon of adhesive intended for bonding wood to concrete.

◆ Embed random lengths of pressure-treated 1-by-2s, or sleepers, in the adhesive, leaving a $\frac{1}{2}$-inch space between the ends of the boards.

◆ Use a 2-pound maul to secure the sleepers with $1\frac{1}{2}$-inch masonry nails about 24 inches apart.

2. Attaching the top sleepers.

◆ Lay sheets of 4-mil polyethylene film over the sleepers, overlapping joints 6 inches.

◆ Fasten a second course of 1-by-2s to each first course with ring underlay nails, sandwiching the film between the two layers.

Laying Floor Boards

Wood flooring is durable and elegant in appearance yet remarkably simple to install because of interlocking tongues and grooves milled on the sides and ends of the boards. Some are lumber, others are laminated. Laminated boards may be glued down instead of nailed, and either type may be purchased prefinished or sanded and finished after installation.

Nailing Techniques: All nailable floors must be installed over a wood subfloor *(page 246)*. In cases where boards are face-nailed, nails are countersunk and concealed with wood putty. Most often, however, the boards are blind-nailed through their tongues to hide the nailheads *(page 270)*.

To speed the work, rent a power nailer, either an automatic or a manual model like the one shown on page 250. You may need an accessory called a wedge adapter for the nailer to fasten $\frac{1}{4}$- to $\frac{3}{8}$-inch-thick laminated boards. On prefinished flooring, wrap the bottom of the tool with duct tape to protect the finish. Before using the nailer on your floor, practice on a scrap of flooring atop some spare plywood.

An Alternative to Nails: Glue-down boards can be affixed directly to almost any smooth, dry surface, including concrete, provided it is free of coatings such as paint and wax that might interfere with the adhesive. Fill in low spots in your concrete slab with flash patch, a cement-sand-epoxy compound. If the slab fails the dampness test *(page 246)*, hire a professional to lay a moisture barrier.

Until you've gained the experience of laying several courses of flooring, spread no more than 40 square feet of glue, or mastic, at a time. And when cutting pieces to fit, work in another room to avoid mixing sawdust with the mastic.

Before You Begin: Prepare the existing surface of the floor as described on pages 246 to 247.

Because wood floorboards, especially those made of lumber, are susceptible to warping and swelling caused by moisture, take delivery of the flooring at least 3 days in advance. Make sure your home is at its normal humidity level, then untie the bundles and stack the boards in loose piles to let them adjust to the climate in the room.

 TOOLS

Circular saw
Dovetail saw
Chalk line
Tape measure
Electric drill with $\frac{1}{16}$" bit
Hammer

Carpenter's nippers
Power nailer and mallet
Pry bar
Hand-screw clamps
Miter box
Backsaw

 **MATERIALS**

Asphalt-impregnated building felt (15-pound)
Tongue-and-groove flooring
Finishing nails ($2\frac{1}{2}$", $1\frac{1}{2}$")
Clamshell reducer strips
Corkboard ($\frac{3}{4}$")

Shoe molding ($\frac{3}{4}$")
Slip tongue
Wood-flooring mastic
1 x 2s
Masonry nails
V-notch trowel
Carpenter's glue
Flooring roller (100-pound)

 SAFETY TIPS

When working with mastic, keep the room well ventilated, and wear rubber gloves while spreading the adhesive. Protect your eyes from flying debris when hammering and sawing, and use earplugs to reduce the noise of the circular saw.

HOW TO BUY HARDWOOD FLOORING

Wood flooring is rated in order of decreasing quality and price as "clear," "select," "No. 1 common," or "No. 2 common," depending on color, grain, and imperfections such as knots and streaks. The boards are sold according to a "flooring board foot" formula, based on their premilled size. To determine the amount of flooring you need, calculate the area of your room in square feet. For $\frac{3}{4}$- by $2\frac{1}{4}$-inch boards, the most common size, multiply the area by 1.383 to convert to flooring board feet and to account for waste. For boards of other dimensions, ask your flooring distributor for the proper conversion factor.

1. Trimming for a new floor.

◆ Shorten each door that opens into the room to account for the new floor height. To do so, simulate the new floor with boards laid next to the doorstop. Add the height of a threshold if you plan to install one—plus $\frac{1}{4}$ inch for clearance above the finished floor—and mark the door. If the door is veneered, score the cut with a utility knife to prevent splintering while sawing.

◆ Using the straight factory edge of plywood as a guide, cut along the marked line.

◆ Cut the doorstop and doorcasings even with the flooring using a flush-cutting dovetail saw *(page 265, photo)*. If adding a threshold, position it on top of the flooring and trim the doorstop to that height.

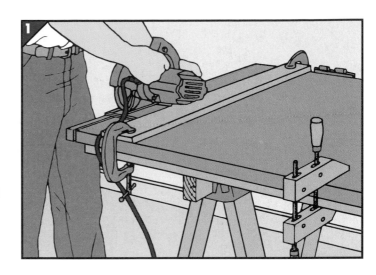

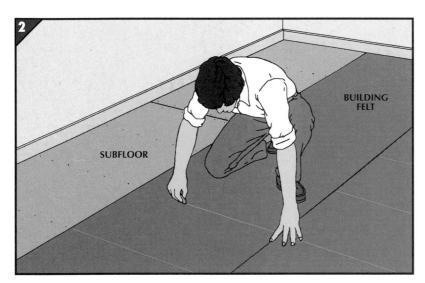

2. Marking the joists.

◆ Choose a wall that runs perpendicular to the joists as the starting wall along which you will lay the first course.

◆ Along the wall opposite the starting wall, unroll a strip of asphalt-impregnated building felt.

◆ On the felt, mark the positions of the joists, using the nailing pattern as a guide if there is a plywood subfloor. If the joists are hidden by existing flooring, and if they cannot be seen from below, use a stud finder to locate them.

◆ Continue unrolling strips of felt—overlapping them 3 inches and marking the joists—until the floor is covered.

3. Aligning the starter course.

◆ Find the midpoints of the walls parallel to the joists and snap a chalk line between them to mark the center of the room.

◆ Measure equal distances from the ends of the centerline to within roughly $\frac{1}{2}$ inch of the starting wall and snap a starting chalk line between those points *(right)*. Laying the starter course along this line ensures that boards in the center of the room look straight even if the room is not quite square. Shoe molding will hide the gap between the first course and the baseboard *(page 252, Step 7)*.

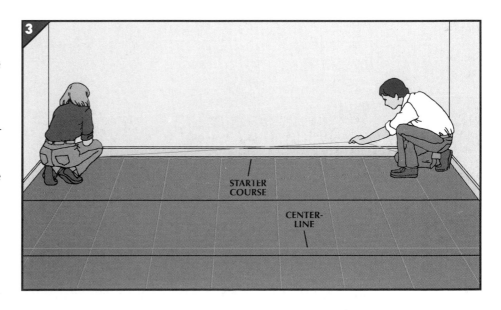

NAILING THE BOARDS

1. Face-nailing the starter course.
◆ An inch from each end of a long flooring board and an equal distance from the grooved side, drill a $\frac{1}{16}$-inch pilot hole.
◆ With a helper, align the grooved side of the board along the starting chalked line, $\frac{1}{2}$ inch from the side wall to allow a gap for expansion.
◆ Countersink a $2\frac{1}{2}$-inch finishing nail through each pilot hole.
◆ Drive and countersink more nails through pilot holes drilled at every joist and midway between them, about an inch from the grooved edge.
◆ Nail the rest of the first course, interlocking tongue and groove ends, and finishing with a piece that fits within $\frac{1}{2}$ inch of the side wall.

2. Arranging the field.
◆ Working out from the starter strip, rack seven or eight loose rows of flooring boards, staggering end joints in adjoining rows at least 6 inches apart and leaving a $\frac{1}{2}$-inch gap along the walls.
◆ Secure the second and third courses, fitting grooves onto tongues, tapping them in place with a mallet and protective block if necessary. Blind-nail them along joist lines.

3. Using the power nailer.
◆ At the fourth course, slip the power nailer's head onto the tongue of the first board, about 2 inches from the wall. Strike its plunger with a rubber mallet to drive a nail through the board's tongue and into the subfloor (inset).
◆ Using your heel to keep the board fitted tightly against the preceding course, drive nails into the tongue at each joist, halfway between joists, and near the board's end. Use carpenter's nippers to snip off nails that do not penetrate completely.
◆ Install boards with the nailer until you get too close to the wall to use it, then blind-nail the remainder by hand.

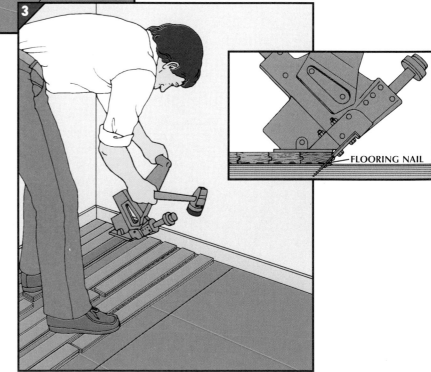

FLOORING NAIL

4. Installing the final boards.

◆ If more than $\frac{1}{2}$ inch of space remains at the far wall, trim boards on the tongue side to fill the gap *(page 252)*.

◆ Drill pilot holes *(page 250, Step 1)*, then position the board on the floor.

◆ Insert a pry bar between the flooring board and the baseboard *(right)*, protecting the baseboard with a scrap of wood. Push the pry bar sideways with your foot to hold the board in place and face-nail the board to joists and the subflooring.

5. Finishing off a doorway.

Drill pilot holes, then face-nail a clamshell reducer strip—so called because its rounded top makes it resemble half a clamshell—at a doorway where a new wood floor meets a lower floor. The reducer strip *(photograph)*, available at flooring distributors, is milled on one side to fit over the tongue of an adjoining board. The strip can also be butted to the ends of floorboards that run at right angles to a doorway.

REDUCER STRIP

6. Laying expansion strips.

Wedge strips of $\frac{3}{4}$-inch corkboard into the space where the floor meets glass sliding doors, ceramic tiles, or a laid stone floor. The cork acts as a cushion that compresses or expands to compensate for shrinkage or swelling of the floorboards.

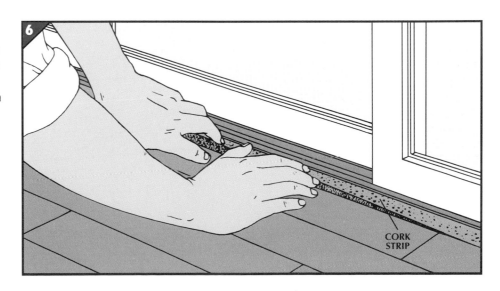

CORK STRIP

7. Installing shoe molding.

◆ Through the center of $\frac{3}{4}$-inch shoe molding, drill $\frac{1}{16}$-inch pilot holes that are angled to direct a nail into the baseboard.

◆ Fasten the shoe molding over the gap between the flooring and the baseboard with $1\frac{1}{2}$-inch finishing nails.

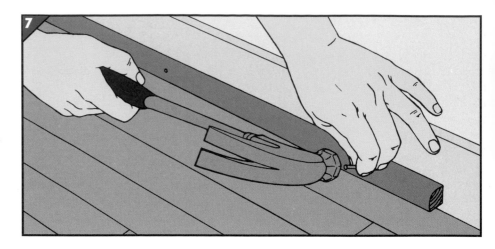

SPECIAL SITUATIONS

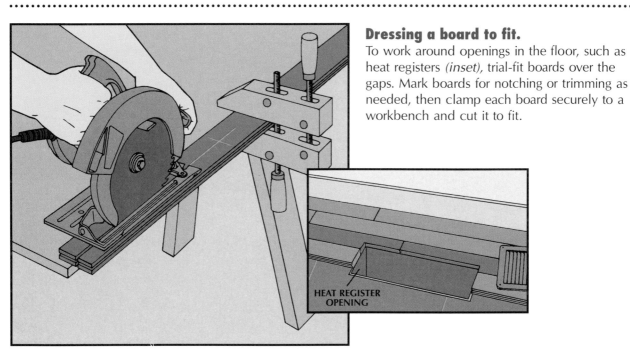

HEAT REGISTER OPENING

Dressing a board to fit.

To work around openings in the floor, such as heat registers *(inset)*, trial-fit boards over the gaps. Mark boards for notching or trimming as needed, then clamp each board securely to a workbench and cut it to fit.

Framing special borders.

Using a miter box, saw boards at 45-degree angles to frame a fireplace hearth *(inset)*. Remove the boards' tongues when necessary to make them fit tightly against adjoining boards, then face-nail them into place.

Reversing tongue direction.
To blind-nail tongue-and-groove boards in a hall or closet opening onto the groove side of the starting course, join groove to groove with a slip tongue, available in 3-foot lengths from flooring distributors. Place the slip tongue into the back-to-back grooves, then position the power nailer over the tongue of the loose board and nail it to the floor.

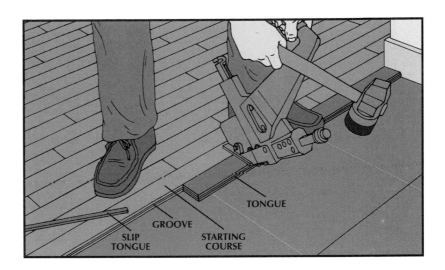

TONGUE

GROOVE

SLIP TONGUE

STARTING COURSE

SECURING BOARDS WITH GLUE

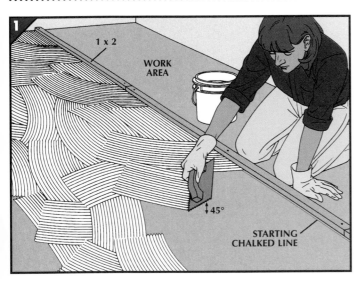

1 x 2

WORK AREA

45°

STARTING CHALKED LINE

1. Spreading the mastic.
◆ Establish a starting chalked line *(page 249, Step 3)* approximately 30 inches from the starting wall. The 30-inch gap serves as a mastic-free work area.
◆ Snap a parallel chalked line as a boundary for spreading mastic for the first courses of boards, remembering not to exceed 40 square feet.
◆ Fasten 1-by-2s along the starting chalked line with masonry nails. They will hold the first course in place while you add succeeding rows, so be sure they are straight.
◆ With a V-notch trowel held at a 45-degree angle, spread mastic between the chalked lines.
◆ Wait for the mastic to become tacky, usually 20 minutes to an hour.

2. Affixing the boards.
◆ At the left end of the starting chalked line, lay a board $\frac{1}{2}$ inch from the wall, tongue side against the 1-by-2s. Tap it with a mallet and protective block to seat it in the mastic.
◆ Apply carpenter's glue sparingly to the tongue end of the next board, fit it in the groove of the first board, and lay the board along the 1-by-2s. Seat it in the mastic, then remove excess glue with a damp cloth.
◆ Continue the first course until you are within 4 feet of the wall, then cut the last board to fit, leaving a $\frac{1}{2}$-inch gap between it and the wall.
◆ Add boards by rows, cutting pieces as necessary to stagger joints *(page 250, Step 2)*. Interlock the sides first, then the glued ends, before seating the board in the mastic.
◆ Fill in the rest of the room, removing the 1-by-2s and flooring the work area last.
◆ Use a flooring roller to bond the boards securely to the mastic, then let it set as the adhesive label advises.

Tiles of Wood or Vinyl

Tile flooring, whether it is made of wood, linoleum, or some synthetic material such as vinyl, lends itself to imaginative design. Moreover, it can be glued to almost any surface. Before laying the tiles, however, you must plan the pattern of the floor and prepare the surface as described in the introduction to "Installing a New Wood Floor" on page 248.

Resilient Tiles: Tiles of vinyl and its relatives come in a vast array of colors, styles, and patterns. Some are available as 12-inch squares, others as 9-inch squares. However, aside from following the instructions that begin at the bottom of this page for planning your floor on graph paper and laying it, there is little about such tiles that requires particular attention.

Wood Parquet: Some aspects of wood tiles require special consideration. They are available, for example, not only as squares, but also as rectangles. This feature permits patterns like the ones shown on page 257, which are impossible with resilient tiles.

Grain also needs to be considered. All the tiles can be laid with the grain in the same direction, but results are often more attractive if grain direction alternates from one tile to the next.

Because wood tiles absorb moisture, allow them 72 hours to adjust to the humidity before laying them. Also, to allow for expansion, leave a $\frac{1}{2}$-inch space between the border tiles and the walls, then fill it with a strip of $\frac{1}{2}$-inch cork, covered by quarter-round molding. In areas that are heavily trafficked, such as doorways, lay a border of whole tiles on the sides of the room where there are doors; partial tiles tend to loosen in the heavy foot traffic there.

 CAUTION *Use a nonflammable, latex-based tile adhesive, and keep the room well ventilated.*

 TOOLS

Chalk line
Flooring roller
  (100-pound)
V-notch trowel
Utility knife
Mallet
Fine-toothed
  handsaw

MATERIALS

Graph paper
Small nails
Tape measure
Adhesive for vinyl
  or wood tiles
Wood block
Cork strip ($\frac{1}{2}$")

 SAFETY TIPS

When spreading adhesive, wear rubber gloves.

INSTALLING RESILIENT TILES

1. Planning on paper.

◆ On graph paper, plot a design for a floor laid on the square *(near right)* or on the diagonal *(far right)*, letting each block represent one tile if they are square (or the width of the tile if they are rectangular). If you plan to use 9- rather than 12-inch tiles, multiply the dimensions of the room by 1.33 to find how many tiles to plot to a side. Always count fractions as whole tiles.

◆ Buy one 12-inch tile for each square foot to be covered. To determine how many 9-inch tiles to purchase, multiply the room's square footage by 1.78. For two colors of tile, subtract the squares of one color from the total to see how many tiles you need of each; add 5 percent for waste and repairs.

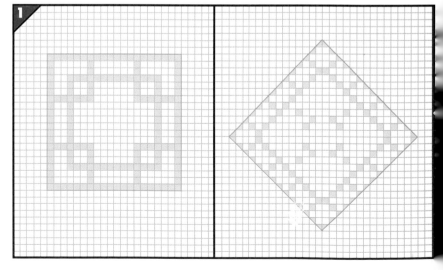

2. Guidelines for the dry run.

◆ Divide the room into equal quadrants with two chalked strings that are stretched between nails set at the midpoints of facing walls.

◆ Make sure that strings are perpendicular by measuring 3 feet from the intersection on one string and 4 feet on the other. The diagonal between the 3- and 4-foot points should be exactly 5 feet. Do not snap the chalk lines yet.

For a diagonal pattern, measure from the intersection to one of the two longer walls, and transfer the distance to the wall on both sides of the guideline nail. Then set nails into the wall. Do the same thing on the facing wall, and stretch chalked strings diagonally between the nails *(inset, red lines)*.

3. Making a dry run.

For a pattern laid on the square—including the Haddon Hall pattern for wood parquet *(page 257)*—place dry tiles along the guidelines defining one quadrant, starting from the intersection and duplicating the plan on your graph paper. If both rows end more than half a tile from the walls, snap the chalk lines. If the border is less than half a tile, shift the rows so you will not have to cut and lay small pieces. Set the chalk lines in the new place and snap them.

To check a diagonal pattern, lay tiles corner to corner along the lines defining one quadrant, and lay another row along the diagonal guideline *(inset).*

When laying a diagonal or herringbone pattern *(page 257)*, arrange for the pattern to end in a sawtooth line of half tiles; add a border of tiles set on the square to fill any space between a wall and the nearby half tiles. If differences in the widths of borders on two adjacent walls are visually disturbing, make the borders at least two tiles wide.

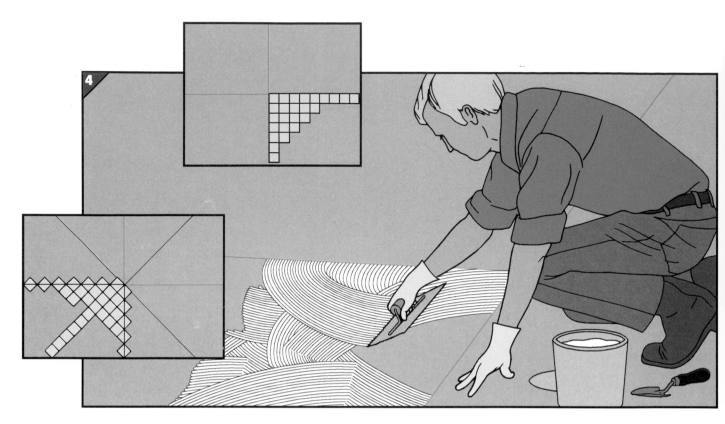

4. Setting tiles and adhesive.

◆ Apply adhesive holding the notched trowel so it is at a 45-degree angle. If you are laying tiles on the square, spread adhesive along one chalked line. Work from the intersection toward a wall, leaving parts of the line uncovered for guidance. Let the adhesive become tacky.

◆ Lay this row of tiles, butting each tile against one already laid and dropping it into place. Press the tile firmly against the adhesive.

◆ Beginning again at the intersection, set a row of tiles at a right angle to the first, then fill in the quadrant as shown in the upper inset.

◆ When you have finished a quadrant, roll it with a rented flooring roller.

To lay a diagonal pattern *(lower inset),* set tiles point to point over the perpendicular chalked lines. Lay another row of tiles with their sides along the diagonal chalked line. Then fill in the area between rows, working from the intersection toward the wall.

5. Trimming a border tile.

◆ Place two loose tiles squarely on top of the last whole tile in a row and slide the upper one across the untiled gap until it touches a wall.

◆ Using the edge of the top tile as a guide, score the one beneath with a utility knife. Snap the tile along the scored line and fit the piece into the gap, snapped edge against the wall.

◆ Trim door moldings to permit tiles to slip under them, and cut tiles to fit around cabinets or other obstacles *(page 281).*

For a diagonal pattern, score tiles from corner to corner and snap them, forming triangular half tiles to fill the sawtooth edge of the pattern. Trim tiles for a square-set border as at left.

LAYING WOOD PARQUET

Setting wood tiles in place.

The procedure for laying a wood parquet floor is identical to the one described on pages 254 to 256 for resilient tile, with a couple of exceptions. First, you must use a mallet, cushioned by a block of wood, to join the tiles—which have tongue-and-groove edges like floorboards *(page 248)*—and to set them in the adhesive. While you are tapping with the mallet, hold adjacent tiles in place by kneeling on them. Second, use a pencil to mark tiles for trimming instead of scoring them, and cut them with a fine-toothed handsaw.

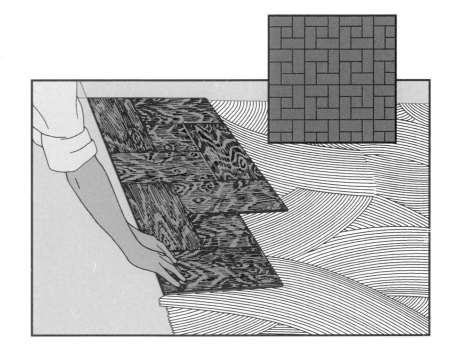

The Haddon Hall pattern.

◆ In the corner of one quadrant, lay two 6- by 12-inch tiles perpendicular to each other.

◆ Set a 6- by 6-inch tile in the corner created by the perpendicular tiles, and position two 6- by 12-inch tiles around it to make a square within a square.

◆ Complete the quadrant pyramidally, then fill in the other quadrants *(inset)*.

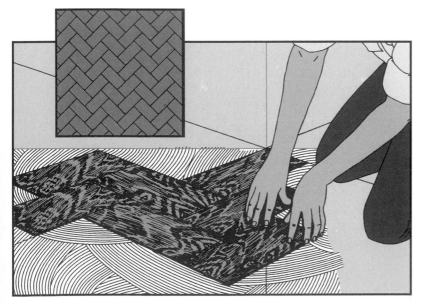

The herringbone pattern.

◆ Establish guidelines as for laying square tiles on the diagonal *(page 255, Step 2)*.

◆ Spread adhesive in one quadrant, extending several inches beyond the guidelines as shown.

◆ Place a 6- by 12-inch tile along a diagonal guideline, with one corner at the intersection.

◆ Lay the second tile across the end of the first, and the third across the end of the second.

◆ Use the chalked lines and these tiles as guides for the next three tiles, and continue in this manner until you reach the wall.

◆ Repeat in the other sections of the room to complete the floor *(inset)*.

Applying Sheet Vinyl Flooring

Durable and stain-resistant, resilient sheet-vinyl flooring is an excellent choice for such high-traffic areas as a kitchen or playroom. It also has a great virtue as replacement flooring: In most cases, sheet vinyl can be laid right over an existing floor. Vinyl-flooring suppliers offer a variety of products to level and smooth the old surface and ensure good adhesion of the new flooring with a nonflammable, water- or latex-based adhesive. If the old floor must be removed, first read the asbestos warning on page 278.

Buying Replacement Flooring: Measure the room at its widest and longest points and add 6 inches at each wall for overlap. Because sheet vinyl comes in widths of up to 15 feet, you may be able to avoid seams. If you do need more than one sheet, buy a small bottle of seam sealer from the flooring dealer.

To fit the new vinyl flooring to your room, either purchase a pattern-making kit when you buy the flooring or use kraft paper and masking tape to make a template *(below)*.

Preliminary Steps: Move all furniture or appliances out of the room, then remove the shoe molding at the base of the walls; remove any door thresholds as well. Lay the new flooring out flat in a convenient space for 24 hours to adjust to the household temperature. The tightness of the inner part of the roll will have compressed the pattern on that part of the sheet; to even out the pattern, reverse the roll briefly.

 CAUTION *Seam sealer is toxic and flammable; follow all safety precautions on the label.*

 TOOLS

Utility knife
Straightedge
Notched spreader
Flooring roller
Screwdriver

 **MATERIALS**

Kraft paper
Masking tape
Vinyl-flooring
  adhesive
Seam sealer

 **SAFETY TIPS**

Protect your hands with rubber gloves when handling adhesive, and wear heavy work gloves when cutting flooring with a utility knife.

MAKING A TEMPLATE

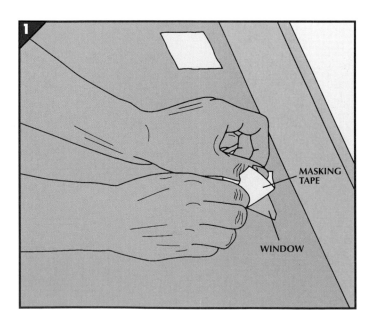

1. Taping down the template.

◆ Cut a length of kraft paper 6 inches longer than the longest floor edge. Position the paper along the floor edge $\frac{1}{8}$ inch from the wall with its ends lapped up the adjacent walls.

◆ With a utility knife, cut windows in the paper along the floor edges; then stick masking tape over the windows *(left)* to secure the paper to the flooring under it.

◆ Working across the floor to the other side, continue to lay down and tape together overlapping lengths of paper to cover the entire floor.

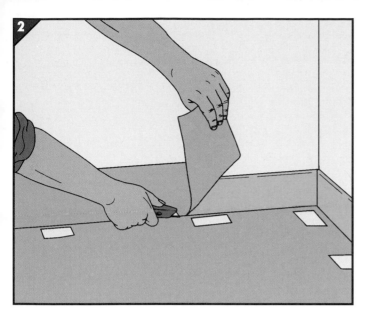

2. Trimming excess edges.
◆ With the utility knife, trim off the paper around any obstructions—radiators or built-in cabinets, for example. Then trim the paper where it is lapped up a wall *(left)*.
◆ Carefully roll up and remove the template in one piece.

CUTTING AND INSTALLING THE PIECES

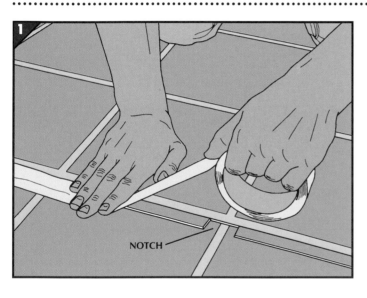

NOTCH

1. Aligning sheets for a seam.
If you need more than one sheet of replacement flooring to cover a room, you must align the patterns and secure the sheets along the seam before installation.
◆ Place the sheets flat in a work area with their seam edges butted together.
◆ With a utility knife and a straightedge, cut rectangular notches along the edge of one replacement sheet: At each pattern line perpendicular to the edge, make a notch 1 inch long and wide enough to reach to the first pattern line parallel to the edge.
◆ Pull the notched edge of the replacement sheet over the edge of the other sheet and use the notches to align their patterns.
◆ Tape the two sheets together securely with masking tape *(left)*.

2. Cutting replacement flooring.
◆ With the replacement sheet or sheets laid out flat, place the template on top of the flooring, centering it with any pattern lines.
◆ Tape the template to the flooring with masking tape. With a felt-tip pen, mark a cutting outline on the flooring around the template edges, then remove the template.
◆ Cut along the outline with a utility knife and a straightedge *(right)*; keep any excess pieces for repairs.
◆ Roll up the flooring and carry it into the room where it is to be installed. Unroll it and check the fit, trimming along the walls and doors and around obstructions, if necessary.

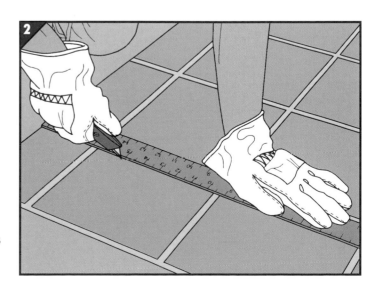

3. Adhering the flooring.

◆ Starting at one edge of the flooring along a wall, roll it back to the floor center. If there is a seam, stop 18 inches from it.
◆ With a notched spreader, coat the underlayment or the old floor evenly with adhesive *(above, left)*, working from the wall back to the center.
◆ Let the adhesive set for the time specified by the manufacturer. Then roll the flooring back out over the adhesive; make any small adjustments immediately.
◆ Roll a flooring roller over the flooring *(above, right)*, making two passes at a 90-degree angle to each other. Secure the flooring edges with a hand roller.
◆ Follow the same procedure to adhere the other half of the flooring. If your flooring has no seam, proceed to Step 6.

4. Cutting a seam.

◆ Remove the masking tape from the overlapped flooring edges along the seam.
◆ On the notched sheet, lay a straightedge along the pattern line at the top of the notches.
◆ Hold the utility knife against the straightedge and make several firm, steady strokes to cut through both flooring sheets and produce clean, even edges.

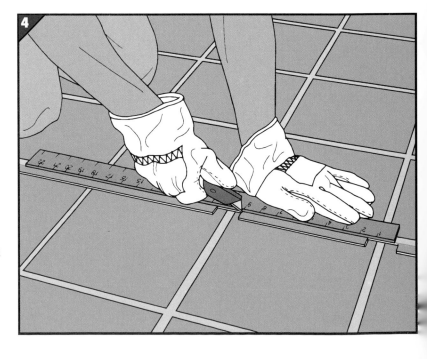

5. Adhering a seam.

◆ Pull the flooring on each side of the seam back 18 inches to expose the old flooring and coat it evenly with adhesive using a notched spreader.

◆ Allow the adhesive to set for the time specified by the manufacturer, then roll the flooring on each side of the seam back over the adhesive.

◆ Push a flooring roller back and forth over the area.

6. Finishing the installation.

◆ Keep traffic off the flooring for 24 hours after you have adhered it.

◆ Seal any flooring seam with a commercial seam sealer recommended for the flooring, following the manufacturer's instructions.

◆ Reinstall or replace the shoe molding you removed. Put back any thresholds removed from doorways, screwing them through the flooring into the underlayment *(right)*.

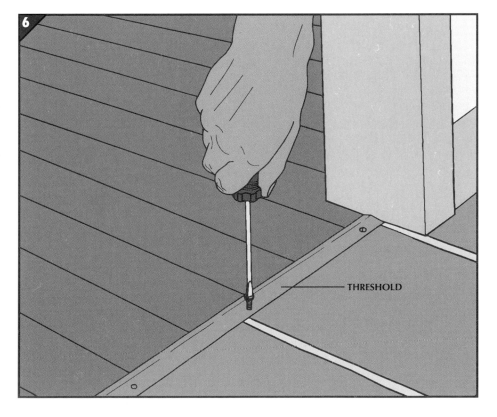

THRESHOLD

Setting Stone and Ceramic Tiles in Mortar

Rigid flooring tiles made of ceramic or a stone such as slate, sandstone, or marble offer greater durability than resilient materials like wood or vinyl. Plan a new rigid-tile floor as explained on pages 254 to 255.

When selecting floor tiles, remember that they become slippery when they are wet. Choose ceramic tiles for the floor of a bathroom, kitchen, or vestibule that have an abrasive grain fired into the glaze in order to reduce slipperiness. Marble tiles are best finished to a soft gloss rather than a high polish. Glazed ceramic tiles are impermeable, but some rigid flooring, such as Mexican and quarry tiles, absorbs liquids and therefore requires a protective sealant to make it resistant to stains.

Preparing the Surface: While rigid tiles are best laid directly on a concrete slab, as described here, you can also use them to cover an existing tile floor in good condition. Furthermore, modern adhesives make it possible to lay rigid tiles on a plywood subfloor using the methods for laying resilient tiles *(pages 254-256)*. After removing baseboards and shoe moldings, however,

you'll need to build up the subfloor to a thickness of $1\frac{1}{4}$ inches. A thinner subfloor is not rigid enough to prevent the floor from flexing and cracking the tiles.

No matter what surface you tile over, it must be flat. Roll a pipe over the floor in several directions, looking for surface undulations greater than $\frac{1}{8}$ inch. Reduce high spots with a rub brick or a rented concrete grinder; fill low spots with mortar.

When tiling an area of concrete that is larger than 125 square feet, cover the concrete with an isolation membrane before laying any tiles. Available as a sheet or a thick liquid, the isolation membrane helps prevent cracks in the concrete from affecting the tiles.

Setting the Tiles: Anchored to a concrete slab with thin set—a type of mortar mix to which you add water—rigid tiles are laid with joints between them. Fill these gaps with grout containing sand if they are $\frac{1}{8}$ inch wide or larger. For smaller spaces or for marble tiles, use unsanded grout. Gray grout made with Portland cement is inconspicuous and does not show dirt, but you can also tint the grout with powdered

coloring available from building-supply dealers.

Finishing the Edges: For ceramic-tile or marble-tile floors, a marble threshold is generally installed in interior doorways. Marble companies cut thresholds to length and bevel them to join the newly tiled floor to its neighbor. Thresholds for bathroom doorways should rise $\frac{1}{4}$ inch above the tiled floor to make a dam against spills. Outside doorways may need new weatherproof metal thresholds.

The job is finished, for most vestibules and hallways, with wood baseboards and base shoes—the ones you removed or new ones. For a formal look or for protection against splashes in bathrooms, make bases of the same material as the floor. Ceramic-tile makers can supply such trim.

For stone floors, you can make your own base trim by sawing 12-by-12 tiles into 4-by-12 strips. Smooth and bevel or round the rough edges with silicon-carbide sanding disks in an electric drill, using grits 80, 150, and 320 in succession. Secure the trim to the wall with thin-set adhesive.

 TOOLS

Chalk line
Square-notch
  trowel
Sponge
Mason's trowel
Level
Mallet
Circular saw with
  silicon-carbide
  masonry blade
Tile cutter
Tile sander
Dovetail saw
Grout float
Small brush
Clamps

 **MATERIALS**

Concrete isolation
  membrane
Thin-set mortar
Tile spacers
2 x 4
2 x 10
Sawhorses
Scrap wood
Grout
Grout sealant

 SAFETY TIPS

Be prepared for dust when cutting stone or ceramic tiles. Work outdoors if possible, and wear goggles, a respirator, and earplugs. Wear rubber gloves when spreading mortar and grout.

FILLING IN THE CENTER OF THE ROOM

1. Making the mortar bed.
◆ When laying tile on bare concrete, dampen it before proceeding.
◆ Divide the room into equal quadrants and snap chalk lines as described on page 255.
◆ At the intersection of the chalked lines, use a square-notch trowel to spread a low mound of mortar, then hold the trowel nearly vertical and drag the teeth on the sub-floor, leaving ridges of mortar *(left)*. Add more of the dry ingredients if the mortar is soupy and does not form ridges. If the mortar is dry and crumbly, add water.

2. Laying the first tile.
◆ Sponge water onto the back of a tile if it absorbs water readily. Place the tile on the mortar at the intersection of the guidelines. Press it down firmly, twisting it slightly several times. Apply your full body weight on big tiles.
◆ Lift the tile off the floor and examine the bottom. If you see a pattern of ridges or that the bottom is less than 90 percent covered with mortar, use a larger notch trowel to make a new bed and re-lay the tile.
◆ With the handle of a mason's trowel, tap the tile to align it with the chalked lines.
◆ Level the tile diagonally and along two adjacent sides. Tap down any high sides with a mallet and a 2-by-4 wrapped in cloth. Scoop up excess mortar.

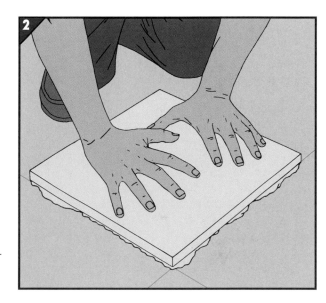

3. Filling in the field.
◆ Lay four tiles around the first tile to form a cross. For tiles without spacing lugs cast on their bottom edges, insert rubber or plastic tile spacers between them. Let the tiles set overnight.
◆ Fill in each quadrant, redampening bare concrete before doing so if it has dried. Since tiles may differ in size, measure frequently from the guidelines *(left)*. Enlarge spacing as needed to keep tiles aligned and rows even.
◆ As you set tiles, check their height against the center tile using a level on a straight 2-by-4. Tap down any high tiles *(Step 2)*.
◆ Use the techniques shown on page 281 to fit tiles around obstacles.

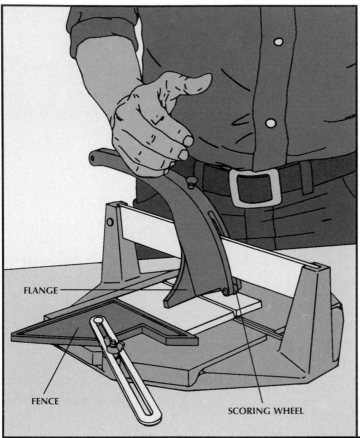

FLANGE

FENCE

SCORING WHEEL

Cutting border tiles.

Mark border tiles for cutting as described on page 256. For most ceramic tiles, rent a tile cutter *(left)*. Set the fence to position the cut line under the scoring wheel, then score the tile surface. Release the handle and gently strike it with your hand. The flanges on the tool will snap the tile along the scored line.

For stone tiles or thick ceramic ones, use a circular saw fitted with a silicon-carbide masonry blade *(below)*. Clamp the tile between a guide board and a 2-by-10 on sawhorses. Beside the tile, place wood scraps no thinner than the tile to carry the saw at the beginning and end of the cut. Cut the tile in two passes, the first $\frac{1}{4}$ inch deep, the second through the tile and $\frac{1}{8}$ inch into the 2-by-10.

⚠️ **CAUTION** *Cut tiles are sharp. Dull the edges with a tile sander, available from tile suppliers.*

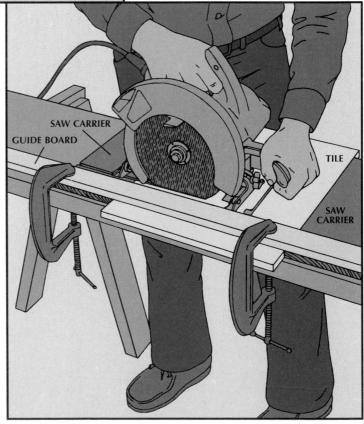

SAW CARRIER

GUIDE BOARD

TILE

SAW CARRIER

Setting a threshold.

◆ Position the threshold in the doorway and mark its height on the doorstops.

◆ With a handsaw—preferably the dovetail variety *(photograph)*—cut the doorstops at the marks.

◆ Set the threshold in a bed of raked mortar just as you would a tile.

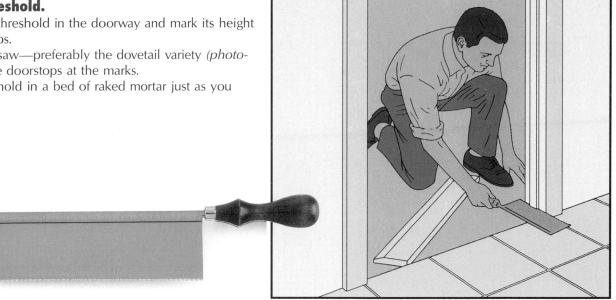

FINISHING THE JOB

1. Spreading grout.

◆ Let the tiles set overnight, then remove the spacers between them.

◆ Pour a cup or two of premixed grout onto the tiles. Working on sections of 5 square feet or so at a time, hold a grout float at a 45-degree angle to the floor and sweep it diagonally across the joints several times, forcing grout between the tiles.

2. Packing grout into the joints.

◆ Turn the float on edge and compact the grout in each section until it is slightly below the surface of the tiles.

◆ When the floor is done, clean the float, then drag it across the surface to remove excess grout.

◆ Wipe the tiles, 10 to 15 minutes later, with a damp cloth to remove any grout haze.

◆ Keep the grout moist as it cures—usually about 3 days—then brush grout sealant over the joints and allow it to dry.

Quick Cures for Wood Flooring

Although durable, wood floors are subject to a variety of ailments—among them, squeaks, bouncing, cracks, stains, and burns. Most maladies can be easily remedied. If the damage is serious, you can replace boards without leaving visible scars.

Problems beneath the Floor: Squeaks are usually caused by subflooring that is no longer firmly attached to the joists or by the rubbing of finish floorboards that have worked loose from the subfloor. Retightening either can be done in a number of ways, explained at right and on page 268.

Squeaks, along with bouncing, may also indicate a lack of bridging—diagonal braces between joists, needed for any joist span of 8 feet or more. If this reinforcement is missing, install prefabricated steel bridging.

Sealing Cracks: Cracks between boards open when humidity and temperature changes cause uneven shrinkage. Plug them with a mixture of sawdust from the floor itself and penetrating sealer. Gather the dust by sanding boards in a corner of a closet. Work 4 parts sawdust and 1 part sealer into a thick paste and trowel it into the crack.

Surface Defects: Stains and burns, if not too deep, can be erased by sanding. To determine the extent of the damage, go over the blemished area with a wood scraper. If the defect starts to lift out, the board can be saved by sanding and refinishing; otherwise, you will have to replace it.

Patching a Damaged Floor: Replacement of ruined boards is best done in the winter, when dry furnace heat will shrink the wood and ease the job of fitting in new pieces. Inspect for decay in the subfloor if you see any sign of rot in the floorboards: With an ice pick or awl, pry up some wood; if it feels spongy or cracks across the grain, rot has set in. Treat lightly decayed subfloors with a preservative containing pentachlorophenol. If the rot has penetrated through the wood, replace the subflooring.

 TOOLS

Hammer
Stud finder
Electric drill
Nail set
Screwdriver
Putty knife
Mallet
Wood chisel
Pry bar

 **MATERIALS**

Construction
adhesive
Finishing nails or
trim head screws
(3")
Wood shingles
Screws and washers
Glazier's points
Steel bridging
Replacement
boards
Flooring nails (3")

 SAFETY TIPS

When hammering nails, wear safety goggles to protect your eyes from flying debris.

Anatomy of a wood floor.

A typical wood floor is constructed in layers. Parallel 2- by 8-inch joists, laid on girders and braced by diagonal bridging, provide structural support. In older homes, the subfloor is often wide planks or tongue-and-groove boards laid diagonally for extra stability. Today, sheets of $\frac{3}{4}$-inch plywood are preferred; they are usually glued as well as nailed to the joists. A moistureproof and sound-deadening underlayment of heavy felt or building paper is laid atop the subfloor. The finish flooring, most commonly strips of oak, $\frac{3}{4}$ inch thick and $2\frac{1}{4}$ inches wide, has interlocking tongues and grooves on the sides and ends. They are attached by driving and setting 3-inch flooring nails at an angle above the tongues, where the nails will be concealed by the upper lips of the adjoining grooves *(inset)*.

FINISH FLOORING

UNDERLAYMENT

SUBFLOOR

GIRDER

BRIDGING

JOISTS

Shimming the subfloor.

If the subfloor is accessible from below, have someone walk on the floor while you look for movement in the subfloor over a joist. To eliminate movement, apply a bead of construction adhesive to both sides of the tapered edge of a wood shingle and wedge it between the joist and the loose subfloor. Do not force the subfloor upward or you may cause boards in the finish floor to separate.

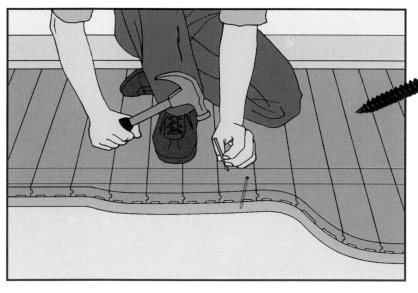

TRIM HEAD SCREW

Securing inaccessible subfloors.

If the ceiling beneath the floor is finished, refasten the loose section of subfloor to the nearest joist through the finish floor above.

◆ Use a stud finder to locate the joist. Then drill pairs of pilot holes angled toward each other and drive 3-inch finishing nails or trim head screws *(photo)* into the subfloor and joist below.

◆ Set the nailheads or countersink the screws and cover them with wood putty that has been tinted to match the color of the boards.

Anchoring floorboards from below.

◆ Select screws that will reach to no more than $\frac{1}{4}$ inch below the surface of the finish floor.

◆ Drill pilot holes through the subfloor, using a bit with a diameter at least as large as that of the screw shanks, so that the screws will turn freely. Avoid penetrating the finish floor by marking the subfloor's thickness on the drill bit with tape.

◆ Drill pilot holes into the finish floor with a bit slightly narrower than the screws.

◆ Fit the screws with large washers, apply a bit of candle wax to the threads to ease installation, and insert them into the pilot holes. As you turn the screws, their threads will bite into the finish floorboards, pulling them tight to the subfloor.

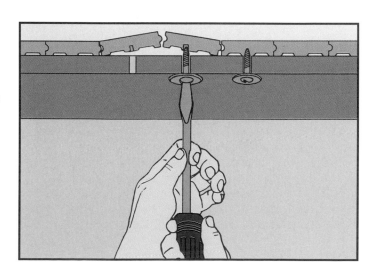

Silencing finish flooring from above.

◆ First, try remedies that do not mar the finished surface. Force powdered graphite or talcum powder into the joints between boards.

◆ If the squeak persists, insert glazier's points—the triangular metal pieces that secure glass into frames—every 6 inches and set them below the surface with a putty knife *(right)*. If the pressure of the knife is insufficient to push the points down, use a hammer and small piece of scrap metal to tap them into place.

◆ Should these solutions fail, drive finishing nails or trim head screws through the floorboards and into the subfloor, angling and concealing them as explained on page 267.

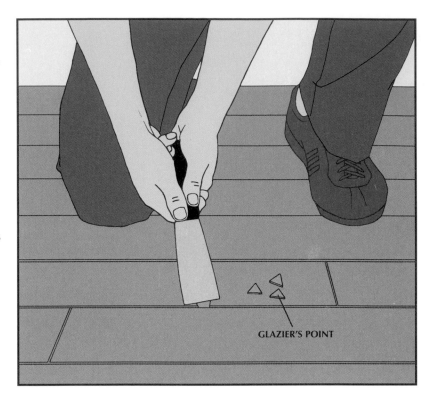

GLAZIER'S POINT

Installing steel bridging.

Prefabricated steel bridging comes in sizes to fit between joists spaced at 12, 16, and 24 inches. To install the braces, hammer the straight-pronged end into a joist near the top. Then pound the L-shaped claw end into the adjacent joist near the bottom. Alternate the crisscross bridging pattern from joist to joist, making sure the pieces do not touch each other.

CUTTING OUT A DAMAGED AREA

1. Making end cuts.

◆ Remove boards in a staggered pattern, with adjacent end joints at least 6 inches apart. At the end of a damaged board, make a vertical cut with a sharp 1-inch wood chisel, keeping its bevel side toward the portion of the board to be removed.

◆ Working back toward the vertical cut, angle the blade and drive the chisel at about 30 degrees *(inset)* along the board.

◆ Repeat this sequence until you have cut all the way through the board. Repeat at the other end.

2. Splitting the board.

◆ With the chisel, make two parallel incisions a little less than an inch apart along the middle of the board from one end to the other.

◆ Use the chisel to pry up the board between the incisions just enough to split the wood.

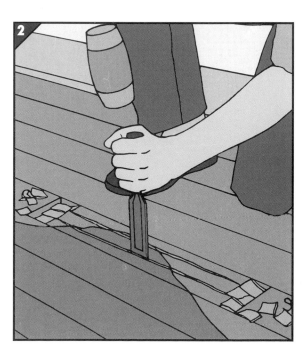

3. Prying the board out.

◆ Working on a board at the center of the damaged area, insert a pry bar into the lengthwise crack created with the chisel. Pry the middle strip out, then the groove side of the board, and finally the tongue side.

◆ Remove adjacent boards in the same way, working toward the edge of the damaged area and taking care not to harm any good boards. Remove exposed nails or drive them down with a nail set.

◆ Take a sample of the flooring to a lumberyard to get matching replacement boards.

PATCHING THE HOLE

1. Inserting a new board sideways.
Cut a replacement board to fill the outermost space on the tongued side of the damaged area. Using a scrap of flooring with a groove that fits the tongue of the replacement piece as a hammering block, wedge the new board securely into place.

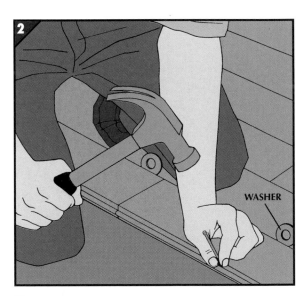

2. Blind-nailing a board.
Drive and set 3-inch flooring nails at a 45-degree angle through the corner of the tongue of the replacement piece. Pilot holes are not essential but may be helpful. If existing boards around the repair have separated slightly, try to match their spacing by inserting thin shims such as metal washers between the new board and the old one while driving the nails.

3. Inserting a new board lengthwise.
To slide a replacement between two boards, lay it flat on the subfloor and work the tips of its tongue and groove into those of the existing pieces. Using a scrap hammering block, tap it all the way in.

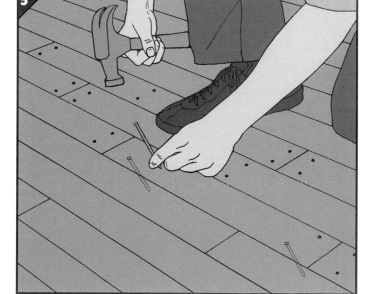

4. Inserting a new board from above.
◆ For the last few spaces where you cannot slide the pieces into place, lay a replacement board upside down on a piece of scrap wood and chisel off the lower lip of the groove as indicated by the blue line on the board at right.
◆ Turn the board faceup and gently tap it into place from above.

5. Face-nailing.
◆ To fasten the last replacement boards, which offer no access for blind-nailing, drill angled pilot holes every 12 inches about $\frac{1}{2}$ inch from the edges of the face. Drive 3-inch finishing nails or trim head screws into the holes.
◆ Set the nails or countersink the screws and cover them with wood putty that has been tinted to match the color of the boards.

Refinishing Hardwood Floors

Restoring the natural beauty of a wood floor, whether it is varnished or painted, necessitates removal of the old finish before the new one can be applied. The first step is to take all furniture out of the room and to seal drapes in plastic bags. Lift off floor registers and cover the vents with plastic.

Fasten loose boards and replace badly damaged ones *(pages 269-271)*. Drive protruding nailheads $\frac{1}{8}$ inch below the floor surface with a nail set. Beginning at a door, remove shoe moldings from baseboards by driving the nails through the molding with a pin punch no larger than the nailhead.

Getting to Bare Wood: Some laminated floorboards are too thin to sand; remove the old finish with a chemical stripper. On thicker boards, use a drum sander *(below)*.

Multiple sandings are required.

For rough or painted floorboards, begin with 20-grit sandpaper, then proceed to 36-grit, 50-grit, and finally 80-grit. Varnished or shellacked floors need only three sandings beginning with 36-grit. Sand parquet floors first with 50-grit followed by 80- and 100-grit.

Removing Stains: First try to remove a stain by hand-sanding. If it remains, apply a small amount of wood bleach to its center. Let the spot lighten, then apply enough bleach to blend the treated area with the rest of the floor. Rinse away the bleach with a vinegar-soaked rag. If the stains remain even after bleaching, replace the boards *(pages 269-271)*.

A Two-Step Glaze: To protect the wood and emphasize the grain, apply a sealer, which is available in both natural wood hues and a clear, colorless form *(page 274, bottom)*. For a final protective glaze over the sealer, select a urethane floor finish, which becomes exceptionally tough as it hardens.

Both oil- and water-based sealers and finishes are available. If you plan to stain the floor, oil-based products provide richer, more even color than water-based products, which dry faster and are easier and safer to handle.

If you choose water-based products, apply and smooth them with tools made of synthetic material, avoiding natural-bristle brushes and steel wool. Use a synthetic abrasive pad instead. Clean the floor with a lint-free rag rather than a tack cloth.

⚠ **CAUTION** *Sanding produces highly flammable dust. Seal the doorways into the work area with plastic, and ventilate the room with a fan (opposite).*

TOOLS

Nail set
Pin punch
Drum sander
Edging machine

Floor polisher
Paint scraper
Paintbrushes
Lambs wool
    applicator
Putty knife

MATERIALS

Sandpaper
Wood bleach
Vinegar
Tack cloth
Lint-free rags

Sealer
Urethane floor
    finish
Abrasive pads
    (steel-wool or
    synthetic)
Tinted wood putty

SAFETY TIPS

Sand floors wearing goggles, ear protection, and dust mask. When applying wood bleach, sealer, or finish, put on goggles and rubber gloves, as well as long pants and a long-sleeve shirt.

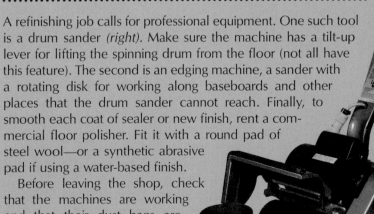

TOOLS TO RENT

A refinishing job calls for professional equipment. One such tool is a drum sander *(right)*. Make sure the machine has a tilt-up lever for lifting the spinning drum from the floor (not all have this feature). The second is an edging machine, a sander with a rotating disk for working along baseboards and other places that the drum sander cannot reach. Finally, to smooth each coat of sealer or new finish, rent a commercial floor polisher. Fit it with a round pad of steel wool—or a synthetic abrasive pad if using a water-based finish.

Before leaving the shop, check that the machines are working and that their dust bags are clean. Take with you any special wrenches for loading the drum sander and plenty of sandpaper—at least 10 drum-sander sheets and 10 edger disks of each grit for an average room. Because sanders need grounding, they must have three-pronged plugs; if your house has two-slot receptacles, you will need grounding adapters.

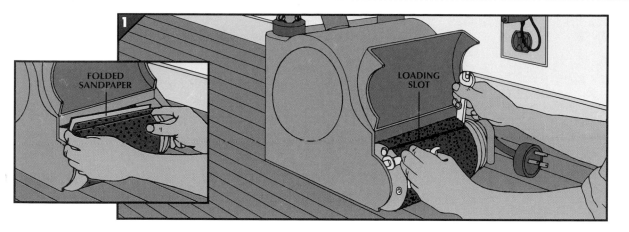

1. Loading the drum sander.

◆ With the sander unplugged, thread a sheet of sandpaper into the loading slot, turn the drum one full revolution, and slip the other end of the sheet into the slot.

◆ To secure the paper, tighten the drum's internal clamp by turning the boltheads at both ends of the drum with the wrenches provided by the dealer. With fine-grit sandpaper, fold a strip of the material in half, grit exposed, and slip it into the slot between the two ends to keep them from slipping out (inset).

TRICKS OF THE TRADE

Filtered Ventilation

A window fan with a furnace filter helps clear the air in a room while you are sanding. Buy a filter large enough to cover the entire fan, and tape it to the intake side; duct tape works well for the purpose. Place the fan in a window with the intake side inward, and turn it on. The filter will catch a large portion of the dust so it does not collect in your fan or blow into the neighborhood.

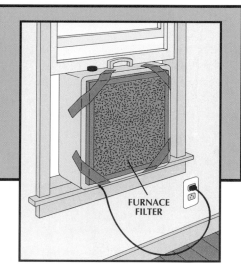

FURNACE FILTER

2. The first sanding.

◆ Standing with a wall about 3 feet behind you, lift the drum from the floor with the tilt-up lever, start the sander, and when the motor reaches full speed, lower the drum to the floor. Let the sander pull you forward at a slow, steady pace. Sand boards along the wood's grain unless they undulate slightly. In that case, or if the floor is patterned with varying grain directions, do the first sanding diagonally.

◆ At the far wall, raise the drum from the floor, move the cord behind you to one side, then lower the drum and pull the sander backward over the area you just sanded.

◆ Lift the drum and move the machine to the left or right, overlapping the first pass by 2 or 3 inches.

◆ Continue forward and backward passes across the room, turning off the sander occasionally in order to empty the dust bag, then turn the machine around and sand the area next to the wall.

⚠ **CAUTION** *Keep the sander in motion to prevent it from denting or rippling the wood.*

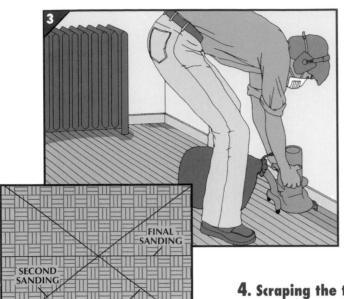

3. Completing the sanding.

◆ Sand areas missed by the drum sander with the edger, loaded with coarse-grit paper.

◆ Repeat both the drum and edge sandings, with successively finer sandpaper. On floorboards, these sandings, like the first, should be made with the grain. On parquet floors, do the second sanding on the opposite diagonal to the first, and the final sanding along the length of the room *(inset)*.

◆ Smooth the floor with a floor polisher *(opposite)* and a fine abrasive pad, suited to sealer and finish. This will lessen the boundary between drum- and edge-sanded areas.

4. Scraping the tight spots.

In areas that neither the drum sander nor the edging machine can reach, remove the finish with a paint scraper. At a radiator, remove collars from around the pipes for a thorough job. Always pull the scraper toward you, applying firm downward pressure on the tool with both hands. Scrape with the grain wherever possible, and replace the blade when it gets dull. Sand the scraped areas by hand.

APPLYING PROTECTIVE COATS

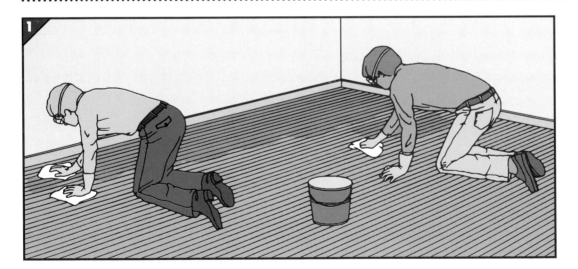

1. Spreading sealer.

◆ Ventilate the room. Vacuum the floor and pick up dust with a tack cloth, or a dry rag if using water-based sealer.

◆ Starting next to a wall and away from the door, apply sealer liberally over a 3-foot-wide strip of floor with a rag. Use long, sweeping strokes along the grain of the wood or along the length of the room if the grain directions vary.

◆ Between 8 and 20 minutes after it is applied, the sealer will have penetrated the wood, leaving shallow puddles of the liquid on the surface. Have a helper, using rags in both hands, mop up the excess sealer.

◆ As your helper works on the first strip, start applying sealer to the second strip. Try to work at a pace that keeps both of you moving together with your knees on dry floor until the job is almost finished. On the last strip, the helper will have to back across wet sealer to the door.

◆ Finally, let the sealer dry according to the manufacturer's specifications.

2

ABRASIVE PAD

SCRUB BRUSH

2. Smoothing the sealed wood.

◆ Fit a floor polisher with a heavy-duty scrub brush and press a fine abrasive pad into the bristles of the brush *(inset)*. Run the polisher over the floor to smooth irregularities in the surface caused by tiny bubbles in the sealer coating.

◆ Scour the edges and corners of the floor by hand with a small abrasive pad, then vacuum the entire floor and go over it thoroughly with a tack cloth or damp rag, according to the finish, to pick up any remaining dust.

3. Finishing the floor.

◆ Apply the finish slowly and evenly with a wide brush. With oil-based finish you may use a lambs wool applicator *(photograph)*. Work along the grain. If grain directions vary, work along the room's length. Stroke in one direction and do not go back over finish that has begun to set. If working alone, do edges and corners first with a small brush, then work on the rest.

◆ When the first coat is dry, smooth the surface *(Step 2, above)*.

◆ Clean the floor with a vacuum and tack cloth or damp rag. Force wood putty, tinted to match, into cracks and nail holes with a putty knife.

◆ Apply a second coat of finish in the same way. Water-based urethane, thinner than oil-based, needs a third coat.

◆ Wait 24 hours. Replace shoe moldings, registers, radiator-pipe collars.

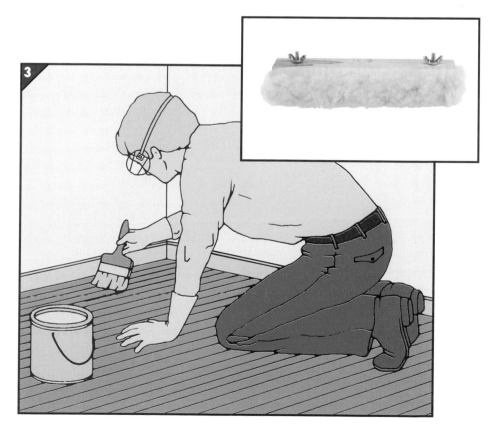

3

The tough surface of vinyl tiles or sheet flooring will resist wear and stains for many years. If damage does occur, you can usually repair or hide it yourself.

Common-Sense Precautions: A resilient floor should be kept as dry as possible, even when being cleaned, so that water does not get underneath and destroy the bond of the adhesive that holds it in place.

Resting furniture feet on plastic or rubber coasters will help protect the floor from punctures and gouges. When heavy furniture or appliances must be moved across the floor, slide them over pieces of plywood.

Curing Minor Ailments: To conceal a shallow scratch, gently rub it lengthwise with the rim of a coin. This will press the edges of the scratch together so only a thin line remains. Deeper cuts can be closed by carefully heating the vinyl as explained on page 279.

If a tile has come loose, first determine whether water from leaking plumbing is the cause; if it is, repair the leak before fixing the floor. Use water-based latex adhesive to glue the tile down.

Mending Major Flaws: The best remedy for a ruined tile is a replacement; similarly, a badly damaged section of sheet flooring will need a patch. If you cannot find any spare matching tiles or sheet flooring, look for replacements in inconspicuous areas of your floor—under a refrigerator or at the back of a closet, for instance. Cut and remove the section from the hidden area and substitute a nonmatching material of equal thickness.

If your resilient floor is glued to an asphalt-felt underlayment, the felt may tear as you remove damaged flooring. Usually you can glue the felt back together with latex adhesive; allow the adhesive to dry before continuing the job. If the felt is beyond repair, cut out the damaged section and glue down enough replacement layers of 15-pound asphalt felt to maintain the same floor level.

⚠ **CAUTION** *CAUTION: If your resilient floor was installed before 1986, the flooring or the adhesive underneath may contain asbestos. Precautions to take with asbestos appear on page 15.*

 TOOLS

Putty knife   Notched trowel
Utility knife   Metal straightedge
Iron

 **MATERIALS**

Latex adhesive
Replacement vinyl tiles or sheet flooring

 SAFETY TIPS

Protect your hands with rubber gloves when working with adhesive.

SIMPLE FIXES

Securing a loose tile.

◆ Lift the loose portion of the tile and spread a thin coat of latex adhesive on the underside of it with a putty knife. If only a corner of the tile has come unstuck, loosen more of it until you can turn the tile back far enough to spread the adhesive.
◆ Press the tile into place, so that it is level with those tiles that surround it. Hold it down with a 20-pound weight for at least an hour.

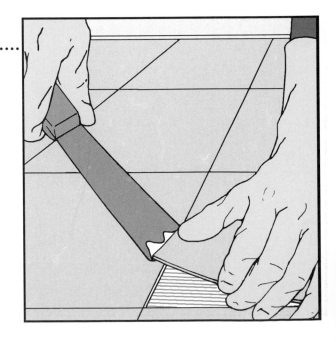

Deflating a blister.

◆ Following a line in the flooring pattern if possible, score then slice along the length of a blister with a utility knife *(right)*. Extend the cut $\frac{1}{2}$ inch beyond the blister at both ends.

◆ With a putty knife, spread a thin layer of latex adhesive through the slit onto the underside of the flooring.

◆ Press the vinyl down; if one edge overlaps because the flooring has stretched, use it as a guide to trim the edge beneath. Remove trimmed-off scrap, then press the edges together and put a 20-pound weight on the repaired area for at least 1 hour.

Dealing with Stains

Most resilient flooring today has a permanent finish as hard, smooth, and shiny as wax, protecting it against stains and dirt. Daily sweeping plus occasional damp-mopping is usually sufficient to remove grime. Limit washing with detergent and water to every 3 to 6 weeks.

Over time, some spillage and staining is almost inevitable. The following treatments are recommended for stains caused by common substances:

STAIN	REMEDY
Alcoholic beverages	Go over the spot with a cloth that has been dampened with rubbing alcohol.
Blood	Sponge with cold water; if that does not work, sponge with a solution of 1 part ammonia to 9 parts water.
Candle wax, chewing gum, or tar	Cover with a plastic bag filled with ice cubes. When the material becomes brittle, scrape it off with a plastic spatula.
Candy	Rub with liquid detergent and grade 00 steel wool unless the floor is a "waxless" vinyl; in that case use a plastic scouring pad, warm water, and powdered detergent.
Cigarette burns	Rub with scouring powder and grade 00 steel wool.
Coffee and canned or frozen juice	Cover for several hours with a cloth saturated with a solution of 1 part glycerine (available at drugstores) to 3 parts water. If the stain remains, rub it gently with scouring powder on a damp cloth.
Fresh fruit	Wearing rubber gloves, rub with a cloth dampened with a solution of 1 tablespoon oxalic acid, a powerful solvent available at hardware stores, and 1 pint water.
Grease and oil	Remove as much as possible with paper towels, then wash the stain with a cloth dampened in liquid detergent and warm water.
Mustard or urine	Cover for several hours with a cloth soaked in 3 to 5 percent hydrogen peroxide, and cover that cloth with another soaked in household ammonia.
Paint or varnish	Rub with grade 00 steel wool dipped in warm water and liquid detergent.
Leather and rubber scuff marks	Scrub with a cloth soaked in a solution of 1 part ammonia to 9 parts water.
Shoe polish or nail polish	Rub with grade 00 steel wool soaked in warm water and scouring powder.

REPLACING A DAMAGED TILE

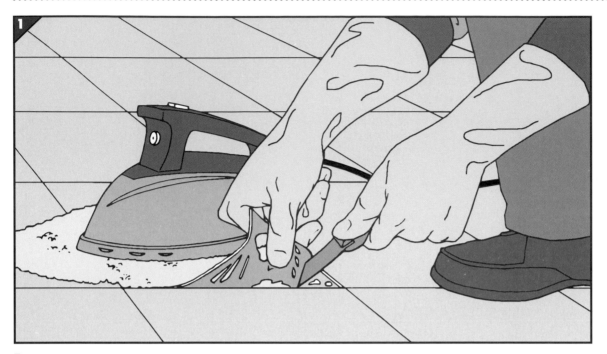

1. Removing a tile.

◆ Lay a towel on the tile and warm it with an iron at medium heat until the adhesive softens and you can lift one corner with a putty knife.

◆ Pull up the corner and slice at the adhesive underneath with the putty knife, reheating the tile with the iron if necessary, until you can take out the entire tile.

◆ Scrape the remaining adhesive from the subfloor (see asbestos warning on page 15).

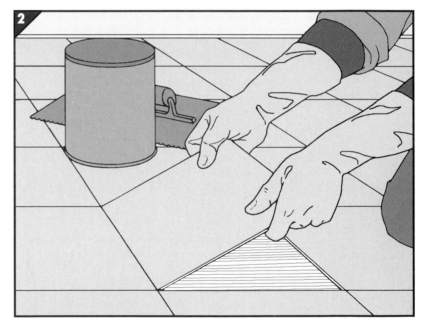

2. Installing a replacement.

◆ Spread a thin layer of adhesive—not more than half the thickness of your tile—on the subfloor with a notched trowel, then butt one edge of the new tile against the edge of an adjoining tile, aligning the pattern.

◆ Ease the tile into place. Make sure it is level with surrounding tiles; if it is too high, press it down and quickly wipe away excess adhesive before it dries; if the tile is too low, gently pry it out with a putty knife and add more adhesive beneath it. Rest a 20-pound weight on it for the length of time specified by the adhesive manufacturer.

PATCHING SHEET FLOORING

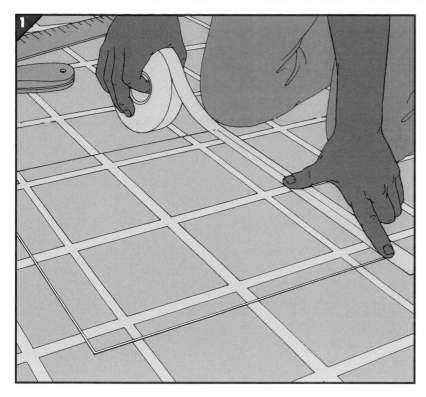

1. Cutting the patch.
◆ Place over the damaged spot a spare piece of matching flooring larger than the area to be patched, aligning the design of the replacement piece with that of the floor. Secure it in position with tape *(left)*.
◆ With a metal straightedge and a utility knife, score the top piece, following lines in the pattern where possible. Using the scored line as a guide, cut through the replacement piece and the flooring underneath. Keep slicing along the same lines until you have cut through both sheets.
◆ Set the replacement piece aside and loosen the adhesive under the section you are replacing as shown in Step 1 on page 278. Remove the damaged section and the old adhesive.

2. Installing the patch.
◆ Spread adhesive over the exposed subfloor with a notched trowel and set the replacement patch in position as you would a tile *(page 278, Step 2)*.
◆ Hide the outline of the patch by a careful application of heat: Cover the edges of the patch with heavy aluminum foil, dull side down, and press the foil several times with a very hot iron *(inset)*. This will partly melt the cut edges of the flooring so they form a solid and almost undetectable bond.

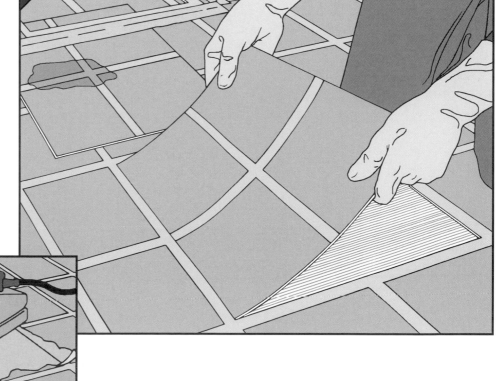

Concrete and marble, slate or ceramic tiles make the most durable floors. They are also the most inflexible and brittle. All of them can be cracked by the fall of a heavy weight. They can also be pulled apart by the normal expansion and contraction of a house.

Underlying Problems: A floor that is cracked throughout a room is usually a sign of trouble in the structure beneath it. If your subflooring is less than $1\frac{1}{8}$ inch thick, you may have to replace it.

When subflooring has localized damage, you can usually tighten or patch problem areas. Repair the cause of any water damage before installing new flooring. Dampness in concrete slabs may not be curable; dry the area as much as possible, and use a waterproof epoxy adhesive to hold the finish surface in place.

Ceramic Tiles: The techniques for replacing a tile at the base of a toilet (below and opposite) work for repairing damage around any permanent fixture, such as a tub, pipe, or kitchen cabinet.

Use organic adhesives to lay new tile on a wood subfloor or on smooth, dry concrete, and epoxy adhesive on a floor that is moist or uneven. Fill joints between tiles with color-matched silicone grout, which comes premixed in squeeze tubes, cures quickly, and adheres to both old and new tile.

Marble and Slate: These tiles are normally butted tightly against each other in a bed of mortar. To cut them, use a saber saw with a tungsten carbide blade instead of scoring the tile as a prelude to fracturing it or shaping it with tile nippers (opposite, bottom). Otherwise, replacing them involves only slight variations in the procedure for ceramic tiles shown here.

Concrete: Fill cracks less than an inch wide with a vinyl or latex patching compound. Use concrete and wire mesh for larger cracks (pages 282-283), and apply an epoxy bonding agent to the old concrete before pouring the patch. This prevents the old, dry concrete from absorbing water the new concrete needs for proper curing.

TOOLS

Grout saw	Grease pencil
Straightedge	Tile nippers
Glass cutter	Carbide-tipped
Electric drill	hole saw
Masonry drill bit	Adhesive spreader
Hammer	Sledgehammer
Cold chisel	Shovel
Compass	Wire brush
	Metal shears
	Trowel

MATERIALS

Replacement tile	Bricks
Emery cloth	Reinforcing wire
Tile adhesive	Patching concrete
Grout	Epoxy bonding
Length of 2 x 4	agent
Gravel ($\frac{3}{4}$")	Plywood sheet
	Bucket
	Polyethylene

SAFETY TIPS

Safety goggles will protect your eyes when you remove tiles, grout, or concrete. Wear rubber gloves when spreading adhesives, and work gloves when breaking up old concrete and mixing or finishing new concrete.

A TIGHT FIT AROUND A FIXTURE

1. Removing the grout.
◆ Run a grout saw along the joints bordering the damaged tile, applying firm pressure as you move the saw back and forth.
◆ To remove grout from very narrow joints, unscrew one of the twin blades supplied with the saw. For extra-wide joints, add a third blade.
◆ Clean fine debris and dust from grooves with a brush or shop vacuum.

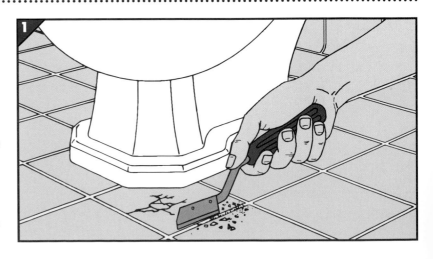

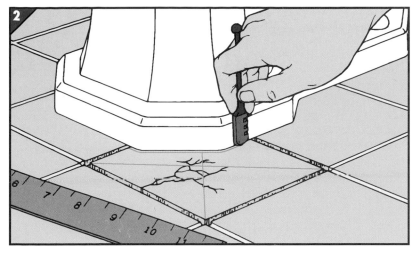

2. Taking out the tile.

◆ For ceramic tile, score an X on the damaged piece with a glass cutter and straightedge, then score along the base of the fixture *(left)*.

◆ Drill a hole through the center of the X with a $\frac{1}{4}$-inch masonry bit. Hammer a cold chisel into the hole, and working toward the edges, break the tile into small pieces. Remove the tile fragments, and scrape off the old adhesive beneath them with a putty knife.

On marble or slate tile, mark an X with a grease pencil. With a masonry bit, drill $\frac{3}{4}$-inch holes every $\frac{1}{2}$ inch along the X and the fixture's base. Break out the tile with a hammer and chisel.

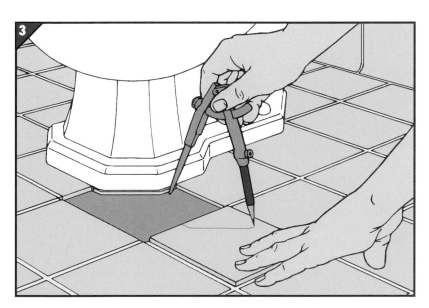

3. Marking the new tile.

◆ Lay a new tile over the tile adjacent to the space you have cleared.

◆ Replace the pencil in a school compass or scribe with a grease pencil, and open the compass to the width of a tile.

◆ Set the pencil at the edge of the new tile and the point of the compass or scribe at the corresponding point on the base of the fixture.

◆ Holding the new tile securely, move the compass slowly along the base of the fixture to mark the shape of the base on the new tile.

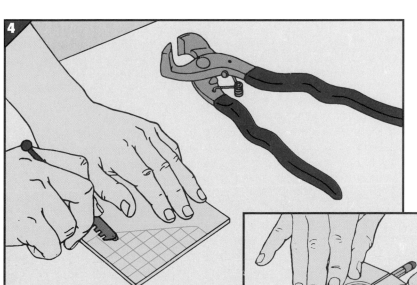

4. Cutting the tile.

◆ Score the fixture outline with a glass cutter, then score a crisscross pattern in the area to be cut away *(left)*.

◆ Using only the corners of the nipper blades, nibble $\frac{1}{8}$-inch pieces of tile away from the scored area with tile nippers. Check the tile for fit, and smooth the edges with an emery cloth.

To replace tile around a pipe, mark the pipe diameter on adjacent edges of the tile, draw lines across the tile, and drill a hole at the center of the square thus formed with a carbide-tipped hole saw. Using a glass cutter, score the tile through the center of the hole, then set the tile on a pencil and break the tile by pressing on both sides *(inset)*.

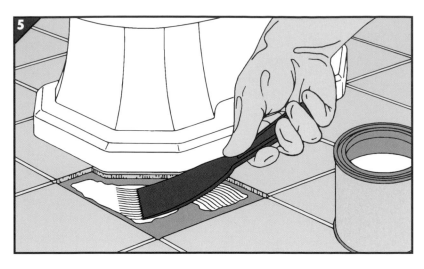

5. Setting the tile in place.
◆ With a notched plastic spreader, apply adhesive to the subfloor or mortar bed. If the new tile has tabs on its back, also add a thin coat of adhesive to the bottom.
◆ Apply enough adhesive to raise the tile slightly higher than the ones around it. Use toothpicks or coins set on edge as spacers to keep the joints between ceramic tiles open and even.
◆ Lay a 2-by-4 across the tile, and tap it down with a mallet or hammer.
◆ Let the adhesive set for 24 hours, remove the spacers, and fill the joints with silicone grout.

DURABLE PATCHES FOR CONCRETE

1. Preparing the area.
◆ Break up the damaged concrete with a sledgehammer or an electric jackhammer *(page 238)*. Cut reinforcing wire in the broken concrete with metal shears and clear away the debris.
◆ With a cold chisel and a hammer, slope the edge of the hole toward the center. Then dislodge loose particles of concrete with a wire brush and remove them.
◆ Dig out the top 4 inches of dirt from the hole and tamp the bottom with the end of a 2-by-4. Fill the hole to the bottom of the slab with clean $\frac{3}{4}$-inch gravel.

2. Reinforcing the patch.
◆ Unroll wire reinforcing mesh over the hole, and cut it with metal shears so that the ends of the wires rest on the sloped edge of the hole.
◆ Reinforcing mesh usually comes in rolls 5 feet wide; if you are patching a wider hole, wire two pieces of mesh together.
◆ Place the mesh in the hole supported by bricks.

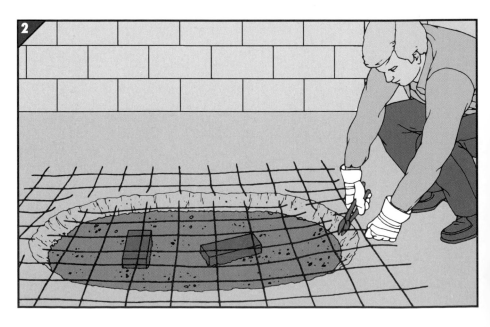

3. Pouring the patch.

◆ Form a cone of premixed patching concrete on a piece of plywood or in a mortar pan. Hollow out the top and add water as specified by the manufacturer. Mix the ingredients thoroughly *(left)*.

◆ Coat the edges of the hole with an epoxy bonding agent. Before the coating dries, shovel the concrete into the hole. Jab with the shovel tip to force the mix against the sides of the hole and through the reinforcing mesh.

◆ Fill the hole to the level of the slab, then add a few extra shovelfuls to allow for settling.

4. Finishing the patch.

◆ With a helper, work a straight 2-by-4 across the surface of the patch with a back-and-forth motion. Fill any surface depressions with concrete and smooth the patch again.

◆ A thin film of water will soon appear on the surface. When it evaporates and the surface sheen disappears, smooth the patch with a metal trowel. To trowel a large patch, kneel on boards laid across it and work backward, moving the boards as you go.

◆ When the concrete hardens, sprinkle it with water and cover it with polyethylene. Let the patch cure for 3 to 7 days, checking it daily and sprinkling it as needed to keep the surface damp.

MAINTAINING THE LOOK OF YOUR CONCRETE FLOOR

After patching the concrete, you can leave your floor unfinished or apply a protective coating to its surface. Penetrating sealers are the least expensive finishes for concrete. They can be easily applied, dry in about 8 hours, and leave a thin film that protects against stains.

You will need to remove stains that might spoil the rough beauty of raw concrete or prevent a finish coat from adhering. Many stains can be scrubbed away with a household detergent. Those listed here require special treatment. To remove these stains, first fold a piece of cheese-cloth several times and lay it over the affected area. Then pour the recommended cleaning agent over the cloth. The chemicals will dissolve the stain, and the cheesecloth will absorb the chemicals.

RUST: 1 part sodium citrate to 6 parts glycerin.

GREASE, OIL, OR MILDEW: 1 pound trisodium phosphate to 1 gallon of water.

COPPER, BRONZE, OR INK: 1 part ammonia to 9 parts water.

IRON: 1 part oxalic acid to 9 parts water.

OLD PAINT: use a commercial paint remover.

7 CARPETS

For Warmth & Softness

Warm and plush, carpet has long been a favorite floor covering in cold climates. It offers a variety of effects, from luxurious to cozy, and comes in many styles, colors, and patterns to make it a vibrant part of a decorating scheme or a muted but lovely background for treasured furniture and other items.

If you decide to install carpeting you'll want to show it to its best advantage, and this chapter will help you do just that. We'll show you how to keep seams away from doorways to prevent them from loosening, running the carpet's longest seam toward the major light source, installing carpeting with the pile leaning toward the main entrance to make it look its best, and making sure the pile of each piece runs in the same direction. This chapter discusses the basics of estimating how much carpet to buy, what kind of padding to buy, and laying a foundation of padding and pins. You'll learn the difference between carpeting made with looped and cut pile; knowing which type of carpet you're working with will help you cut it properly. After cutting you'll learn how to seal edges with hot-melt seaming tape and a seaming iron, and then you'll stretch and fine-cut your carpet to finish installing it. Planning on carpeting stairs? You'll learn the fine points of special padding, dealing with corners, and installing runner rods. This chapter also shows you how to repair different types of damaged carpet to keep the whole expanse looking as beautiful as the day you install it.

Take advantage of all the decorating possibilities of soft flooring with throw rugs over your wall-to-wall. This Chinese Aubusson rug contrasts beautifully with the carpet's soft, pale-blue grids and pulls together all the colors of the room in its elaborate design.

Because darker walls tend to make a room look smaller, you may want to use a light-colored carpet to maintain a spacious feel. To keep it clean, try small carpet mats in entranceways to catch unwanted dirt.

A striking carpet creates a warm, cozy atmosphere in this large room. The cranberry color repeated throughout the furniture fabrics and curtains, unifies the stylish decor.

Carpeting your stairs will cut down on the noise of creaky steps as well as help prevent slips. This understated cream carpet allows the dramatic sweep of an exquisite stairwell to shine. The gold stair rods provide an elegant accent.

Working with Texture

Saxony

Historically, carpeting appeared only in very wealthy homes, where it was sometimes draped on furniture or hung on walls to display its marvelous colors and textures. Over time, the development of synthetic materials and cost-effective manufacturing processes made carpeting more affordable, and today it can be one of the least expensive flooring options. Carpeting has always been popular in cool climates because of its insulating properties. It deadens sound, too, which makes it a good choice for home offices, living rooms, bedrooms, libraries, and other peaceful rooms. Despite its plushy texture, it's an extremely hard-wearing floor treatment that can stand up to a lot of foot traffic. Like wallpaper, it comes in a broad range of colors, patterns, and textures to give home decorators a versatile palette to work with. It can be vibrantly colored and patterned to become the focal point of a room, or can be installed in neutral colors to become the background for a decorating scheme. As with paint, the choice of carpeting color can alter a room's perceived dimensions; light tones open up a room, while dark, jewel-toned colors make it more cozy. Those dark colors are particularly good for hallways, which are subject to lots of wear and tear. Other options for hallways are carpets that contain tiny flecks of color or stylized designs to help hide wear from foot traffic. Wall-to-wall

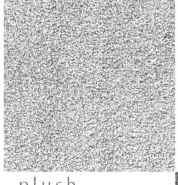

plush

Frieze

short cut pile

carpeting is a warm, inviting way to unify a decorating theme from room to room. Patterned carpeting works well in heavily used rooms, since its design tends to hide wear. It comes in an enormous range of designs; geometric patterns work best with rectangular rooms, while abstract designs help disguise irregularly shaped spaces. Floral motifs can lend either a formal or a casual look to a room, depending on the size of the pattern.

level loop

Carpeting comes in a variety of textures. The most familiar are Saxony and plush, which are thick, rich cut piles ideal for formal settings. They do show footprints and vacuum marks, however. To avoid this choose Frieze, a textured cut pile, which is a little less thick and less susceptible to marks. Stores and commercial buildings often use a short cut pile, which is thin and easy to clean. It's a good choice for a patio. For a play room or entranceway, a level loop carpet works best, as it is the most hard-wearing. Multi-level loop are just as sturdy, but add a touch of elegance. Level tip shear, a combination of cut and loop, has stylish texture and pattern and will stand up to heavy traffic. A Berber style level loop, made of fine natural fibers, works well with contemporary decorating schemes. Most Berbers come in their natural, beige tones, yet dyed Berbers are also available for a bolder effect.

multi-level loop

level tip shear

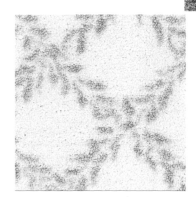

patterned

Planning Wall-to-Wall Carpet

Carpet laying was once an art performed by skilled workers who stitched every seam and placed each hidden tack to carpet even a small room. Today's special tools and materials—tackless strip *(page 292)*, heat-sealing seaming tape *(page 298)*, and the knee-kicker and power stretcher *(pages 299 and 300)*—have so simplified laying carpet that even an amateur can do it.

Styles of Piles: Most carpets are tufted: that is, their pile—the fibers that make up the cushiony surface—is machine stitched into a backing. Carpets may be made with loop pile or cut pile *(bottom left)*, a distinction that is important when cutting carpet *(page 295)*.

When new carpet is rolled up as it comes off the machine, the pile fibers are pressed down, acquiring a "pile direction" that permanently affects appearance and installation technique *(checklist, right)*.

Measuring the Room: The first step in a carpeting project is to determine how much carpet you will need to buy. Begin by drawing the room to scale on graph paper, letting each square equal 1 square foot. Measure the length of each wall and the distances between doorjambs and other features, and plot the measurements on the graph paper. Also measure between the walls in several places to see if they are skewed or bowed. Add 4 inches to the length and the width of the floor to allow for error and for trimming each factory-cut edge.

Estimating Carpet Needs: Cut a strip of graph paper 12 squares wide to represent the standard 12-foot width of broadloom carpet. Snip pieces from the strip and arrange them on your room diagram to keep wasted carpet to a minimum. Consult the checklist and the illustrations at right for tips on how to place seams and position the pile.

With patterned carpet, you must take into account the repeat—the distance from the point where a pattern begins to where it begins again—in order to be sure of matching the pattern along a seam.

Padding and Tackless Strip: Your scale drawing will also tell you how much padding and tackless strip you need. Padding comes in rolls $4\frac{1}{2}$ to 12 feet wide; compute the square footage of the room and buy just a little more than will cover the area. Determine the type of tackless strip needed *(page 292)*, and buy a few feet more than the room's perimeter. (If you are replacing a carpet with one that is of similar thickness, use the existing strip. Make sure the strip pins are at the proper angle and that the strip is nailed down securely.)

Before starting, reattach loose flooring, remove grilles from heating vents, and sweep the floor. You might wish to remove shoe moldings; if you do not plan to reinstall them, repaint the baseboards before laying the carpet.

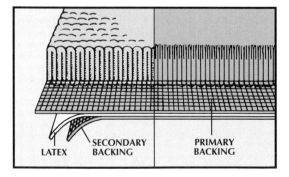

Tufted carpet.
The pile yarn of tufted carpet is stitched through a layer of open-weave fabric—the primary backing. A second fabric backing is stuck onto the underside of the first with a coating of latex. When the yarn is left uncut, the result is loop-pile carpet *(left)*. But the tops of the loops are often split or cut off, making cut-pile carpet *(right)*.

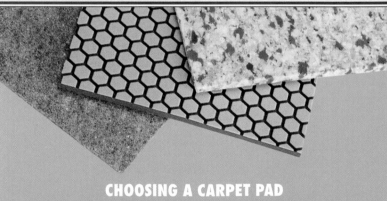

CHOOSING A CARPET PAD

Most carpet padding is made either of synthetic felt, a mix of foam and rubber scraps bonded together in sheets, or a continuous sheet of urethane foam. Felt, a hard padding, is now rarely used in homes, having been supplanted by the other two. Bonded and urethane padding come in a variety of densities and thicknesses. Urethane is the more expensive of the two, but either in higher grades will outlast most carpets.

Buy a pad $\frac{7}{16}$ inch thick or less; thicker pads flex too much, causing damage to the carpet backing. Medium- or high-density pads extend the life of a carpet.

FITTING CARPET TO THE ROOM

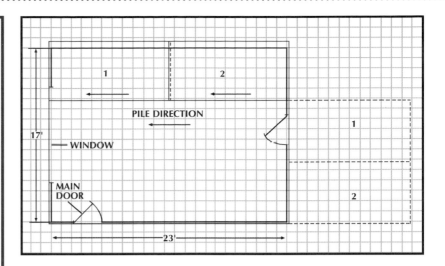

Lengthwise installation.

In this typical room, 17 feet by 23 feet, the best plan is lengthwise installation of broadloom 12 feet wide; the rest is filled with two pieces (1 and 2) from an extra 4 yards of carpet (dashed lines, far right). The major seam will run into the main light source—the window at the left. The pile should lean toward the main door. Most of the room's traffic will pass between the two doors, over the large section of full-width carpet. The seams will be out of the way, and probably partly hidden by furniture.

In a smaller room, fill the gap between the main run of carpet and the wall at the top of the drawing with narrow sections cut from the 12-foot broadloom width. You will have to make more seams but pay for less carpet.

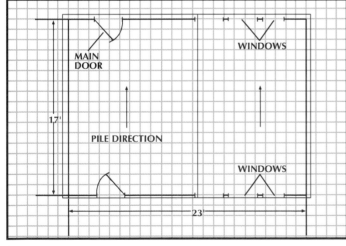

Adding a seam to avoid a door.

This room is much like that above, center, except that a door is in the middle of one wall and the seam of a normal short-sheeting installation would run directly into it, taking the wear of heavy traffic. To avoid this undesirable seam location, cut one of the full widths of carpet lengthwise into two pieces and seam them to both sides of the remaining full-width section. The result is two seams instead of one, but neither of them runs directly into a door.

Short sheeting a room.

This room (left), while the same size as that above, has an arrangement of doors and windows that makes it preferable to install the length of the carpet across the shorter dimension of the room—a technique that is called short sheeting. That way, the major seam will be aligned with the light from the windows and will be away from the bulk of traffic that passes between the doors. The pile should lean toward the main door.

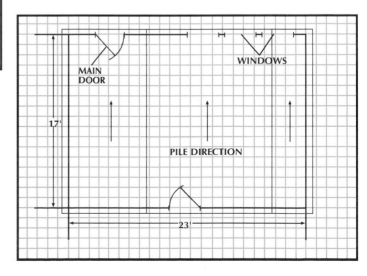

A Foundation of Padding and Pins

Although hidden when the job is done, tackless strip and padding are essential to the carpeting of a room. The tackless strip goes around the perimeter of the room to hold the carpet taut *(below);* the padding provides cushioning.

Get the Correct Strip: Tackless strip comes in three main types, all 1 inch wide and $\frac{1}{4}$ inch thick, with two rows of pins. Type C strip, with pins $\frac{1}{4}$ inch high, is used for thick shag carpeting. Type D strip has $\frac{3}{16}$-inch pins suited for thin-backed carpets. Type E has medium-sized $\frac{7}{32}$-inch pins that are right for the great majority of carpets.

To select the right type of strip, place a sample of carpet over the pins and press your fingers into the carpet. The carpet and strip are ideally matched if you can discern the tips of the pins without being pricked by them. If the pins feel sharp, use strip with shorter pins.

A fourth type, called architectural strip, is $1\frac{1}{2}$ inches wide and has three rows of pins to grasp carpet more firmly. This strip is better for laying heavy-backed or woven carpets, and for installing carpet in very large rooms.

Installing the Strip: The tackless strip is nailed to most floors but can be glued to tiles. You can nail it through vinyl tiles, but if a concrete floor lies under the tile, use strip that has masonry nails.

Place strip in front of obstacles such as radiators, under which it would be difficult to stretch the carpet. Where carpet will end in a doorway, use special metal edging *(opposite, bottom).*

Laying Carpet Padding: Always put padding down smooth or shiny side up. With wood sub- or finish flooring, all forms of padding are stapled in place after being cut *(page 294).* However, other circumstances require different measures.

On concrete or ceramic tile, use linoleum paste to cement down felt padding. Affix foam-rubber padding to concrete or tile using an adhesive made for that purpose. Secure the seams between sections with padding tape, and tape the pad to the strip by pushing the tape over the pins across the strip's full width.

 TOOLS

Hammer	Staple gun
Saw	Utility knife
Garden shears	

 **MATERIALS**

Tackless strip	Sandpaper
Cardboard	Water-based
Metal edging	adhesive

 SAFETY TIPS

Wear goggles when hammering nails and when cutting tackless strip. Gloves protect your hands when you are working with tackless strip.

Holding carpet without tacks.

Tackless strip is made of a three-ply strip of wood 1 inch wide and $\frac{9}{32}$ inch thick, with sharp pins protruding at a 60-degree angle from the face to grip the carpet. When the strip is installed correctly, the pins point toward the wall, and the printing on the strip can be read from the room. It comes in 4-foot lengths and is fixed to the floor with preset nails. Strip with masonry nails for concrete floors is available.

When carpet is stretched over the strip, the pins hold it under tension. A gully formed between the wall and the strip holds the tucked-in edge of the carpet. The strip comes beveled along the wall edge to create a gully if you leave quarter-round shoe moldings in place.

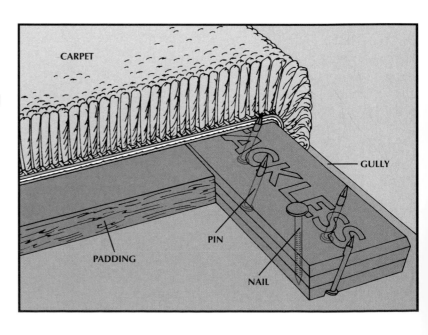

NAILING TACKLESS STRIP TO THE FLOOR

1. Fastening strips along a wall.

◆ Glue pieces of cardboard together to make a spacer two-thirds the thickness of the carpet.

◆ Starting in a corner, use the spacer to position a length of tackless strip next to the wall, and drive the nails into the floor.

If you cannot keep from battering down the carpet-holding pins with a regular hammer, try a tack hammer, which has a smaller head. When nailing into concrete, you will need a ball-peen hammer with a 24-ounce head.

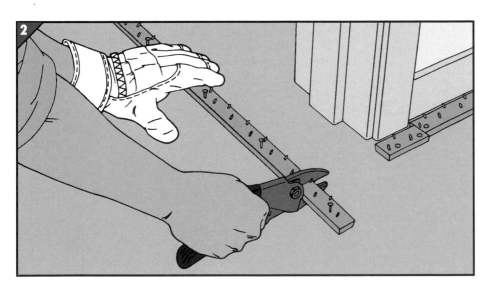

2. Cutting tackless strip.

With a saw or garden shears, cut pieces to fit around a doorjamb *(left),* or to fill gaps. If using shears, grip the strip in the jaws, position the lower handle against the floor, and lean on the upper handle to make the cut. At door openings install small pieces to maintain the correct spacing between the strip and each section of door molding. Drive extra nails so that each piece of strip is held by at least two.

3. Metal edging for doorways.

Nail metal edging to the floor so that its binder bar—the flange that folds down over the carpet edge—is directly under the door. In doorways where the door opens away from the area to be carpeted, as shown at right, notch the flat part of the strip to accommodate the doorstop.

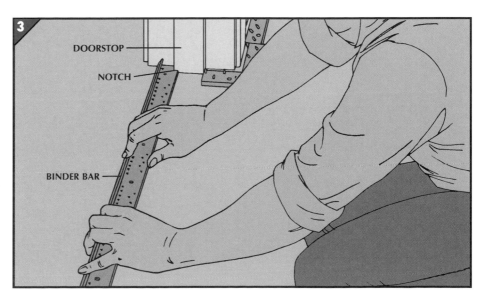

FASTENING TACKLESS STRIP WITH GLUE

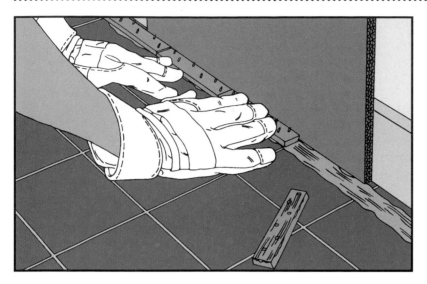

Cementing strip.

◆ On an uneven, nonnailable surface such as a ceramic tile floor, cut the strip to the width of each tile—if the tiles are very small, cut the strips about 4 inches long.

◆ Clean and sand the floor surface, then fasten each strip with a water-based adhesive, tapping each piece with a tack hammer in order to make a strong joint.

LAYING THE PAD

1. Stapling padding in place.

◆ Cut from the roll of padding a piece large enough to cover one end of the room, slightly overlapping the tackless strip.

◆ Drive staples at 6-inch intervals around the edges of the piece.

◆ Cut and staple down more padding, butting the pieces together, until the floor is covered.

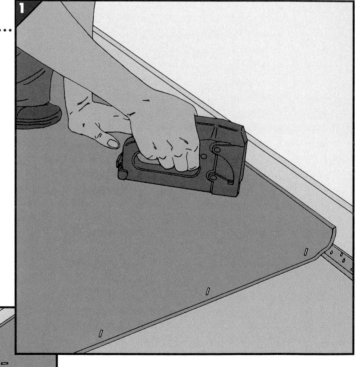

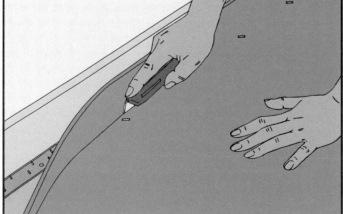

2. Trimming.

With a utility knife make a vertical cut along the inside edge of the tackless strip all around the room. For foam padding that is thicker than the tackless strip, tilt the knife away from the wall to make a beveled edge. Doing so will ensure that the padding will not ride up over the strip when you stretch the carpet over it.

Unroll the carpet and cut it according to the graph-paper plan you made earlier *(page 291)*, then stack the pieces and give them time to flatten.

Lay out the pieces in the area to be carpeted so that the pile leans in the same direction on all of them.

Cutting Techniques: Cutting on the pile side of the carpet, called front-cutting, is used on loop-pile carpet *(page 290)* to be sure the carpet does not remain joined by uncut loops across the cut. Front-cutting is also preferred for cut-pile

carpet if you can find the space between rows of pile. Cutting carpet across its backing—back-cutting—is reserved for cut-pile with indistinct rows of pile.

Seams across the width of the carpet require special care to ensure a perfect fit *(page 297)*.

In a doorway, make the seam only after the carpet on one side has been stretched and fastened to metal edging *(page 302)*.

Carpet Tools: Front-cutting is easier when you use a row-running cut-

ter *(below)*. This inexpensive tool has a runner that slips between rows of pile while a sharp blade behind the runner cuts the carpet backing without harming the pile.

A utility knife suffices for other cutting jobs, but a carpet knife, available where you buy carpet, has a two-edged, flexible blade that makes some cutting tasks easier.

Seams are sealed with hot-melt seaming tape and a seaming iron *(page 298)*, available for rent. The tape glues seams tightly together from the underside.

 TOOLS

Row-running cutter
Straightedge
Chalk line
Utility knife or carpet knife
Seaming iron

 **MATERIALS**

Hot-melt seaming tape (6" wide)
Edge sealer

TWO WAYS TO CUT CARPET

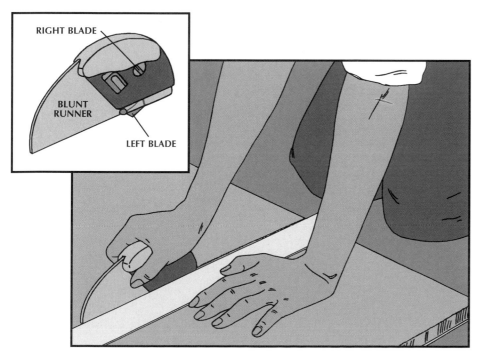

Front-cutting.
◆ Measure and mark the carpet.
◆ Retract both blades of a row-running cutter *(inset)*. Place the runner between two rows of pile, and slide the runner across the carpet.
◆ After making a path through the pile, extend the blade on the side of the tool next to the section of carpet you will use and make the cut, guided by a straightedge.

Back-cutting.

◆ Measure along the face of the un-rolled carpet, cut notches in the edges to mark the cutting location, then fold the carpet back.

◆ Stretch a chalk line taut between the notches, then snap the line.

◆ Extend the blade of a carpet knife enough to cut the backing only, and slice along the chalked line guided by a straightedge.

MANEUVERING THE CARPET

1. Kicking carpet into place.

◆ Lay a cut piece of carpet on the section of floor it will cover. Lift a corner, straddle it, and kick the carpet to shift it into its final position *(right)*. Kick with your toe or the side of your foot; using your heel may tear the carpet.

◆ At both inside corners and outside corners, slit the carpet vertically where it laps up against the baseboard *(inset)*. Cut only as far as the bottom of the baseboard. Doing so allows the carpet on both sides of the corner to lie flat on the floor.

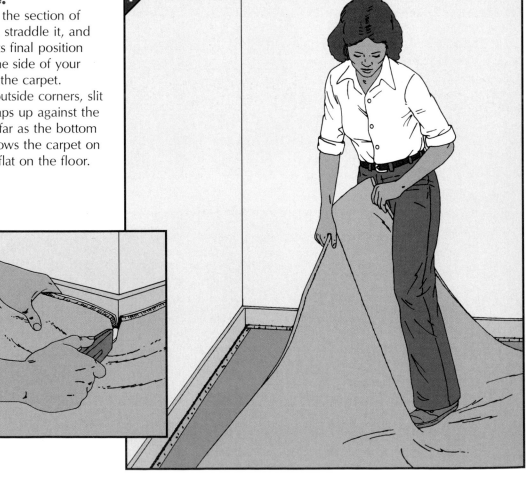

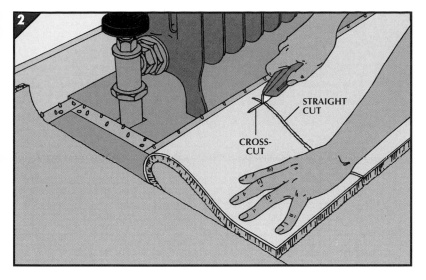

2. Cutting to fit around obstacles.

◆ Fold the carpet so that the backing touches an obstacle, such as the foot of a radiator, and mark the backing there. Make a straight cut from the mark to the carpet's edge.

◆ Then make a crosscut just long enough for the carpet to lie roughly flat around the obstacle until final trimming. For a radiator this may involve several cuts out to the edge and several crosscuts to accommodate all the feet and pipes.

MAKING A HOT-MELT SEAM

1. Cutting for a cross seam.

◆ Where you need to make a seam across the width of the carpet roll, overlap the pieces 1 inch, placing on top the piece that has its pile leaning toward the joint. Make sure the edge of this piece is positioned between pile rows on the piece below and parallel to them.

◆ With the edge of the top piece as a guide, cut the underlying carpet with a row-running cutter (inset).

◆ Cut the part of the carpet that laps the wall with a utility knife.

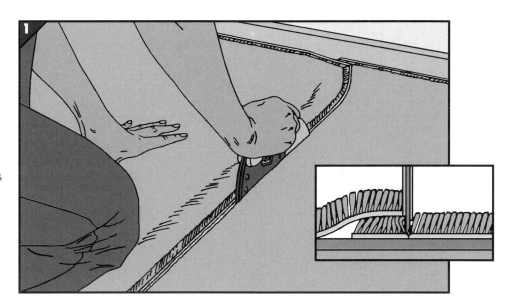

Wavy Seams for Sculptured Carpet

Because sculptured carpet's multilevel surface and swirl design are difficult to match at a seam, straight seams are unpleasantly obvious. A serpentine tool allows you to cut a wavy edge for a less apparent seam.

When cutting the two adjoining pieces, offset the tool the width of one "hump" from one piece to the next so that the convex cutouts on one side of the seam fit into the concave portions on the butting piece.

The opposite edge of the tool serves as a long straightedge for other types of cuts.

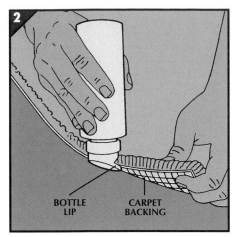

BOTTLE LIP **CARPET BACKING**

2. Sealing the cut edge.

Edge sealer coats carpet backing along a cut with a fast-drying liquid, preventing the edges from fraying. Practice with the sealer on a piece of scrap carpet so that you can apply it evenly and without getting the liquid on the pile. Apply sealer as follows:
◆ Push the activator button on the sealer bottle, then invert the container.
◆ Place the lip of the bottle against the backing. Squeeze the bottle lightly as you move it at a smooth and consistent speed along the carpet edge.
◆ Seal all cut edges of carpet.

3. Positioning seaming tape.

Slip a length of hot-melt seaming tape, adhesive side up, under one edge of carpet where two pieces will be joined. Align the tape's printed centerline with the carpet edge.

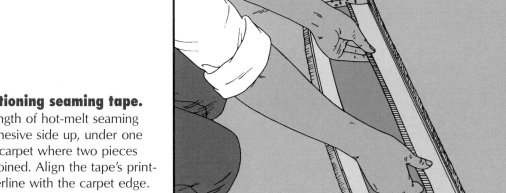

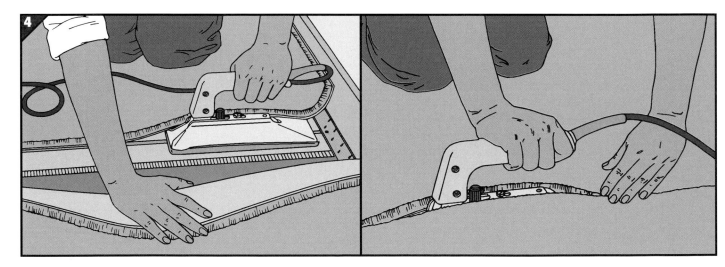

4. Ironing the tape.

◆ Warm a seaming iron to 250°—setting number two on some models.
◆ Holding back the carpet on one side of the joint, slip the preheated iron onto the tape at the end that lets you work along the direction of the pile *(above, left)*. Center the iron on the tape; allow the carpet to flop down.
◆ Let the iron rest for 30 seconds. Then draw it slowly along the tape for a distance of about 1 foot while you press the carpet into the softened adhesive behind the iron *(above, right)*.
◆ Separate the pile along the seam to check that the carpet backings touch; if not, force them together with your hands, then weight the seam with a board at least 6 inches by 2 feet.
◆ Continue seaming about a foot at a time, moving the board along the seam and kneeling on it as you go. Work as close as you can to the wall, then wait 5 minutes for the adhesive to set.
◆ To finish the final few inches of seam at the carpet edge, slide the carpet away from the wall to free the iron.

Do not use a household iron on seaming tape. A seaming iron has a heat shield to direct heat against the tape and away from the carpet's underside.

CAUTION

Stretching and Fine-Cutting

After you have rough-cut and seamed a carpet, you will need two tools, available at rental agencies, to make it smooth and taut. The first, a knee-kicker, secures an edge of the carpet to the tackless strip and to metal edging across doorways along one wall. The second is called a power stretcher. Used in concert with a knee-kicker, it pulls the carpet across the room and secures it to the strip along the opposite wall.

Hooking the Carpet on the Pins: The knee-kicker has an adjustable gripping head on one end, a cushion on the other, and an adjustable telescoping handle in between. Forced into the pile at one edge of your carpet, tiny hooks in the gripping head catch the nap and longer teeth extend through the carpet backing. When you bump the kicking cushion, or pad, with your knee, the knee-kicker scoots forward, carrying the carpet toward the wall; if you have placed the tool correctly, the carpet will remain against the wall, caught by the pins in the tackless strip.

Stretching It Tight: After securing the carpet at one wall, stretch it across the room with a power stretcher. Like a knee-kicker, a power stretcher has a toothed head, but it is a larger device—as much as 26 feet long when fully extended. A smaller version, called a ministretcher, is intended for narrow places such as hallways.

Instead of jerking the carpet into position like a knee-kicker, stretchers have a smoothly operating lever action that pulls the carpet and locks the toothed head in place to hold the carpet at the correct tension. A 2-by-4 and a 2-by-8 come in handy when using a power stretcher opposite a doorway and in very large rooms *(page 300)*.

Trimming and Tucking: After attaching the carpet to the tackless strip all the way around the room, trim the excess and tuck the edge into the gully between the baseboard and the strip. This hides the cut edges of the carpet and locks it securely to the strip.

You can do the trimming with a utility knife, but a special tool called a wall trimmer—which can be rented—does the job more precisely. Finally, trim the carpet around floor duct openings (making sure that grilles cover raw carpet edges) and plane doors so they clear the carpet.

TOOLS

Knee-kicker
Ministretcher

Power stretcher
Wall trimmer
Screwdriver
Hammer

USING A KNEE-KICKER

Hooking the first edge of the carpet.
◆ Before using the kicker, adjust its head until you can feel the teeth on the underside of a scrap of carpet.
◆ Place the head of the kicker in the carpet no more than 4 inches from the wall. Then push the extension release trigger to adjust the handle to a comfortable length.
◆ Lean on the handle with one hand, and bring your knee smartly against the kicking cushion *(right)*. The carpet, shoved forward, should catch on the tackless strip, and the excess will lap farther up the wall.
◆ As you move along the wall, hold the already secured carpet in place with your free hand so that it does not come unhooked as you kick.

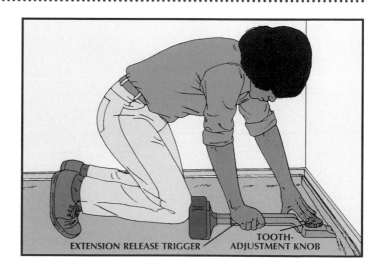

EXTENSION RELEASE TRIGGER   TOOTH-ADJUSTMENT KNOB

Knee-kicking in narrow places.
In restricted spaces like hallways, strike the pad with the side of your knee *(far left)* or adjust the handle so that you can place your foot against the wall and your knee against the kicker pad *(near left);* then force the kicker to move by pushing against the wall with your foot.

POWER STRETCHER TECHNIQUES

Stretching a carpet.
◆ Set the stretcher's teeth for your carpet thickness, and adjust its extension tubes so that it reaches from the wall where you used the knee-kicker to a point 6 inches from the opposite wall. In narrow places, use a ministretcher *(photograph)*.
◆ Press the lever down gently to avoid tearing the carpet. If the lever locks before the carpet is fully stretched, release the tension and extend the stretcher one notch. When the lever will not lock without overstretching the carpet, reset the head with the lever partly lowered.
◆ Use the face of a hammer to press the carpet firmly onto the pins in the tackless strip.

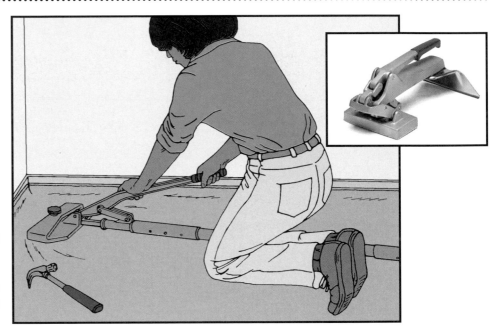

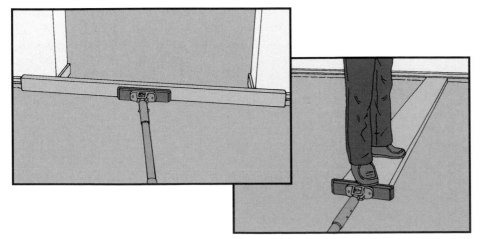

Ways to brace the stretcher.
◆ If there is a doorway in the wall you are stretching from, bridge it with a 2-by-4 *(far left)*, which will serve as a brace for the tail block.
◆ If your room is longer than the maximum length of the stretcher—usually 26 feet—use a 2-by-8 between the tail block and the wall to extend the reach of the device *(near left)*. Have a helper stand on the board so that it will not slip out of place during the stretch.

WHEN AND WHERE TO KICK AND STRETCH

Fitting a taut carpet.

These pictures show the sequence in which to use a knee-kicker and a power stretcher to lay a carpet in a typical room.

◆ Begin by hooking the carpet in one corner *(1)* with a knee-kicker and stretch it to an opposite wall with the power stretcher at a slight angle.

◆ Then secure the carpet against the perpendicular wall near the same corner *(2)* with a knee-

kicker and stretch it to the opposite wall with the power stretcher.

◆ Next, hook the carpet with the knee-kicker the full length of the top and right-hand walls *(3 and 4)* at about a 15-degree angle, then use the power stretcher along the bottom wall *(5)* at a similar angle.

◆ Finally, stretch from the right-hand wall to the left-hand wall *(6)*.

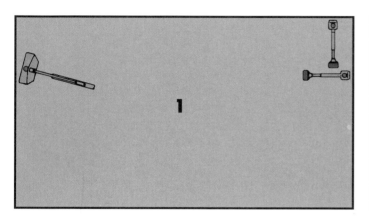

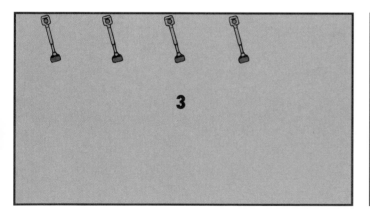

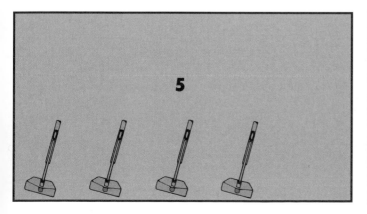

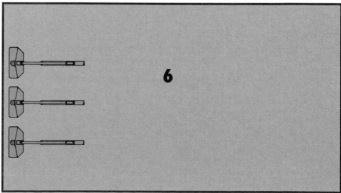

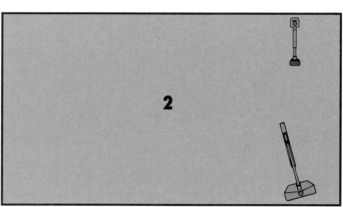

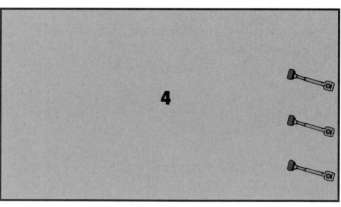

THE FINAL TRIM AND FIT

1. Trimming the carpet.
◆ Adjust a wall trimmer for the thickness of carpet and trim the edges of the carpet all around the room. Start the trimmer in the up-lapping carpet at a 45-degree angle and level it out when you reach the floor.
◆ Trim the last few inches approaching a wall with a utility knife.

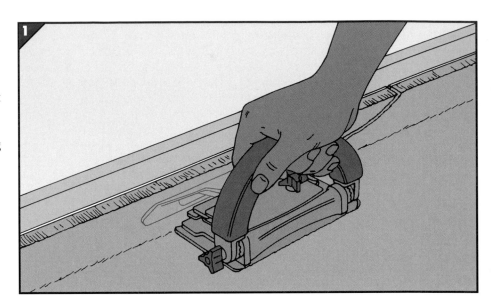

2. Tucking in the carpet.
Put masking tape on the tip of a screwdriver, and use it to tuck the carpet into the gully between the tackless strip and the baseboard and to snare any loose strands of yarn in the gully. If the carpet edge bulges after tucking, pull it out of the gully and trim it a bit shorter before retucking.

3. Clamping the carpet at a metal edge.
◆ Trim the carpet to fit under the binder bar of a metal edging strip.
◆ Tuck the carpet under the binder bar and bend it against the carpet by gently tapping a block of wood with a hammer *(right)*. Bend the bar down a little at a time by moving the block of wood along it after each hammer blow to avoid deforming the edging.

BINDER BAR

Stairs deserve high-quality carpeting. The nap of a cheap carpet with a low pile density will soon wear away there, exposing the carpet backing in an effect called "grinning."

Help preserve your carpet by using a high-density padding beneath it *(page 290)*. Another way to increase carpet life, by up to half, is to let the pile of the carpet lean toward the nosing.

How Much Carpet to Buy: When estimating the amount of carpet needed, first measure the width of a stair baluster-to-baluster, baluster-to-wall, or wall-to-wall. Add $2\frac{1}{2}$ inches to allow for a $1\frac{1}{4}$-inch roll-under on each side *(page 306, Step 4)*, then deduct twice the height of the pile. Doing so assures that the pile will just brush walls and balusters when the carpet is installed. If the result is 36 inches or less, you can get four stair-width pieces from a standard 12-foot-wide roll of broadloom.

To estimate the number of running yards of broadloom to buy for a straight flight of stairs, first divide the number of steps by the number of stair-width pieces you can obtain from a standard roll of carpeting. Next multiply the result by the amount of carpeting needed to cover one step *(below)*, and add a foot or so as a safety margin. After buying a piece of carpet this length, cut it into strips as shown on pages 295 and 296.

Dealing with Corners: When a stairway turns a corner, find the amount of carpet you will need for its wedge-shaped steps by cutting paper templates. Make a separate template for each tread and the riser below, adding 1 inch to allow for the bulge of padding over tread nosings. Cut the templates to a width that takes into consideration pile height and a $1\frac{1}{4}$-inch roll-under next to balusters, but not next to walls.

Cover each template with a piece of carpet, then grasp both carpet and template and turn them over. Align the template's bottom edge between two rows of pile and cut around the template.

Attach the carpet cutout to the tackless strip on the riser and stretch it over the tread. If the wall has a pronounced curve on its closed side, cut the tackless strip into small pieces that follow the arc. On an open side, roll the carpet edge under and tack it into place.

The Runner Option: A runner can be tufted carpet or an Oriental rug. Both work best on a straight stairway; leave a curved one to professionals. Measure as shown below, but do not cut an Oriental runner to fit; it will unravel. Instead, fold under any excess at the top, then tack it to the last riser. Add a decorative touch by affixing stair rods at the crotch of each step *(page 307)*.

 TOOLS

Tape measure
Hammer
Utility knife
Staple gun

Chalk line
Awl
Knee-kicker
Stair tool
1 x 3 gauge
   block

Electric drill with
   bits ($\frac{3}{32}$", $\frac{1}{8}$")
Handsaw
Screwdriver

 **MATERIALS**

Carpet
Tackless strip
Carpet tacks
   (24-ounce)

 SAFETY TIPS

Wear goggles when hammering nails and when cutting tackless strip. Gloves protect your hands when you are working with tackless strip.

PREPARING THE STAIRS

1. Determining the stairway length.

◆ Measure from the back of one tread to the bottom of the riser below *(right)* and add 1 inch for the bulge of padding at the tread nosing.
◆ Multiply this figure by the number of steps to be carpeted.

If you intend to carpet the landing at the top of the stairs, subtract the height of one riser.

In an old house the steps may be of varied sizes; in this situation measure each step individually and add the measurements together.

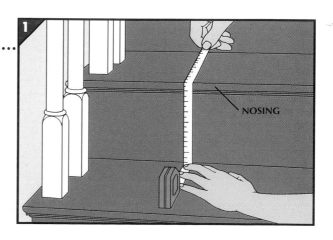

NOSING

2. Installing tackless strip.

◆ For each step, cut two pieces of tackless strip *(page 293, Step 2)* $2\frac{1}{2}$ inches shorter than the width of the steps.

◆ Make two spacers by pulling the nails from short pieces of tackless strip and taping them together, pins to pins *(inset)*.

◆ Rest a piece of tackless strip on the spacers and nail it to the riser, with the pins pointing down *(right)*. Nail tackless strip to the tread, $\frac{5}{8}$ inch from the riser and with the pins pointing toward it.

◆ Repeat the process for each riser and tread.

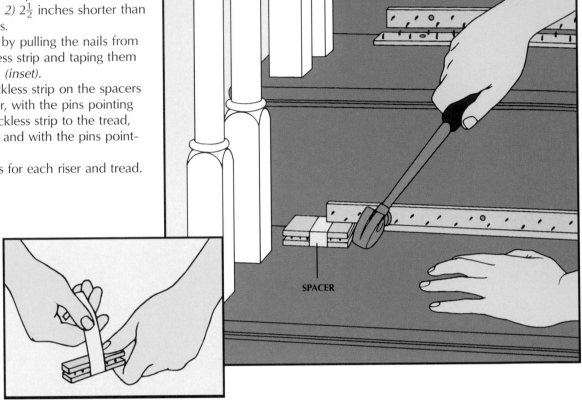

SPACER

3. Fitting the padding.

◆ Cut a piece of padding $2\frac{1}{2}$ inches shorter than the width of a step. If one side of the stairway is open, cut the riser portion of the padding away from the nosing at an angle on the open side so that it will not be seen when carpeting is installed.

◆ Butt the padding against the tackless strip on a tread and staple it there.

◆ Pull the padding over the nose of the tread and staple it about 2 or 3 inches down the riser *(left)*.

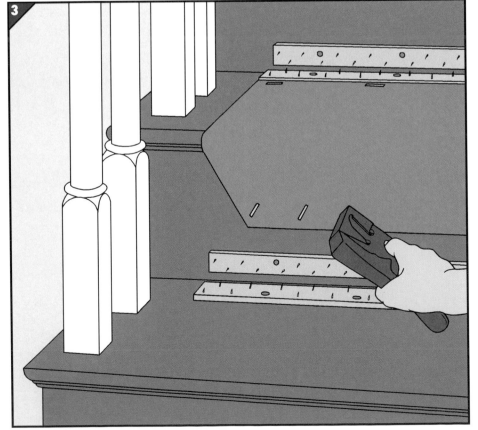

LAYING THE CARPET

1. Rolling the edges.

◆ Lay the carpet facedown and snap a chalk line $1\frac{1}{4}$ inches from each side to mark the crease of the roll-under.

◆ Score the carpet backing along the chalked lines with an awl, folding the carpet with your fingers as you do so *(right)*.

◆ Position the carpet roughly on the stairway, with the pile leaning down the stairs.

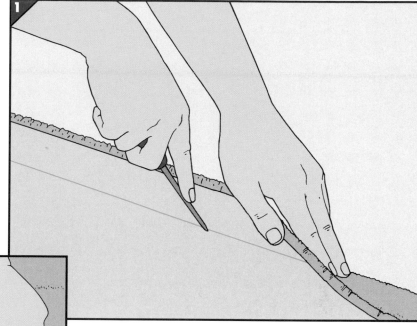

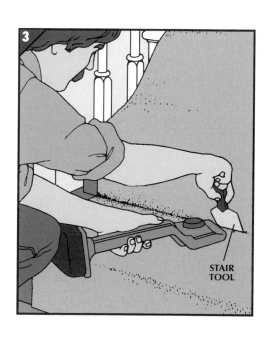

2. Securing the bottom edge.

◆ With an awl, pull the lower edge of the carpet over the tackless strip on the bottom riser until about $\frac{3}{8}$ inch laps onto the floor, then press the carpet onto the pins with your fingers *(left)*.

◆ Tuck the carpet edge into the gully between the tackless strip and floor. Run the head of a hammer along the gully to iron any bulges out of the carpet.

◆ Secure the rolled-under edge on each side with a 24-ounce carpet tack driven through both thicknesses of carpet and into the riser, just above the tackless strip.

3. Covering the tread.

◆ Beginning at the center of the bottom tread, stretch the carpet toward the stair riser with a knee-kicker. At the same time, push it into the gully behind the tackless strip with a stair tool, hooking the carpet backing on the pins of the strip *(right)*.

◆ Angle the knee-kicker slightly to stretch the carpet away from the center of the step, alternating left and right sides until you have done the entire step.

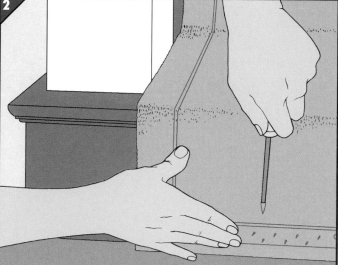

STAIR TOOL

4. Adjusting the width.

If the width of a tread varies from front to back, push an awl through the top layer of the carpet's rolled-under edge, pierce the lower layer with the tip, and, using the awl as a lever, shift the rolled-under edge to make the carpet fit the width at every point.

5. Forcing the carpet into the crotch.

When you have adjusted the carpet the way you want it—trying to move it after this step will damage the backing—hammer the stair tool into the space between the tackless strips on the tread and riser *(right)*. Doing so tightens the carpet and fixes it securely to the tackless strip on the riser.

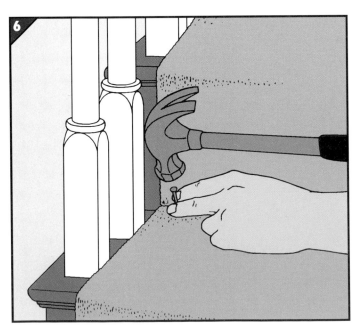

6. Tacking at the crotch.

◆ Secure the rolled edges at the tread-riser crotch with 24-ounce carpet tacks driven through the carpet and into the crotch at a point $\frac{5}{8}$ inch or less from each edge.
◆ Finish driving the tacks with a nail set if necessary.

Proceed up the stairs, one step at a time. When you reach the end of a length of carpet, drive a tack through each rolled-under edge near the rear of the tread, and trim off any carpet that extends beyond the tackless strip there. Begin fitting the next piece at the bottom of the next riser *(Step 2)*.

STAIR RODS FOR A RUNNER

1. Drilling rod-bracket holes.

To align the stair-rod brackets, make a gauge block for drilling the holes:

◆ Cut a piece of 1-by-3 equal in length to the width of a riser.

◆ Measure from the edges of the riser to the spot where the bracket will go—between $1\frac{1}{2}$ inches and 3 inches from balusters and walls and about $\frac{3}{4}$ inch above the tread.

◆ Transfer the measurements to the 1-by-3 and drill a $\frac{1}{8}$-inch hole through the board at each bracket location.

◆ Holding the block firmly in position against the riser, use the holes to guide a $\frac{3}{32}$-inch bit into the riser *(right)*.

◆ Drill holes on both sides of the step with the gauge block. For brackets that also screw into the tread, use the gauge block to drill holes there.

GAUGE BLOCK

STAIR ROD

RUNNER

2. Installing the runner.

◆ Screw the brackets onto each step, nail tackless strip between the brackets, and staple padding over the stair noses *(page 304, Steps 2 and 3)*.

◆ Starting at the bottom of the stairs and working one step at a time, install the runner as shown in Steps 2, 3, and 5 on pages 305 and 306.

◆ After securing the runner to a step, slide a stair rod into the corresponding brackets *(left)*. Screw one of the decorative caps provided onto each end of the rod.

◆ At the top of the staircase, tack the runner to the last riser, just below the nose of the landing.

The most carefully tended carpets can suffer accidental damage such as burns, rips, and stains. But with a few scraps of matching carpet and some inexpensive tools and materials, you can make durable, almost invisible repairs.

Set scraps aside when the carpet is laid or ask for some from the seller when you buy a carpeted house. If no scraps have been saved, take them from unseen areas such as a closet floor.

Carpet Repair Basics: Many repair jobs call for a tuft-setter, a special tool for embedding bits of pile yarn in the carpet backing. If you cannot find one at a carpet supplier, you can make your own *(opposite)*.

Before you begin to repair a damaged carpet, familiarize your-

self with its special characteristics. Loop pile, for example, may require a different cutting technique *(page 295)* from the one that is used for cut pile, and the repairs for carpeting installed over padding are different from those for cushion-back carpeting *(page 313)*.

Always use the smallest piece of scrap carpet first, so that if you make a mistake there will be larger scraps available to correct it. Practice on carpet scraps before tackling the actual repair.

Cushion-Back Considerations: This type of carpet is glued to the floor instead of being stretched over tackless strips *(page 293)*, so some techniques cannot be used. For example, cushion-back carpet has only a single layer of woven backing

(conventional carpet has two), so mending a surface tear, as shown on page 312, will not work; the tear must be repaired by patching.

Cushion-back carpet is different in another way, as well: Although pile rows run straight along its length, as on a conventional carpet, the rows of pile running across the width of the roll sometimes meet the long rows diagonally.

Before cutting a patch, run the tip of a Phillips screwdriver along the crosswise rows at various angles until you can easily clear pathways for a utility knife. The resulting shape may be a parallelogram instead of a rectangle. Cut out the damaged area to fit the patch as you would on conventional carpet *(page 310)*, slicing through the cushion back all the way to the floor.

 TOOLS

Nail scissors
Tweezers
Cotton swabs
Tuft-setter
Hammer

Utility knife
Knee-kicker
Awl
Putty knife
Notched trowel
($\frac{3}{32}$")

 **MATERIALS**

Scrap carpet
Latex cement
Nails ($1\frac{1}{2}$")
Seam tape

Latex seam
  adhesive
Multipurpose
  flooring adhesive
Cushion-back seam
  adhesive

 SAFETY TIPS

Rubber gloves protect your hands when you are working with liquid adhesives.

RESTORING A SMALL AREA

1. Removing damaged pile.
Using nail scissors *(right),* cut the damaged pile down to the carpet backing, then pick out the stubs of the tufts or loops with tweezers. For replacement pile, pick tufts or unravel lengths of looped yarn from the edge of a carpet scrap.

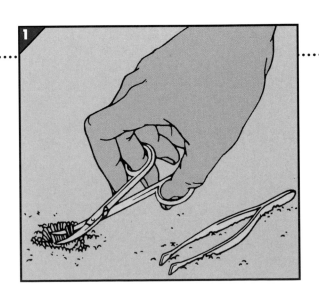

2. Applying the cement.

Squeeze a small amount of latex cement onto the back of a carpet scrap, dip a cotton swab into it, and lay a spot at the point where you will begin setting new tufts or loops. The cement dries rapidly—apply it to one small area at a time, and avoid getting it on the carpet pile.

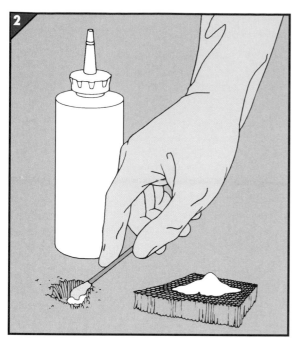

A TOOL FOR SETTING CARPET TUFTS

The makings of a tuft-setter consist of a large needle of the type used for sewing squares of knitting together and a $\frac{3}{8}$-inch wooden dowel. Cut a 4-inch length of dowel and drill a $\frac{1}{16}$-inch hole about 1 inch deep into one end. Insert the needle point into the hole and tap it with a hammer, driving the point into the wood. Using wire cutters or the cutting section of a pair of long-nose pliers *(right)*, clip most of the eye from the needle, leaving a shallow V-shaped end *(inset)*. To complete the tuft-setter, round and smooth this end with a small file or sharpening stone.

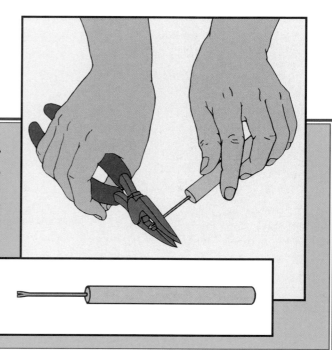

3. Replacing the pile.

◆ For cut-pile carpet, fold a tuft into a V over the tip of the tuft-setter and punch it into the latex-swabbed backing with one or two light taps of a hammer *(right)*.

◆ Repeat the process, setting the tufts close together and spreading more cement as needed. For best results, set the new pile so that it protrudes above surrounding fibers, and trim it flush with scissors.

◆ For loop-pile carpet *(inset)*, punch one end of a long piece of yarn into the backing with a tuft-setter, then form successive loops from the same piece and set the bottom of each loop.

◆ Check each loop to be sure it is the same height as the existing pile. Pull a short loop up with tweezers; punch a long one farther into the backing with the tuft-setter.

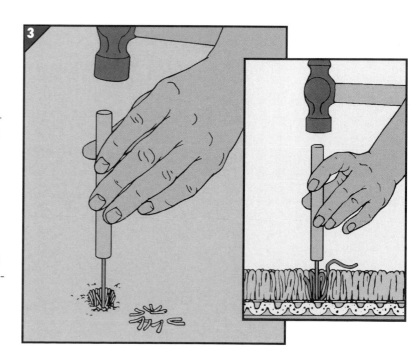

1. Stay-tacking.

◆ To reduce carpet tension for patching, set the teeth of a knee-kicker about a foot from the area to be patched and push the kicker forward. Be careful not to raise a hump in the carpet.

◆ Lay a strip of scrap carpet upside down just ahead of the knee-kicker and tack it to the floor with $1\frac{1}{2}$-inch nails at 3- to 4-inch intervals. Later, this strip of scrap carpet simplifies pulling out the nails without damaging the carpet.

◆ Release the knee-kicker and repeat the process on the other three sides of the damage.

2. Cutting a patch.

◆ From scrap carpet, measure out a patch slightly larger than the damaged area.

◆ Open a pathway through the pile with a blunt tool, such as a Phillips screwdriver, then pull the pile away from the cutting line with your fingers as you cut.

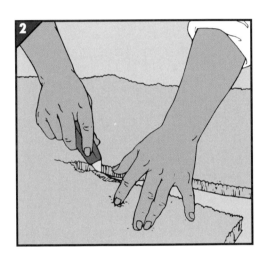

A COOKIE CUTTER FOR SMALL REPAIRS

If the damaged area is less than 4 inches in diameter, rent a tool like that at left, which cuts both a hole in the carpet and a patch to fit, consolidating Steps 2, 3, and 4.

Four spikes penetrate the backing to hold the tool in place as you twist it to work the sharp, serrated edge through. Do not cut the underlying carpet pad except with cushion-back carpet *(page 313)*. Use the same technique to cut a matching patch, then glue it in place as explained in Step 6 on page 312.

3. Cutting a hole.

◆ Place the patch over the damaged area, matching pattern and pile direction.

◆ With one edge of the patch acting as a guide, cut through the carpet and backing to a point about $\frac{1}{2}$ inch from each edge of the patch. Open a pathway for the knife between rows of pile as you cut. Do not cut the pad beneath the carpet.

◆ Lift the patch and cut completely around the damaged area to create a hole about $\frac{1}{2}$ inch smaller than the patch on three sides, as shown by the light gray lines in the illustration *(right)*.

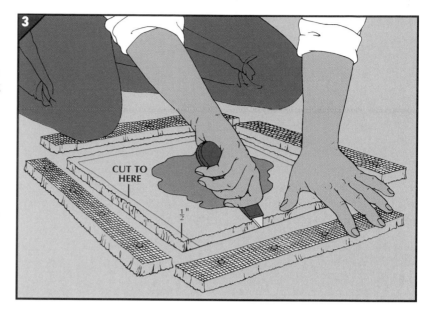

CUT TO HERE

$\frac{1}{2}$"

4. Trimming the hole.

◆ Position the patch to overlap the hole evenly on three sides, and stay-tack the edge used in Step 3 as a guide for the first carpet cut *(left)*.

◆ Cut around the anchored patch to enlarge the hole in the carpet to fit snugly around all sides of the patch.

◆ Pull the nails used to secure the patch and remove it from the hole.

5. Placing seam tape.

◆ Cut four strips of seam tape about an inch longer than the sides of the hole, and spread each strip with a thin layer of latex seam adhesive—just enough to fill in the weave of the tape.

◆ Slip each strip beneath an edge of the hole so that the cut edge of the carpet lies on the centerline.

◆ Squeeze a thin bead of adhesive along the edges of the carpet backing; avoid getting any adhesive on the pile.

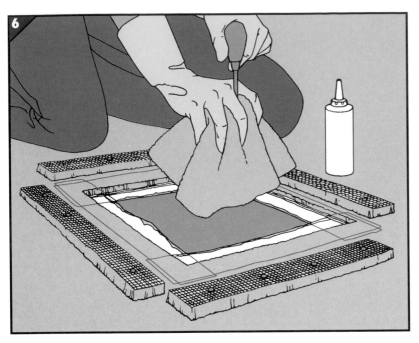

6. Putting in the patch.

◆ Cup the patch in your hand if it is small enough. Otherwise, push an awl through the center of the patch, then fold the patch downward into a tent shape *(left)*.

◆ Position the patch over the hole, and push it off the awl. As the edges of the patch move toward the sides of the hole, they will pick up small amounts of adhesive from the tape.

◆ Push the edges of patch and carpet together and press on the seam around the patch with the heel of your hand. With the awl, free tufts or loops of pile crushed into the seam, and brush your fingers back and forth across the seam to blend the pile of carpet and patch.

◆ After about 5 hours, tug the carpet scraps to remove nails from around the patch, and restore the overall tension on the carpet by using the knee-kicker opposite the patch at all four walls of the room.

MENDING A SURFACE RIP

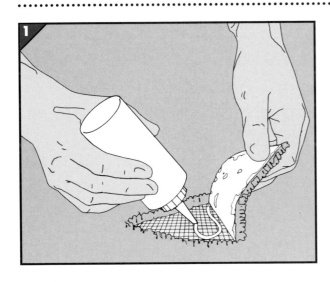

1. Sealing the flap.

◆ If the backing is undamaged, lift the torn section of carpet pile and clean out any loose pile or dried cement.

◆ Apply latex seam adhesive to the exposed backing *(left)*, then spread it in a thin coating over the backing.

2. Hiding the seam.

◆ Press the ripped pile against the adhesive and hold it in place with one hand while you rub the carpet surface with a smooth object, such as the bottom of a glass bottle *(right)*. Rub firmly from the rip toward the sound carpet to work the adhesive into the backing. If any adhesive oozes to the surface, clean it off immediately with water and detergent.

◆ After 4 or 5 hours, when the adhesive has dried, replace any pile that is missing *(page 309)*.

REPAIRS FOR CUSHION-BACK CARPET

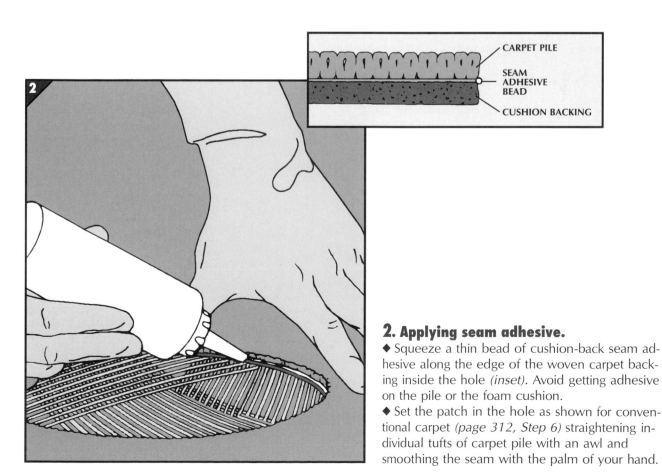

1. Applying floor adhesive.
◆ After cutting out the damaged area and a patch to fit, scrape any dried cement from the floor with a sharpened putty knife.

◆ Spread multipurpose flooring adhesive on the clean floor using a $\frac{3}{32}$-inch notched trowel. Press firmly on the trowel to leave a pattern of adhesive ridges separated by bare floor.

CARPET PILE

SEAM ADHESIVE BEAD

CUSHION BACKING

2. Applying seam adhesive.
◆ Squeeze a thin bead of cushion-back seam adhesive along the edge of the woven carpet backing inside the hole *(inset).* Avoid getting adhesive on the pile or the foam cushion.

◆ Set the patch in the hole as shown for conventional carpet *(page 312, Step 6)* straightening individual tufts of carpet pile with an awl and smoothing the seam with the palm of your hand.

APPENDIX

Several important topics play background roles in almost any redecorating or remodeling project. The information in this appendix will help you deal with such issues, from choosing a ladder—even an extension ladder may be needed for working in a house with high cathedral ceilings—to purchasing the right amount of an appropriate paint. And some ventures, such as installing wood paneling or a tile ceiling, benefit from a knowledge of wall and ceiling construction.

Choosing and Using a Ladder

You will need at least one ladder to complete many painting and wallpapering jobs. The following pages describe the various types of ladders that are available and how to work safely with each.

Construction: Ladders are available in wood, aluminum, and fiberglass. Aluminum ladders offer several advantages. They are no more expensive than the other types, weigh about 20 percent less, and are durable and easy to maintain. Their major drawback, however, is that they conduct electricity. If you plan to work near electrical cables, purchase a wood or fiberglass ladder instead.

Strength: A ladder's rating number indicates its strength. Type IA is the strongest; it can bear loads up to 300 pounds. IA is followed, in order of decreasing strength, by Type I, Type II, and Type III, which can support 200 pounds. For added assurance, look for an "ANSI" seal, which means the ladder has been approved by the American National Standards Institute.

Platforms and Scaffolds: Ladders by themselves may be insufficient for certain jobs. Stairwells, for example, may be impossible to paint or paper without a platform like the one shown on page 317. Exterior painting, particularly with a sprayer, is facilitated above level ground by using brackets called ladder jacks to support a platform of planks from two extension ladders *(page 318)*. Use only specially fabricated planks that are available at scaffold- and ladder-rental stores. If your yard is uneven—or if the house structure prevents setting up the ladders within reach of the work—hire a professional to erect scaffolding.

Maintenance: Before climbing a ladder, inspect it for components that are cracked, twisted, jammed, or loose. If you find any defects, do not attempt repairs; get a new ladder. When you are not using the ladder, store it horizontally on at least three large, strong hooks in a dry place. To ensure smooth operation, periodically lubricate all its movable parts.

BUCKET SHELF

SPREADER BRACE

Some Ladder "Don'ts"

✔ Don't set up a ladder in front of a closed, unlocked door; either lock the door or open it.

✔ Don't level a ladder's feet by placing objects under them.

✔ Don't use a ladder in a high wind.

✔ Don't stand a ladder on ice, snow, or any other slippery surface.

✔ Don't lean the top of a ladder against a windowpane or screen.

✔ Don't link ladders to add height.

✔ Don't place a metal ladder near electrical wires.

✔ Don't step from one ladder to another.

✔ Don't carry tools in your hands or pockets while climbing. Set them on the shelf of a stepladder; if you are working on an extension ladder, place them in a bucket and hoist them up with a rope.

✔ Don't hold a paint bucket with one hand while painting. Instead, place it on the shelf of a stepladder or hang it from a rung of an extension ladder with a hook.

✔ Don't stand above the third-highest rung of an extension ladder or the second-highest step of a stepladder.

✔ Don't overreach to either side of the ladder.

✔ Don't take both hands off the ladder at once.

The versatile stepladder.
◆ Open the ladder to its fullest extent, lock its spreader braces into place, and push the bucket shelf down as far as it will go.
◆ Place the four legs on level ground or a level floor.
◆ Mount the ladder one step at a time, always facing the ladder and holding onto upper steps—not the side rails—with both hands as you climb.

Setting up an extension ladder.

◆ Place the ladder flat on the ground, with its feet a few inches from the vertical surface to be painted.

◆ Raise the top end. Then, grasping the rungs hand over hand, "walk" the ladder to a vertical position *(right).*

◆ Lift the bottom slightly and shift the ladder outward so it leans firmly against the wall. You can compensate for uneven ground with leg levelers *(page 317).*

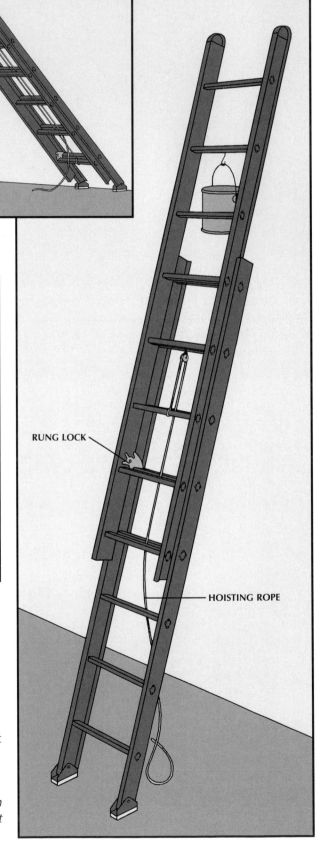

RUNG LOCK

HOISTING ROPE

TRICKS OF THE TRADE

The Right Angle for a Ladder

Use the following technique to set an extension ladder against a wall at a safe angle. After raising the ladder, move the base away from the wall so that your outstretched arms comfortably reach the rung nearest to shoulder height when you stand with your toes touching the ladder feet *(right).*

Extending the ladder.

◆ Pull the hoisting rope to raise the upper section to the desired height. Check to see that the rung locks on the upper section have fully engaged against the rungs on the lower section.

◆ Set the ladder at a safe angle against the wall using the procedure that is described above.

⚠ **CAUTION** *Make sure the upper section overlaps the lower one by at least 3 feet.*

CLAMP

NONSKID PAD

Ladder accessories.

A ladder stabilizer *(above)* provides a broad, sturdy base for the top of an extension ladder. It also lifts the ladder away from the wall to provide easier access to roof overhangs. Stabilizers are available in a variety of materials and designs; the one shown above is made of square aluminum tubing bent into a shallow U that is wide enough to bridge a window. The stabilizer clamps to the ladder rails at the highest rung, and has nonskid pads that prevent the ladder from slipping or marring the wall.

Leg levelers *(photograph)* allow you to set a ladder on uneven surfaces. Fasten one to each rail of the ladder according to the manufacturer's instructions, then adjust them independently to make the rungs level.

A platform for a stairwell.

To paint the ceiling and walls above a staircase, fashion a platform from a straight ladder, a stepladder, and scaffold planks. Protect the wall above the stairwell by fitting the ladder rails with foam-rubber protectors.
◆ Place the straight ladder on the staircase and lean it against the wall as shown on page 316.
◆ Set the stepladder at the top of the stairs.
◆ Lay the planking on a lower rung of the stepladder and on whichever rung of the straight ladder makes the planks level, or nearly so.

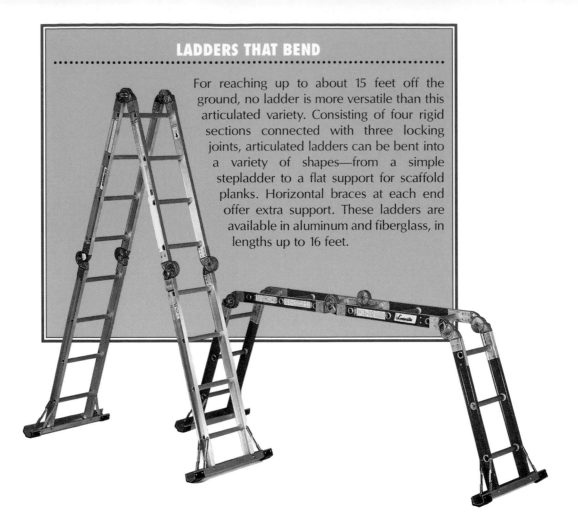

Turning ladders into scaffolding.

Two Type I or IA extension ladders, two 2-by-10 scaffold planks 10 feet long, and a pair of ladder jacks like those at right are the ingredients for this one-person painting scaffold.

◆ Adjust the lengths of the ladders so that the rung at the height you wish to stand—no more than 20 feet—will lie about $2\frac{1}{2}$ feet from the wall ($3\frac{1}{2}$ feet for spraying).

◆ Lean the ladders against the wall no more than 8 feet apart and attach the ladder jacks to the rungs (right) or rails, depending on the model. Level the arm of each jack with its brace.

◆ With a helper, carry the planks one at a time up the ladders and lay them across the arms of the ladder jacks.

Be careful when working from this kind of platform; there are no handholds or safety rails to keep you from falling.

⚠ CAUTION

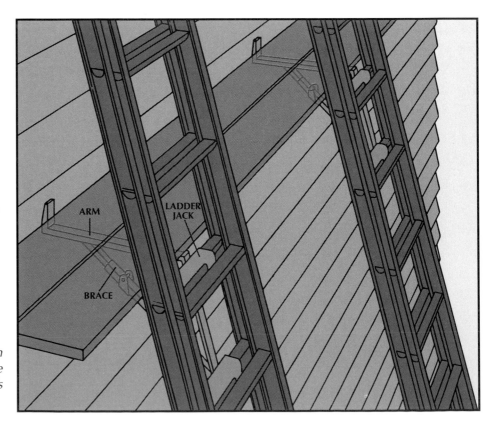

ARM

LADDER JACK

BRACE

ESTIMATING PAINT AND WALLPAPER QUANTITIES

PAINT

To estimate the amount of paint you will need for a job, first calculate the area to be painted *(below)*. Next, divide the result by the area that a gallon of paint will cover—400 square feet of previously painted wallboard or plaster, 350 square feet of textured or previously unpainted walls. When applying a light color over a dark one—or vice versa—two coats may be needed. For the second coat, use a figure of 450 square feet per gallon on a smooth-surface wall and 400 square feet per gallon for a rough wall. Estimate the amount of trim paint you will need in the same way.

WALLPAPER

To calculate the amount of wallpaper necessary to cover a room, first find the room's area *(below)*. Wall coverings are measured in units called single rolls. Though the width of papers may range from 15 to 54 inches, a single roll contains approximately 28 to 30 square feet of covering. Expect to waste about 3 to 5 square feet per single roll on odd-shaped areas, on points where the wall ends before your pattern does, and in trimming excess paper from the top and bottom of a strip. Therefore, divide your total wall area by 25 square feet to find the number of single-roll units you will need. Don't underbuy; wallpaper is printed in dye lots that might be difficult or impossible to match later.

Calculating Area

For a rectangular room *(below, left)* measure the length and width, round up each figure to the nearest foot, and add them together. Multiply that total by the wall height—measured from baseboard to ceiling or top molding—and double that result. Subtract doors and windows, allowing 21 square feet for each door and 15 square feet for an average window. The final figure is the wall area in square feet. If the room is an unusual shape, measure the height and width of each wall section. Then multiply each set of figures, and add the products for the total wall area. Ceiling area is the length times the width of the room. Measure and figure trim and door areas separately, especially if you are using a different color or type of paint.

A stairwell *(below, right)* often forms a triangular shape. For the area of a triangle, multiply the length of the horizontal leg by the length of the vertical leg and divide by two.

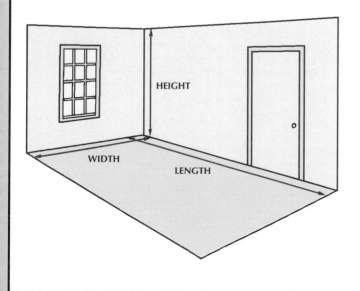

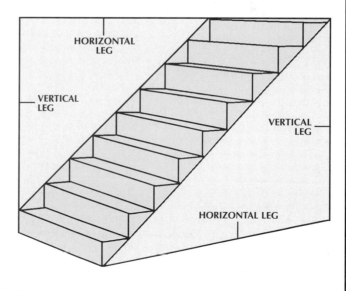

A COATING FOR EVERY SURFACE

Not all paints are compatible with every surface. Alkyd-base paints, for example, are the wrong coating for fresh plaster; as the plaster dries, moisture and salts migrate to the surface and push paint away. A better choice in this case would be latex-base paint, which breathes better than alkyds.

Furthermore, the wrong paint can actually damage a surface. Latex paint, which is thinned with water, promotes rust if it is applied directly to iron or steel. And the thinners in other coatings may dissolve glue; if paint containing such a solvent is used over wallpaper, both paper and paint could peel right off the wall.

The chart on these pages is intended to help you avoid such errors. To learn more about these finishes—what they are made of, what kind of preparations they require, how fast they dry—turn to pages 322 to 325.

Surfaces	GLOSSY ALKYD PAINT	GLOSSY LATEX PAINT	FLAT ALKYD PAINT	FLAT LATEX PAINT	LATEX SHINGLE PAINT	ALKYD SHINGLE PAINT	RUBBER-BASE PAINT	CEMENT PAINT
Raw Wood								
Wood or plywood	✔		✔	✔				
Particle board	✔		✔					
Hardboard	✔	✔	✔	✔				
Raw Masonry								
Plaster		✔		✔		✔		
Gypsum wallboard		✔		✔				
Concrete		✔		✔			✔	✔
Cinder block		✔		✔			✔	✔
Brick		✔		✔			✔	✔
Stucco		✔	✔	✔			✔	✔
Ceramic tile or glass								
Bare Metal								
Steel or iron	✔							
Galvanized metal								
Aluminum	✔	✔	✔	✔				
Copper or bronze								
Previous Surface Covering								
Wallpaper		✔	✔	✔				
Flat alkyd paint or primer	✔		✔			✔		
Flat latex paint or primer		✔		✔	✔		✔	
Alkyd glossy paint or varnish	✔		✔					
Glossy latex paint		✔		✔				
Epoxy paint or varnish	✔		✔					
Urethane paint or varnish	✔		✔					
Rubber-base paint	✔	✔	✔	✔			✔	
Cement paint								✔
Zinc-rich metal primer	✔	✔	✔	✔				
Aluminum paint	✔	✔	✔			✔		
Block filler	✔	✔	✔	✔			✔	✔
Wood filler	✔		✔			✔		
Wood preservative	✔		✔			✔		
Masonry sealer	✔	✔	✔	✔			✔	✔

EPOXY PAINT	URETHANE PAINT	PORCH AND FLOOR PAINT	MARINE PAINT	MULTICOLOR PAINT	LATEX SAND PAINT	LATEX TEXTURE PAINT	DRIPLESS PAINT	FIRE-RETARDANT PAINT	ALKYD VARNISH	EPOXY VARNISH	URETHANE VARNISH	SPAR VARNISH	ALKYD STAIN	EXTERIOR LATEX STAIN	ALKYD PRIMER	LATEX PRIMER	ALKYD CEMENT PRIMER	ZINC-RICH METAL PRIMER	ALUMINUM PAINT	WOOD SEALER	MASONRY SEALER	SILICONE WATER REPELLENT	BLOCK FILLER	WOOD FILLER	WOOD PRESERVATIVE
✔	✔	✔	✔				✔	✔	✔	✔	✔	✔	✔	✔	✔	✔			✔	✔				✔	✔
	✔		✔				✔	✔	✔		✔	✔	✔	✔	✔	✔			✔	✔				✔	✔
✔	✔	✔	✔		✔	✔	✔	✔	✔	✔	✔	✔			✔	✔			✔	✔					
				✔	✔	✔		✔							✔	✔					✔				
				✔	✔	✔		✔								✔									
✔	✔	✔		✔	✔	✔		✔							✔	✔					✔		✔		
	✔	✔		✔	✔	✔		✔							✔	✔					✔		✔		
✔		✔		✔	✔			✔		✔					✔	✔					✔		✔		
				✔	✔	✔		✔							✔	✔					✔		✔		
✔			✔							✔	✔														
✔		✔								✔					✔	✔	✔	✔	✔						
															✔	✔	✔	✔							
✔	✔									✔					✔	✔		✔	✔						
✔	✔		✔							✔					✔			✔							
				✔											✔	✔									
	✔	✔	✔				✔	✔	✔		✔				✔	✔			✔						
	✔	✔		✔	✔	✔	✔	✔			✔				✔	✔									
	✔	✔	✔				✔	✔	✔		✔				✔	✔			✔						
	✔	✔			✔	✔	✔	✔							✔	✔									
✔		✔	✔				✔																		
	✔	✔									✔														
		✔					✔																		
	✔	✔																		✔	✔				
		✔	✔				✔	✔													✔				
✔	✔	✔		✔	✔	✔		✔									✔					✔	✔		
✔	✔	✔	✔				✔			✔	✔	✔	✔	✔	✔									✔	
	✔						✔			✔	✔	✔	✔	✔							✔				
	✔			✔	✔	✔		✔													✔				

SELECTING A COATING

Here and on the pages that follow, the interior coatings listed in the chart on pages 320 to 321 are discussed in detail. They are grouped in three categories: finishing paints; primers, sealers, and fillers; and special finishes.

Finishing Paints: After color, gloss is the most important factor in choosing a finishing paint. The four gloss types available are high gloss, semigloss, low sheen (or eggshell), and flat. High-gloss paints are the most wear-resistant because they contain a great deal of resin, the ingredient that solidifies into the coating film. The more resin, the tougher the film. This toughness makes glossy paints ideal for areas subject to heavy use or frequent washing—particularly kitchens and bathrooms. Semigloss and low-sheen paints afford moderate durability with a less obtrusive shine for most woodwork. Flat paints provide a desirable low-glare finish for surfaces that do not need frequent washing.

Primers, Sealers, and Fillers: If a surface is incompatible with the paint you want to apply—or is too rough to yield a smooth finish—the solution is to first use an undercoat like a filler, sealer, or primer. Fillers smooth uneven or damaged wood surfaces, and sealers close the pores of wood or masonry. Most common of all undercoatings are primers, which serve as a bridge between a finishing coat and an incompatible surface. Primers always have a flat finish in order to provide the rough texture, or "tooth," needed for good topcoat adhesion.

Special Finishes: There are also a number of paints designed for special needs, like hiding a flaw in a wall or ceiling (page 43). These paints usually cost more and are harder to use than conventional paints, but are often worth the time and expense.

FINISHING PAINTS

Latex Paint

SIMPLIFIES CLEANUP
VIRTUALLY ODOR FREE
QUICK DRYING

The most widely used covering for walls and ceilings, latex paint consists of plastic resins and pigments suspended in water. Having water as its solvent gives latex a number of advantages over other kinds of paints: Tools, spills, and hands can be cleaned with soap and water; it is nearly free of odor and harmful fumes; and a coat usually dries in little more than an hour.

Latex adheres well to most surfaces painted with flat oil or latex paint, but it does not adhere to some alkyds and tends to peel away from any high-gloss finish. It can be used over unprimed wallboard, bare masonry, and fresh plaster patches that have set but are not quite dry. Before applying it to new concrete, wash the surface with a 10 percent muriatic acid solution, then rinse it clean. (Always wear goggles and rubber gloves when using muriatic acid.) You can even paint over stain with latex, provided the stain does not have a topcoat of varnish. If it does, use alkyd paint instead (right).

For all its advantages, latex also has drawbacks. Although it can be applied directly over wallpaper, the water in the paint may soak the paper off the wall. On raw wood, the water solvent swells the fibers, roughening the surface—a disadvantage where a smooth finish is desirable.

And if you apply it to bare steel, it rusts the metal.

Alkyd Paint

DURABLE
NEARLY ODORLESS

Made from organic solvents such as mineral spirits and synthetic resins called alkyds, these paints are more durable than latex paints. They are also quite versatile; many painted or wallpapered surfaces—and even bare wood—can be covered with alkyds. They do not, however, adhere to bare masonry or plaster, and should not be used on bare wallboard because they raise the nap on the wallboard's paper covering. Most alkyds are dry enough for a second coat in 4 to 6 hours.

Latex paints will not bond well to alkyd paints, but most other paints can be applied over them. If you plan to spread a new coat of alkyd paint over an old one, make sure that the solvent in the new paint is not any stronger than mineral spirits; a stronger solvent may dissolve the old paint and lift it off the surface. Alkyd paints are best for painting over varnish, though you must first wash the varnish with a strong detergent and then sand it so that the new paint will stick.

While alkyd paints have traditionally had a strong smell, recent formulations are nearly odor free. But keep in mind that alkyd fumes and the organic thinners used for cleanup are toxic and highly flammable whether you can smell them or not. For this reason, use alkyds only in well-ventilated areas and wear gloves while painting.

Rubber-Base Paint

GOOD FOR MASONRY
MOISTUREPROOF
FAST DRYING

This waterproof coating, made from liquefied rubber, is excellent for masonry, especially concrete basement floors. Prepare bare brick to accept this paint by sealing it with clear varnish, and new concrete by washing it with a 10 percent muriatic acid solution. (Wear goggles and rubber gloves when you are working with muriatic acid.)

Rubber-base paint is far more durable than latex, but it is only available in flat and low-gloss finishes and a narrow range of colors. It is also expensive, has a strong smell, and needs special solvents. But its durability, water-resistance, and quick drying time—a coat normally dries in an hour—make it an excellent choice for high-traffic, moisture-prone areas.

Cement Paint

RENEWS MASONRY
APPLY TO DAMP WALLS

This inexpensive coating gives a facelift to brick, stucco, or concrete by adding a thin layer of cement to the old masonry. Some types also act to retard water seepage—an advantage in basements. To get the best results, be sure to work the paint into every pore and crevice with a rough-surface applicator specially made for painting masonry.

Though some manufacturers make ready-mixed formulations, cement paint is also available as a powder, which is a mixture of white Portland cement, pigment, and often a small amount of water repellent. This powder is mixed with water just before use. To help the cement set, the wall must be kept moist during the job and for at least 48 hours thereafter. Tools and spills must be rinsed off before the paint sets.

Cement paint forms a poor base for all other finishes.

Epoxy and Urethane Paints

VERY DURABLE
TRICKY TO USE

These coverings, referred to collectively as plastic paints, are exceptionally elastic and resistant to abrasion, grease, dirt, and most chemicals. Although they are expensive, they are often the best covering for surfaces subject to chemical and physical stress—like floors, stairs, and the walls of kitchens and bathrooms.

In some respects the two types of paint differ. Urethanes can be used on bare wood or over latex, alkyd, or oil paint. Epoxies produce a slick, impervious coating on nonporous materials such as ceramic or metal tile, glass, porcelain, or fiberglass; they can also be used on concrete or wood floors, but they will not adhere to latex, alkyd, or oil paint.

The most durable plastics are two-part paints, which must be mixed just before use because they dry and harden rapidly. Both types require special solvents, which are listed on the package labels, for cleanup.

Alkyd paints can be used over an epoxy or urethane, but the surface must be roughened first by sanding, to provide a coarse texture onto which the paint can adhere.

PRIMERS, SEALERS, AND FILLERS

Latex Primer

QUICK DRYING
ODOR FREE
EASY TO CLEAN UP

This water-base primer is especially valuable in preparing bare plaster, concrete, gypsum wallboard, or cinder block. Such masonry contains alkalis that destroy alkyd finishing coats; the latex primer forms a barrier between the alkalis and the finish. In addition, this primer serves as a bridge between incompatible types of paint, since almost all paints will adhere to it and it will adhere to almost any surface—even to glossy oil paint if you sand it first. You can use latex primers on raw wood, though they will roughen the grain.

A latex primer has many of the advantages of latex paint: it is virtually odor free, it dries in 2 to 4 hours, and cleaning up requires only soap and water.

Alkyd Primer

BEST UNDERCOAT FOR WOOD
GOOD BASE FOR ALL PAINTS
NOT RECOMMENDED FOR WALLBOARD

This type of primer is the best undercoat for raw wood, because it does not raise the wood grain. Some alkyd primers are also compatible with masonry, though it is a poor first coat on gypsum wallboard because alkyd raises a slight nap on the wallboard's paper covering. Most finishing coats —including all types of latex paint— adhere well to an alkyd base coat. Alkyd primers take overnight to dry; tools and spills can be cleaned with the solvents used for alkyd paints.

Metal Primer and Paint
PREVENT PEELING AND RUST

The most commonly painted metals are steel and aluminum. Steel must be kept painted or it will rust. And while aluminum does not rust, it eventually pits if left uncoated or exposed to harsh weather. There are two ways to cover either type of metal: you can use a metal primer followed by a finishing coat of paint, or a single coat of metal paint that acts as its own primer.

If you choose the former, the best primer for steel is an alkyd type that contains zinc, which rustproofs the metal. This formulation also works well for aluminum, or you can apply epoxy or urethane finishes directly to the bare metal as self-primers. Any compatible finish can then be applied over these primers. The only exception is for painting a radiator; in this case, use only flat paint because glossy finishes trap heat.

In metal paints, primer and top coat are combined in a single mixture. These latex or alkyd paints come in high-gloss and semigloss versions and are available in a wide range of colors. They are applied by

brush, and cleaned and thinned with the conventional solvents used for alkyd coatings.

All metal primers and paints must be applied to a surface that is absolutely free of dirt, grease, and corrosion. Before painting the metal, clean off grease with paint thinner. If there are any rust spots, either remove them or seal them with rust-converting sealer.

Copper, brass, and bronze hardware are not normally painted. Instead, the fixtures are usually lacquered at the factory to preserve their original appearance. If the lacquer wears away unevenly, first clean the finish off completely with a lacquer remover. Then, in the case of copper and brass, remove tarnish with fine steel wool and metal polish—or, for a mirror finish, metal polish alone—and apply a protective coating of polyurethane or epoxy varnish. Uncoated bronze develops an attractive patina that you can protect with varnish; if you prefer bright bronze, treat it like brass. To paint over these metals, use an alkyd metal primer containing zinc and any compatible finishing paint.

Sealers and Primer-Sealers
SEAL PORES OF WOOD AND MASONRY
PRESERVE NATURAL LOOK OF WOOD

These liquids, made of synthetic resins mixed with a high proportion of solvent, seal the pores of wood and masonry.

Transparent wood sealers sink into the wood's pores, binding the fibers

together and making them easier to sand. They protect wood against dirt and moisture, and seal in the natural dyes and resins that can seep through paint. They dry more rapidly than most primers and do not alter the appearance of the wood. Stain, varnish, and alkyd paints may be brushed directly over a clear wood sealer, since sealed wood can still absorb liquid.

Masonry sealers—often tinted a translucent blue to make it easier to see the areas that have been coated—are used on concrete, cinder block, or plaster to prevent chalking. They also slow the passage of water through basement walls. Masonry sealers vary greatly in their composition; consult the label of the package for cleanup instructions and for compatible topcoats if you intend to paint over them.

Wood Filler
SMOOTHS WOOD
CAN BE MIXED WITH STAIN

A combination of synthetic resins and wood-toned pigment, wood filler is used to plug holes and build up rough or damaged sections in wood. It is available in either paste or liquid form. The paste type is usually thinned with a small amount of turpentine (or with a special solvent recommended by the manufacturer) and used to repair open-grain woods such as walnut, ash, oak, or mahogany. Liquid filler, which is simply a prethinned paste, is generally applied to woods with a closer grain, such as maple or birch. Neither the paste nor the liquid protect the wood; you must cover the filler with a coat of sealer and, in a surface subject to heavy use, a final coat of shellac, varnish, or paint.

You can repair minor damage in an already-painted piece of wood by patching it with paste filler colored with stain to match the wood finish.

SPECIAL FINISHES

Multicolor Paint
DISGUISES FLAWS
DISTINCTIVE AND DECORATIVE
These latex-base coatings contain two nonmixing pigments. Depending on the formulation, they produce either a tonal variation or a flecked appearance ideal for concealing uneven or slightly damaged surfaces. For indoor use, choose a brand that can be brushed or rolled on and does not require spraying. Any alkyd or latex paint can be applied over a multicolor paint, but two coats may be needed to hide it.

Sand and Texture Paints
DISGUISE FLAWS
YIELD ATTRACTIVE, ROUGH FINISH
DIFFICULT TO PAINT OVER
These paints give walls and ceilings a coarse texture that, like multicolor paint, conceals surface flaws. Sand paint is simply regular latex paint mixed with sand or a sandlike synthetic. It creates a fine-grained, glare-free texture that is attractive on ceilings but has a grittiness that limits its use to areas not likely to be touched. Texture paint is an extra-dense flat latex or alkyd paint. You can apply it as you would conventional paint to get a stuccolike finish, or follow the instructions on page 43 to get a deeply stippled finish.

These paints can be applied to surfaces compatible with their latex or alkyd base. The latex type is often used on wallboard ceilings, since it adheres without a primer and helps conceal the wallboard seams. Painting over them, however, presents special difficulties: you will need as much as 25 percent more paint than usual, and the rough texture will always show through the new coat.

Dripless Paint
GOOD FOR CEILINGS
EXPENSIVE
Formulated so thick that it does not drip from a brush or roller, dripless paint is an ideal finish for ceilings and other high, hard-to-reach places. It will usually cover any surface in a single coat, but it is considerably more expensive than conventional alkyds and covers less area per gallon.

Though dripless, this paint will spatter if it is carelessly applied, and its thickness makes it more difficult to clean up.

Fire-Retardant Paint
A WORTHWHILE PROTECTION
This paint slows the spread of fire by puffing up into a foamy, insulating layer when exposed to high temperatures. It is especially valuable in garages and basements, where many house fires start.

Be sure to follow the manufacturer's instructions when painting, especially in controlling the thickness of the coating: if it is too thin, it will not provide adequate protection; too thick, and it may fall away in case of a fire. And since the puffing ingredients in some types of fire-retardant paint remain water soluble even after the paint dries, check the label for cleaning instructions.

Available in latex flat and semigloss finishes, as well as in both urethane and epoxy formulations, fire-retardant paints can be applied over any surface that is suitable for latex. You can also cover bare wood with it, provided a perfectly smooth finish is not essential. But you should never apply conventional paints over fire-retardant paint, because they impair its effectiveness.

Inside Walls and Ceilings

There's more to walls and ceilings than meets the eye. As the illustrations on the following pages show, the wallboard or plaster surface is nothing more than an attractive skin for the skeleton of a house.

Wood-Framed Construction: Of the four surface-and-structure combinations presented, wood-framed walls and ceilings covered by wallboard are the most common. The walls consist of vertical members, called studs, and horizontal members, the top plates and sole plates —all usually cut from 2-by-4 stock.

Larger boards called joists *(box, below)* define every ceiling and support the floor of any living space overhead; hence the terms "ceiling joist" and "floor joist" are often used interchangeably. The box describes several techniques for finding studs and joists in a finished wall or ceiling.

Masonry Walls: Older houses with exterior walls built of solid masonry are often finished inside with plaster laid on brick, but most such dwellings have ceilings and partition walls framed with wood joists and studs. Studs also lie behind the brick facades of many houses that are actually brick veneer, in which a single layer of brick is added to the outside of wood-framed walls.

Walls That Bear Weight: A wall that supports the roof or other upper structural parts of a house is known as a load-bearing wall, or bearing wall. In masonry houses, interior bearing walls are usually built of masonry. In a few frame houses, the studs of bearing walls are closer together than the standard 16-inch spacing for greater strength. Ceiling joists run perpendicular to bearing walls.

Finish Surfaces: Plaster over a bonding surface known as lath, most often made of wood or wire mesh, was once the most common wall surface. Wallboard made from gypsum sandwiched between heavy paper is now standard. Because wallboard requires neither lath nor drying time, it is more easily and quickly installed.

An attractive alternative to a plaster or wallboard surface is wood paneling, which is made of solid-wood boards or sheets of wood veneer. The paneling may cover the entire wall or just a portion of it as in wainscoting. Decorative molding conceals joints and provides a finished look to the room.

LOCATING CONCEALED STUDS AND JOISTS

For most wall and ceiling work, you need to know where studs and joists are. Typically they are 16 inches apart; finding one helps locate others. One way of detecting studs and joists is to tap the wall or ceiling, listening for the solid sound of wood behind wallboard or plaster.

Alternatively, check for visual clues to stud and joist locations. Examine wallboard close up for traces of seams or nailing patterns; this is best done at night with a light shining obliquely across the surface. If the work you plan requires removing the baseboard, look behind it for seams or nails that hold wallboard panels to studs.

The easiest approach is to use an electronic stud finder *(photograph)*, which indicates changes in structure density with a column of lights. As the tool is guided across wallboard or plaster, the lights turn on sequentially as it approaches a stud or joist. The top light glows when the stud finder reaches the edge of a framing member. You can approximate its center by finding the midpoint between the two edges.

No method is perfect. In each case small test holes drilled in an inconspicuous spot may be needed to pinpoint a stud or joist and to confirm the spacing between them.

WOOD FRAMING BEHIND THE SURFACE

Wallboard over studs and joists.
On this wood-framed wall, 4-by-8 panels of wallboard are secured horizontally with adhesive and nails or screws to vertical 2-by-4 studs. The studs are nailed between the sole plate (a horizontal 2-by-4 at floor level) and the top plate (doubled horizontal 2-by-4s at ceiling level). Studs are normally spaced at 16-inch intervals, center to center. Short pieces of 2-by-4 called firestops are sometimes nailed horizontally between studs at staggered levels to retard the spread of the flames in case of fire.

Alongside door and window openings, studs are doubled, and a heavy, beam-like assembly called a header forms the top of each opening. Short sections known as cripple studs extend above each header and below each window opening's rough sill, a 2-by-4 that runs across the bottom of the opening.

On the ceiling, wallboard covers 2-by-10 joists, 16 inches apart. Joist ends are toenailed to the upper surfaces of the top plates of two bearing walls.

Most pipes that run upward inside a wall pass through the sole and top plates; holes in the centers of studs or joists—or notches cut in the edges—accommodate horizontal pipes. Vertical runs of electrical cable are stapled to the sides of the studs or joists; horizontal cables are threaded through $\frac{3}{4}$-inch holes.

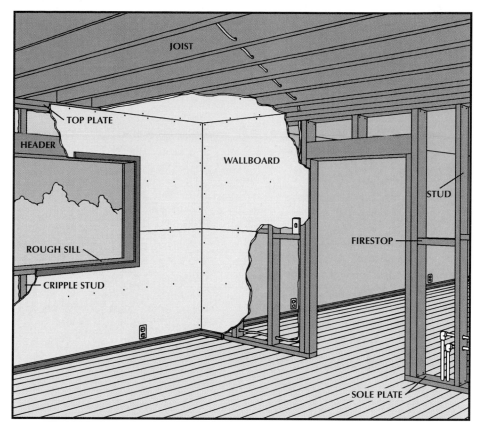

JOIST

TOP PLATE

HEADER

WALLBOARD

STUD

ROUGH SILL

FIRESTOP

CRIPPLE STUD

SOLE PLATE

DIFFERENT STYLES OF JOISTS

Instead of joists made of solid lumber like the ones illustrated above, your home may have one of the more modern kinds of joist shown here. Both types are stronger and lighter than lumber joists. I-beams (*below, left*) consist of two 2-by-4s joined by a plywood web. Open-web trusses (*below, right*) are built like bridge girders from 2-by-3s or 2-by-4s.

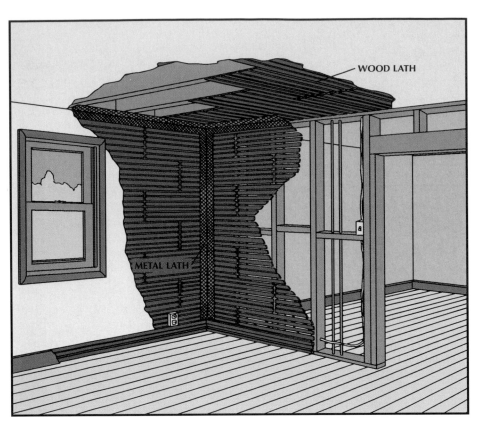

Plaster over wood lath.
The plaster finish that covers this wood-framed wall and ceiling is typical of house construction before 1930. The layout of wall studs and ceiling joists here is identical to modern frame construction *(page 327),* except that spacing between the framing members varies from 12 to 24 inches.

A pattern of wood strips, called lath, anchors the plaster. Generally $\frac{5}{16}$ inch thick and $1\frac{1}{2}$ inches wide, the strips span up to four studs or joists, in staggered groups of four to six. The strips are spaced $\frac{1}{4}$ inch apart so that the plaster can ooze between them for a good grip. At corners, the wood lath is strengthened with a 4- to 6-inch-wide strip of metal lath.

MASONRY WALLS WITH WOOD-FRAMED CEILINGS

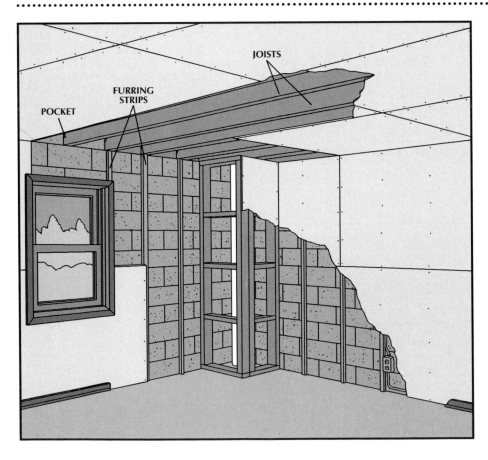

Furring strips under wallboard.
On a concrete-block wall, wallboard is nailed to vertical 1-by-3 wood strips, called furring strips. They are spaced at 16-inch intervals and secured to the blocks with masonry nails, adhesive, or a combination of the two. Enclosures built of 2-by-3s or 2-by-4s hide any exposed pipes.

On the ceiling, wallboard is attached to 2-by-10 ceiling joists whose ends rest in pockets made in the masonry walls at the time of construction.

Plaster over masonry walls.

In this masonry house, typical of the early 1900s, all exterior walls as well as interior bearing walls consist of two layers of brick separated by a narrow air space. Nonbearing interior walls are framed with wood studs. The ends of the ceiling joists rest in pockets that were made in the brick walls at the time of construction.

The plaster finish on the interior masonry walls is applied directly to the bricks; on walls and ceilings, the base underlying the plaster is wood lath, reinforced at corners with metal lath.

WOOD PANELING AND TRIM

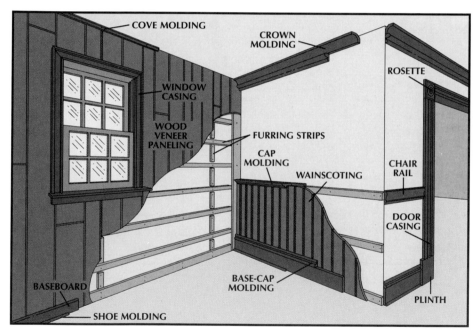

Paneling over furring strips.

Sheets of wood veneer paneling may be attached directly to the wall or to a grid of furring strips as shown here. Grooves in the panel appear to be random but are actually placed every 16 or 24 inches to coincide with furring strips or studs. Decorative moldings and trim (photograph) smooth joints and provide finishing touches to the room. For example, where paneling meets the ceiling, cove molding, a convex wood trim, conceals the joint; baseboard and shoe molding cover the joint at the base of the wall.

Wainscoting is paneling that extends only partway up a wall. Attached and finished at the bottom like full-height paneling, wainscoting is topped with cap molding. Instead of wainscoting, a chair rail, originally created to protect the wall from furniture, may be set 36 inches from the floor.

Crown molding often trims the tops of walls. Made from a single molding or a combination of them, crown molding often detracts from fully paneled walls. At doorways, a plinth smooths the transition between the baseboard and door casing, and a rosette block decorates the upper corner of the doorway.

Complete Book of Redecorating & Remodeling

Time-Life Books is a division of Time Life Inc.

PRESIDENT and CEO: George Artandi
PRESIDENT: Stephen R. Frary

Time-Life Custom Publishing
VICE PRESIDENT and PUBLISHER: Terry Newell
Vice President of Sales & Marketing: Neil Levin
Project Manager: Jennifer M. Lee
Director of Special Sales: Liz Ziehl
Managing Editor: Donia Ann Steele
Production Manager: Carolyn Clark
Quality Assurance Manager: James King
Photo Researcher: Kimberly Grandcolas

Adapted from Time-Life Books **Home Repair & Improvement** Series

SERIES EDITOR: Lee Hassig
MARKETING DIRECTOR: James Gillespie

Art Directors: Kathleen Mallow, Barbara M. Sheppard
Associate Editor/Research and Writing: Karen Sweet
Marketing Manager: Wells Spence
Picture Coordinator: David A. Herod
Editorial Assistant: Patricia D. Whiteford

Special Contributors: George Constable (text); Jill Tunick
  (chapter introductions & *decorating ideas* text);
  John Drummond (illustration); Karen Leeds (gallery designs);
  Jennifer Gearhart, William Graves, Craig Hower, Marvin Shultz,
  Eileen Wentland (digital illustration); Janet Syring
  (composition); Jennifer Rushing-Schurr (index).

Correspondents: Christine Hinze (London), Christina
  Lieberman (New York), Maria Vincenza Aloisi (Paris).

Director of Finance: Christopher Hearing
Director of Book Production: Marjann Caldwell
Director of Publishing Technology: Betsi McGrath
Director of Photography and Research: John Conrad Weiser
Director of Editorial Administration: Barbara Levitt
Chief Librarian: Louise D. Forstall

**Library of Congress
Cataloging-in-Publication Data**
Complete Book of Redecorating & Remodeling /
  by the editors of Time-Life Books.
      p.   cm.
  Includes index.
  ISBN 0-7835-5251-3
    1. Dwellings—Remodeling—Amateurs'
  manuals.   2. Interior decoration—Amateurs'
  manuals.   I. Time-Life Books.
TH4816.C644   1997   97-20562
643'.7—dc21   CIP

Books produced by Time-Life Custom Publishing are available at special
bulk discount for promotional and premium use. Custom adaptations can
also be created to meet your specific marketing goals. Call 1-800-323-5255.

PICTURE CREDITS

Illustrators: Art Great, Inc., Jack Arthur, George Bell, Frederic F. Bigio from B-C Graphics, Adolph E. Brotman, Jean-Guy Doiron @ St. Remy Multimedia, Roger Essley, Nicholas Fasciano, Forta, Inc., Elsie Hennig, Walter Hilmers, Jr., HJ Commercial Art, Fred Holz, Fred Holz, Peter McGinn, John Massey, Eduino J. Pereira, Greg De Santis, inked by Walter Hilmers Jr., Nick Shrenk, Snowden Associates, Inc., Ray Skibinski, Tyrone Taylor, Drew Toth, @ Totally Incorporated, Vantage Art, Inc., Vicki Vebell, Whitman Studios, Inc.

Photographers: (Credits from left to right are separated by semicolons, from top to bottom by dashes) **6, 7:** Steven Mays/Rebus. **8:** Steven Mays/Rebus—© Beth Singer, CBI Design/Rob Clarke, Zelinski Builders Incorporated; Aldo Ballo, Milan/design by Flavio Albanese, Vicenza, Italy. **9:** Giovanna Piemonti, Rome. **10, 11:** Larry Sherer. **12, 13, 22, 37, 38, 41:** Renée Comet. **43:** Renée Comet; William Zinsser & Company. **50, 51:** Explorer Collection, Imperial Wallcoverings, Inc. **52:** © Beth Singer, Keenan & York/Joe Keenan. **53:** A Man's World II, United by Imperial Wallcoverings, Inc.—Botanical Wallpaper and Border from Thibaut's Notions Collection; Di Lewis for Kids Collection, by Sunworthy Wallcoverings. **54, 55:** Mrs. Mitchell's Collection by Sunworthy Wallcoverings; Imperial Wallcoverings, Inc.; George Ross—Steven Mays/Rebus. **56, 57, 60:** Renée Comet. **100, 101:** Dub Rogers, courtesy Safdie Rabines Architects. **102:** Tim Street-Porter, from Elizabeth Whiting and Associates, London/Arquitectonica, architects, Miami; Dub Rogers, courtesy Safdie Rabines Architects—Steven Mays/Rebus. **103:** © Beth Singer, Teich-Davis Interiors/Mark Davis—Steven Mays/Rebus. **105:** Norman McGrath, courtesy Peter Gisolfi Associates, Architects and Landscape Architects—Norman McGrath, courtesy Charles Marks Associates, Architects—© Beth Singer, Schearer Design, Inc./Bob Schearer. **108:** Robert Chartier @ St. Remy Multimedia. **118, 119:** George Ross. **120, 121:** Courtesy Custom Decorative Moldings (CDM) (top molding); Rick Patrick; Larry Sherer/location, courtesy Ernst Chase Alexander—Steven Mays/Rebus; J. Curtis. **122:** George Ross (2). **123:** Courtesy Custom Decorative Moldings (CDM)(4)—George Ross (2). **125:** Porter-Cable Professional Power Tools. **133:** Renée Comet. **135:** PANELLIFT ® brand dry-wall lift manufactured by Telpro, Inc. **139, 140, 141, 149, 150:** Renée Comet. **155:** Design Brick Products. **159:** Renée Comet, prop courtesy the Door Store, Washington, D.C. **163, 165-167:** Renée Comet. **170:** Laser Tools Co. **177:** Renée Comet. **184, 185:** © James Yochum Photography. **186:** © Beth Singer, Kennedy & Company/Diane Howting. **187:** Steven Mays/Rebus—Rick Patrick; Pavillion Border from Thibaut's Notions Collection. **188, 189:** Courtesy Georgia-Pacific Corporation (5). **197, 206, 219:** Renée Comet. **226, 227:** © Beth Singer, Brian Killian & Company/Brian Killian. **228:** Proclaim Tile 8521 courtesy of Tarkett, Inc.—HomeLife 52042 courtesy of Tarkett, Inc.—courtesy of Laufen Ceramic Tile. **229:** Steven Mays/Rebus. **230:** Steven Mays/Rebus (3). **231:** Simeone Ricci (3)—© Beth Singer (3). **236:** Porter-Cable Professional Power Tools. **240, 244, 248, 251, 265, 267:** Michael Latil. **272:** Clarke Industries, Inc. **275:** Michael Latil. **284, 285:** © Beth Singer, Riemenschneider Design Assoc./Alice Riemenschneider. **286:** © Beth Singer, Interiors by Design/ Barbara Gimesky—courtesy of Carpetmax—courtesy of DuPont Stainmaster™ carpet "For Beauty That Lasts". **287:** © Beth Singer, Custom Designed Woodwork, Inc./Bruno Trentacost, Thad Galvin of Galvin & Co., Deerwood Development Group, Martha Noonan Interiors/Martha Noonan. **288:** Courtesy of DuPont Stainmaster™ carpet "For Beauty That Lasts" (2)—photos courtesy of AlliedSignal Fibers, makers of the Anso® brand nylon family of carpet fibers (2). **289:** Courtesy of DuPont Stainmaster™ carpet "For Beauty That Lasts" (2)—photos courtesy of AlliedSignal Fibers, makers of the Anso® brand nylon family of carpet fibers (2). **290:** Michael Latil. **297:** Renée Comet. **300:** Roberts Consolidated Industries, Inc. **310:** Michael Latil. **317:** Werner Ladder Company. **318:** Louisville Ladder Corporation. **326:** Renée Comet. **327:** TruJoist MacMillan; Southern Pine Council.

ACKNOWLEDGMENTS

The editors also wish to thank the following individuals and institutions:
Crescencio Batalla, Trussway, Inc., Fredericksburg, Va.; Joseph Biber, Dutch Boy Paints, Cleveland; Jeanne Byington, Sumner, Rider & Associates, New York; Ken Charbonneau, Benjamin Moore Paints, Montvale, N.J.; Bill Cochran, Home Depot, Alexandria, Va.; Rob Cooksey, Louisville Ladder Corporation, Louisville, Ky.; Mike Dawson, A & A Rental, Alexandria, Va.; Esther del Rosario, Silver Spring, Md.; Kimberly A. Fantaci, National Guild of Professional Paperhangers, Dayton; Jeff Fantozzi, Western Wood Products Association, Portland, Oreg.; Debra Fedasiuk, William Zinsser & Company, Somerset, N.J.; Teri Flotron, National Decorating Products Association, St. Louis; Steve Francis, American Brick Company, Detroit; Marcy Graham, F. Schumacher & Company, New York; Frank Granelli, William Zinsser & Company, Somerset, N.J.; Kirk Grundahl, Wood Truss Council of America, Madison, Wis.; Kevin and Kate Hardardt, Alexandria, Va.; Steve Harman, DAP, Inc., Dayton; Glen Hasenyager, TruJoist MacMillan, Boise, Idaho; Tony Hedgepeth, Fairfax, Va.; John Hollern, Dodge-Regupol, Inc., Lancaster, Pa.; Uel Johnson, Prince Georges County Office of Central Services, Forestville, Md.; Jim Keener, J&J Industries, Dalton, Ga.; Martin Kobsik, Werner Ladder Company, Greenville, Pa.; Joseph Koppi, Koppi Communications, West St. Paul, Minn.; Todd Langston, Porter-Cable Professional Power Tools, Jackson, Tenn.; Susan Levine, Prescott Healy Co., Ltd., Chicago; Mac Mackay, The Rug Man, Alexandria, Va.; Timothy K. McCool, National Wood Flooring Association, Manchester, Mo.; Frank Magdits, Benjamin Moore Paints, Montvale, N.J.; David Marlinski, Morristown, N.J.; Doug Mingst, Northeast Industries, Midland Park, N.J.; Ruth Pestorius, Decorating with Paint, McLean, Va.; Bill Price Jr., Preferred Products, Inc., Seattle; Glen Robak, TruJoist MacMillan, Boise, Idaho; Judy Rodde, Roberts Consolidated Industries, Inc., City of Industry, Calif.; Biff Roberts, Senco Products, Inc., Cincinnati; Richard C. Robertson, Covey's Carpet and Drapes, Springfield, Va.; Bob Snitzer, Century Stair Company, Haymarket, Va.; Leopoldo Soto, Trussway, Inc., Fredericksburg, Va.; David Stone, Styleline Systems Division of Daston, Inc., Walworth, Wis.; Gary Sweatt, Trussway, Inc., Hurst, Tex.; Jim Thomas, Trussway, Inc., Fredericksburg, Va.; Carroll Turner, The Carpet and Rug Institute, Dalton, Ga.; Wagner Consumer Products Division, Minneapolis; Shelley Walk, Dutch Boy Paints, Cleveland; Rick Watson, Duron Paints, Beltsville, Md.; Bill West, Metropolitan Rolling Door, Inc., Columbia, Md.; Diane Wood, William Zinsser & Company, Somerset, N.J.; Murphy Wright, A & A Rental, Alexandria, Va.

INDEX

long overlap method for, 82-83
short overlap method for, 84-85

Wainscoting: 187, 189;
  installing, 224-225; materials for,
    224; tools for, 224;
  molding for, 224
Wallboard: 132, 327; attaching, 135;
    braces for damaged, 25;
    cutting out damaged, 25-26;
    dimensions of, 132;
    fasteners for, 132;
    fitting, 134;
    hanging, 132-137;
    hiding seams in, 138-141;
    holes in: filling, 23-24; large,
      25-27; patching, 20, 23;
      sealing; 24
    joints of: filling, 22; retaping,
      22-23;
    openings in, 134;
    panels of: attaching, 137;
      shortening, 134;
    patching, 27;
    for plaster flaws, 32-33;
    repairing, 20-27;
    for soundproofing, 177-179;
    tapered joints for, 136
Wallboard trowel, 141
Wall panels: 158-161; frame for, 158
    materials for, 158; tools for, 158
Wallpaper
  adhesives for, types of, 66
  aligning, 69, 78
  borders, 94-95; horizontal, 94;
    mitering corners of, 95;
    preparing, 95
  cleaning, tools for, 57
  creasing, 71
  cutting, tools for, 57
  drop-match pattern, 72
  dry-scraping, 59
  edging, tools for, 57
  estimating quantities of, 319
  first strip of, 68-70; brushing,
    69-70; smoothing, 70
  flattening bubbles in, 96, 98;
    curved cuts for, 99
  holes in, patching, 96
  large pattern, 52
  loosening, 60
  maintaining, 99
  marking, tools for, 56
  materials of, 54-55
  measuring, tools for, 56
  painting over, 19

paper, around casement
    windows, 81-82
  pattern of, aligning, 62, 65
  patterns of, 52-54; for   difficult
    areas, 86;   matching, 72
  perforating, 59-60
  prepasted, 50, 67
  repairing, 96-99; double-cut
    method for, 97; tools for,
    56; torn-patch method for, 96
  rolling, tools for, 57
  scraping, 59; tools for, 56
  scraps, uses for, 55
  seams of: joining, 74; types of, 73
  selvages of, trimming, 68
  smoothing, tools for, 57
  soaking, 59-60
  steaming off, 61
  straight-match pattern, 72
  stripping, 58-60
  trimming, 71
  vinyl, around casement
    windows, 82-85
  wallpapering over, 58
Wallpapering: 50-99;
  corners: inner, 76-77;
  corners: outer, 77-78;
  decorating ideas for, 54-55;
  difficult areas, 86-91;
  around fixtures, 92-93;
  around openings, 76-85;
  preparing for, 58-61;
  seams in, 68;
  techniques for, 50-53, 68-75;
  tools for, 56-57, 68;
  over wallpaper, 58;
  around windows, 78-85;
  where to end, 62, 64
  where to start, 62-63;
Walls
  anatomy of, 326-329
  checking for defects in, 124
  double, for soundproofing,
    178, 183
  false: over masonry, 128-129;
    pipe/duct enclosures in, 129-
    130
  metal frame: plumbing in, 165;
    wiring in, 164-165
  metal framing, 162-165;
    components of, 162;
    doorway in, 164; materials
    for, 162; tools for, 162
  mirrored, 146-149
  painting, 44
  slanted, papering, 89-91
  sound-resistant, 176-183;
    sealing gaps in, 176, 183

truing, 124-131
Wall scraper, 56
Wall treatments, 118-183
Warm colors, 10-11
Water-base stain, 215
Water box, 57, 67
White, 11
Window glass, protecting from
    paint, 34
Windowpanes, edging, 49
Windows
  casement: painting, 46;
    wallpapering around, 81-85
  double-hung: painting, 45;
    wallpapering around, 78-80
  painting, 44-45
  paneling around, 194-195
Window scraper, 13
Window stool, removing, 130
Wire seam, 73
Wiring
  for brick wall, 157
  for ceiling fan, 117
  for dimmer switch, 109
  for metal partition wall, 164-165
  for recessed lighting, 114
  for track lighting, 113
Wooden paddle: 12; holes in, 38
Wood filler, 324-325
Wood flooring: 230-231;
  anatomy of, 266;
  damaged area in, cutting out
    269-270;
  holes in, patching, 270-271;
  parquet, 231, 257;
  protective coats for, 274-275;
  refinishing, 272-275;
  smoothing, 275;
  squeaks in, 267
Wood knots
  preparing, 18
  sealing, 18
Wood lath, 328
Wood paneling: 184-225. *See also*
    Solid-wood paneling; anatomy
    of, 329;
  attaching, 190, 193
  color combinations in, 187
  cutting, 190-194;
  decorating ideas for, 188-189;
  door in, for service panel, 197;
  at electrical box, 196;
  finishes for, 215
  fitting to corner, 194;
  herringbone pattern in, 201;
  for high-ceilinged room, 200;
  materials for, 190;
  moldings for, 202-203;

around obstacles, 198-201;
  for oddly shaped openings,
    195-196, 199-200;
  painted, 187;
  pipes and, 197;
  plumbing, 192
  raised, 186, 216-223; assembly
    of, 223; bevels in, 222; dowel
    holes in, 221; frame for,
    219-221; installation of, 223;
    making, 221-222; materials for,
    216; molding for, 218; parts of,
    216; patterns of, 216; plywood
    facsimile of, 217-218; tools for,
    216; trim for, 218
  recycled, 188-189
  at rounded windows, 194-195
  scribing, 200
  tools for, 190
  types of, 190

Yellow, 8, 10